MORAL AND POLITICAL EDUCATION

NOMOS

XLIII

NOMOS

Harvard University Press

I   *Authority* 1958, reissued in 1982 by Greenwood Press

The Liberal Arts Press

II   *Community* 1959
III   *Responsibility* 1960

Atherton Press

IV   *Liberty* 1962
V   *The Public Interest* 1962
VI   *Justice* 1963, reissued in 1974
VII   *Rational Decision* 1964
VIII   *Revolution* 1966
IX   *Equality* 1967
X   *Representation* 1968
XI   *Voluntary Associations* 1969
XII   *Political and Legal Obligation* 1970
XIII   *Privacy* 1971

Aldine-Atherton Press

XIV   *Coercion* 1972

Lieber-Atherton Press

XV   *The Limits of Law* 1974
XVI   *Participation in Politics* 1975

New York University Press

XVII   *Human Nature in Politics* 1977
XVIII   *Due Process* 1977
XIX   *Anarchism* 1978
XX   *Constitutionalism* 1979
XXI   *Compromise in Ethics, Law, and Politics* 1979
XXII   *Property* 1980
XXIII   *Human Rights* 1981
XIV   *Ethics, Economics, and the Law* 1982
XXV   *Liberal Democracy* 1983
XXVI   *Marxism* 1983

NOMOS XLIII

Yearbook of the American Society for Political and Legal Philosophy

MORAL AND POLITICAL EDUCATION

Edited by

Stephen Macedo, *Princeton University*
and
Yael Tamir, *Tel Aviv University*

NEW YORK UNIVERSITY PRESS • *New York and London*

NEW YORK UNIVERSITY PRESS
New York and London

Library of Congress Cataloging-in-Publication Data
Moral and political education /
edited by Stephen Macedo and Yael Tamir.
p. cm. — (Nomos ; 43)
Includes bibliographical references and index.
ISBN 0–8147–5675–1 (cloth : alk. paper)
1. Education and state. 2. Politics and education.
3. Moral education. 4. Democracy.
I. Macedo, Stephen, 1957– II. Tamir, Yael. III. Series.
LC71 .M67 2001
307.11'4—dc21   2001004297

New York University Press books are printed on acid-free paper,
and their binding materials are chosen for strength and durability.

Manufactured in the United States of America
10 9 8 7 6 5 4 3 2

CONTENTS

PART II: NEUTRALITY, INDIVIDUAL AUTONOMY, AND EDUCATIONAL REFORM

PART III: PRISONS, PUNISHMENT, AND MORAL EDUCATION

PART IV: EDUCATION AND THE IDEAL OF RACIAL INTEGRATION: RENEWAL OR RETREAT?

PREFACE

The contributions to this forty-third volume of NOMOS center around a group of papers and commentaries presented at the 1998 meeting of the American Society for Political and Legal Philosophy, held in conjunction with the Eastern Division Meeting of the American Philosophical Association in Washington, D.C., December 1998. My thanks to our original paper writers (Amy Gutmann, Michael W. McConnell, and Lawrence Blum), and to our commentators and other contributors for their care and patience throughout.

The excellence and timeliness of this volume owes in part to our authors' ability to use theory to illuminate practice. My coeditor, Yael Tamir, contributed at every stage, and did much of the work of thinking through the overall structure of this volume. In the midst of the production process she was called upon to serve in the government of Israel. It has been a great pleasure to work with Professor/Minister Tamir!

Thanks to Stephen Magro and Despina Papazoglou Gimbel at NYU Press, who have provided expert, timely, and enthusiastic production support. NOMOS Managing Editor, John Holzwarth, a busy Ph.D. candidate in the Princeton Politics Department, has always made time to compensate for my near total lack of organization. He devoted many hours to staying in touch with authors, and to preparing the manuscript for publication, doing a terrific job at every stage.

My thanks to the membership of ASPLP for their continued support, to association officers for their leadership and guidance, and to Secretary-Treasurer Judith Wagner DeCew for her critical role in helping to produce ASPLP meetings and these volumes.

STEPHEN MACEDO

CONTRIBUTORS

ANITA L. ALLEN
Law and Philosophy, University of Pennsylvania

LAWRENCE BLUM
Philosophy, University of Massachusetts, Boston

HARRY BRIGHOUSE
Philosophy of Education, London Institute of Education, and Philosophy, University of Wisconsin, Madison

RANDALL CURREN
Philosophy and Education, University of Rochester

PETER DE MARNEFFE
Philosophy, Arizona State University

JAMES G. DWYER
Law, College of William & Mary

CHISTOPHER L. EISGRUBER
Program in Law and Public Affairs, Princeton University

WILLIAM A. GALSTON
School of Public Affairs, University of Maryland

AMY GUTMANN
Politics and University Center for Human Values, Princeton University

MICHAEL W. MCCONNELL
  Law, University of Utah

STEPHEN MACEDO
  Politics and University Center for Human Values, Princeton University

ROB REICH
  Political Science, Ethics in Society, and Education, Stanford University

NANCY L. ROSENBLUM
  Political Science, Brown University

YAEL TAMIR
  Ministry of Immigration Absorption, Israel, and Philosophy, Tel Aviv University

JOHN TOMASI
  Political Science, Brown University

ANDREW VALLS
  Political Science, Morehouse College

INTRODUCTION

STEPHEN MACEDO

What are the proper aims of education in a liberal democracy? Given the deep disagreement about moral and religious values in modern societies, what is the proper balance between public and private claimants to educational authority? Should parents be given greater control over their children's formal education—and perhaps a share of public resources to support that control—or is there already too much latitude for parental tyranny over children? Are today's public schools promoting a culture of rootless individualism? Do we increasingly resort to prisons and punishment instead of schools and moral education to control young people, and the adults whose education was never taken seriously? And what, finally, should be the fate of the great project of racially integrated schooling: a project that energized a vast expenditure of hopes and resources in the latter half of the 20th century in America? Should we recommit ourselves to the ideal of integration, or should we embrace other, perhaps better, ways to help the disadvantaged and promote social integration? Should we go further, and affirm that predominantly black educational institutions have intrinsic benefits, such as preserving black culture and providing role models for black youngsters?

These are among the questions and problems addressed by the important essays gathered in this volume. These are not the only questions associated with moral and political education throughout the ages, but they do implicate some of the most

1

vexing moral, political, and legal conflicts of our time, and they furnish ample ground for serious moral reflection and lively debate. Our essayists are determined to bring philosophical, political, and legal reflection to bear on the practical question of how education should be reformed. These essays are the fruit of intellectual engagement with the real world: they display a determination to illumine educational choices that lie before modern democracies.

In politics no less than in the academy, fundamental questions concerning the proper aims of education, and the proper balance of authority between governments, parents, and particular moral and religious communities, have attracted increasing attention over the past 15 years. Three broad sets of reasons for the turn to education form the background for the essays in this volume. First is the renewed attention to the quality of citizenship in modern liberal democracies, attention sparked by communitarian and civic republican charges that liberalism is corrosive of virtuous citizenship and good forms of community. Second is the challenge presented by the growing concern with multiculturalism. Third is the renewed attention being paid to educational reforms emphasizing parental choice. Let me say a bit about each of these.

The attention of political philosophers shifted somewhat in the 1980's from the project of promoting basic rights and distributive (or economic) justice toward the fate of community and the character of citizens in liberal political regimes. Conservatives had long warned that the decline of traditional sources of authority would lead to incivility and aimless individualism, and that welfare would undermine the character of aid recipients. In the 1980's conservative critics of liberalism were joined by "communitarians" and civic republicans who also argued that the liberalism of the 1960's and 1970's had become corrosive of essential elements of the good society: it had become a court-oriented anti-politics of equal individual rights and economic redistribution. Liberal politics freed individuals from inherited roles and unchosen ties to others, while ignoring the centrality of community to the good life. Liberalism's hallmark, these critics alleged, is the insistence that government should remain neutral on contested conceptions of the good life.[1]

It is possible to sympathize with some of the concerns of liberalism's critics while insisting on the paramount political importance of equal basic rights for all: for blacks, for women, for gays and lesbians, and others pushed to the margins of society. Granting the primacy of justice, there can be no doubt that the political agenda of a self-governing republic must involve more than equal rights and justice for all. The democratic pursuit of justice requires a measure of citizen competence and engagement. It was natural, therefore, that as the dust settled from the liberal revolution of the 1960's and 1970's, renewed attention would be given to a wider political agenda, including the project of forming citizens. The concerns of liberalism's critics may have helped intensify the salience of education, but signal contributions to constructive reflection on educative questions have been made by democrats and liberals, as well as their critics.[2]

Concerns about the perceived thinness of the individual rights-oriented agenda of liberalism pushed political thinkers to take education more seriously: to think more about citizen virtues, and how public educational policy should or should not promote public values and virtues. A second development has also raised the stakes around education while often pushing the substance of the debate in opposite directions: sometimes toward a thickening and sometimes toward a thinning of the public education agenda.

This second development is the swelling tide of concern with multiculturalism and the politics of identity and "recognition."[3] Multiculturalism, like communitarianism and civic republicanism, often appears as a response to the perceived failings of liberal educational and political aims. Multiculturalists of all stripes argue for the inadequacy of politics of equal rights for all. They argue that liberal justice unfairly universalizes certain interests and needs, which are not in fact valued equally by all groups in society: divergent group-based perspectives need to be taken more seriously. Greater weight should be given to the distinctive voices, interests, and self-conceptions of groups outside the cultural mainstream. Debates over multiculturalism have invigorated educational thinking in America and abroad.

Two very different ways have emerged of taking multicultural concerns seriously. The first, inclusive form of multiculturalism

looks toward the reform and improvement of common institutions: it seeks to make public institutions fairer by making them
more truly inclusive. In education, inclusive multiculturalism
seeks to promote greater respect for the distinctive identities of
traditionally marginalized groups in the common curriculum: in
textbooks and in classroom and extra-curricular exercises,
thereby publicly affirming the importance and value of group
identities.

Greater inclusiveness in the commons—a more truly *common*
commons—is one face of the multicultural challenge to traditional educational practices. Inclusive multiculturalism is a reformist impulse: a way of taking more seriously the traditional liberal value of equal concern and fairness (this is clearest in the
case of Will Kymlicka). The other face of multiculturalism is
quite different: it challenges the fairness of the commons however conceived, and suggests that public educational institutions
should not be reformed but abandoned. Public educational requirements should be slimmed down so that we can give much
greater weight and scope to deep value pluralism and institutional diversity. The educational upshot of this second, separationist form of multiculturalism is not to rework the terms of inclusion but to argue for the greater justice of allowing parents
who disagree about educational aims—just as they disagree about
religious and intellectual aims—to go their own way, opt out of
public educational requirements with which they disagree, and
to choose their own schools. According to this view, in the face of
parental disagreement, the legitimate overriding educational interests of the liberal democratic polity are minimal: far more
minimal than the values that have been asserted by overweening
advocates of democratic education from Horace Mann to John
Dewey to Amy Gutmann. Children must learn to be literate, tolerant, and decently well informed about the constitutional order.
These limited ends can be secured by the regulation of publicly
supported private schools. Today's public schools go beyond the
necessary core of civic virtues. Public schools promote secular-
ism, and reflect the values of a popular youth culture that many
parents wish to oppose: a culture of materialism, moral non-judg-
mentalism, and premature sex. Supporting only public schools
with tax dollars is unfair.

The political potency of this second version of multicultural-ism has been enhanced in recent years as a consequence of its growing appeal to religious groups upset with the values of pub-lic schools. The old strategy of religious opponents of public, sec-ular schooling was a variant of the first, inclusive version of multi-culturalism: that strategy involved efforts to re-introduce prayers into public schools, and to get "equal time" for the teaching of "Creation Science" alongside the teaching of evolution, thus making public schools fairer to religious parents via the inclusion of religious exercises. Religious critics of public schooling appear to be increasingly interested not in reforming but in abandoning public schools, in favor of tax-supported systems of parental choice among public and private, religious and secular schools. Some argue for vouchers based on the claim that greater compe-tition among public and private schools would improve educa-tional effectiveness. Others (including Michael McConnell, in chapter 3) argue that a system of publicly supported educational diversity would be fairer: getting rid of the common-school mo-nopoly on public funding and substituting a system of publicly supported educational vouchers for parents to spend on the schools of their choice would be fairer to the diversity of view-points in our society and truer to the traditional values of equal liberty for all. Thus, the traditional concern to protect religious freedom is increasingly wedded to the newer emphasis on group rights and multiculturalism.

If the concern with citizenship pushed liberal democrats to take public educational aims more seriously, the concern with multiculturalism has been more complicated in its effects: it sometimes appears to provide a basis for reforming the common curriculum of public schools to make them more inclusive, and at other times it is interpreted as providing a basis for abandon-ing common schools in favor of educational pluralism.

A third reason for the greater concern with education is what has appeared to be a growing willingness to experiment, on grounds in addition to multiculturalism, with various forms of ed-ucational reform emphasizing parental choice. Parental choice has been a growing feature of public school policy for some years now. In the 1970's and 1980's, "magnet schools" were formed within the public system to promote voluntary racial integration.

More recently, "charter schools" are increasingly popular ways for states to provide opportunities for groups of public school teachers and administrators to establish smaller schools, often with a special focus, and a measure of autonomy from local school boards, within the public system. These forms of public school choice remain variations on the traditional American system of common schooling, according to which public monies support free public schools at the primary and secondary levels, with parents being free to choose private schools if they wish but at their own expense. The far more revolutionary reform would channel state education dollars to parents, in the form of a check or voucher, to be spent on the qualified public or private school of the parents' choice, generally including religious schools. The voucher idea, which has been discussed off and on since Milton Friedman advanced it in the 1950's, gained ground in the 1990's, as voucher experiments were undertaken in Milwaukee and Cleveland.[4] Voucher proposals suffered court setbacks and electoral reversals in the fall 2000 elections. While the future of vouchers appears uncertain, they remain an important challenge to educational practices in America.

The voucher debate is important because this reform represents a fundamental shift of educational authority away from public institutions and toward parents. Part of the motivation for this shift of authority is the conviction, supported by some policy researchers but hotly denied by others, that the shortcomings of public schools could be remedied by allowing private schools to compete for students. Educational choice including vouchers, the argument sometimes seems to be, would help us pursue our public educational aims more effectively. But other arguments for vouchers owe more to the second version of multiculturalism mentioned above: allowing parents with divergent educational aims to choose among public and private schools, including religious schools, would be fairer to parents, perhaps especially those parents who worry that the education provided by today's public schools undermines their children's religious beliefs.

These large themes—the concern with citizen virtue, multiculturalism, and educational reform movements emphasizing parental choice—form the background for most of the essays that follow.

The appearance of Amy Gutmann's *Democratic Education* in 1987 provided an important impetus for the turn toward educational questions among philosophers and political theorists. It is appropriate that Gutmann opens our volume with a defense of democratic education.

Democratic governments should, according to Gutmann's book, subsidize and require schooling that prepares students for exercising their "civil, political, and social rights and responsibilities." Citizens' educational decisions are limited by the two bedrock requirements of non-repression and non-discrimination: neither the state nor any group within the state may use education to restrict "rational deliberation of competing conceptions of the good life and the good society," and all educable children must be educated. Democratic deliberation about educational aims gives citizens the opportunity to engage in "conscious social reproduction," and this contributes to the political education of adults as well as children. Democratic governments should also allow that outside of schools, "parents are and should remain the primary educators of children." In addition, parents ought to be able to choose private schools so long as they "supplement but do not supplant" the requirements of civic education.[5]

In chapter 1, Gutmann defends the democratic educational ideal against three sets of critics: against "parentalists" who argue that democratic education is too demanding, and against cosmopolitans and defenders of patriotic education who argue that democratic education is not demanding enough. Parentalists such as Stephen Gilles argue that because educational ends are controversial, public educational requirements should be limited to a "civic minimum." Against this view, Gutmann argues that every conception of educational authority is controversial, including every conception of a "civic minimum." This fact is not an argument for deferring to parents, who have ample opportunity to influence their children's education even under the democratic educational model. Against cosmopolitans like Martha Nussbaum, and advocates of an education for patriotism, such as Maurizio Viroli, Gutmann grants that some versions of moral universalism and love of country are morally admirable, but they are not uniquely admirable and democratic citizens are not required to adopt either of these moral ideals. Thus Gutmann argues that democratic education is neither too demanding (as parentalists argue) nor insufficiently demanding (as universalists and patriots argue): it is just demanding enough.

In chapter 2, Christopher L. Eisgruber argues that what is at stake in many educational controversies may be less than Gutmann and others believe. When parents take the local school board to court to challenge material in textbooks or the content of the curriculum (as they did in the somewhat famous case of *Mozert v. Hawkins County School Board*),[6] observers like Gutmann leap too quickly (according to Eisgruber) to interpret the controversy in terms of a clash of basic principles: democratic education versus parentalism. In fact, Eisgruber argues, choices about textbooks and curricular materials do not determine what children learn. Since conflicting lessons can be drawn from the same story, it is implausible to think that any particular reading assignment will be crucial to teaching children important democratic virtues. Eisgruber argues that the role of the teacher is liable to be far more important than the particular reading selections, and judges attempting to articulate constitutional standards will not have an easy time controlling teachers' discretion. Teaching democratic values may depend crucially on the teachers' classroom style—how different children are treated—and such intangible factors as the school's ethos or moral environment.

In chapter 3, Michael McConnell issues a radical challenge to the basic legitimacy of democratic education as Gutmann defends it, and as we have known it in America over the past 150 years and more. McConnell (who has argued more than a dozen cases involving church-state controversies before the United States Supreme Court) argues that democratically controlled public schooling violates basic liberal and constitutional principles: in place of an educational system that is "democratic and collective," we should adopt one that is "private and pluralistic." Given the range of reasonable disagreement in our society about the moral and religious viewpoints relevant to education, "it is time to discard the notion that democratic control over education is *in principle* the form best suited to a liberal, pluralistic society. The opposite is true." A system of publicly subsidized parental choice among schools (all of which would have to satisfy minimal civic standards) would be fairer.

It would be more democratic and more liberal, McConnell argues, for educational policy to allow citizens who disagree deeply, permanently, and reasonably about their educational visions to educate their own children in their own way. Imposing one official educational vision on all is akin to maintaining an established church: public schooling is inconsistent with the "disestablishmentarian" values of the First Amendment. Public schools have always sought to assimilate children to a preferred religious view, or a close equivalent to a religious view: in the 19th century, the schools promoted Protestantism; nowadays they favor "secular self-actualization." Now, as before, dissenters from the official educational orthodoxy are treated as second-class citizens. Paradoxically, McConnell concludes, some studies show that children get a better civic education in religious schools nowadays, whereas in public schools they are imbued with "crass consumerism, materialism, premature sexualization, rebellion, and nihilism." Thus McConnell argues that educational choice, including publicly funded school vouchers that could be used by parents to pay for religious as well as secular private schools, would be fairer as a matter of basic First Amendment values of intellectual freedom, pluralism, and disestablishment.

Nancy Rosenblum notices some important ambiguities in McConnell's powerful indictment of the educational status quo. For one thing, she argues, it is unclear whether McConnell's proposals amount to an effort to improve American democracy or to supplant fundamental democratic values in favor of what would be better understood as a "regime of pluralism." If McConnell's argument is based on the fundamental importance of respecting pluralism, why stop with schools? A wider program of respect for pluralism would extend beyond schools into civil society, and would justify granting groups and subgroups within the polity a "wide range of accommodations and opt-outs from general obligations." Churches and religiously affiliated organizations could be exempted from anti-discrimination laws. By stopping with schools, Rosenblum argues, McConnell fails to fully confront the possible dangers of reconceiving our polity as one founded on value pluralism. To really take pluralism seriously could, Rosenblum suggests, flirt with anarchy.

Rosenblum additionally notes a possible trade-off that advocates of educational pluralism may need to face. McConnell is sanguine that educational pluralism will not lead to social "Balkanization," but others may not be so sure. Advocates of social pluralism like McConnell should beware its possible unintended side effects: if they succeed at moving school policy away from the promotion of democratic aspirations, the reaction could be in the form of efforts to constrain pluralism in society. The safest course, argues Rosenblum, is to continue to use common schools to promote our democratic aspirations.

Amy Gutmann follows in chapter 5 with a rejoinder to McConnell and Eisgruber. She emphasizes, first of all, that the democratic educational ideal is not a unified, "one-size-fits-all" system. Democratic education stands for the decentralized control of schools, and so for a great deal of local variation, as well as a mix of public and private schools: "no one who defends democratic education argues for a *comprehensive* set of prescriptive standards that would make all schools the same." There is, on the other hand, no reason to regard maximum diversity among schools as a basic value. Voucher schools must serve public purposes or else the public has no reason to fund them. The chief unfairness of our current system is not the lack of vouchers but public inattention to poverty, and the absence of a real public safety net. Helping poor children would at least be one good justification for vouchers, Gutmann asserts, but that is not McConnell's justification, and there is no evidence, she argues, that voucher plans, as opposed to smaller class sizes, help poor children.

Gutmann applauds Eisgruber's attempt to moderate the clash between contending principled commitments to democratic education and parentalism, and to find a pragmatic ground for compromise, but she is doubtful that principled conflicts can be avoided. School boards are not, as Eisgruber allows, choosing textbooks and stories in order to indoctrinate children by insisting on a single orthodox interpretation. It is the parents who object to particular reading assignments (as in the *Mozert* case) who want the courts to step in to force public schools to tailor classroom practices to particular parental preferences and convictions (in *Mozert,* the *parents* insisted that their children could be allowed to read certain stories only if the readings were accompanied by a disclaimer as to the falsehood of the lesson the parents imputed to the stories). Democratic education does not depend on giving public officials the authority to assign "one and only one particular set of texts," Gutmann allows. But effective democratic education does depend on "the authority to pick some reasonable set of texts and not to be required by another authority to substitute other texts whenever any parent objects on conscientious grounds."

And so, the debate over democratic control of education, and the values and ideals that should justify, limit, and guide that control, continues.

The essays in Part II take up questions concerning the influence of public educational values over private moral and religious communities. The principal questions addressed here include: How far may liberal governments go in promoting the value of individual autonomy and critical reflectiveness? Should public educational policies that have the effect of undermining some traditional forms of life and religious belief be curbed?

John Tomasi notes that the values embedded in public institutions and policies often have broad and deeply non-neutral consequences for private moral and religious communities, making it hard for some to survive. Public school curricula often seem to emphasize such values as critical thinking and the autonomy of free individuals, and these values may stand in tension with biblical literalism and the moral codes of some conservative religious families. When public schools embody these values, some communities of adults—including religious fundamentalists—may find it harder to pass along their religious beliefs to their children. Tomasi allows that it would be impossible for public policies to be neutral with respect to these "spill over" effects (as he calls them), but he argues that these non-neutral consequences should be minimized. Indeed, he argues that "political liberals"—those like John Rawls who advocate liberalism as a public morality rather than a comprehensive worldview—should be especially concerned to limit these cultural spillovers. If parents are willing to affirm basic constitutional principles, then political liberals should defer to them if they complain that aspects of the public school curriculum are unfair to their religious or cultural views.

Peter de Marneffe takes up the question of the role of value neutrality in public ethics and public policy. The idea of neutrality should serve as a constraint on the sorts of reasons that can justify coercive government policies: some principled bases for government action are simply illegitimate. The important truth in the idea of neutrality is that the bare belief in the worthlessness of a way of life is by itself not a justification for prohibiting it. But the role of the idea of neutrality in public debates over education policy should not be exaggerated. The proper standard of evaluation of different policies is not which is most neutral but, rather, the burdens that different policies impose on individuals. De Marneffe sketches a theory of moral rights according to which it is wrong for a government policy to impose a burden on one person that is substantially worse than any burden that someone else would bear in the absence of this policy. With respect to voucher proposals, de Marneffe insists that the idea of neutrality properly understood is extremely unlikely to settle the dispute between voucher advocates and opponents. The relevant question is far more likely to be whether choice plans for school reform improve education, especially for the least advantaged children who currently bear the heaviest burdens.

Harry Brighouse agrees with de Marneffe that vouchers violate no plausible principle of neutrality (which is neutrality of aim or intent). To the extent that voucher plans appear to involve public subsidies to religion, he argues that they are really no different in this respect from tax deductions for charitable contributions to religious institutions. But would a system of publicly supported parental choice among public and private, secular and religious schools, violate the autonomy of children: their independence, and ability to make their own reflective decisions about how to live? Brighouse offers a distinctive account of the proper role of the value of personal autonomy in public education policy: state policy should "facilitate" but not promote the value of autonomy. Autonomy should not be promoted because it is not necessary for every good way of life: if Mother Teresa was not especially reflective about the choice of her vocation, her life was no less valuable for that. It is important that people are able to live their lives "from the inside," and that requires that they are able to exit from ways of life that are at odds with their fundamental desires. Education should focus on knowledge and skills, not virtues. Children should acquire "epistemically reliable" ways of evaluating different ways of life so they can understand the costs associated with alternatives. But schools should beware promoting autonomy or any account of the virtues of good persons: the state should refrain from putting its authority behind any controversial conceptions of the good life. Children should be provided with the opportunity to live as autonomous individuals if they want, but state policy must also take account of the fact that nonautonomous lives—including those involving adherence to unquestioned religious beliefs—may be lived well. Voucher plans that allow parents to choose schools for their child need involve no violation of the child's interests, so long as voucher schemes are accompanied by proper public regulations.

Rob Reich argues that greater attention needs to be paid to the growing popularity of home schooling. While tens of thousands of children are enrolled in voucher experiments, and some religious groups such as the Amish are exempted from mandatory high school attendance, the number of children being home schooled has skyrocketed (estimates range as high as 1.3 million as of 1998). Is home schooling a cause for concern? Reich argues that all children have an interest in acquiring a capacity for "minimal autonomy": many children will reject the ideal of Socratic critical reflection, but all should have the capacity to develop and pursue their own interests and to participate as equal citizens if they choose. It is possible, Reich allows, that home schooling may increase children's ability to resist some peer pressures and the domination of mass culture, thereby increasing the autonomy of home-schooled children. Nevertheless, Reich notes evidence suggesting that most home-schooling parents want to control the moral and spiritual upbringing of their children, and many are eager to prevent their children from being exposed to conflicting moral and spiritual values. Home schooling should be regulated to guard against parental domination, but regulating home schools is extremely problematic: who will complain to public officials if regulations are ignored? And how will violations be punished? Public officials are extremely unlikely to be willing to remove children from their homes. Home schooling is troubling because it is so intrinsically hard to monitor and regulate. Reich argues that in practice the best solution may be to insist on the vigorous enforcement of some fairly minimal but essential regulations by testing and other means.

James Dwyer concludes Part II with a sweeping indictment of most of those who write about educational policy and principles. Dwyer argues that educational theorists and policy makers fail to give "full effect" to the independent personhood of children. Anything other than a "child-centered" perspective on education is misguided. Arguments over education such as those in Parts I and II of this volume are, says Dwyer, far too concerned with adults' interests in education: typical education controversies pit adults as parents against adults as citizens. Children's interests in their own education are wrongly subordinated to the interests of competing groups of parents.

Dwyer concludes by turning to the voucher debate and argues that what is crucial is not whether schools are public or private but whether they are serving children's interests. Insofar as private or public schools do not serve children's educational interests, they have no right to exist. Where children's education is suffering because they are in resource-poor private schools, the government is not only permitted but required to provide financial aid to those schools.

The essays in Parts I and II range across many of the most prominent fissures in contemporary education policy. But do these essays wrongly discount children's educational interests? I will take the liberty of offering two observations. First, what most adults are disagreeing and arguing about with respect to education in this volume and elsewhere is (in large part) not their own interests in education but *the education they think is best for children,* and *who they think ought to be entrusted* to make educational decisions for children. Second, insofar as educational thinkers and policy makers are concerned about such matters as the health of democracy, it is far from clear that these interests are being pursued *at the expense* of children. There is nothing wrong with designing education policy partly with an eye toward the health of our liberal democratic citizenship, so long as this also conduces to the good of children, who are after all future citizens as well as future adults. Thinking about civic virtue is often a way of thinking about children's interests. Civic ends should not be pursued at the expense of children's basic interests as human beings. Finally, for a "best interests of the child" perspective on education to be useful we need an account of the best interests of the child, and Dwyer does not provide one. In advancing and defending a particular conception of children's interests Dwyer will have to face the same conflicts addressed by others in Parts I and II, including how to divide educational authority between parents and citizens, given the fact of disagreement among adults *about* children's educational interests. Maybe Dwyer is right that children's interests have not always been explicitly at the center of debates over education. It remains to be seen how much difference it will make to place Dwyer's favored conception of children's basic educational interests at the center of educational debates.

Part III contains only one essay, which takes an unusual but interesting perspective on the debates over education: the perspective of the criminal justice system and its increasingly frequent application to children. Randall Curren's essay is a reflection on the growing popularity of the maxim "adult time for adult crime." Under what conditions can a society rightfully apply adult standards of criminal responsibility to children and adolescents? Curren does not seek to provide an exhaustive answer, but he insists on the centrality of one standard that is relevant to this volume: justice demands that serious efforts be made to ensure that all children receive an adequate moral education, and only when these efforts have been exhausted can it be proper to resort on a massive scale to criminal sanctions. Society must provide a fair chance for children to overcome their immaturity and lack of self-control before it subjects them to the massive apparatus of official violence that is our criminal justice system. Curren argues in effect that our society's readiness to adopt and pursue a punitive paradigm with respect to youth misconduct is a grave injustice. Taking moral education more seriously is a pre-requisite to applying criminal sanctions in good conscience. To pursue this more humane approach properly, Curren urges the value of an "Aristotelian" perspective that takes seriously the importance of habit and character.

Curren's observations add to the moral urgency of debates over education. He is right that one of the prime ways in which our society in effect cleans up after its collective failure to educate all children adequately is an ever-expanding resort to incarceration and parole, in which criminal sanctions are applied to ever-younger children. To respond properly to Curren's pointed assault on our punishment-centered model of behavior control, we will need to think about moral education in a broad sense, as involving greater attention to the morally educative dimensions not only of schooling but of public policy and the social environment broadly. Curren clarifies the urgency of insuring a basic moral education for all.

Nothing has done more to change the practice of primary and secondary education in the United States over the past half century than the pursuit of racial desegregation.[7] While racially segregated schools are no longer permissible as a matter of government policy, racial integration as a lived reality is far from being achieved. The formal color blindness of our laws coexists—with increasing comfort it appears—with the fact of racially segregated housing patterns, class and race divisions across most inner cities and suburbs, and the persistent poverty of many inner-city blacks. How should we feel about racial integration as a positive ideal? Can we muster enthusiasm for a renewed push for school integration? Or should we give in to the sober dispiritedness that is one rational response to the persistence of racial division and put our energies into other projects to improve the prospects of the least well off in our society?

Part IV takes up these vexing questions. Lawrence Blum urges that we reconsider, reappreciate, and renew our commitment to the positive ideal of racial integration. The retreat on school integration witnessed in the 1990's is partly the consequence of an overly narrow focus on the benefits of desegregation gauged from the point of view of economic opportunity. School administrators and teachers should be guided by an ideal of deliberate racial mixing, rather than resting with the mere "co-presence" of racial groups once formally separated by law. Blum notes that racial mixing is already the norm in inner-city public schools, where large numbers of blacks and Latinos are educated with smaller but significant numbers of white students. The average suburban white student, however, attends a school that is over-whelmingly white: most white students attend schools in which there is not a critical mass of non-whites, and these schools cannot really be considered racially plural. Most white students are missing out on the moral, social, and civic benefits of racially plural schools.

Ethnoracially plural schools would encourage and support the expression and recognition of ethnic and racial identities, but they would also foster cross-group friendships. It is no good to ignore or suppress the plurality of identities that exist in our society, but it also thwarts our central moral, civic, and social aims as an ethnoracially plural democracy if these identities are expressed in isolated enclaves whose boundaries are reinforced by suspicion and distrust of outsiders. Schools should be set up to reflect the diversity of identities in our society and to foster cross-group conversations and friendships; such schools would help break down the stereotypes and hostility that plague our society. This is especially important for white students, whose horizons will be expanded as they learn to "read" citizens of different races better, and they will gain the opportunity for friendly acquaintance with those they now too often regard with suspicion.

William A. Galston accepts Blum's integrationist aims but doubts that Blum's proposals stand a realistic chance of succeeding. Galston identifies and challenges Blum's implicit empirical assumptions, namely, that school integration is effective in reducing social distance among students, and that the benefits of a renewed focus on school integration will outweigh the costs. Galston argues that the realistic focus in schools should be on improving safety and academic achievement. Integration can be pursued by other means. School integration has not improved over the past 25 years, Galston notes, but racial attitudes have improved. Increased integration in various settings outside the schools—including the military and the workplace—have likely contributed to improving racial attitudes. Racial intermarriage has also increased. So the reality is, according to Galston, that a great push toward racial integration in the schools would be hard to accomplish and very costly, given the ability of whites to flee to the suburbs if they wish. Racial integration may not do much good unless school policy also tackles the crucial problem of class segregation. And, finally, we should not underestimate the great sensitivity and difficulty of bridging deep feelings of racial victimization. As things stand, schools may be less well suited than other institutions to promote integration.

Anita Allen seeks to salvage a realistic faith in integrationist ideals. She allows that integration is out of favor, and acknowledges that more adequate educational facilities should be provided for all children independently of whether their schools are integrated. She also recognizes that measures to promote integration will likely have to be voluntary (such as the use of "magnet schools" within the public system). Nevertheless, Allen argues that integrationists should take heart from the fact that in recent decades in America and societies around the world diversity has become more apparent and more publicly valued. Even in America, diversity is increasingly recognized as a central value in universities and many workplaces and other institutions: diversity is a "welcome mat" that advances the pursuit of excellence. In the end, Allen asserts that Americans remain a "nation of habitual segregationists," and so they may not take Blum's argument seriously enough. Nevertheless, human diversity is a "cultural bounty" that can be reaped only through the conscious pursuit of integration.

Andrew Valls leaves the benefits of integration to one side (without denying them) and focuses on what the celebrators of integration ignore. Predominantly black educational institutions have, according to Valls, positive benefits for blacks: they can help reproduce black culture, provide leadership role models for young blacks, and offer a refuge from a society that remains deeply racist. Valls also notes that arguments for integration such as Blum's often focus on the benefits to whites. The costs of integrationist policies have, moreover, often fallen disproportionately on blacks: black children were bussed farther and more frequently than whites.

Valls insists that no one should be required to attend a predominantly black institution. And he insists that arguments for predominantly black institutions cannot be mustered on behalf of all-white institutions: Valls's argument stresses the vulnerabilities of blacks in America on account of their minority status. Public policy should, as Will Kymlicka suggests, affirmatively support those minority cultures that, on account of their minority status within a larger culture, find it especially costly and difficult to sustain themselves. Given the failures and costs of past efforts at integration, the persistence of racism, and the difficulties faced by any effort to renew integration, Valls urges that we should appreciate the benefits to blacks of preserving some predominantly black institutions. The debate among our essayists closes, therefore, on a sobering note.

The essays gathered in this volume address some of the liveliest and most important conflicts facing modern democracies. Admittedly, the focus of these essays is often (though not always) on the American context, and the questions raised here will be answered by different societies in different ways. But both the conflicts and the principles discussed herein have a relevance that goes far beyond North America. Educational debates remain vexing in part because the very terms of inclusion in modern liberal democratic societies are contested: they are contested everywhere, though the particulars of the conflicts and the intensities of the conflicts vary widely. Should public educational institutions and policies do more to preserve some of our differences? If so, which differences, and why? Are policies designed so as to preserve particular identities best understood as options that may be considered in democratic deliberation, or are some forms of group accommodation and preservation required by basic justice? No society will soon put these questions to rest. Lucky are the societies—as my co-editor well knows—in which disagreements over education and identity are confined to peaceful intellectual and political contest.

NOTES

1. Among the notable critiques of liberalism identified with communitarianism are Alasdair MacIntyre, *After Virtue* (Notre Dame, Indiana: University of Notre Dame Press, 1981), Charles Taylor, "Atomism," and "What's Wrong with Negative Liberty?" in *Human Agency and Language: Philosophical Papers, 1* (Cambridge: Cambridge University Press, 1985); Michael Sandel, *Liberalism and the Limits of Justice* (Cambridge: Cambridge University Press, 1982). I discuss these communitarian and civic

republican critics in *Liberal Virtues: Citizenship, Virtue, and Community in Liberal Constitutionalism* (Oxford: Oxford University Press, 1990).

2. Notable contributions by liberal democrats include Amy Gutmann, *Democratic Education* (Princeton: Princeton University Press, 1987; reissued in 1999); Eamonn Callan, *Creating Citizens: Political Education and Liberal Democracy* (Oxford: Oxford University Press, 1997); Meira Levinson, *The Demands of Liberal Education* (Oxford: Oxford University Press, 1999). In addition see Stephen Macedo, *Diversity and Distrust: Civic Education in a Multicultural Democracy* (Cambridge: Harvard University Press, 2000).

3. Iris Marion Young, *Justice and the Politics of Difference* (Princeton: Princeton University Press, 1990); Charles Taylor, *Multiculturalism* (Princeton: Princeton University Press, 1994); Will Kymlicka, *Multicultural Citizenship: A Liberal Theory of Minority Rights* (Oxford: Oxford University Press, 1996); Melissa S. Williams, *Voice, Trust, and Memory* (Princeton: Princeton University Press, 1998).

4. I discuss the voucher experiments in Milwaukee and Cleveland, and the legal challenges to them, in "The Constitution of Civil Society: School Vouchers, Religious Nonprofit Organizations, and Liberal Public Values," in Symposium on Legal and Constitutional Implications of the Calls to Revive Civil Society, *Chicago-Kent Law Review,* vol. 75, no. 2 (2000), pp. 417–452.

5. Amy Gutmann, chapter 1 in this volume, and see *Democratic Education,* pp. 39, 44–45.

6. See *Mozert v. Hawkins County School Board,* 857 F.2d. 1058 (6th Cir. 1987); I discuss this case at length in *Diversity and Distrust.*

7. See for example the account in Gerald Grant, *The World We Created at Hamilton High* (Cambridge: Harvard University Press, 1988).

PART I

DEBATING DEMOCRATIC EDUCATION

1

CIVIC MINIMALISM, COSMOPOLITANISM, AND PATRIOTISM: WHERE DOES DEMOCRATIC EDUCATION STAND IN RELATION TO EACH?

AMY GUTMANN

Defenders of democratic education argue that democratic governments should publicly subsidize and mandate schooling that tries to prepare students for exercising their civil, political, and social rights and responsibilities. They also argue that democratic governments can and should do this consistently with respecting parental authority to educate their children in their family and in other civic associations of their choice. Parents may also choose private schools that supplement but do not supplant the requirements of civic education.[1]

Some critics charge that democratic education is too demanding and others that it is not demanding enough. Defenders of civic minimalism argue that the civic educational requirements imposed by governments must be minimal so that parental control over children's education can be close to comprehensive. Democratic education is unjust insofar as it imposes educational requirements that exceed what critics call the civic minimum.

In contrast to civic minimalists who argue that democratic education is too demanding of parents, cosmopolitans suggest that democratic education is not demanding enough of citizens, educators, and parents. Whereas civic minimalists challenge democratic education from the perspective of "familial reproduction,"[2] cosmopolitans challenge it from the perspective of cultivating "citizens of the world."[3] Democratic education, cosmopolitans charge, mistakenly focuses on cultivating the skills and virtues of citizenship specific to a single country. A morally good education should aim to educate citizens of the world. Still worse than educating citizens of a single country, according to cosmopolitans, would be educating unreflective patriots. What is the relationship of democratic education to the claims of cosmopolitanism and patriotism? Does democratic education aim to educate cosmopolitans or patriots, neither, or both?

In this essay, I examine the relationship between democratic education, understood as an ideal, and civic minimalism, cosmopolitanism, and patriotism. Civic minimalism, on close scrutiny, does not offer either a substantive or formally coherent challenge to democratic education. The challenge of civic minimalism turns out to be either empty or self-defeating. The challenge of cosmopolitanism, by contrast, is substantive and formally coherent. Democratic education is compatible with a kind of cosmopolitanism, but the kind—egalitarian cosmopolitanism—should not be confused with cosmopolitanism in all its forms. Democratic education is also compatible with a kind of patriotism, but not with a kind that advocates unqualified love and devotion to country. Democratic education is compatible with educating patriots who love their country because—and to the extent that—it makes liberty and justice possible. But democratic education makes neither cosmopolitanism nor patriotism morally mandatory. It recognizes that there are multiple self-identifications that are compatible with being a moral person and living in a way that is compatible with liberty and justice for all.

The response of democratic education to the challenges of civic minimalism, cosmopolitanism, and patriotism suggests its strength as a publicly defensible philosophy. In the first part of this essay, I argue that civic education need not be minimal to be justified to democratic citizens. Democratic education is more defensible both in form and in content than civic minimalism. Democratic education does not make the mistake of confusing the basic rights of parents with the power to deny children an education adequate to exercising their basic rights and responsibilities as free and equal citizens. In the second part of this essay, I argue that democratic education should welcome the kind of cosmopolitanism and patriotism committed to treating all people, regardless of their citizenship, as free and equal beings. But cosmopolitanism and patriotism per se do not necessarily entail such a commitment. We therefore need to define a particular interpretation of cosmopolitanism, egalitarian cosmopolitanism, and a particular interpretation of patriotism, republican patriotism. And we also need to rid these "isms" of their exclusivist claims to being the only morally right modes of self-identification.

Before I consider the challenges of civic minimalism, cosmopolitanism, and patriotism, I should briefly characterize the perspective of democratic education. At the core of the democratic ideal that informs democratic education is a commitment to treating adults as free and equal beings, and therefore to educating children so that they become free and equal beings, and so that they can relate to one another as citizens as such. Free and equal beings should offer one another morally defensible reasons for the laws that mutually bind them.[4] A deliberative conception of democracy highlights this ideal of reciprocal reason giving, but the ideal is not unique to deliberative democracy. All defensible conceptions of democracy underscore the importance of a universally available education that develops the capacity to deliberate among adults who should treat one another and be treated as civic equals. Deliberative accountability and decision making (including the decision not to deliberate about some matters) presuppose a citizenry whose education prepares them to deliberate, to evaluate the results of the deliberations of their representatives, and thereby to hold their representatives accountable. A primary aim of publicly mandated schooling is therefore to cultivate the skills and virtues of deliberation. Prominent among the deliberative virtues is the ability to think, reason, and discuss public matters publicly.

Why should deliberation be considered primary when the opportunity for most citizens to live a good life today requires many more basic skills than public deliberation? The capacity to deliberate about civic matters presupposes many other skills and virtues, a bundle that certainly includes the basics of literacy and numeracy. But just as certainly literacy and numeracy are not enough. The basic liberties and opportunities of individuals and their collective capacity to pursue justice also rest on virtues such as veracity, nonviolence, practical judgment, civic integrity, and civic magnanimity.[5] By cultivating these and other deliberative skills and virtues, a democratic society treats its members as free and equal citizens, rather than (more simply but less justifiably) as deferential subjects or self-interested individualists.

The willingness to deliberate about mutually binding matters distinguishes democratic citizens from self-interested individualists who argue merely to advance their own interests and deferential citizens who turn themselves into passive subjects by failing to argue, out of deference to political authority. Justice is far more likely to be served by democratic citizens who reason together in search of mutually justifiable decisions than by people who are not interested in politics or interested in it only for the sake of power. Even when deliberative citizens continue to disagree, as they often will, their effort to reach mutually justifiable decisions manifests mutual respect, which is itself a civic good. Because ongoing disagreement among reasonable people of good will is inevitable in any free society, mutual respect is an important virtue. Good-willed deliberation manifests mutual respect; it demonstrates a good faith effort to find mutually acceptable terms of social cooperation, not merely terms that are acceptable only to the most powerful, or for that matter to the most articulate.

If civic education should aim to cultivate the deliberative skills and virtues of democratic citizenship, it does not follow that these skills and virtues should be the focus of all educators of children. Outside of schooling, parents are and should remain the primary educators of their children. Parents should not be constrained to focus their educational efforts on preparing their children to become citizens or cosmopolitans. Civic education that is publicly mandated is all the more justifiable in a constitutional democracy where educational authority is divided among parents, citizens, and professional educators. I turn now to the challenges, first of civic minimalism, and then of cosmopolitanism and patriotism.[6]

I. Civic Minimalism or Democratic Education?

In a "parentalist manifesto," Stephen Gilles argues that the authority of parents over the schooling of their children should be treated in the same way as their custodial authority:

> States do not substitute their judgments for parental ones when it comes to nourishing or nurturing children; they assert the narrower power to condemn some parents' conduct as inconsistent with any reasonable conception of good nourishment or nurturing.[7]

Analogously, civic minimalists argue, states may outlaw certain clearly unreasonable educational practices but they must otherwise support the preferences of parents with regard to their own children's schooling. Civic minimalism says that the requirements of publicly mandated (and subsidized) education must be minimal so that parental authority over the schooling of their own children may be correspondingly maximal.

A major attraction of civic minimalism, most advocates argue, is that by virtue of minimizing the civic component of schooling, it can resolve the problem of achieving a consensus about civic education under conditions of reasonable pluralism. Parents can decide for their own children how best to interpret the demands of civic education, its ends as well as its means above the mandatory minimum. Democratic disagreement over public schooling can thereby be minimized.

But what are the minimal requirements of civic education? Like ordinary people, philosophers disagree about what the civic purposes of schooling should be. Disagreement per se is no reason for abandoning our efforts to develop and defend a conception of civic education. Quite the contrary. Within a democratic society, the project of defending a conception of the public purposes of schooling is all the more important in the face of reasonable disagreement. The theoretical and practical alternative to publicly defending a controversial conception is imposing one without defending it.

The fact of disagreement per se does not favor a minimalist position over a maximalist position or over a moderate set of requirements for civic education. Civic minimalists argue that the publicly mandated requirements of civic education in schools must be minimal for two reasons: to diminish democratic disagreement and to increase parental control over schooling. Requiring anything more than the civic minimum, they claim, constitutes an illegitimate exercise of political authority on the part of citizens, and therefore should be constitutionally prohibited.[8] A prohibition on publicly imposing more than a minimum set of requirements on schools does not follow from the fact of disagreement over what constitutes a good civic education in schools, even though civic minimalists often argue as if it does.

Civic minimalism is at least as controversial a position as democratic education. Democratic education gives citizens the discretion to mandate more than a civic minimum. Civic minimalism prohibits citizens from mandating more than the civic minimum. The ideal underlying civic minimalism is therefore more plausibly a defense of near-comprehensive parental control over education, including the publicly subsidized schooling of children, rather than an avoidance of public controversy. A defense of civic minimalism is almost always accompanied by a defense of parental choice over schools, often through a voucher system. Many civic minimalists argue that the government should give every set of parents a stipend to use at the school of their choice, public or private, secular or religious. Some civic minimalists do not defend vouchers but argue that dissenting parents, especially those parents who dissent on religious grounds, should be exempted from any educational requirement that cannot be demonstrated to be a necessary part of the civic minimum.

Civic minimalism thereby tries to amalgamate near-comprehensive parental authority with a minimalist civic education. Civic educational requirements are justifiable if but only if they do not exceed the minimum. Beyond the minimal requirements, parental authority must be supreme. Is civic minimalism a defensible alternative to democratic education, which permits democratic governments to mandate more than the civic minimum and thereby to limit parental authority correspondingly?

Let's consider the different implications of the two perspectives in the context of American constitutional democracy. Some
school districts in the United States support standards of civic education that civic minimalists say are above and beyond the civic
minimum. A school district in Tennessee, for example, teaches
elementary school students from basic reading texts that expose
them to the idea that boys as well as girls can enjoy cooking. One
story reads: "Pat reads to Jim. Jim cooks. The big book helps Jim.
Jim has fun."[9] Civic minimalists deny democratic citizens the discretion to require this reading if a student's parents object.
Judges should overrule the teaching in the name of the constitutional right of parents to determine all parts of their children's
education, including their schooling at public expense, except
the civic minimum. (Note that whereas democratic education
permits but does not require any school district to mandate this
curriculum, civic minimalism requires that no school district
mandate the curriculum. A position that recommends but does
not require a civic minimum is therefore inconsistent with civic
minimalism.)

Whereas civic minimalism authorizes, indeed requires, judges
to override any democratic decision that enforces more than the
civic minimum, democratic education grants democratic governments discretion over how to interpret the demands of civic education, provided the demands are not discriminatory or repressive. Parents do not have a general right to override otherwise legitimate democratic decisions concerning the schooling of their
children.[10] But why, civic minimalists might ask, are democratic
decisions to mandate more than the civic minimum legitimate?

Civic minimalists offer a grab bag of reasons for challenging
the idea that there is a range of democratic discretion over civic
education. One recurring reason is that "the child belongs to its
parents." In *Democratic Education*, I criticize this idea, upon which
civic minimalists rely when all else fails.[11] Children are no more
the mere creatures of their parents than they are the mere creatures of the state. Moreover, claiming that children belong to
their parents proves too much for civic minimalism, since the
claim leaves no principled room for mandating a civic minimum.

The second recurring argument offered by civic minimalism
against democratic discretion is that it opens the door to heated

public debates over schooling, which could be settled simply by ceding parents the right to decide how to educate their own children (over and above the civic minimum). For civic minimalism to be preferable to democratic education on this ground, however, we must believe that avoiding heated public debates is an overriding value (which it is not, in light of the possibility of settling heated public debates by instituting injustice). But if for the sake of argument we set aside the (important) issue of the value of avoiding argument in a democracy, civic minimalists still would need to show that their position is distinctively capable of avoiding heated public debate. To do this, they need to persuade democratic citizens that the civic minimum as they substantively understand it—and nothing more than the civic minimum as they substantively understand it—may limit parental authority. Civic minimalists have failed to do so, and they are probably bound to fail for several reasons.

First, competing conceptions of the civic minimum itself are reasonably contestable. Some of the reasonable conceptions will be more minimal than others, and there is no logical or moral sense to the claim that the most minimal is the constitutionally correct interpretation of the civic minimum. Not surprisingly, civic minimalists themselves disagree on what counts as the civic minimum. Deciding in theory to institute civic minimalism will not close the door to heated public debates over schooling.

Second, reasonable contestation about the content of public schooling is not limited to debates among civic minimalists. Not only civic minimalists reasonably disagree among themselves. Critics of civic minimalism also reasonably disagree with them about whether citizens must be constrained by a civic minimum. Civic minimalists cannot therefore credibly promise that their conception of schooling is the key to ending heated public debates over schooling.

Suppose some citizens at a school board meeting argue that mandating reading texts that teach children about gender equality is within the legitimate authority of their public schools even though a civic minimum might be less demanding of students. Civic minimalists offer no compelling reason why it should be beyond democratic disagreement for citizens to claim the constitutional right to legislate more than what they claim to be the correct civic minimum. Who in a constitutional democracy has the legitimate authority to impose a reasonably contestable conception of a civic minimum on publicly subsidized schools in the face of such deliberative disagreement? To this question advocates of democratic education defend their answer, that citizens and their accountable representatives have this legitimate authority provided they do not use it in a way that is repressive or discriminatory.[12] Civic minimalists do not defend their answer because they resist the most logical and morally consistent answer: citizens and their accountable representatives have the legitimate authority to choose among reasonably contestable conceptions of the civic minimum, of which there are many, including many (such as teaching gender equality) that many civic minimalists refuse to recognize as reasonable.

Suppose civic minimalists grant that democratic governments may decide among reasonably contestable conceptions of the civic minimum, including those to which some parents object, as some parents objected to the Tennessee school district's assignment of the story showing Jim cooking while Pat read to him from the cookbook. If civic minimalism opened itself to citizens' collectively deciding upon a civic minimum for their school districts, then civic minimalism would be far more compatible with democratic education. On this understanding, civic minimalism is no longer a challenge to democratic authority over civic education within any reasonable understanding of the civic minimum. Democratic education certainly authorizes citizens to decide among competing conceptions of the civic minimum. (It authorizes more discretion than this, within the principled constraints of non-discrimination and non-repression, but this discretion—as I will soon show—can credibly be translated into an interpretation of the civic minimum.)

Some of the requirements of civic education that citizens reasonably propose may not present themselves as "minimalist." (It is not clear why they should be required to present themselves as minimalist, but let's set this problem aside for the moment.) Some requirements will be more demanding of schools than others. But the demands—by the very terms of democratic education—are all likely to be made, and credibly so, in the name of civic education. Each competing conception of the requirements of civic education may be interpreted without distortion as the "minimally justifiable requirements for educating free and equal citizens." One thing to be said in favor of making arguments for civic education in the name of a "civic minimum" is that arguing in these terms may help place some self-restraint on citizens—not to claim more authority over publicly subsidized schooling than civic education *requires*. But there is also something to be said on the other side: Why limit citizens to instituting just the minimum necessary for civic education?

If what civic minimalists are seeking is self-restraint on the part of citizens so that democratic governments do not overstep the boundaries of their legitimate authority, then they should say so and present a more defensible understanding of the legitimate authority of democratic governments. Advocates of democratic education and civic minimalists presumably share the aim of defending mutually justifiable institutions and policies. Civic minimalists have not justified requiring citizens to support only the most minimal form of civic education in schools at public expense. Furthermore, civic minimalists have yet to offer a defensible account of what the most minimal form of civic education would be.

In order to avoid emptiness—to be a real alternative to democratic education that makes good on its claim that democratic citizens have no right to mandate a civic education above the minimum—civic minimalists need to specify what the civic minimum is and why. Without a substantive defense of a specific civic minimum, civic minimalism becomes a hollow conception into which everyone can insert a reasonable understanding of civic education and credibly call it the civic minimum. Alternatively, citizens can reasonably resist being bound by civic minimalism. Civic minimalists offer no good reason for citizens to be bound by the civic minimum since it is so lacking in content, on the one hand, and in constitutionally mandated legitimacy, on the other.

Civic minimalists repeatedly criticize conceptions of democratic education for being controversial and for claiming to justify the imposition of controversial curricula on unwilling parents. But civic minimalists cannot take the avoidance of controversy or the imposition of a curriculum on unwilling parents to be a criterion of justification without rendering their own conception of the civic minimum self-defeating. If civic minimalism cannot be given substantive content, it is hollow, and not a real alternative to democratic education.

But what happens when civic minimalists specify a substantive conception? Some defend no more than the 3R's (and then argue about the minimum amount of reading, writing, and arithmetic that is adequate for citizenship). Others defend teaching toleration as well as basic skills. Still others defend teaching racial and gender nondiscrimination, mutual respect, and other virtues of democratic citizenship. For civic minimalism to avoid emptiness, it must be substantive, and substantive conceptions of the civic minimum are subject to the same sort of reasonable disagreement that minimalists invoke as reason to oppose democratic education.

Since civic minimalists fail to justify the comprehensive educational authority of parents over their children, they cannot claim legitimacy for the most minimal conception of civic minimalism. And even if they could, they would still reasonably disagree about what the most minimal conception is. On its own terms, a conception of civic minimalism must require neither less nor more education than what democratic citizenship demands. Choosing the most minimal of the controversial conceptions is therefore not a defensible default position. Any substantive conception of the civic minimum will impose something controversial on some unwilling parents, and there is no good reason (even internal to civic minimalism) to claim that the conception that imposes the least on the fewest parents is the best. By its own terms of avoiding controversy and not imposing any controversial requirements on parents, a civic minimalism that avoids being hollow (and therefore no real alternative to democratic education) becomes self-defeating (and therefore no real alternative either).

Can civic minimalism be made more defensible than this? A prominent defense of parental choice, by John Chubb and Terry Moe, argues that it is "not built to enable the imposition of higher-order values on the schools, nor is it driven by a democratic struggle to exercise public authority."[13] Can civic minimalism do without imposing "higher-order values" on schools? Only if it does not say what constitutes a school entitled to public subsidy or accreditation. Why should citizens mandate schooling for all children if they are constitutionally forbidden to require that schooling have the civic content that they believe is necessary for democratic education? If citizens are constitutionally entitled to expect some civic content from schooling, then they are authorized to impose some values on schools.

Suppose the Constitution were amended (or radically reinterpreted) to conform to the mandate of civic minimalism. Let's imagine that as of today citizens are constitutionally forbidden to impose any values on schools, but they are still permitted to give parents the means to educate their own children as they choose. Under these conditions, it makes far more sense for citizens to mandate a general subsidy to parents for child support, which would let parents decide how to spend it on their children. If publicly subsidized schooling cannot have any publicly mandated content, it ceases to make sense as a public good. Civic minimalism implicitly concedes this much by mandating a civic minimum. But civic minimalists like Gilles, Chubb, and Moe take away what they concede: they empty the civic minimum of substantive content in order to advocate near-comprehensive parental authority over schooling that is publicly mandated and subsidized.

Civic minimalism cannot have it both ways. A parental choice plan must satisfy some standard of mandatory schooling to be publicly defensible. Civic minimalists therefore must call for some public oversight over publicly subsidized schools to ensure that schools satisfy the mandatory standards of schooling. Otherwise, a parental choice plan could not even identify what counts as a school for the purpose of satisfying the civic minimum. To avoid being empty, the minimum must be given content. Once given content, it is subject to the very same critique that Chubb and Moe direct against democratic education: a parental choice plan establishes values to be imposed on schools that are to count as legitimate recipients of public tax dollars, and those values are controversial. Not all citizens or parents accept them. The critique makes civic minimalism self-defeating. Civic minimalists would therefore do well to de-escalate their rhetoric.

Might civic minimalism be defended on grounds that a more minimal set of requirements for civic education is likely to be less controversial and therefore better able to achieve a social consensus about schooling? It would be relatively easy, I assume, to reach a social consensus in the United States today on a positive program of permitting states to mandate a very minimal set of requirements, such as the 3R's. But what is distinctive about civic minimalism is not its attempt to justify a minimal set of civic educational requirements. What is distinctive about civic minimalism is its negative program, *which forbids citizens and their accountable representatives to mandate anything more than the civic minimum* (in the case we are considering, anything more than the 3R's). This negative program—which amounts to a prohibition on any public authority mandating anything more than the minimum—is at least as controversial as its opposite, leaving citizens and their accountable representatives with the discretion to mandate more than the minimum. Mandating civic minimalism would entail *constitutionally prohibiting* citizens from requiring any more of schools than teaching the 3R's, or some other clearly specified minimum. This is probably more rather than less controversial than the claims of democratic education. And it is not a morally neutral or defensible default position. (No position is.)

To be a defensible alternative to democratic education, civic minimalism must publicly justify denying citizens the legitimate authority to mandate more than a specific civic minimum. I have suggested that civic minimalists have yet to offer such a justification; the arguments they have offered render civic minimalism either empty or self-defeating. If civic minimalism, as I have argued, cannot publicly justify the constitutional restriction of public authority and the correlatively broad parental right over publicly subsidized schooling, then it ceases to be an alternative to democratic education. Citizens and public officials are welcome to defend their conception of a civic minimum as the best educational option to institute within a system of democratic education. But so presented, civic minimalism is not an alternative to democratic education but an alternative for democratic citizens to consider within a system of democratic education.

What would a system of democratic education look like that makes room for this alternative to be considered within it? I offer only a brief sketch here to highlight some of the similarities and differences with civic minimalism. (In *Democratic Education*, I offer more details and a more systematic defense.) Democratic education defends decentralization and diversity among public and private, religious and secular schools not as ultimate ends but as means to their achieving civic educational ends. Civic educational ends are publicly binding; they therefore need to be publicly defended.

Deliberation, which takes place at a variety of levels, including individual schools, local school districts, and state legislatures, is a way of publicly defending a civic educational program. Citizens and their accountable representatives deliberate about educating children in ways conducive to their becoming free and equal citizens in a democratic society. Schools may teach more than the mandated civic curriculum. Parents may send their children to public or private schools, religious or secular schools, although only public schools receive complete public subsidy. (I return to address the issue of poor parents not being able to afford private schooling.)

All schools should be constrained to respect the constitutional rights of students, which include rights against repression and discrimination. The basic liberties of individuals must be protected against repression, and their basic opportunities protected against discrimination. If a school, school board, or state legislature fails to respect these individual rights, other institutions, such as courts, should step in to ensure that they are protected.

By contrast, in a regime of civic minimalism, courts and parents together would have almost exclusive control over children's schooling. Judges would enforce the mandated minimum, no more nor less. Parents would control the rest of publicly subsidized schooling. Civic minimalism therefore presumes—before democratic deliberation even begins—that constitutional legitimacy rests on enforcing a single conception of the civic minimum. This presumption, I have argued, has not been defended, much less defended in a way that gives clear content to the idea of a civic minimum or puts it beyond reasonable disagreement. Civic minimalists are therefore presumptuous when they denounce democratic decision making over publicly subsidized schools as illegitimate.

We have yet to consider what the most morally defensible content of a civic minimum would be. The least controversial parts of a mandated civic minimum in the United States—those that can elicit nearly universal agreement among Americans as necessary (but not sufficient) for every citizen to learn—are some (hard to specify) minimal degree of literacy and numeracy. But it would be morally arbitrary, indeed rather ridiculous, for any of us to conclude that literacy and numeracy—at some minimal level— therefore suffice for an adequate civic education in the United States, and that nothing more can be legitimately mandated of schools in the name of civic education.

A more popular and promising start for defining the civic minimum is identifying it with what is necessary to make liberal democracy work well. If "well" means fairly or justifiably, then the content of civic minimalism converges with what democratic education identifies as a good civic education. For a liberal democracy to work fairly, with liberty and justice for all, the civic minimum would need to be robust. It would need to include teaching literacy and numeracy at a high level. It would also need to include teaching—not indoctrinating—civic values such as toleration, nondiscrimination, and respect for individual rights and legitimate laws. Teaching includes both experiencing the practice of these virtues in schools, and helping students develop the intellectual skills necessary to evaluate these practices along with their alternatives.

Schools cannot possibly remain neutral in their practices— they practice either tolerance or intolerance, racial discrimination or nondiscrimination. Moreover, it is desirable that schools practice toleration and nondiscrimination. But as they mature intellectually and emotionally, students also need to learn to evaluate such practices in the open-minded and deliberative spirit that prefigures the way in which democratic citizens ideally govern themselves, deliberatively rather than dogmatically. Civic education should therefore also include helping students to develop the ability to deliberate about their political disagreements with others. Helping students develop this ability also entails helping them cultivate the deliberative virtues of being well informed, open-minded, and opinionated about politically relevant issues and the performance of officeholders.

I present this conception of civic education not as authoritative but as a reasonable alternative that democratic citizens should have the option to institute. If it is a reasonable alternative, then civic minimalism—which says that citizens should not be permitted to institute the alternative of democratic education because it imposes more than a specific civic minimum on parents—is deeply problematic. Civic minimalism does not grant democratic citizens the moral or political room to pursue the civic purposes of schooling as best they can. And it denies citizens this room even if their civic purposes are both reasonable and consistent with parents having a large realm of authority over their children's education in the family.

Democratic education does not impose a single set of civic educational purposes on citizens. It grants citizens (morally bounded) authority to pursue civic educational purposes. The moral bounds that I have defended—non-repression and nondiscrimination—express the ideal of free and equal citizenship at the core of liberal democracy. If other bounds are more publicly justifiable, then they should govern. Not only the theoretical principles but the practical implications of those principles should also be subject to critical scrutiny.

William Galston defends liberal democratic principles but disagrees with some of the practical implications that others and I draw from them. Citizens, Galston agrees, should institute standards of civic education that support the ideal of liberal democracy, not just the status quo. This is a high standard, and probably not well captured by calling it a civic minimum.[14] Galston and I disagree about what a civic education adequate to the ideal of liberal democracy would decide in the case of *Mozert v. Hawkins County Board of Education*, where a group of fundamentalist parents claimed the right to exempt their children from a reading curriculum whose content—although neither religious nor anti-religious—conflicted with their religious convictions. Galston argues that the Sixth Circuit Court of Appeals failed to recognize a constitutional right of the Mozert parents—based on their right of free exercise of religion—to exempt their children from the mandated reading curriculum of the public school that they attended.[15] Reasoning from the principles of democratic education, I have argued that courts should not overturn the decisions of public school boards on matters of reasonable curricular requirements.[16] The right to free exercise of religion does not entail the right of parents to near-exclusive or comprehensive authority over their children's schooling. Galston agrees with these principles but not with the application of them in the *Mozert* case. Children, Galston and I agree, are not the mere creatures of the state or their parents. We also agree that the curricular requirements at issue in the *Mozert* case were reasonable ways for the Hawkins County public schools to engage in civic education. The required reading to which the parents objected ranged from the picture of Jim having fun cooking while Pat (a girl) read to him to an excerpt from Anne Frank's *Diary of a Young Girl* to a passage describing a central idea of the Renaissance as belief in the dignity and worth of human beings. None of the requirements entailed forcing the profession of belief by any student (or parent). Where Galston and I disagree is in our answers to the following question: Should the judiciary set the precedent of routinely requiring school boards to exempt children from curricular requirements that their parents regard as inconsistent with their religious beliefs? Galston recognizes the general legitimacy of such curricular requirements but would give greater weight to the religious convictions of parents. I would not. This disagreement, while important and consequential, is far more limited than the disagreement between Galston and civic minimalists.

Civic minimalists criticize Galston's substantive conception as not recognizing a near-comprehensive right to parental control over schooling, but civic minimalism—as we have seen—is far less defensible than a substantive understanding of the civic purposes of schooling. When civic minimalists try to interpret the United States Constitution to cede parents such comprehensive rights over their children's education, the results are even more disturbing. Gilles at first concedes that civic minimalism lacks support in "our existing Constitution, rightly interpreted." But undaunted, he goes on to argue that judges should make parental authority over education into a free speech right. Here is what he advises judges:

> [E]ducational messages to their children, whether delivered directly by parents in the home or indirectly through their agents in the school, should be treated as parental educative speech, and should receive a high level of First Amendment protection similar to that currently afforded to political speech.[17]

The right to free speech, so interpreted, would become an exercise of parental power over all educators. Judges would evaluate educational regulations "in terms of their impacts on parents" rather than on children.[18] The needs, interests, and rights of children would fade from this picture, as the free speech rights of parents are converted into a constitutional authority over everyone who educates children, including for public purposes and at public expense. The suggestion highlights the extent to which civic minimalism fails to give independent consideration to protecting the needs, interests, or rights of children. Civic minimalism radically re-interprets the First Amendment so as to cede comprehensive control of all educators' speech to parents.

Advocates of civic minimalism typically presume that comprehensive parental authority is a default position. They criticize other positions by saying that they do not command a consensus.[19] But no conception—including civic minimalism—can claim a social consensus. Nor would a consensus settle the issue since the interests of children are centrally at stake in this matter, and young children are not part of a meaningful consensus, indeed by virtue of their age they could not be. We have no better alternative but to defend a controversial substantive conception.

Here and elsewhere I have defended a conception of democratic education that respects parental authority over the education of children in the family, and also respects democratic authority over a civic education that aims to prepare students for exercising the rights and responsibilities of democratic citizenship. Democratic education welcomes reasonable disagreement, and legitimates a democratic process of adjudicating disagreements over the content of civic education, as civic minimalism does not. Democratic education invites citizens to argue about alternative requirements of publicly subsidized schooling, including what an adequate civic minimum would be.

Democratic education offers no simple procedural panacea to the problems that beset America's inner-city schools. Proponents of parental choice, by contrast, do. "Choice *is* a panacea," Chubb and Moe say. It is "not like other reforms and should not be combined with them as part of a reformist strategy for improving

America's public schools." Choice should be viewed as "a self-contained reform":

> with its own rationale and justification. It has the capacity *all by itself* to bring about the kind of transformation that, for years, reformers have been seeking to engineer in myriad other ways.[20]

If a single sweeping procedural reform could cure all of America's educational ills, or even most or many of them, we should all jump on the procedural bandwagon. But the idea that there is an educational panacea is a recurring theme in the politics of American education. What has changed radically over the years is the nature of the panacea that is promoted as such.

Educating children, whether with the aim of helping them become good citizens or good people more generally, remains so complex that no single procedural reform—whether it be in the direction of democratic education or school choice—can promise to be anything close to a panacea. Kant's cautionary claim remains as true today as it was when he wrote it: "[T]here are two human inventions which may be considered more difficult than any others—the art of government, and the art of education."[21]

Nothing I say is intended to deny the legitimate appeal of parental choice over schools in the context of the United States today. Too many public schools—especially in American inner cities—fail to offer an adequate education to too many children. Democratic education calls for the choice of an effective school for every parent whose child is not now receiving an adequate education in a neighborhood public school. Improving public schools and increasing choice among them is more defensible than subsidizing private schools in a society like ours that constitutionally separates church and state. But as long as a substantial number of public schools are failing to provide an adequate civic education to a substantial number of children, there will be something to be said for subsidizing private schools that are willing and able to provide these children with an adequate civic education on a nondiscriminatory basis.

Morally defensible standards of civic education for citizenship in the United States today go far beyond numeracy and literacy at a minimal level. Morally defensible standards should include nothing less than what is necessary to supporting free and equal citizenship for all adults. In addition to a high level of numeracy and literacy, teaching civic values such as racial nondiscrimination and religious toleration is certainly necessary to supporting free and equal citizenship in the United States today. It follows that a program of parental choice among schools should be constrained not to increase racial discrimination or religious intolerance. Since students also learn from one another, and students from less educated families tend to achieve more if they attend schools with students from more educated families, parental choice plans also should not increase the segregation of most advantaged and least advantaged students.[22] Schools are probably the best place for children of different socioeconomic, ethnic, racial, and religious backgrounds to learn to respect one another as future free and equal citizens. Publicly subsidized schools therefore should be nondiscriminatory in their admissions and they should try to teach these civic values by their practices.

Parental choice is certainly not a panacea. Neither is public control. The efforts at privatizing the Hartford (Connecticut) school system were disappointing in their results. So were the efforts at centralizing public control in the Newark (New Jersey) school system. The results of the recent private-public school voucher experiment in Milwaukee (Wisconsin), which wisely targets the least advantaged students in the city, fall far short of supporting the claim that choice is a panacea. Voucher school students in Milwaukee show very modest improvements in their mathematics test scores but no improvement in their English test scores over non-voucher-school students.[23] More time is needed to judge the reliability of these very preliminary findings (which are also contested). But one preliminary conclusion is almost certain to be sustained: if school systems do nothing more than change mechanisms of control from public to private (or vice versa), the results are likely to be modest at best.

The challenge of adequately educating children who are socially and economically disadvantaged is so great that neither private nor public control, by itself, can promise schools that effectively educate all children for free and equal citizenship. A democratic society needs to offer not only choices among schools but good choices if it is to fulfill its educational obligations to children. Some competition among schools is likely to be educationally productive, perhaps even necessary to prevent schools from atrophying.[24] But a largely unconstrained voucher plan as defended by civic minimalists almost certainly cannot solve the major problems of inner-city school systems.

There is no procedural substitute for improving schools, and judging them on their educational merits, where those merits include their capacity to contribute to civic education. To what extent do schools succeed in effectively educating every child to literacy, numeracy, economic opportunity, toleration, mutual respect, and the other fundamental skills and virtues of a free and equal citizenry?

Judged by these standards, the school systems of the United States and other contemporary democracies are lacking. But their shortcomings are not attributable primarily to public control. When a democratic government says to parents that they are free to use the public schools at taxpayers' expense or to use any accredited private school at their own expense, it is not being unfair to those who choose private schools for their children, at extra cost. (Nor is a democratic government being unfair when it funds state universities and makes them less costly than private ones.) What is unfair is that some children are not provided with an adequate education judged by any reasonable standards of civic education, while other children are, whether because their parents can afford to live in a better public school district or because they can opt out of a bad one by paying for private schooling. This problem calls not for paying for private schools but for improving public schools and eliminating the poverty and unemployment that make the task of democratic education such an uphill struggle.

Civic minimalists grant that schools should serve civic purposes, and that citizens may therefore mandate teaching the civic minimum. Having granted that schools should serve civic purposes, civic minimalists lack good reasons for insisting that the civic purposes of schooling be minimal. The reasons that they offer—minimizing the pursuit of public purposes and avoiding public controversy—render civic minimalism either empty or self-defeating, or both. The conception of democratic education that I have defended encourages citizens to support high standards for civic education in schools that therefore do their part to enable all children to enjoy the status, rights, and responsibilities of free and equal citizens. Whether those high standards are called the civic minimum of constitutional democracy is far less important than whether schooling that is publicly mandated and subsidized tries to educate all students as future free and equal democratic citizens.

II. COSMOPOLITANISM OR PATRIOTISM?

But any single democratic society, which oversees democratic education only within its borders, can confer the status of citizenship only on some portion of the world's people. According to the principles that inform democratic theory, all people deserve the status of equal citizens, regardless of whether that status is actually recognized by their society. We all deserve equal consideration when matters of justice are at stake regardless of whether we have been granted the status of democratic citizen somewhere. A democratic education that is true to its basic premise of the civic equality of persons must therefore teach students to consider not just their fellow citizens but all people as equals. The same value that supports the teaching of mutual respect among diverse individuals within a single society also supports the teaching of mutual respect beyond borders, among individuals throughout the world, who represent an even wider range of cultural affiliations and identifications.

Students need to learn a lot about their own society to function as well-informed citizens, but learning only about their own society is not enough to satisfy the moral demands of a democratic education. In an interdependent world, recognizing the rights of all people to live a good life is as important as recognizing the rights of one's fellow citizens. Teaching students to understand foreign people and ways of life presents a similar challenge to teaching them about cultural diversity within their own society. For the sake of achieving greater justice in the world as in our own society, we need to understand people not merely as abstractions but in their particularity, with their own lives to lead and their own ideas of what constitutes a good life to lead. Such understanding should precede the practical political judgments we make as citizens, whether about our own entitlements, those of our fellow citizens, resident aliens, or foreigners. Understanding other people's ways of life is also important in its own right because how we understand *our* own society and *our* own world is inseparable from how we understand all the other people whose ways of life influence our own. Other people's (and societies') ways of life—including their literature, music, trading, spending and saving habits—influence (and in some instances are part of) ours just as ours influence (and in some instances are part of) theirs.

Global interdependence increases the democratic importance of learning about foreign people and societies, but it does not correspondingly decrease the practical challenge of extending mutual respect among individuals beyond national borders. The challenge beyond borders is considerably greater because the domestic politics of a constitutional democracy, with all its flaws, tends to be more conducive to cultivating mutual respect among citizens than world politics is to cultivating mutual respect among people who live in often hostile societies with radically different cultures and kinds of government. (Recent events in American politics strain this distinction, but it is probably still true over time.) The asymmetrical support of mutual respect offered by domestic and world politics is all the more reason for schools to teach students about people and politics of other societies with which they would otherwise be unfamiliar (or prejudicially hostile), and also about their own society as it interacts with others.[25]

With the ever-increasing interdependency of societies, teaching the history and politics of a single country like the United States lends itself all the more to introducing students to the moral challenge of cultivating mutual respect across borders. One way of cultivating mutual respect while teaching American history and politics is to introduce students to moral exemplars of citizens who reached beyond national boundaries to respect the equal rights of all people. Martin Luther King's speech opposing the Vietnam War is one prominent example. King presumed to speak from a moral perspective available to all human beings:

[A]ll of us who deem ourselves bound by allegiances and loyalties
which are broader and deeper than nationalism and which go beyond our nation's self-defined goals and positions. . . . are called to
speak for the weak, for the voiceless, for victims of our nation and
for those it calls enemy, for no document from human hands can
make these humans any less our brothers.[26]

Democratic education should also help students understand
and assess the contributions of institutions that are not specific to
a single society, such as the United Nations, Amnesty International, the European Economic Community, and the International Monetary Fund. The United Nations' Declaration of
Human Rights is a prominent example of an institutionalized
recognition of human rights extending beyond national borders.
Students should be encouraged to think about what values are
(and are not) mutually defensible in an international context
and why. Such reasoning is a prologue to civic deliberation on an
international scale, and it is also directly relevant to a great deal
of domestic democratic politics (such as the politics of free trade
versus protectionism, the disposal of toxic wastes, standards of
medical experimentation at home and abroad, and immigration
policy).

Should (or must) democratic education therefore support
cosmopolitanism rather than patriotism? Cosmopolitanism and
patriotism are used in such radically different ways by their defenders and critics that we need to stipulate their meanings before evaluating them. We would beg the question in favor of cosmopolitanism to use it as a synonym for moral universalism and
to use patriotism as a synonym for moral particularism or
parochialism. Besides, as commonly used and as defined in the
dictionary, cosmopolitanism and patriotism are not moral perspectives in their own right. They are sentiments referring to social attachments and self-identifications beyond the self.

Cosmopolitans are worldly individuals who identify with many
places and a culture, traditionally a high culture, that spans many
societies. They do not identify solely with a single state or solely
with the culture of a single society. It does not follow that cosmopolitans are undiscriminating in their attachments. Not only
is life too short for anyone to be attached to every place and every

culture but cosmopolitans are committed to discriminating on the basis of criteria—either aesthetic or moral or both—that themselves span the culture of a single society. It is important to recognize that cosmopolitans need not be *moral* universalists. Historically, most cosmopolitans were not moral universalists. They were aesthetic universalists, aficionados of high culture. Whether a cosmopolitan's discriminations turn out to be compatible with *moral* universalism—and therefore with the democratic ideal of free and equal persons—is not foreordained by the fact of being cosmopolitan. The worldly attachment of a cosmopolitan who identifies with aristocrats or aesthetes the world over has little to recommend itself from a universalistic moral perspective, which supports democracy and democratic education.

When Martha Nussbaum recommends cosmopolitanism over patriotism, she defends a particular, morally admirable kind of cosmopolitan. Nussbaum's cosmopolitan is someone whose worldly attachments follow the mandates of moral universalism, someone who is attached to human beings as such wherever they may live and therefore accords equal respect to all human beings, whatever their nationality, ethnicity, religion, race, or gender. This is not the cosmopolitan who is attached to high culture, and is largely indifferent to the everyday problems—such as poverty—of ordinary humanity. A morally admirable, egalitarian attachment to the community of humankind is what Nussbaum defends in the name of cosmopolitanism, tracing this sort of cosmopolitanism back to the Stoics.[27]

Egalitarian cosmopolitanism should not be confused with cosmopolitanism more generally. Not all cosmopolitans are so egalitarian in their attachments.[28] The kind of cosmopolitan sentiment conducive to extending the reach of mutual respect among individuals worldwide incorporates an egalitarian commitment. Egalitarian cosmopolitans are attached to all human beings regardless of their more particular identities. Egalitarian cosmopolitanism flows from the same moral source as democratic education: equal respect for, and mutual respect among, persons.

Democratic education is compatible with—even conducive to—cultivating egalitarian cosmopolitans. But cultivating egalitarian cosmopolitans is not the primary aim of democratic education. Why not? Because there are multiple ways of being attached to people that are compatible with a democratic commitment to mutual respect among persons. Egalitarian cosmopolitanism is one, but only one, of those ways. One need not feel similarly attached to all people regardless of their culture to live a morally good life. One can feel more attached to a certain culture and to the people who identify with that culture, and still treat all people with equal respect, and do one's part in furthering justice. Schools can engage in moral education without trying to cultivate cosmopolitans.

Can they engage in moral education with or without trying to cultivate patriots? To answer this question, we need to ask another: Is there a form of patriotism that is compatible with mutual respect among persons across national borders? A common contemporary understanding of patriotism—loyalty to country above all other political obligations—is incompatible with cultivating mutual respect across borders. But there is an egalitarian patriotism that, like egalitarian cosmopolitanism, is compatible with the moral aims of democratic education. To see what egalitarian patriotism entails, we need to understand patriotism more generally.

Patriotism, like cosmopolitanism, is a sentiment rather than a moral perspective. Patriotism is commonly defined as love of, and therefore loyalty to, one's country, where one's country is either a nation or a state. There is a big difference between love of a mass institution, whether it be a nation or a state, and love of a single person, the object of love in its most fundamental form. We need to examine that difference to understand why an unqualified kind of patriotism is problematic from the perspective of democratic education.

Love is a notoriously difficult passion to control. If lovers are unqualified or blind in their loyalty to loved ones, the danger to other people pales in comparison to the danger of the unqualified or blind loyalty of millions of people to nations and states. This is the danger of patriotism as it is commonly defended in politics. Nations and states possess massive institutionalized powers to kill, torture, maim, starve, humiliate, demean, and otherwise deny innocent people the most fundamental prerequisites of a decent life. Nations and states not only frequently threaten to employ these powers; they actually do employ them with terrifying and devastating frequency. A democratic education opposes blind patriotism when its curriculum encourages students to think critically, in moral terms, and its practices encourage students to treat all individuals, whatever their gender, race, religion, or nationality, as entitled to equal respect.

But patriotism need not (and should not) be unqualified or blind. Maurizio Viroli asks us to consider a patriotism that ties love of principle to love of country. A patriot, according to Viroli, loves his country because it is a republic that uniquely permits the pursuit of liberty and justice for all.[29] Love of liberty and love of country (in the form of a republic) are compatible, Viroli argues, indeed intimately interconnected, because liberty and justice for all are made possible by a world of republics. Liberty and justice will be forsaken without the active support of citizens, and citizens' active support will not be forthcoming unless they love their country (because liberty and justice are demanding moral causes).

Republican patriots love their country because—and to the extent that—it makes liberty and justice possible. Because this kind of patriotism is fueled primarily by love of justice and only secondarily by love of country, republican patriots are more discriminating than ordinary patriots in what they will do for their country. They will oppose injustices such as slavery, ethnic cleansing, anti-Semitism, racial segregation, and gender discrimination. They will also oppose nationalistic forms of patriotism that subordinate justice to the nationalistic cause of creating states that are thought to be ethnically, religiously, or racially pure. Republican patriotism is anti-nationalistic, and defined in contrast to nationalism.

But republican patriotism includes a requirement that would limit the basic liberty of persons were it to become the only socially acceptable self-identification: "if our country is unfree we have to work to make it free instead of leaving to look for liberty elsewhere . . ."[30] Just as faithful lovers do not leave their loved ones except out of necessity, so republican patriots do not leave their countries unless they are forced to do so: "[I]f we are forced to leave, we have to continue to work in order to be able to go back to live in freedom with our fellows."[31] But there is no moral mandate to work for the good of your compatriots rather than

for some other equally worthy good. If one identifies as a republican patriot, this is surely an acceptable way of discharging one's
moral obligations to other people. It is a morally admirable way.
But it is not the only morally admirable way; it is one among such
ways. Other ways include leaving one's country and helping
equally or more oppressed people in other countries. To treat republican patriotism as morally mandatory is as misguided as
treating love as morally mandatory. Democratic education should
treat republican patriotism as one self-identification that is consistent with its principles, but only by virtue of its not being made
a mandatory form of self-identification.

Democratic education may legitimately cultivate both republican patriotism and egalitarian cosmopolitanism. As non-manda-
tory forms of self-identification, both are compatible with equal
respect for persons. But democratic education need not directly
aim at cultivating either, or one to the exclusion of the other. In
the spirit of open-minded inquiry, democratic education should
teach students the history and philosophy of patriotism and cosmopolitanism in its various forms. Its aim in this regard would be
to help students understand these internally complex sentiments
and attachments of the self to people and places. But democratic
education should not convey the sense that only one kind of attachment, whether it be patriotic or cosmopolitan, is compatible
with living a moral life or one that is consistent with equal respect
to persons.[32]

Democracy should welcome diverse ways of identifying with
others as civic equals. Egalitarian cosmopolitans and republican
patriots alike respect the equal dignity and basic liberty of all persons. But they manifest their respect in different ways. Some people "nurture the culture and politics of their homes."[33] Others
dedicate themselves to helping people abroad. Democratic education can and should prepare students for different ways of living a moral life.

Nobody needs to be a patriot or a cosmopolitan to be a moral
person. Many people who are consistently committed to opposing oppression, as best they can, do not identify themselves as (or
fit the description of) either. Others do. We are all, as Hilary Putnam describes us, "situated intelligences." But our situation, as
Putnam recognizes, doesn't determine our moral outlook:

[W]ithout inherited ways of life, there is nothing for criticism to operate on, just as without critical reason there is no way for us to distinguish between what should be saved (perhaps after reinterpretation) and what should be scrapped from our various traditions.[34]

Democratic education has the potential for being far more ecumenical and effective if it does not insist on teaching students that all moral beings must identify themselves in any single way, whether as citizens of the world, Kantian ends-in-themselves, Millean progressive beings, cosmopolitans, or republican patriots. Democratic education instead should try to teach students to understand public values such as liberty, opportunity, and justice from multiple perspectives. Why? Because there are multiple ways of reasonably understanding these values, and there are many self-identifications that converge on the idea that individuals the world over are entitled to the liberties and opportunities necessary to live a good life consistent with their own identities and with respect for the equal rights of other individuals. Democratic education welcomes all identifications that are compatible with pursuing justice for all people.

When the aim of democratic education is framed broadly—to encourage the pursuit of justice for all—it embraces a wide range of attachments and identities at the same time as it recognizes that the moral obligations of citizenship do not stop at state boundaries. It also enables students to expand the horizons of their own lives by learning about lives that otherwise would be less accessible. Teaching students about foreign countries and cultures need not be a recipe for homogenizing the world. It is consistent with every society giving greater attention to the history, cultures, and politics of its own country than to any other.

What then, if anything, makes it legitimate for citizens to support a system of public schooling that focuses disproportionately, although not exclusively, on the history, culture, and politics of their country? Homogenization of world culture is not a credible consequence of public schools in the United States focusing on world history rather than American history. But there are at least three other reasons why citizens may legitimately support schooling that focuses disproportionately on the history, culture, and politics of their own country.

The first reason is so basic that it is easy to overlook. Schooling, even more than life, is too short to teach everything. And teaching a very little about a lot of different places is a recipe for conveying very little by way of understanding. It makes more educational sense to focus enough on a few places to learn something in depth.

But this reason does not provide anything positive about an educational focus on one's own country. The second reason does. Although publicly supported schools could randomly select the history, culture, and politics that they teach, teaching children about who they are—besides being human beings as such—is part of what democratic education (and equal respect of individuals) can and should be about. American students are appropriately taught the history, culture, and politics of their country because it is *their* country, just as they are appropriately taught (by their parents) about their family's particular customs, habits, and stories because it is their family.[35] Learning about oneself is part of what education is and should be.

There is nothing wrong with identifying as members of particular families or citizens of particular countries as long as these identities do not carry a sense of moral superiority, particular desert, or privilege with them. Civic education should demonstrate that particularistic identifications are no excuse whatsoever for oppressing or otherwise denying the equal rights of individuals. Quite the contrary, it should teach students in such a way that they understand that their right to enjoy a particularistic identity presumes the equal rights of their fellow human beings.

A third reason for schools in the United States to focus disproportionately on domestic politics is that American citizens can more readily enlist the politics of their own country rather than the politics of another country if they are committed to doing their part to further justice, even beyond the borders of their own country. It is of course not easy to enlist any actual politics in pursuit of justice. And it is also true that less local forms of politics are increasingly important in the pursuit of justice throughout the world. But the politics of our own country (especially when it is a relatively rich and powerful country like the United States) is still the most indispensable collective means to furthering the cause of justice. Students need to learn how they can enlist the assistance of their own country's political institutions to do what they believe to be right. From the perspective of acquainting students with the most effective means of their doing good in the world, there is no practical substitute to their being educated for effective citizenship in their own society.

These reasons justify teaching students more about their own society than about any other single society, but they do not justify neglecting the politics, histories, and cultures of other societies. To further mutual respect among all people, schools also need to teach about different societies, not all other societies, but enough other societies in enough depth so as not to convey the message that people who live beyond our borders do not count, or count less, or are entitled to less concern or respect than members of our own society.

Democratic education should convey respect for all people regardless of their nationality, ethnicity, gender, color, class, or religion. This civic aim seems to me morally mandatory. It is not a minimal aim. But if I were to defend a civic minimum, I could defend nothing less.

NOTES

1. This is a very short synopsis of the more detailed understanding of democratic education found in *Democratic Education* (Princeton: Princeton University Press, 1999).

2. Stephen Gilles, "On Educating Children: A Parentalist Manifesto," 63 *University of Chicago Law Review* 937 (Summer 1996), p. 941.

3. Nussbaum, "Patriotism and Cosmopolitanism," in Joshua Cohen, ed., *For Love of Country: Debating the Limits of Patriotism* (Boston: Beacon Press, 1996), pp. 6, 15.

4. The principle and practice of reciprocal reason giving is defended as central to democracy in Amy Gutmann and Dennis Thompson, *Democracy and Disagreement* (Cambridge: Harvard University Press, 1996).

5. For a discussion of deliberative virtues in education, see *Democratic Education* (Princeton: Princeton University Press, 1999), pp. 50–52. For a discussion of civic integrity and magnanimity, see *Democracy and Disagreement*, pp. 81–85.

6. My arguments in this essay build on the conception of democratic education that I develop and defend in *Democratic Education*, second edition (Princeton: Princeton University Press, 1999).

7. Stephen Gilles, "On Educating Children," p. 962.

8. There is a weaker form of civic minimalism that makes it discretionary rather than mandatory. It recommends that citizens support only the minimum requirements of democratic education for schools but recognizes the constitutional right of citizens to require more than the minimum. I focus on the stronger form of civic minimalism because the weaker form is not really inconsistent with *Democratic Education*.

9. The case is real, not hypothetical, and it divides civic minimalists and advocates of democratic education. The story is one to which some fundamental Christian parents objected (on grounds that "it denigrates the differences between the sexes" that are affirmed in the Bible) in the case of *Mozert v. Hawkins County Board of Education*, which I discuss in "Civic Education and Social Diversity," *Ethics*, vol. 105, no. 3 (April 1995), pp. 557–579. It is certainly plausible to say—as I later suggest—that this kind of teaching should be part of the civic minimum, but then we would need to ask how the perspective of civic minimalism differentiates itself, except nominally, from that of democratic education.

10. In *Democratic Education*, I defend this position. It is a position that is critical of much educational practice in the United States today, but it is far more consistent with a long line of court cases than is civic minimalism. The American judiciary has quite consistently recognized broad democratic authority over public schooling, consistent with not regarding children as "mere creatures of the state." In *Pierce v. Society of Sisters*, the Court recognized "the power of the State reasonably to regulate all schools," 268 US 510 at 534 (1925). Lower courts therefore have typically assessed the legitimacy of state regulation of schools, including regulation of home schooling, under the rational basis test, the easiest test to pass. In *Prince v. Massachusetts*, the Court found that: "The state's authority over children's activities is broader than over like actions of adults." 321 US 158 at 168 (1944).

One significant limit that the Court places on state authority over schooling tracks the constraint that I call "non-repression." The Court has struck down educational practices that compel students to profess belief against their convictions, and it has not rested this restriction on a right of parents to dictate the content of their children's schooling. The state's legitimate power of schooling, the Court argued in *Board of Education v. Barnette*, does not extend to compelling a profession of belief. The legitimacy of the laws of the state are limited to those that do not "force citizens to confess by word or act their faith therein." 319 US 624 at 642 (1943). Even in *Wisconsin v. Yoder*, where the Court exempts Amish children from two years of compulsory schooling on the basis of their parents' right to the free exercise of religion, Justice Burger argues that the Amish are an unusual exception to the general rule. Burger notes that: "Nothing we hold is intended to undermine the general applicability of the State's compulsory school-attendance statutes . . . " 406 US 205 at 236.

I discuss the religious freedom of parents as it relates to the state's authority over schooling in "Religion and State in the United States: A Defense of Two-Way Protection," in Nancy L. Rosenblum, ed., *Obligations of Citizenship and Demands of Faith: Religious Accommodation in Pluralist Democracies* (Princeton: Princeton University Press, 2000).

11. See *Democratic Education*, pp. 28–33, 64–70.

12. Ibid., esp. chs. 1–5.

13. See John E. Chubb and Terry M. Moe, *Politics, Markets, and America's Schools* (Washington, D.C.: Brookings, 1990), p. 189.

14. See William A. Galston, *Liberal Purposes* (New York: Cambridge University Press, 1991), esp. pp. 224–227.

15. *Mozert v. Hawkins County Board of Education*, 827 F.2d 1058.

16. "Undemocratic Education," in Nancy L. Rosenblum, ed., *Liberalism and the Moral Life*, Cambridge: Harvard University Press, 1989, pp. 71–88.

17. Stephen Gilles, "On Educating Children," p. 944.

18. Ibid., p. 1018.

19. Gilles writes, for example, "there is no consensus in favor of Gutmann's conception of liberal democracy," p. 972. I agree. No consensus exists that favors my conception—or any other conception—of liberal democracy, deliberative democracy, or democratic education. But a person who proposes to convert the First Amendment right to free speech into a right of parents to control the speech of everyone who educates their children cannot consistently count lack of consensus as a criticism.

20. Chubb and Moe, *Politics, Markets, and America's Schools*, p. 217.

21. Immanuel Kant, *Kant on Education* (*Ueber Padagogik*), trans. Annette Churton (Boston: D. C. Heath and Co., 1900), p. 12.

22. This was a major (although disputed) finding of the pathbreaking study by James S. Coleman, et al., *Report on Equality of Educational Opportunity* (Washington, D.C.: U.S. Government Printing Office, 1966).

23. See, for example, Cecilia Elena Rouse, "Private School Vouchers and Student Achievement: An Evaluation of the Milwaukee Parental Choice Program," *The Quarterly Journal of Economics*, May 1998, pp. 552–602; and John F. Witte and Christopher A. Thorn, "Who Chooses?

Voucher and Interdistrict Choice Programs in Milwaukee," *American Journal of Education 104* (May 1996), pp. 186–217. See also John F. Witte, "Reply to Greene, Peterson and Du: The Effectiveness of School Choice in Milwaukee: Secondary Analysis of Data from the Program Evaluation," unpublished paper, August 23, 1996; and Paul E. Peterson, Jay P. Greene, and William Howell, "New Findings from the Cleveland Scholarship Program: A Reanalysis of Data from the Indiana University School of Education Evaluation," unpublished paper, May 6, 1998.

24. For a balanced overview and analysis of the merits of school choice, see Jeffrey R. Henig, *Rethinking School Choice: Limits of the Market Metaphor* (Princeton: Princeton University Press, 1995).

25. Nussbaum argues for "making world citizenship, rather than democratic or national citizenship, the focus of civic education" (*For Love of Country*, p. 11). But she also seems to agree that world citizenship should not be considered a substitute for democratic citizenship and that democratic citizenship should be committed to respecting the dignity and rights of individuals the world over. It is therefore somewhat misleading to say that world citizenship *rather than* democratic citizenship should be the focus of civic education. We should also recognize that the idea of world citizenship is significantly more metaphorical than the idea of democratic citizenship. No one is (yet or soon to be) enfranchised as a world citizen. This does not detract from the importance of teaching students to identify with human beings the world over. Indeed, I think it makes such an education all the more important because there are fewer institutional incentives that encourage citizens to consider the well-being of non-citizens and people who live beyond their country's borders.

26. Martin Luther King, Jr., "A Time to Break Silence," in *A Testament of Hope: The Essential Writings of Martin Luther King*, ed. James Melvin Washington (New York: Harper & Row, 1986), p. 234.

27. See Nussbaum's essay "Patriotism and Cosmopolitanism," in Cohen, ed., *For Love of Country*, pp. 2–17.

28. See Anthony Appiah, "Cosmopolitan Patriots," in *For Love of Country*, p. 23.

29. Maurizio Viroli, *For Love of Country: An Essay on Patriotism and Nationalism* (Oxford: Clarendon Press, 1995).

30. Ibid., p. 9.

31. Ibid.

32. See Viroli, who writes that "the cause of liberty against oppression does not need cosmopolitans; it simply needs patriots." Ibid., p. 144. The cause of liberty does not need either cosmopolitans or patriots. It needs morally motivated people who can but need not be either.

33. Anthony Appiah, "Cosmopolitan Patriots," and Hilary Putnam, "Must We Choose?" in *For Love of Country*, pp. 22, 95.

34. Ibid., p. 96.

35. Susan Wolf rightly highlights this implication of equal respect of persons for multicultural education within a single society in her "Comment" on Charles Taylor's "The Politics of Recognition," in *Multiculturalism* (Princeton: Princeton University Press, 1994), pp. 75–85.

2

HOW DO LIBERAL DEMOCRACIES
TEACH VALUES?

CHRISTOPHER L. EISGRUBER

Can liberal democracies mandate a curriculum for the purpose of teaching civic values? People often suppose that this question requires us to elect between two broad conceptions of the state's authority over civic education. Under one of these conceptions, the state may insist that children receive instruction in fields such as reading, writing, mathematics, history and science, but the state has no authority to teach values to children if their parents object. Under the other conception, parents and the state have shared authority over the moral upbringing of children, and the state may accordingly demand that students read texts and take courses which are assigned for the purpose of teaching particular values (such as tolerance).

In this essay, I argue that this debate about *whether* liberal democracies may teach values overlooks an important question about *how* liberal democracies teach values. In particular, I contend that civic education in a liberal democracy will depend only minimally upon the assignment of texts or courses beyond those needed to teach reading, writing, and certain basic facts about American government. For that reason, many conventional arguments about civic education are misleading. They exaggerate the importance of moral questions about the rights of parents and the authority of communities, and they underestimate the importance of strategic questions about the design of educational institutions—questions such as, "to what extent can we rely upon judges to ensure that the bureaucrats who run school systems behave in a way that is democratically accountable?"

Section I of this paper analyzes *Mozert v. Hawkins,*[1] in which the United States Court of Appeals for the Sixth Circuit held that parents have no constitutional right to exempt their children from portions of the public school curriculum which they find objectionable on moral or religious grounds. *Mozert* is usually regarded as raising moral questions about the scope of parental authority over children; I reconceive it to emphasize pragmatic questions about how best to supervise the behavior of school bureaucrats. Section II extends the treatment of *Mozert* to reach other controversies about whether the state can require children to read particular texts or take particular courses. The argument of Section II depends heavily on a theory about how liberal democracies teach values. Section III offers some more general reflections about the relative importance of moral and institutional arguments for educational policy decisions in liberal democracies.

I.

Mozert v. Hawkins dealt with some parents' religiously motivated objections to the readings assigned their children, who attended public school in Tennessee. For example, the Holt-Rinehart series of readers contained a story which I'll refer to as "Jim Cooks." The story went like this:

> Pat reads to Jim. Jim cooks. The big book helps Jim. Jim has fun.

Robert Mozert complained that "Jim Cooks" interfered with his ability to control his children's religious upbringing. More specifically, he contended that "Jim Cooks" taught children that men cook, and hence conveyed the improper suggestion that "there are no God-given roles for the different sexes . . ."[2] Mozert also objected to many other assigned readings, and he demanded that the school provide his children with alternative assignments. For a time, the school district tried to accommodate

Mozert's requests. Eventually, however, the district refused to make further exceptions to its standard curriculum. The district said, among other things, that teaching sexual equality was a legitimate part of its educational mission.[3]

People commonly believe that cases like *Mozert* force us to choose between two grand visions of education in a democratic society. One vision emphasizes the importance of parental autonomy. On this view, the state's authority to teach children is limited to equipping them with basic intellectual skills (such as reading, writing, and mathematics), and the state should make great efforts to maximize parental control over the teaching of values. A competing vision bestows the state with the authority and the responsibility to teach values that are constitutive of democratic citizenship. On this view, the state may permissibly endeavor to teach children certain values, such as self-critical rationality and tolerance for diverse viewpoints, even if the parents of the children disapprove.

For example, elsewhere in this volume Professor Amy Gutmann declares that the controversy in *Mozert* "divides civic minimalists from advocates of democratic education."[4] In Professor Gutmann's vocabulary, "civic minimalism" holds that "civic educational requirements imposed by governments must be minimal so that parental control over children's education can be close to comprehensive."[5] Civic minimalism calls upon judges to protect parental authority against infringement; hence, "in a regime of civic minimalism, courts and parents would have almost exclusive control over children's schooling."[6] Civic minimalists therefore "deny democratic citizens the discretion to require ["Jim Cooks"] if a student's parents object."[7] By contrast, defenders of "democratic education," which is Gutmann's own position, "argue that democratic governments should publicly subsidize and mandate schooling that tries to prepare students for exercising their civil, political, and social rights and responsibilities."[8] The theory of democratic education invites public deliberation over the content of school curricula:

> Whereas civic minimalism authorizes, indeed requires, judges to override any democratic decision that enforces more than the civic minimum, democratic education grants democratic govern-

ments discretion over how to interpret the demands of civic education, provided the demands are not discriminatory or repressive.[9]

In particular, democratic education endows "citizens at a school board meeting" with discretion to decide whether public schools should "mandat[e] . . . texts that teach children about gender equality."[10]

Under civic minimalism, Robert Mozert wins his lawsuit: judges should intervene to ensure that Mozert enjoys "close to comprehensive" control over his children's schooling. Under democratic education, he loses: democratic bodies have discretion to deliberate about how best to educate children in the public schools. Or so it might seem. As it turns out, matters are not that simple. Mozert might lose his suit under civic minimalism, and he might win within a regime of democratic education. When we appreciate why that is so, we can begin to see a new way to conceive of *Mozert v. Hawkins*—not as a case that depends upon a confrontation between incompatible philosophical positions like "civic minimalism" and "democratic education" but as a case that turns upon pragmatic questions about how to ensure that school bureaucrats will faithfully serve goals which are shared by civic minimalists and defenders of democratic education alike.

Consider first the position of the civic minimalist. As Gutmann notes, some civic minimalists might consider gender equality to be part of the "civic minimum"—part, in other words, of the minimal curriculum which the state may enforce over parental objections.[11] Gutmann's observation applies, however, only to some, relatively moderate versions of civic minimalism. I am interested in a different problem with Mozert's claim, one that exists even under more radical versions of civic minimalism. To see that problem, we must first notice that Mozert's claim in fact involves two components. One component is Mozert's assertion that the state has no authority to teach children about gender equality if their parents object to the state's message. This component of Mozert's claim excites the division between civic minimalists and proponents of democratic education. But Mozert's claim has a second, equally crucial component: Mozert contends that "Jim Cooks" in fact teaches a principle about gender equality which subverts his authority over his children's upbringing.

This second component of Mozert's claim is sometimes taken for granted, but its truth is far from self-evident.[12] After all, the school district was not forcing Mozert's children to swear that there are no "God-given roles for the different sexes." Nor was the school district forcing the students to write essays celebrating gender equality. If the school district were to have taken any of these steps, defenders of democratic education might well join civic minimalists in finding the district's behavior unconstitutional—not on the ground that the district had intruded upon the right of parents to control their children but on the ground that the district had failed to respect the children's own right to free expression.[13]

The school district did not even ask students to read an essay arguing that men *ought* to perform domestic tasks—it required students to read "Jim Cooks," a simple story in which a man *did* perform (and enjoy) a domestic task. Apparently, both the parents and the school district assumed that "Jim Cooks" is a radically subversive story. They took for granted that the story had the power to disrupt or transform students' views about gender roles. But that shared premise seems fanciful. Is there really some sub-culture within the United States in which men never cook? Even the most masculine jock tosses a steak on the grill occasionally. More importantly, "Jim Cooks" is subject to radically antifeminist interpretations. So, for example, a chauvinist reader might say, "'Jim Cooks' indicates that men are good cooks. The only reason that women cook is that men are busy doing other things, which are more important and more difficult. Women are lucky, because cooking, like other housework, is fun and easy. Women owe a lot to men." No story is self-interpreting. If Jim behaves in feminine fashion, then students might condemn Jim as a wimp or a miscreant. If the story's narrator praises Jim, students might repudiate the narrative perspective.

These observations point to a radical problem with Robert Mozert's claim. Civic minimalists concede that the state may teach children to read. In order to teach students to read, the state will have to assign texts, and most (if not all) texts will be open to interpretations that might subvert a particular parent's values. So, for example, Robert Mozert objected to many stories other than "Jim Cooks." One of the stories that bothered him was "Goldilocks and the Three Bears"; he complained that "Goldilocks" undermined respect for property rights because the protagonist was treated sympathetically even though she trespassed upon the property of the bears.[14] Must the Tennessee school district defer to Mozert's interpretation of "Goldilocks"? That suggestion seems absurd. On the contrary, to be a good reader, one must understand that "Goldilocks" is not necessarily an endorsement of trespass, theft, and vandalism. And, likewise, to be a good reader, one must understand that "Jim Cooks" is open to multiple interpretations—including the anti-feminist interpretations suggested above.

Even texts written from Mozert's own perspective will admit interpretations that he would find subversive. Suppose, for example, that the school assigns a story about a woman who cooks: "Pat cooks. Pat likes to cook. Many women like to cook." Suppose that the teacher wants to test whether students have understood the passage. Suppose, in particular that she asks her students whether the story's author might believe that men as well as women like to cook. That is a perfectly reasonable way to test comprehension of the passage, but the query invites students to entertain the possibility that men do, in fact, like to cook. Would commentators sympathetic to Mozert think that the teacher was doing something impermissible? Or suppose that one of the second-grade students says in class discussion, "Pat is silly. Cooking is hard work. Women shouldn't have to cook all the time. Don't men like to cook?" What would civic minimalists ask the teacher to do? Excuse the Mozert children from the classroom? Refuse to answer the question? Condemn the student's interpretation?

School districts cannot teach students to read unless they assign passages which are open to interpretations with which the students (or their parents) disagree. Of course, different texts pose different kinds of interpretive challenges. Some texts disclose possibilities which children lack the maturity or experience to handle. Nearly all parents would object, for example, if a teacher exposed young children to sexually explicit literature. It is utterly irrelevant that students could repudiate the author's perspective. Exposure to sexual images can confuse and harm children. Other texts might shock only students from particular cultural or religious backgrounds. For example, *Grove v. Mead*

School District No. 354 dealt with a controversy that arose after a religious student was asked to read a novel in which characters referred to Jesus Christ as a "long-legged white son-of-a-bitch," and boasted about a girlfriend with a "keester that would make old Rev'rend Broadnap throw his Bible in a privy hole."[15]

To make Robert Mozert's complaint plausible (even under a regime of civic minimalism), one cannot construe it to allege simply that school officials asked the Mozert children to read texts which were open to interpretations that might subvert their parents' religious and philosophical perspective. That would hold true of virtually any text (including the Bible). One must instead understand Mozert to claim that school officials improperly assigned some texts—including "Jim Cooks" and "Goldilocks"—which were especially disrespectful or shocking to certain children. In fact, though, "Jim Cooks" seems mild by comparison to readings which most civic minimalists would permit the state to assign. So consider the following passage, which is composed of true statements about Supreme Court Justice Ruth Bader Ginsburg:

> Ruth is a famous judge. Martin is her husband. Martin likes to cook. Martin cooks often.

If Robert Mozert is correct to think that "Jim Cooks" will cause his children to reject his views about gender roles, then presumably the first sentence of "Ruth Judges" is even worse: it accurately asserts that a woman holds one of the highest political offices in the United States.[16] Yet, I suspect that even radical civic minimalists would permit schools to teach children the names and identities of American political officials. It is less obvious, but still plausible, that civic minimalists would permit the state to teach students something about the biography of these political figures—such as, for example, that when Ruth and Martin throw dinner parties, he does the cooking.

Let's suppose, though, that we believe that "Jim Cooks" crosses the line—that it is an especially provocative or inflammatory text, and that parents ought to be able to exempt their children from that particular reading assignment. Does it follow that judges should uphold Robert Mozert's constitutional claim? Not necessarily. Presumably, school officials ought to have some discretion to exercise their professional judgment about which texts to assign. One might think that their discretion should include the freedom to make good faith mistakes; or, alternatively, one might doubt whether judges will be able to determine when teachers have exercised their discretion badly. Indeed, many of the people who react sympathetically to Robert Mozert's claims are quick in other contexts to warn us about the dangers that result when federal judges attempt to "micro-manage" the decisions of local officials.

Robert Mozert might thus lose his case even under a regime of radical civic minimalism in which the state's authority is limited to the teaching of reading and other basic intellectual skills. Conversely, Mozert might win his suit under a regime of democratic education. Defenders of democratic education insist that the state may try to inculcate in children values that are necessary to prepare children to "exercis[e] their civil, political, and social rights and responsibilities," but it does not follow that democratic education is unconcerned with protecting the ability of parents to supervise their children's upbringing. One can defend the state's authority to teach values and simultaneously affirm both that the parent/child relationship is a human good which the state must respect, and that policies which respect parental autonomy will often (though not invariably) be the best means to promote the welfare of children. Thus Gutmann contends that the state "can and should" respect "parental authority to educate their children in the family and in other civic associations of their choice."[17] She says that, within a regime of democratic education, parents should be able to choose whether to "send their children to public or private schools, religious or secular schools . . ."[18] More generally, in her book *Democratic Education*, Gutmann reaffirms both "the right . . . of parents to educate their children as members of a family . . ."[19] and "the value of parental freedom . . ."[20] She observes that "we shall want some assurance from even the wisest educational authority that our good as *parents* and as citizens, and not just the good of our children, will be considered in designing the educational system for our society."[21] She concludes that "[t]he only acceptable form of assurance is for *parents* and citizens both to have a significant share of educational authority."[22] It seems plausible to think that this "assurance" should yield a judicially enforceable constitutional right.

Proponents of democratic education therefore have reason to care about Robert Mozert's complaint. It would be better, all things considered, if the schools were able to accomplish their goals without compromising Mozert's relationship with his children. Of course, if gender equality is part of what students must learn in order to become effective citizens, and if schools cannot teach gender equality without assigning "Jim Cooks" or some similar story, then (under a regime of democratic education) school districts must have the discretion to assign "Jim Cooks." They must have that discretion to assign the story even if doing so would intrude upon the parent/child relationship in some families (like the Mozert family). Yet, at this point, the ambiguity of "Jim Cooks" once again becomes important. As we noticed earlier, "Jim Cooks" is open to multiple interpretations, including some anti-feminist interpretations. Those interpretations made it unclear whether "Jim Cooks" was in fact a threat to Robert Mozert's authority and value system; they make it equally unclear whether "Jim Cooks" is a useful vehicle for teaching gender equality. If it is unclear whether "Jim Cooks" is *at all* helpful to the project of teaching gender equality, it becomes less plausible for a district to assert that the assignment is *essential* or even *important* to that task. Indeed, "Jim Cooks" is fiction, and it is discomforting to think that democratic citizenship depends crucially upon whether states can force particular fictions upon children.

We therefore should not be surprised to find that theorists who defend the state's authority to assign controversial texts nevertheless suggest that it would be prudent for the state to accommodate parental objections. For example, both Gutmann and Stephen Macedo have suggested that if the state ignores parents' curricular wishes, it may impel parents to move their children from public schools to private ones.[23] The school district would then win the battle only to lose the war. More generally, educational policy within a regime of democratic education must pursue multiple goals: it must prepare students for citizenship but it must also respect the authority of parents within families. Often, school districts will best be able to serve these plural goals if they accommodate parents who ask that their children be exempted from particular assignments.

Still, somebody might say, none of this establishes what Mozert demanded: a judicially enforceable right to a special accommodation for his children. Democratic education gives "discretion" to "democratic governments"[24] so that citizens have "the moral or political room to pursue the civic purposes of schooling as best they can."[25] All I have done in the past two paragraphs is to argue that proponents of democratic education should use their discretion to accommodate Robert Mozert's objections; I have not given any reasons why judges should compel them to do so.

That deficiency is easily remedied. School districts might have at least three different kinds of reasons for refusing to accommodate parental requests for exceptional treatment. First, the district might believe that the request cannot be accommodated without compromising the student's education (as would be the case if, for example, a parent said that she did not want her child to learn how to read). Second, the district might believe that the request cannot be accommodated without extraordinary expense or difficulty (as might be the case with Robert Mozert's objections, which applied to a very large number of assignments). Third, the district might refuse the request out of sheer bureaucratic indifference or even discriminatory animus. A school official might, for example, refuse to accommodate Robert Mozert because she thinks that Mozert's religious beliefs are silly, or because she considers him to be an annoying pest who takes up too much of her time.

If a school district were to deny Robert Mozert's claim on the basis of neglect or hostility, proponents of democratic education might well hope that judges would intervene on Mozert's behalf. After all, if the school district has acted out of bias, then there has been no good faith effort by any democratic body to determine what course of action would best serve the goals of democratic education. How should judges search for procedural miscarriages of this kind? Judges might demand direct evidence of discrimination or insensitivity. Direct evidence is, however, often hard to obtain, even in cases where discrimination has occurred. So judges might also ask whether or not the school district is able to give a persuasive explanation for its refusal to accommodate Mozert's demands. By asking for such an explanation, the judiciary can "smoke out" impermissible motives: the district's failure to make a persuasive defense of its decision may indicate that its decision was actually based on other, unacceptable reasons— such as a dislike for Robert Mozert or his religion.

It is useful at this point to juxtapose Professor Gutmann's analysis of *Bd. of Education, Island Trees School District v. Pico*[26] to her analysis of *Mozert v. Hawkins. Pico* dealt with an instance of library censorship in a Long Island school district. Some parents persuaded the school board to remove various books—including Kurt Vonnegut's *Slaughterhouse Five* and Richard Wright's *Black Boy*—from the high school library. Students sued, and the case went to the Supreme Court, which splintered. The constitutional claim in *Pico* is a kind of mirror image of the claim in *Mozert*. The constitutional claim in *Pico* insists upon student freedom and the open exchange of controversial ideas; the constitutional claim in *Mozert* champions parental authority and the need to insulate students against subversive ideas. People who sympathize with the claim in *Pico* tend not to like the claim in *Mozert*, and vice versa.

Gutmann believes that the students in *Pico* deserved to win their suit.[27] That leaves her with a challenge. The theory of *Pico* is somewhat mysterious. Few people would maintain that judges should compel school libraries to add controversial books to their holdings, and that is certainly not Gutmann's position.[28] Yet, if the school district is free to decide, for pedagogical reasons, never to purchase *Slaughterhouse Five*, why can't the school district decide to remove that book later? Do books get tenure? Are school districts hostage to whatever decisions were made by librarians in the past? That does not seem very sensible.

Gutmann has a reasonable answer to these questions. She emphasizes that "[m]any decisions to ban books are made or applied in an 'erratic, arbitrary, and free-wheeling manner.'"[29] That was the case, she tells us, in *Pico*. Had the school board acted on the basis of a "consistently applied procedures" that resulted from "deliberative democratic procedures," then we would be obliged to recognize that the school board had a "democratic 'right to be wrong.'"[30] When, however, a school board censors libraries haphazardly, judicial intervention is justifiable.

Yet, if proponents of democratic education can license judges to intervene to correct for failures of "consisten[cy]" and "deliberati[on]," then surely they can do so when the constitutional interest at stake pertains to parental autonomy (as in *Mozert*) as well as when the constitutional interest at stake pertains to student speech (as in *Pico*). Viewed this way, *Mozert* and *Pico* are not so different from each other as people commonly suppose. Instead, the two cases raise similar questions. In both cases, the question is how judges can fashion a doctrine which protects individuals against the irresponsible exercise of power by citizens and school officials but which simultaneously respects the discretion of citizens and responsible officials to make the ultimate judgment about contestable pedagogical issues.

I do not mean, of course, that proponents of democratic education must believe that Robert Mozert enjoys a judicially enforceable claim for the accommodation he seeks, or that they must endorse Mozert's claim if they embrace the claim in *Pico*. My point is more modest—namely, that a judge could subscribe to the position that Gutmann calls democratic education (or any other position which likewise affirms the authority of the community to teach civic values) and simultaneously rule in Robert Mozert's favor. Whether or not Mozert ultimately loses will depend crucially not upon any of the basic propositions that are constitutive of Gutmann's theory but, rather, upon a supplemental theory about how and when judges should intervene to protect individuals against abuses of discretion by school officials. The content of that supplemental theory will depend upon whether one trusts judges to do a good job ferreting out bad behavior by bureaucrats. People who agree about the merits of democratic education (or civic minimalism) can disagree quite sharply about that question of judicial competence.

Our analysis of *Mozert* under the regime of democratic education has thus arrived, by a slightly different route, at exactly the same conclusion we reached when examining *Mozert* through the lens of civic minimalism. That is no accident. There is a substantial and important moral common ground which is obscured by debates about the limits of parental autonomy. Both sides accept that parents have some authority to control the upbringing of their child, and neither side believes that this authority is absolute or comprehensive. In particular, both sides believe that the state is entitled to (and probably obliged to) demand that children learn how to read (and to do so well). Both sides should be able to agree that school officials, in order to do their job, must have some discretion about which texts to assign. Finally, neither side has any reason to insist that this discretion should be totally free from judicial supervision. This common ground is sufficient, I think, for us to conclude that the crucial issues in *Mozert* are not issues about the scope of parental autonomy or community authority but, rather, more pragmatic issues about whether and how judges can improve the quality of decision making by school officials.

II.

Mozert illustrates a general feature of philosophical debates about civic education. Participants commonly assume that if the liberal democratic state could control the formal schooling of American children, it could effectively use that control to shape children's values. This assumption raises the stakes in debates about the relative extent of community and parental authority over education. If the state must defer to parental wishes, then the state may find itself unable to prepare children for the responsibilities of citizenship. If, conversely, the state may trump the wishes of parents, then parents lose their capacity to direct the upbringing of their children. So we are faced with a hard choice among competing philosophical positions, such as "civic minimalism" and "democratic education."

But how much does it really matter whether the state controls schooling? Or, to put the question more precisely, how much control over schooling must the state have in order to inculcate liberal values? Some aspects of the state's authority undoubtedly do matter. A few parents might want to keep their children illiterate and ignorant. It surely matters whether the state can insist that all children be educated. Conversely, a few public officials might think it desirable for the state to seize children at an early age and take over their upbringing entirely, so that their formal education becomes comprehensive. It surely matters whether parents can resist such policies. But American disputes about civic education rarely deal with such extreme possibilities. They more commonly deal with questions like the one in *Mozert*, about whether the state may compel students to read particular texts, or with questions about whether the state may use financial incentives to induce parents to send their children to public, secular schools rather than religious schools or other private schools. To what extent does the state's power to inculcate values depend upon how we resolve issues of that kind?

On first impression, that question may sound not only empirical but hopelessly indeterminate, dependent upon sociological data of a sort almost impossible to gather. If that were so, we might have no choice but to assume, for purposes of both philosophical argument and public policy making, that the state's control over formal schooling does indeed have a crucial impact upon its ability (and hence upon parents' ability) to influence children's values.[31] But descriptive questions about mental processes—such as, "How do children come to have liberal democratic values?"—are not immune to theoretical analysis. Indeed, we cannot begin to analyze such a question sociologically until we refine it philosophically. We must decide what it means for somebody to "have" a "value," and what it means for a value to be a "liberal democratic value." Even after such refinement, theory has another crucial role to play. To interpret data about learning, we will need a model of human behavior. We can analyze the coherence of such models. Not all of us will use the same models, but often the models will share overlapping assumptions. It may therefore be possible to make statements such as, "Given what most people believe about how texts acquire meaning, it does not seem plausible to suppose that exposure to stories like 'Jim Cooks' will play a crucial role in determining either the likelihood that children will become good citizens, or the likelihood that they will embrace their parents' religion." I think that it is possible to make at least two important, general claims of this kind.

1. Teaching the "3 R's" Is a Way of Teaching Democratic Virtues

Almost everybody agrees that the state has the authority to require children to study the so-called "3 R's": reading, writing, and mathematics. In a liberal democracy, there is an essential connection between these intellectual skills and the virtues needed for good citizenship, and it is quite impossible to teach the former without simultaneously conveying something of the latter. Take, for example, writing. Can the state mandate advanced classes in English composition? Somebody might say that students can "write" so long as they can string together sentences which are both comprehensible and syntactically correct. That is, however, a singularly ungenerous view about what it means to write. If students are to become good writers, they must learn to write good essays.

To write good essays, students must become reflective about their own views, so that they can avoid self-contradiction and obscurity; they must learn to be sensitive to other people's perspectives, so that they can anticipate and address potential misunderstandings of their ideas; more generally, they must prepare themselves to enter a discursive forum within which they will be judged by the precision, clarity, and cogency of their reasons rather than by who they are.

Conceptions of goodness are usually laden with politically significant values, and the ideal of "good writing" is no exception. In our society, the values that constitute competence within the discursive realm mirror those that define the political order: an emphasis upon reason giving; respect for the opinions of others; and the equality of persons. Similar points apply to reading and mathematics. One cannot read well without engaging in the sympathetic reconstruction of perspectives different from one's own. The logic of mathematical argument is ruthlessly egalitarian: a bad geometric proof is a bad proof, no matter how rich your parents are or what church they attend. These convergences between democratic values and intellectual skills are no coincidence. Liberal democratic government is in many respects an effort to constitute the political order on the same terms that govern rational speech. One of the defining characteristics of liberal democracy is that persons must give reasoned justifications for the power they seek to exercise; they behave undemocratically insofar as they rely only upon personal status or authority. Another characteristic is that one can be a good citizen of a liberal democratic state even if one disagrees with principles that are fundamental to the regime. Liberal democratic citizens may embrace heretical goals; they need not swear allegiance to the community's values, so long as they defend their positions reasonably and recognize their obligation to comply with the law even when they disagree with it.

These reflections are borne out if we consider more closely the virtues which Gutmann insists the state ought to be able to teach even over parental objection. She writes that publicly mandated schooling should "cultivate the skills and virtues of deliberation"; that "literacy and numeracy are not enough"; and that students should also be taught "virtues such as veracity, nonviolence, practical judgment, civic integrity, and civic magnanimity."[32] She explains elsewhere that "civic integrity" and "civic magnanimity" each have three subcomponents. "Civic integrity" requires that persons demonstrate "consistency in speech[,] . . . consistency between speech and action[,] . . . and integrity of principle."[33] "Civic magnanimity" deals with people's attitudes toward the positions taken by their fellow citizens; it demands that people give "moral reasons for rejecting [moral] position[s]"; that they be "open-minded"; and that they should "seek the rationale that minimizes the rejection of the position they oppose."[34]

Two things are noteworthy about this list. The first is that much of it is rather uncontroversial. How many parents would object to their children being taught "veracity, nonviolence, [and] practical judgment," or being taught to strive for "consistency between speech and action"? The second point is that many of Gutmann's democratic virtues are exactly the sorts of things we might expect students to learn in order to become good writers. Surely a good essay will manifest "consistency in speech." Gutmann's idea of "civic magnanimity" bears a strong resemblance to the principle of "interpretive charity": the idea that, when criticizing an argument, one should first put it in its most powerful form. One could probably learn all of the virtues which Gutmann describes by learning how to write sincere, tautly reasoned essays defending a patriarchal, repressive, theocratic political order.[35]

Of course, somebody can be a great writer, a brilliant mathematician, and an intemperate racist. Intellectual refinement does not guarantee tolerance. But no form of education will wipe out bigotry. Students can read "Jim Cooks," or a whole boatload of feminist literature, and still be sexists (indeed, it is even possible that, with some audiences, a boatload of feminist writing might cause a backlash and *increase* the likelihood that somebody will become a sexist). My point is a limited one: teaching intellectual skills will not be a perfectly successful way of teaching democratic virtues, but it is one important way of doing so.

This point gets lost in the ideological crossfire between people who insist that the community should be able to teach democratic values and others who insist that the community should have no more authority than is necessary to teach intellectual skills. Consider the debate between Gutmann and Stephen Gilles, who is her paradigmatic example of a "civic minimalist." Gutmann insists that "deliberation should be considered primary" among the goals of educational policy even though living a "good life today requires many more basic skills than public deliberation[.]"[36] Gilles, on the other hand, criticizes Gutmann at some length for attaching too much importance to "critical deliberation."[37] Yet, Gilles himself suggests that the state's obligation to respect parental authority over a child's education applies only if "the child has been educated in a tradition in which reasoning and deliberation, at least within the framework of that tradition, is valued and encouraged[.]"[38]

As framed by Gutmann and Gilles, the competition between their positions appears to turn on the choice between "public deliberation" (Gutmann's phrase) and "deliberation . . . within the framework of [a] tradition . . ." (Gilles' phrase). That slices deliberation very finely. I have summarized Gutmann's conception of "public deliberation" above, and I do not see much to distinguish it from "deliberation" in general. If there is an important difference between Gutmann and Gilles on this point, it is a difference not about kinds of deliberation, but about degrees of proficiency. They agree that the state may teach children to deliberate but they disagree about whether the state must be satisfied with rudimentary deliberative skills, or whether the state instead has the authority to compel children to undergo instruction intended to refine further their deliberative capacities.[39] That is a significant difference, and it is a difference of moral principle, but it is not the product of sharply differing moral perspectives about whether the state may teach values or whether it may instead teach only intellectual skills.

2. The Liberal State Teaches Mainly by Example

Gutmann has claimed that "[i]f public schools cannot require students to read about the religious orthodoxy of a New Mexican Indian settlement, or about a boy cooking, or about Anne Frank's unorthodox religious opinions, or about the dignity and worth of human beings, then liberal democracy might as well give up on civic education beyond teaching literacy and numeracy."[40] Is it reasonable to believe that the liberal democratic state's capacity to teach values will depend upon whether it has the authority to assign particular texts? I have already expressed my doubts about whether it matters whether the state is free to assign "Jim Cooks." I want now to generalize that argument.

The most effective way for the state to teach gender equality is not by assigning feminist readings but by treating girls and women equally, and by making that fact of equal treatment known to students. The state should reward and encourage academic achievement by girls, and it should take steps to make sure that girls feel welcome in the classroom. Schools should insist that girls have equal opportunity to receive advanced training in fields like mathematics and the sciences, which some people continue to view as male domains. The state should also make sure that girls have equal opportunities to participate in athletic and extracurricular programs.

Initiatives of this kind secure benefits for female students, but they also teach important lessons to girls and boys alike. How teachers treat girls and boys in the classroom will provide much more powerful lessons about gender equality than will any text— whether it be "Jim Cooks" or something much more sophisticated. The state has a powerful capacity to teach by example— that is, by the way it rewards or punishes particular behaviors. This capacity extends, of course, to actions and policies which the state pursues outside of schools. So, for example, the fact that two Supreme Court Justices are women is powerful evidence that women can have successful and satisfying careers outside their home. The fact that there are federal and state laws prohibiting sex discrimination tends to undermine the legitimacy of views which suppose that people should be judged on the basis of their sex. If schools report these facts to children, they will make an impressive point about gender equality.

In principle, I suppose, civic minimalists could deny that the state has authority to teach children about these basic features of our political system. Children might receive instruction in the so-called "3 R's" (reading, writing, and arithmetic) without learning anything about their government. American children could, for example, learn to read and write without ever learning the name of the President of the United States—or even that there is such a thing as the President of the United States. I suspect, however, that most people—including most "civic minimalists"—would permit the state to demand that students learn something about the American government and American history.[41] If so, that is an important concession. Lessons in law and history can have a powerful influence upon children, since they tell children what values the state will use its awesome power to vindicate.

Somebody might concede all this but insist that the state could do better if, in addition to exemplifying a commitment to sexual equality, schools could demand that students read some feminist texts (or texts selected with a feminist purpose in mind). Is that a reasonable position? Empirical studies provide surprisingly little support for such claims. For example, Gutmann acknowledged in her 1987 book that "[w]hen students who have taken [civics] courses are tested for political knowledge, political interest, sense of political efficacy, political trust, and civic tolerance, the findings offer 'strikingly little support for the impact of the curriculum.'"[42] She also noted that "[m]ost theories of child development converge on the conclusion that early socialization shapes the fundamental moral and political values of children to a much greater extent than subsequent schooling."[43] Indeed, high school civics requirements seem to do a shockingly ineffective job at conveying even simple factual information about the American government.[44]

Nevertheless, we should grant Gutmann's observation that "[e]mpirical studies measure the results of civic and history courses as they are, not as they might be."[45] Likewise, we should agree with her that "[h]owever students have been socialized outside of school, there should be room within school for them to develop the capacity to discuss and defend their political commit-

ments with people who do not share them."[46] As I suggested earlier, if the issue were purely empirical, we might simply have to
trust the discretion of educational policy makers. But there are
theoretical reasons to doubt whether the state's capacity to teach
liberal democratic values is much enhanced by the authority to
assign controversial texts.

Texts are open to multiple interpretations and can provoke
complex and varied reactions in different readers. Suppose, for
example, that a school decides to require a course on "gender
equality," in which students are assigned various "mainstream
feminist" texts.[47] How would students react to such a course? My
suspicion is that any student old enough to understand such a
course would also be old enough to recognize it as propaganda—
and to resent the course for that reason. If the state controlled all
of the sources of information available to students, students
might lack the critical resources by which to recognize, criticize,
and dismiss the state's efforts to preach to them. In a liberal
democracy, however, children will be able to contrast what they
hear in school with what they hear from other sources—including their parents and the news media. Indeed, insofar as the
school's democratic mission requires it to teach students to deliberate critically about the public good, the school's own teaching
will make it difficult for the state to indoctrinate students with an
orthodox view about any subject, including gender equality.

Perhaps a skillful teacher could mediate these difficulties and
teach an effective course about—and in favor of—gender equality. But this observation deepens, rather than resolves, the problem we have been discussing, for it highlights the decisive role of
the teacher. It seems inevitable that the teacher will in fact matter
more than the texts she assigns. Her attitude and insights will determine whether students approach the text with enthusiasm or
boredom, sympathy or hostility, imagination or torpor. As any
teacher knows, it is exceedingly difficult to teach values. If a
teacher is gifted enough to teach gender equality, then she is
probably capable of doing so from a wide variety of texts. If a
teacher lacks that skill, a feminist reading list will not help. Yet,
while the state can easily mandate particular texts, it will have an
exceedingly hard time controlling the way in which teachers
present those texts. Supervising teachers requires sitting in on

their classes. In general, neither parents nor administrators have time to do that (and if some parent or administrator does sit in on a particular class and complain about the teacher's behavior, a question immediately arises as to whether the rest of us should trust the teacher or the observer). As a practical matter, teachers have a great deal of freedom in the classroom—whether they teach in public schools or private ones.

Still, isn't it *possible* that the assignment of particular texts could enhance the ability of schools to teach democratic values? Of course it's *possible.* Assigning feminist literature might to some modest extent increase the likelihood that students will embrace principles of gender equality. Still, whatever benefits might flow from adding value-laden assignments or practices to the curriculum, they seem marginal by comparison to the lessons that are conveyed by ensuring that girls receive equal educational opportunities, and by communicating the fact that women in the United States are not only legally entitled to equal treatment in the workplace but in fact now occupy important government offices. If these are the principal means by which the state teaches equality and other values, then the debate over whether or not the state can mandate the assignment of feminist texts becomes a distracting sideshow. One would have to embrace an extreme version of civic minimalism to deny that the state has authority to tell students about anti-discrimination laws, or to disclose that, after centuries of discrimination, women for the first time now have held such important offices as Attorney General and Secretary of State. Conversely, one would also have to be an extremist to believe that it is worthwhile to mandate the imposition of feminist literature upon children in the face of heartfelt parental objections.

III.

Non-liberal political theorists are free to consider a rich menu of questions about civic education. If freed from the constraints of liberal democratic principle, the state can manipulate the social environment in comprehensive ways, all with an eye to making sure that children eventually develop into good citizens. The state can prohibit the dissemination of unhealthy ideas. It can conduct show trials. It can exile poets and musicians; rip children from their families; deny formal education for some children and mandate it for others; decide which children can enter which professions; and make laws about who can marry whom. It can delegate portions of this authority to matriarchs, patriarchs, generals, or bishops. The constitution of the state can be revised and refined with an eye to improving the character of the people who inhabit the state.

Within liberal political theory, by comparison, the topic of civic education is highly circumscribed. I have thus far focused upon a limited subset of questions about civic education: namely, controversies about whether the state can demand that students take particular texts or courses which are intended to teach them "liberal values" unconnected to intellectual skills. Such questions do not exhaust the range of controversy about educational policy. So, for example, disputes have arisen about whether the state may insist that children achieve high levels of literacy, or whether it must instead defer to parents who wish to pull their children from school once those children have developed rudimentary reading and writing skills.[48] I see no way to resolve such issues without entering moral debates about the scope of parental autonomy. Disputes have also arisen about what steps the state may take in order to encourage—or even force—students to attend integrated schools. If indeed students learn tolerance by seeing the state treat diverse people equally, then it may be crucial that students mix with classmates from other races, religions, social classes, and perhaps with classmates of differing abilities. If so, and if parents insist that they should have the discretion to educate their children in a segregated environment, there will be no way to resolve their dispute with the state without addressing moral arguments about parental autonomy.

We should, however, avoid exaggerating the number and importance of these stark moral conflicts. There are many principles, justified without regard to their impact on the formation of citizen character, which constrain what the liberal democratic state can do. For example, liberal democrats respect the right of parents to have and care for children; the right of adults to decide for themselves what to think and how to live their lives; the existence of a free press; and the equality of persons. These shared principles have profound consequences. So, for example,

American parents are under no obligation to send their children to school before the age of five. During that period, parents have virtually unfettered control of their children's development. These early years are widely thought to be the most important formative period in a person's life. Once children reach age five, parents are constitutionally entitled to send them to the private school of the parents' choice (provided they can afford the tuition). On the other hand, in a liberal democracy like the United States, it is extremely difficult for parents to shield their children from exposure to ideas or information they consider harmful. If, for example, Robert Mozert's kids ever got their hands on a copy of *USA Today* or *People* magazine, they would discover all sorts of things that would curl their father's hair (they might not even have to read—they might just see a photo of Wolfgang Puck standing over a hot stove).

This moral common ground inevitably channels policy debates toward two pragmatic questions. The first question is "How can the state best muster resources to provide high quality instruction in intellectual skills to all students, including poor students?" The second question is "How can the state structure its institutions to ensure that those resources are used well, rather than squandered or misapplied by (for example) school boards and administrators?" These questions are heavily, though not exclusively, strategic. They are, in other words, largely about which means will best enable us to pursue shared goals, rather than about which goals we should pursue. As such, the questions call for a kind of political theory that is intensely concerned with institutional questions as well as moral ones.

One of the most valuable contributions that political theory can make is to caution against resolving complex educational policy disputes on the basis of simple moral formulae or stark ideological positions. For example, elsewhere in this volume, Professor Gutmann considers and refutes several blunt arguments which purport to prove that it would be desirable for the state to subsidize private education through a voucher system. Gutmann rejects arguments which contend that a voucher system can be defended solely on the basis of the bogus claim that it is "morally neutral." She likewise dismisses the idea that "market competition" would inevitably improve educational quality. Gutmann persuasively argues that voucher plans can be justified, if at all, only by a difficult all-things-considered strategic judgment about their impact upon the capacity of American schools to educate children.

On the other hand, Gutmann occasionally writes as though educational policy will be "democratic" if made by "individual schools, local school districts, and state legislatures" rather than by judges. She characterizes school districts and legislatures as fora in which "citizens and their accountable representatives deliberate about educating children."[49] That will sometimes be so, but we will often need a more complex account of the institutions that decide educational policy. Legislatures, after all, are subject to capture by special interest groups. So are school boards; indeed, very few citizens attend school board meetings, and voter turnout in school board elections is often dismal. The need for a nuanced theory of democratic decision making becomes even more evident when we turn our attention from citizens' elected representatives to teachers, school principals, district administrators, and the numerous state and federal bureaucrats who regulate schools. It seems precipitous to regard these officials as "accountable representatives" of citizens, or to assume that their decisions will be founded upon public "deliberation." School principals, for example, are not publicly elected; they are hard to supervise on a day-by-day basis; and they may be difficult to remove from office. Conversely, as Gutmann's own analysis of *Pico* illustrates, judicial intervention may sometimes enhance public deliberation and improve the accountability of school officials. Moreover, judges themselves have a kind of democratic pedigree. Some state judges are elected or subject to recall. Federal judges are not, but their appointments often receive careful political scrutiny—more scrutiny, one might suspect, than the appointment of a state bureaucrat or a high school principal. In addition, judges are obliged to justify their decisions publicly. Their opinions may goad public deliberation—as the extensive discussions of *Mozert v. Hawkins* in this volume nicely illustrate.

Institutional questions about the relationship among judges, legislators, and bureaucrats arise in many policy domains. Political theorists who aspire to produce an institutionally sensitive model of civic education will also face another, less familiar challenge: they must take into account the discretion enjoyed by classroom teachers. On the one hand, student-teacher interactions will likely be the most important determinant of the quality of the education a student receives in school; on the other hand, these day-to-day interactions are almost impossible for either parents or public officials to monitor, much less control. That is true of private schools as well as public schools: parents who send children to private schools will be able to select among schools, and perhaps among teachers, but they may find themselves upset by (or utterly ignorant of) what actually happens in their child's classroom.

This pedagogical autonomy is not necessarily a bad thing. I suspect that, for the most part, teachers care more deeply about the interests of children than do school board officials, principals, state bureaucrats, or "taxpayers," to name a few of the "accountable representatives" who might control teachers. Indeed, good teachers will sometimes understand and care for their students in ways that even the students' parents are unable to do.

Yet, whatever one thinks about the pedagogical autonomy of teachers, it has two consequences for political theorizing. First, as we have already seen, the unreviewability of teachers' behavior limits the importance of the debate about parental autonomy and community authority with respect to questions of curricular content. Teachers are at best imperfectly accountable to either parents or the community. Second, by recognizing the discretion of teachers, we uncover another set of philosophic questions. These questions ask how teachers should use the discretion they inevitably have, rather than how public officials or citizens should try to limit teachers' discretion.

Indeed, in a liberal democracy, questions addressed to teachers may be the richest questions about civic education. Teachers are in a position to respond not only to ideas about how liberal principles constrain the state's authority over education but also to ideas about what education is ideal for children who will become citizens in a liberal democracy. Ideal conceptions of education will require subtle adjustments to educational practice. Such nuances are impervious to the clunky regulatory mechanisms of the liberal state, but they may be within the grasp of those (like parents and teachers) who educate individual children on a day-to-day basis, and so can change their own pedagogy in response to thoughtful conceptions of what it means for an education to be excellent.

IV.

In this essay, I have sought to highlight the existence of moral common ground in disputes about civic education. I have focused in particular upon disputes about whether the state can mandate imposition of a curriculum designed to teach liberal democratic values. In liberal democracies, there is a deep connection between the improvement of intellectual capacities and the inculcation of civic values. Moreover, the liberal democratic state teaches most powerfully by example, not by sermonizing. These observations, when combined with liberal democracy's baseline respect for parental autonomy, generate the following conclusion: the kinds of publicly mandated curricula which are arguably consistent with liberal principles are neither likely to make substantial new inroads upon parental authority nor likely to make substantial contributions to the state's efforts to prepare children for citizenship.

Given the chronic failures of American publicly financed education, the most crucial issues of educational policy today are questions of institutional design and pedagogical approach. How well are judges positioned to weigh the merit of state intrusions upon parental control? How is it possible to criticize a child's mistakes without destroying her self-esteem? How can one motivate children to read Dickens rather than watch *Dawson's Creek?* How can we enable schools to attract teachers who are good at these delicate and difficult tasks? How can we best ensure that children from poor families and poor neighborhoods enjoy access to a good education? Until American schoolchildren are well taught in such subjects as English composition and geometry and natural science and history, Americans should put aside ideological disagreement and make common cause against the daunting practical obstacles which stand in the way of the state's educational mission, regardless of how that mission is conceived.

NOTES

I thank Stephen Macedo for comments on a draft of this essay. I am also grateful to the Filomen D'Agostino and Max Greenberg Research Fund at the New York University School of Law, which provided generous financial support for this research.

1. 827 F.2d 1058 (6th Cir. 1987).

2. Robert Mozert, Letter to the Editor, *Tennessee Times News* (Oct. 18, 1983) (quoted in Nadine Strossen, *"Secular Humanism" and "Scientific Creationism": Proposed Standards for Reviewing Curricular Decisions Affecting Students' Religious Freedom*, 47 Ohio St. L.J. 333, 340 & n. 44 (1986)).

3. In his suit against the school district, Mozert claimed that the district had violated his right to the free exercise of religion. For purposes of this essay, I will treat the claims in *Mozert* as dependent upon a general right of parental autonomy which would enable all parents, religious or secular, to control the moral education of their children. I will put to one side questions about when religiously motivated conduct should be constitutionally exempt from the application of an otherwise valid law. Lawrence Sager and I have addressed that question elsewhere. See, e.g., Christopher L. Eisgruber and Lawrence G. Sager, *The Vulnerability of Conscience: The Constitutional Basis for Protecting Religious Conduct*, 61 U. Chi. L. Rev. 1245 (1994).

4. Amy Gutmann, *Civic Minimalism, Cosmopolitanism, and Patriotism: Where Does Democratic Education Stand in Relation to Each?*, this volume, n. 9, 000.

5. *Id.* at 54.

6. *Id.* at 23.

7. *Id.* at 36.

8. *Id.* at 29.

9. *Id.* at 29.

10. *Id.* at 30.

11. *Id.* at 31.

12. One of the Sixth Circuit judges said that "mere exposure" to ideas could not amount to a burden on religious practice. *Mozert*, 827 F.2d at 1065 (Lively, J.). Stated so broadly, that claim is false. It is also quite different from the issue explored here. At issue in this essay is whether exposure to "Jim Cooks" is likely to transform children's values. It is possible that exposure to "Jim Cooks" might burden religious practice even if it does not teach any principle whatsoever. If God can tell people not to eat particular foods, then surely God can tell people not to read (or not to permit their children to read) certain books—regardless of how little impact those books might have.

13. In her contribution to this volume, Gutmann emphasizes that "[n]one of the requirements [at issue in *Mozert*] entailed forcing the profession of belief by any student (or parent)." Gutmann, 39.

14. Strossen, 47 Ohio St. L.J. 333, 340 & n. 44.

15. 753 F.2d 1528, 1547, 1551 (9th Cir. 1985). The school district excused the religious student from the obligation to read the novel. The case ended up in court when the student's parents sought to prohibit the district from assigning the book to other students; the parents contended that inclusion of the book within the school's curriculum amounted to an establishment of "secular humanism."

16. In fact, Mozert did object to the assignment of "biographical material about women who have been recognized for achievements outside their homes." *Mozert*, 827 F.2d at 1062. Not surprisingly, this facet of the case has received relatively little attention from those who are sympathetic to Mozert's claim; it is hard to see how the public schools could be prevented from conveying true historical information about the achievements of women.

17. Gutmann, this volume, at 23.

18. *Id.* at 36.

19. Amy Gutmann, *Democratic Education* 29 (Princeton: Princeton University Press 1987).

20. Id. at 32.

21. *Id.* at 27 (emphasis added).

22. *Id.* (emphasis added).

23. *Id.* at 122; Stephen Macedo, *Liberal Civic Education and Religious Fundamentalism: The Case of God v. John Rawls*, 105 Ethics 468, 488 (1995).

24. Gutmann, this volume, at 29.

25. *Id.* at 38.

26. 457 U.S. 853 (1982).

27. Gutmann, *Democratic Education* at 98–99.

28. *Id.* at 98.

29. *Id.*

30. *Id.* at 99.

31. Macedo, 105 Ethics at 485.

32. Gutmann, this volume, at 26.

33. Amy Gutmann and Dennis Thompson, *Democracy and Disagreement* 81 (Cambridge: Harvard University Press 1996).

34. Id. at 83–85.

35. Whatever Gutmann means by "open-mindedness," it cannot entail any sweeping version of relativism. Open-mindedness must, for example, be consistent with Gutmann's own condemnation of "civic minimalism" as "either empty or self-defeating." Gutmann, this volume, at 35.

36. *Id.* at 25–26.

37. See, e.g., Stephen G. Gilles, *On Educating Children: A Parentalist Manifesto*, 63 U. Chi. L. Rev. 937, 972–983 (1996).

38. *Id.* at 978.

39. So, for example, Gutmann says that democratic governments are not required "to recognize a 'right' of Amish adolescents to leave school after eighth grade if this right would result in a significant shortening of the time that Amish adolescents were exposed to knowledge and ways of thinking essential to democratic deliberation." *Democratic Education* at 123. Gilles, by contrast, says that the Amish should be able to remove their children from school after "[e]ight years of conventional schooling" because that much time is "sufficient to equip children with basic skills such as reading, writing, and numeracy, and to provide them with basic knowledge about our society, its history, and its institutions." Gilles, 63 U. Chi. L. Rev. at 993. For Gilles, it does not matter that "two or three years of high school would . . . enable Amish children to develop these skills and knowledge more fully . . ." *Id.*

40. Amy Gutmann, *Civic Education and Social Diversity*, 105 Ethics 557, 572 (1995).

41. For example, Gilles defends the power of the state to insist that "all seventh-graders . . . take a year-long course in American history," even if some parents object that the "course should come later in the curriculum . . ." 63 U. Chi. L. Rev. at 987.

42. Gutmann, *Democratic Education* at 105, quoting M. Kent Jennings, Kenneth P. Langton, and Richard Niemi, "Effects of the High School Civics Curriculum," in Jennings and Niemi, eds., *The Political Character of Adolescence: The Influence of Families and Schools* 181 (Princeton: Princeton University Press 1974).

43. Gutmann, *Democratic Education* at 107.

44. A useful recent study is Richard G. Niemi and Jane Junn, *Civic Education: What Makes Students Learn* (New Haven: Yale University Press 1998). Niemi and Junn report that "the accepted wisdom in the political science profession is that civics classes have little or no effect on the vast majority of students." *Id.* at 16. At least one recent study has concluded that not merely civics education but formal education in general have "no effect on 'political sophistication' about political candidates and parties." *Id.* at 13. Niemi and Junn argue that high school civics classes, if properly taught, can improve political understanding. *Id.* at 117–46.

45. Gutmann, *Democratic Education* at 106.

46. *Id.* at 107.

47. The example belongs to Gilles, who uses it to illustrate the sort of course which the state might try to impose, but which he thinks it ought not to have the authority to mandate. Gilles, 63 U. Chi. L. Rev. at 987.

48. See, e.g., *Wisconsin v. Yoder*, 406 U.S. 205 (1972). For the divergent views of Gutmann and Gilles regarding *Yoder*, see note 38, *supra.*

49. Gutmann, this volume, at 36.

3

EDUCATION DISESTABLISHMENT: WHY DEMOCRATIC VALUES ARE ILL-SERVED BY DEMOCRATIC CONTROL OF SCHOOLING

MICHAEL W. McCONNELL

Liberals and progressives in the United States usually argue for a system of democratically controlled education: a system of public schools, supported by public taxation, controlled by publicly elected school boards, teaching a curriculum designed (among other things) to inculcate the values necessary for the perpetuation of democratic institutions. Families who choose to send their children to nonpublic schools, they have argued, should have to pay the full cost of that education, in addition to paying through taxation for the support of the public school system.

I argue that this traditional liberal and progressive position is wrong—or at least, wrong as a matter of liberal principle. Rather than organizing education along democratic lines, I will argue, a liberal pluralistic society committed to nonestablishment of religion should organize education along pluralistic lines.[1] The precise details of the educational choice plan may vary, but the core of the idea is that families would be permitted to choose among a range of educational options, including but not limited to government schools, using their fair share of educational funding to pay for the schooling they choose.[2] The government's educational role would continue to be significant: it would require accreditation to ensure that schools satisfy basic requirements of educational quality, and perhaps of minimal civic responsibility; it would provide funding to ensure that all children, poor as well as rich, have an adequate opportunity for education; and it probably would continue to operate its own set of schools.[3] But government schools would no longer enjoy monopoly privileges over their competitors in the marketplace of educational ideas.

In addressing this question, I make three assumptions. First, I assume that within the society are many different and reasonable, but for practical purposes irreconcilable, viewpoints that bear on education. These differences might be religious, moral, ideological, or pedagogical. This is what is meant when we say the society is pluralistic. Second, I assume that the society is committed, above all else, to peaceful coexistence among adherents of many such views, and where feasible without the undue sacrifice of other public goods, to the freedom of adherents of these different views to be able to conduct their lives in accordance with their own conscience and convictions.[4] This is what is meant when we say the society is liberal. Third, I assume that the society is committed to a constitutional principle under which the government will not officially adopt or espouse any *religious* doctrine or worldview in preference to other religious or nonreligious doctrines or worldviews. That is what is meant by nonestablishment.

The pluralist ideal of educational organization is often defended on the basis of parental rights, on the theory that parents have a natural or constitutional right to raise their children in accordance with their own understanding of the good, within certain constraints.[5] It should be obvious that pluralistic education is preferable from this parentalist point of view. In this paper, however, I will put aside these parentalist arguments and rely instead on the interests of liberal democratic society as a whole. Of course, to the extent that liberal democratic society depends on families as a core social institution, the well-being of families may play an instrumental role. However, my defense of educational pluralism is based not on the rights of parents as such, but on maintaining a free and liberal society in the face of cultural, ideological, and religious differences.

Let me be clear about the limited nature of my argument. Proponents of democratic control offer some prudential, contingent, and empirical arguments that cannot entirely be dismissed, and that rightly suggest a degree of conservative caution regarding the restructuring of education. These arguments deserve respectful consideration in the legislative arena, and suggest that the best approach to reform may be to encourage experimentation in certain places (presumably, large cities, like Milwaukee or Cleveland, where the public school establishment has most clearly failed children from the most impoverished backgrounds) rather than immediate adoption of educational choice in every school district in the nation. But it is time to discard the notion that democratic control over education is *in principle* the form best suited to a liberal, pluralistic society. It is the public school establishment—not educational choice—that is inconsistent with disestablishmentarian liberal values.

The argument will proceed in four parts. The first part will explain the attractions of establishmentarianism, and the reasons disestablishmentarianism prevailed in the United States, and apply these principles to religious establishments, freedom of the press and other institutions for the propagation of ideas, and elementary and secondary education. The next three parts will show that each of the three most prominent reasons for disestablishment of religion have strong parallels to educational establishments. Part II will discuss the problem of choosing a single curriculum in the face of strong conscientious disagreements about educational and moral philosophy. Part III will discuss liberal theory and its aversion to government-fostered orthodoxy, and apply that theory to the experience of public education in the United States. Part IV will explore reasons why decentralized control over education might serve democratic purposes better than democratic control. My thesis is that the argument for democratic, collective control of educational choices is similar to the classic argument for an established church, and the reasons that defeated official religious establishments in this country should also be persuasive in defeating official educational establishments.[6]

I. ESTABLISHMENT AND DISESTABLISHMENT

A. *Religious Establishments*

Every society needs some means by which to inculcate its values and commitments among the populace, and particularly among the next generation. This generally goes by the antiseptic label of "social reproduction," but the actual tools of social reproduction, which involve appeals to the loyalties and affections of the populace, are anything but antiseptic. Parades, pomp, and pageantry play as large a role as that played by appeals to reason—perhaps larger. Until modern times, the most important tool of social reproduction was the state church. Civil religion—as both Hobbes[7] and Rousseau[8] cogently argued—was the means by which nations could inculcate the virtues and habits of loyalty and obedience necessary to preservation of good order. Divine sanction would serve as a supplementary support for the laws. In Rousseau's words, the role of religion in politics is to "bind the hearts of the citizens to the State."[9]

At the time of the American founding, churches were the primary institutions for the formation of democratic character and the transmission and affirmation of community values. That is why, in the turbulent and depressing years between independence and the creation of a new constitutional order, so many patriotic Americans (like Patrick Henry) believed that the want of public virtue could be traced to the decline in the preaching and teaching of the Christian religion. That is why, in newly independent and republican America, the question of disestablishment was bitterly contested in almost every state. Arguments for public support of religion were based not on obscurantism or bigotry but on the civic and republican claim, as expressed in the much-admired Massachusetts Constitution of 1780, that "the happiness of a people and the good order and preservation of civil government essentially depend upon piety, religion, and morality," and that "these cannot be generally diffused through a community but by the institution of the public worship of God and of public instruction in piety, religion, and morality."[10]

Disestablishment of religion, by contrast, meant that democratic politics in America would be deprived of a key instrument for social reproduction. The primary responsibility for development and transmission of community values would be left to a diverse set of private institutions, outside democratic control. From our vantage point of more than 200 years, we may not realize what a dangerous experiment this was. If, as Washington stated in his Farewell Address to the Nation, religion and morality are "indispensable supports" for republican government and the "firmest props of the duties of men and citizens,"[11] then in leaving religious training to the vagaries of the private sphere the new nation was taking a grave risk. Churches might preach the wrong virtues and fail to preach the right ones. A religious free-for-all might exacerbate divisions among the people rather than providing a source of unity and common aim. Disestablishment could imperil the moral and social preconditions for the new nation.

Yet an established church was never a serious option for the United States. At a national level, the religious complexion of the nation was already too diverse to permit agreement on a national creed. Under conditions of deep disagreement about religious fundamentals, any attempt to forge a united institution for worship would produce dissension, hostility, and possibly even bloodshed. Even the states with religious establishments at the time of the founding gradually moved toward disestablishment. Massachusetts' establishment was the last to go, in 1833. It is nice to think that bringing worshipers of diverse backgrounds and convictions into communion with one another under the aegis of a broad latitudinarian church would breed toleration and mutual respect—as Justice Scalia recently argued in defense of public prayer[12]—but the actual effect was a struggle for dominance. To bring peace to warring religious factions it is better to let each of them go its own way.

Moreover, disestablishment of religion was more in keeping with the liberal presuppositions of the new American republics. In a regime of free speech, free press, private property, and limited government, it seemed natural to insist upon liberty of conscience as well. There was something wrong—Jefferson called it "sinful and tyrannical"—with requiring citizens to support and attend institutions propagating doctrines they do not believe.[13]

The structure of American liberty was based on pluralism and diversity—the balance of power among sects and factions—rather than on a contrived homogeneity.[14] Indeed, it became the aspiration of liberal government to refuse to use state power to impose any particular understanding of the good life upon one's fellow citizens.[15] That is the distinctive claim of liberalism to superiority over other regimes: liberalism enables the people—as individuals, as families, as voluntary groups—to pursue happiness in their own way. Disestablishment of religion was the harbinger and quintessence of liberalism.

Finally, even accepting the proposition that religion and morality are indispensable supports to republican government, Americans of the founding era widely recognized that establishing religion—granting it exclusive privileges and emoluments and protecting it from the need to compete in the marketplace of ideas—would weaken religion, not strengthen it. Adam Smith devoted a section of his *Wealth of Nations* to showing that clergy of the established church, like other monopolists shielded from the forces of competition, would "repos[e] themselves upon their benefices" and "neglect to keep up the fervour of faith and devotion in the great body of the people."[16] Madison, more pungently, declared that established religion tends toward "indolence in the clergy and servility in the laity."[17] Moreover, the likely result of forcing diverse groups to come to agreement on the content of creeds and prayers is to foster a watered-down religion that offends few because it stands for little. A "least common denominator" approach has the effect of trivializing religion, while allowing each group to be "sectarian" in its own way tends to preserve religious distinctiveness and vitality. Just as free markets tend to produce a strong economy, disestablishment and free exercise tend to produce strong religion.

Thus disestablishment carried the day. Strong religion may be an essential precondition to republican government, but established religion tended to produce discord, conflicted with liberal principles, and weakened religion. It foundered on the *fact* of irreducible pluralism, the *principle* of liberalism, and the *ineffectiveness* of religious monopolies. Two generations later, Tocqueville described religion as "the first" of America's "political institutions," reported that religion was stronger in America than in any

other country, and attributed this strength to the separation between church and state.[18]

B. *Freedom of the Press and Other Institutions for the Propagation of Ideas*

Other means by which the society might control the propagation
of ideas posed much the same institutional question. And in each
case, the founders of the American republic opted for the same
resolution: disallowing government control. Consider freedom
of the press, which is the closest cousin to disestablishment of religion. Control over the press, like established religion, is in theory an excellent tool for shaping public opinion. A free press can
be subversive of community values and good order. But from the
beginning, Americans refused to allow their government to license the press, and later—unlike some other Western democracies—decided not to create state radio or television networks.
Even publicly supported radio and television stations are carefully insulated from democratic control. Despite the enormous
power of mass communications to shape the ideas and moral tex-
ture of the nation, we leave this important function to decentralized, and mostly private, institutions. The BBC is the telecommu-
nications equivalent of the Church of England. In America—for
better or worse—we have neither BBC nor C of E.

  In other areas involving the propagation of ideas, opinion,
and culture—such as higher education, science, and the arts—
the United States has followed a similar course. The government
may provide financial support. It may even be a participant, as in
the case of higher education. But we have gone to considerable
lengths to ensure that the actual production and dissemination
of academic, scientific, and artistic work cannot be controlled by
the central authorities. In all these fields, diverse actors, many of
them private, are responsible for the shape and content of our
culture. No one speaks of these institutions as instruments for
the inculcation of democratic values. The structure of the national endowments for art, science, and the humanities, and the
tradition of academic freedom, all can be seen as versions of the
principle of disestablishment. Our constitutional tradition is one
that denies our collective selves the power to engage in conscious

social reproduction through political control over the institutions for dissemination of ideas.

C. Education: The Great Exception to
Disestablishmentarian Principles

Primary and secondary education stands out as the great exception to our disestablishmentarian tradition. In the present age, schools have become the primary institutions for the formation of democratic character and the transmission and affirmation of community values. We depend on elementary and secondary schools to inculcate the values and ideals necessary for the next generation to become responsible citizens in our democratic society. The Supreme Court has referred to the "importance of public schools in the preparation of individuals for participation as citizens, and in the preservation of the values on which our society rests,"[19] and has stated that one objective of public education is "to inculcate fundamental values necessary to the maintenance of a democratic system."[20] In perhaps the most important recent book on the relation between education and the American political regime, Amy Gutmann notes that "education . . . shapes the political values, attitudes, and modes of behavior of future citizens."[21]

Yet unlike religion, press, mass communications, art, science, and higher education, this important means for the transmission of ideas and formation of values has not been insulated from democratic control. More than eight out of every ten children in the United States attend schools organized and financed by the state and controlled by elected school boards.

To be sure, the American public school system has traditionally been a localized establishment, akin to the congregationalist establishments of New England, rather than a national establishment like the Church of England. From the beginning, American public schools have been controlled by locally elected school boards, not by national or state agencies. That meant that schools tended to reflect local community norms. A localized establishment is less dangerous to pluralistic values, since it permits differences of approach and philosophy within the nation as a whole. To be sure, the individual family living in a particular location has no realistic choice of schools, but it is more difficult for centralized authorities on a national level to control the content of education for all the children. More recently, however, this safeguard against centralized control has diminished in importance. As a result of many factors, including an increasing assertion of state authority, school district consolidation, increased federal funding and attendant regulatory controls, the movement for national standards and testing, and the economies of scale in textbook publishing, local variations in educational approach and philosophy have become more difficult to sustain. Increasingly, public education has taken on the attributes of a nationally homogenous system, with local administration.

The decision to adopt a collective, democratic system of education was not one made at the Founding. Public education was almost nonexistent when the First Amendment was written. To be sure, some prominent voices (Benjamin Rush, for example) urged creation of a system of republican schools on the French model, but these proposals fell on deaf ears.[22] Prior to 1830, most schools were private. Almost all (even those organized by towns) were conducted under religious auspices.[23] Governmental financial support for education (especially in the more religiously diverse big cities) typically took the form of grants to private schools for the education of the poor, with the choice of schools left to the families involved. For example, in New York in 1805 there were schools conducted by Presbyterian, Episcopalian, Methodist, Quaker, and Dutch Reformed groups, as well as the "Free School Society," a nondenominational charitable group, all receiving public support. Later these groups were joined by Baptists, Catholics, and Jews.[24] Early federal aid, which typically took the form of land grants, went to private as well as public schools, including religious schools. Until 1864, education in the District of Columbia was provided entirely through private and semi-private institutions, including denominational schools, partially at public expense.[25]

By the Civil War, most northern and western states had established public school systems, and most ceased to support nonpublic education. In the South, rudimentary public school systems were created as part of Reconstruction. Most of the schools for the former slaves in the South, funded by Congress under the

Freedman's Bureau Act, were run by Protestant missionary societies, including Presbyterians, Methodists, Baptists, and Congregationalists.[26]

Yet by 1900, about 92 percent of the school population attended public schools, which were created, financed, and governed by the state. Public schools had become the cornerstone of moral and economic uplift, and perhaps the most important function of local government. They were justly called "Pillars of the Republic."[27] To be sure, in the 1925 decision of *Pierce v. Society of Sisters*,[28] the Supreme Court held that families could not be *compelled* to send their children to public schools, but the Court did not question the assumption that any nonpublic alternatives would be at private expense. This meant that, for most families, children received an education whose basic content and ideological stance was determined by the community as a whole. Until quite recently, that generally meant an education based on traditional Protestant values, capitalism, and patriotism. Today, it is more likely to mean an education based on vaguely leftist secular egalitarian values. Whatever the ideological content, dissenters are faced with the choice of seeing their children educated according to normative premises they do not share, or paying for an alternative. Education thus stands as the great exception to the principle of disestablishment in America. Alone among the various institutions for the propagation of ideas, the education of the young is almost exclusively under the control of the government.

The public school establishment thus bears a strong functional similarity to the more overtly religious establishments of yore. Like religious establishments, public schools are designed to undergird and impart to the younger generation the values and ideals of the regime. How else can we assure that future generations will remain committed to our democratic way of life? But like religious establishments more than 200 years ago, the public school establishment faces powerful obstacles arising from the *fact* of cultural and religious pluralism, the *principle* of liberalism, and the *ineffectiveness* of public education. Not surprisingly, the public schools are the most bitterly contested arena in our nation's culture wars. How can a common curriculum accommodate the deep disagreements that legitimately exist in American society, regarding not only issues of religion (narrowly understood) but of pedagogy, morality, equality, patriotism, gender roles, ethnicity, sexuality, economics, and justice? Can common schools be operated without effectively establishing an official orthodoxy regarding questions of legitimate disagreement? Even assuming the need for social reproduction and inculcation of the habits of heart and mind needed for democratic citizenship (which I, for one, do not doubt), does it help to give a single system of schools a monopoly on public funds and protection from the need to compete for students?

II. DEMOCRATIC VALUES AND THE REALITY OF PLURALISM

As noted, one reason that establishment of a national religion was never a serious option for the United States was that, even by the time of the Founding, religious diversity was too great to permit agreement on the content of the establishment. Much the same problem faces advocates of common schools. If students of different cultures and creeds are to be educated according to a common curriculum, then it is necessary to determine what the content of that curriculum is. The diversity of opinions about the content of education makes that difficult. What is taught to children—be it cooking or transubstantiation, safe sex or the pledge of allegiance—is of intense interest to parents. They will not accept modes of education with which they disagree without a fight. Consider the battle in New York over the Rainbow Curriculum, the continuing bitterness over school prayer, and the recent outbreak of controversy over phonics and whole language education. If families are able to choose schools consistent with, or responsive to, their convictions—with progressives choosing progressive schools, traditionalists choosing traditionalist schools, and the religious choosing religious schools—then there is no need for differences of opinion to break out into conflict. Everyone can live and let live. But if one curriculum will be imposed upon all the conflicting groups, the predictable result will be conflict, with attendant hostility and intolerance among the contending groups.[29] As Supreme Court Justice Robert Jackson observed: "Probably no deeper division of our people could proceed from any provocation than from finding it necessary to choose what doctrine and whose program public educational officials shall compel youth to unite in embracing."[30] And the losers will be put to a choice between seeing their children educated in ways deeply disturbing to their convictions, or being forced to dig deep into their pockets to pay for an education the winners get for free. That will breed further alienation and division—and probably make out-groups more antagonistic toward the mainstream values of the community. It is difficult to see how this arrangement can be expected to increase toleration and social harmony.

An even more probable scenario is that public schools, under conditions of pluralism, will attempt to avoid conflict by watering down the curriculum and avoiding any teaching that might be offensive to any significant group. In other words: mush. This is the educational equivalent of the least-common-denominator religion that seems to be the result of official establishment. But this result is neither neutral (mush, too, reflects an ideological perspective that sharp differences and clear opinions are either dangerous or pointless) nor calculated to provide a firm basis for democratic citizenship. The mush alternative is effectively an abdication of the responsibilities of value inculcation. It is a capitulation to the often anti-social values of mass youth culture, as conveyed in television, movies, and popular music.

How do the theorists of democratic education deal with the issue of pluralism? At the outset, we must confront a fundamental ambiguity in their argument. Does the call for education in democratic values refer to values that have been adopted, in fact, by the people through democratic processes? Or does it refer to the content of the values—values necessary or appropriate to a democratic society (such as tolerance)? It should be obvious that democratic values in the first sense (call them "democratically derived values") will not necessarily be the same as democratic values in the second sense (call them "substantively democratic values"). Indeed, there is no particular reason to expect a strong correlation between the two. But it is far from clear that the argument for democratic values is legitimate if the values to which it refers are merely majoritarian, and not democratic in content.[31] And it is equally far from clear that the argument for substantively democratic values supports the claim for democratic control of education if those are not the values which will, in fact, be adopted by democratically controlled school boards. Democratic control is a reasonable guarantee that the values taught in school will be democratically derived, but it is no guarantee that they will be democratic in substantive content.

Let us consider both versions of the argument.

A. *Democratically Derived Values*

Amy Gutmann argues that our society is committed to a collective model of education embodying "the practices and authorities to which we, acting collectively as a society, have consciously agreed." "Although we are not collectively committed to any particular set of educational aims," she argues, "we are committed to arriving at an agreement on our educational aims." This process of obtaining collective agreement on educational aims is "minimally problematic," she says, because society "has a compelling response to those adults who object to the form or the content of education on grounds that it indirectly subverts or directly conflicts with their moral values." The response is to say that "'[t]he values we are teaching are the product of a collective decision to which you were a party. Insofar as that decision deprives no one of the opportunity to participate in future decisions, its outcome is legitimate, even if it is not correct."[32]

This argument falls short in four ways. First, it rests on an assertion about the actual nature of our democratic commitments: "we are committed," Gutmann says, "to arriving at an agreement on our educational aims." But this assertion appears to be empirically false. More than 40 percent of the people now support educational choice,[33] a number that rises to 70 percent in the case of "failing schools" and "poor" families.[34] Black and Hispanic parents, whose children are the worst served by the public school establishment, now favor educational choice rather than collective decision making by a majority that exceeds two-thirds.[35] Even opponents of genuine educational pluralism often support limited pluralism *within* the public school system—charter schools, magnet schools, and the like. These approaches eliminate the need for collective "agreement on our educational aims." There does not seem to be any social consensus that educational aims should be established collectively.

Second, even if it were true that majorities prefer majority-controlled education, why should majoritarian preferences be compelling in this context? There are, of course, some things upon which we *must* agree collectively—such as whether to go to war or where to build a highway. But why is it necessary to determine educational aims collectively? Why not allow families to choose their own educational philosophy (at least within certain limits), just as we allow them to choose their own religion? In a democratic society, a collective decision will approximately reflect the preferences of the mainstream or median voter. But why should mainstream or median citizens be able to impose their ideas about the education of the next generation on everyone else?

Third, the democratic argument fails to recognize the particular problem posed for families whose understanding of "educational aims" includes the idea that religious faith is an essential aspect of education, which should be integrated into the curriculum. This is not an unreasonable view, and it is one that the liberal state is bound to respect. Under the Establishment Clause of the First Amendment, however, this religious educational premise cannot serve as the basis for democratic decision making. Government schools may not engage in education according to this religious ideal. But when this perspective is excluded from collective deliberations, families who adhere to the religious perspectives are deprived of the right other citizens have to seek incorporation of their ideas about educational aims into the curriculum. From these families' point of view, the values taught in the schools are the product of a collective decision to which they are not equal parties. It is one thing to say that losers in the political process can be compelled to give way because they had a full and fair opportunity to persuade a majority, and they failed. It is quite another matter to tell people they must submit to an educational philosophy contrary to their beliefs, when their own beliefs were constitutionally excluded from the outset.[36]

This is not an insignificant objection to the argument, since a very large proportion of those who dissent from the ideology of the public schools, and of those who form alternative schools, do so from religious motivation. The democratic argument can have no force for these citizens.

Finally, the insistence on obtaining collective agreement on educational aims begs the question even from the point of view of democratic social reproduction. The objective of social reproduction is to reproduce, in the next generation, the set of values and beliefs that constitute the character of the society. In a homogeneous society, that might well entail collective deliberation over the aims of education, since pluralistic education tends to undermine social homogeneity. But if society is pluralistic in character, collective educational decision making will distort, rather than reproduce, the social condition of the society. America is made up of people of diverse cultures and beliefs, and the best way to ensure that the next generation will be of similarly diverse character is to allow subgroups to pursue their own understanding of educational aims, within bounds of reasonableness (as expressed through accreditation standards).

B. Substantively Democratic Values

The alternative theory of democratic education is that it must impart certain values that are necessary to, or inherent in, a democratic way of life. The most immediate problem with this argument, however, is that there is no set of agreed-upon values for democratic citizens, except perhaps at a level of vagueness that ceases to be controversial because it ceases to be meaningful. Let us imagine two approaches to identifying the set of essential democratic values: thick and thin.

The thick approach is highly prescriptive. A familiar conservative version would teach patriotism, free enterprise, industry, thrift, respect for law, respect for parents and other authorities, self-restraint, veneration for the Constitution and our Founding Fathers, the English language, the classics of Western and American culture, and so forth. A familiar left-progressive version would teach egalitarianism with respect to race, sex, ethnicity, creed, color, disability, and sexual orientation, self-expression and assertion, the ability and willingness to criticize authority, an appreciation for the many ways in which this nation has fallen short of its supposed ideals, linguistic and cultural diversity, an emphasis on the voices of the oppressed, safe sex, and so forth. At this level of prescriptive specificity, however, the imposition of substantively democratic values contradicts the premise of a liberal pluralistic society: that there be no official orthodoxy. Of course, conservatives believe that certain values and virtues are essential to the democratic way of life: that is why they are conservatives. And of course, left-progressives believe that certain other values and virtues are equally essential: that is why they are left-progressives. But neither of these groups (or any of the other perspectives we could identify) is entitled to label its own view as "democratic" and coerce the others to conform. A thick version of democratic values cannot support the argument for a uniform system of schools because any particular thick version is too partisan and sectarian.

Gutmann's argument serves as a convenient example. Gutmann is very quick to label "conservative moralists" as setting their "moral sights too low," and "liberal moralists" as setting them "too high." The "democratic perspective," as she labels her own educational philosophy, is apparently just right.[37] From a pluralist perspective, however, this clash of values appears to be an instance of legitimate disagreement among presumptively reasonable citizens. Why must we assume there is a single "democratic" right answer?[38]

Adoption of a thick understanding of "democratic" values relegates reasonable dissenters to the status of second-class citizens. Their views are not merely rejected but assumed to be undemocratic. This approach thus fails the test of liberal democracy, because it fails to treat other Americans as civic equals. In both its left-wing and its right-wing forms, it contradicts the premise of American pluralism.[39]

The thin approach is far less prescriptive. Certain values and virtues are essential to a democratic society, but they are relatively few and they are subject to many different interpretations. It may be necessary for all citizens to be literate and numerate, but reading and math can be taught in many different ways. It may be necessary for all citizens to have a rudimentary understanding of United States history and civics, but this can be taught from a variety of perspectives. Conservative celebratory history is permissible; so is left-progressive critical history; and if Mormons want to teach that American history is the working out of the providential hand of God, that is permissible too. It may be necessary for all citizens to be tolerant, but this need not mean much more than to recognize that other citizens have an equal right to freedom to hold their beliefs. We do not need to think those beliefs have merit.[40]

The thin approach to democratic values has much to commend it, but it is not an argument for democratic control over education. Beyond the scant essentials, a democratic society can let a thousand flowers bloom. There is no need for uniformity. The only need is for a modest form of regulation, to weed out those schools that do not even make an attempt to meet these basic democratic norms. Even then we should tread lightly; many a movement thought disturbing or abhorrent in its day turned out to make a positive contribution to American democratic culture.

The argument for democratic control of education seems to be: we know what principles are best for democracy, and therefore we should ensure that all schools adopt them. The premise, however, is questionable, and the conclusion does not follow from the premise. Maintaining a pluralism of reasonable answers may be more in keeping with our liberal principles even if we are confident that we know what democratic values are best, precisely because pluralism is a seemingly essential social precondition for genuine liberal government. But even if we were confident of our ability to deduce the right answer, and even if we thought that imposition of that right answer would be worth the cost to pluralism and diversity, we should still be hesitant to vest our elected officials with the authority to decide these questions for all of us. Enlightened leaders will not always be at the helm. Behind a veil of ignorance where we do not know what philosophy of education those who control the schools will hold, who would gamble on collective decision making? In 1789, few Americans (with the notable exceptions of Baptists and Quakers) were disestablishmentarian as a matter of principle. Most were adherents of establishmentarian traditions: Congregationalism (the established church of most of New England), Presbyterianism (the established church of Scotland), or Anglicanism (the established church of England). In theory, many members of these denominations might have supported a national establishment if they could be confident it would be theirs. But none could be sure—and accordingly all were in agreement that it was better not to have a national established church. Similarly, many people would choose a system of collective control over education if they knew their own views would prevail. But allowing a reasonable pluralism should be everyone's solid second choice, both for individual reasons (so that our children will not be forced to endure indoctrination in pernicious doctrines) and for societal reasons (so that no single pernicious doctrine can gain sway over the entire educational system).

As a collective matter, therefore, we should impose only a thin understanding of democratic values, and not attempt to require all schools to conform to a thick version of democratic virtue. This is the most pragmatic way of dealing with the realities of pluralism in the United States.

III. Liberalism, Majoritarianism, and the Problem of Dissenters

Not only did the realities of American pluralism make religious establishments difficult to sustain, establishment also appeared inconsistent with the emerging liberal principles of the American regime. No matter how tolerant they might be of dissenters, establishments required the political community to make a collective democratic judgment regarding controversial questions of the good life, supported those judgments with the financial and symbolic weight of official approval, required dissenters to support those judgments through taxation, and denied dissenters an equal share in public benefits. Democratic control of education creates much the same problem. Collective judgments about the ideological and philosophical content of the curriculum must be made; dissenters as well as believers will be forced to pay for it; and dissenters must either allow their children to be educated according to precepts they dispute or finance the alternative from their own resources. This is an inherently coercive arrangement, seemingly at odds with liberal principle.

It may be objected that even the more reduced role for the state in the model of pluralistic education that I am defending—

the role of financing and of quality control—carries dangers of the establishment of orthodoxy. The power to deny accreditation to schools could indeed be used as a weapon against dissenting viewpoints. But there is a major difference between an educational regime in which the government owns and controls a single set of schools and one in which the government sets limits on the activities of private schools. In the former, the government must perforce adopt a particular stance, whereas in the latter the government may allow a wide (even if not an infinite) range of educational options. That is almost certainly more consistent with the pluralistic character of our society. If we understand liberalism not as neutrality among all possible conceptions of the good life but as a reasonable pluralism among a wide range of competing worldviews, this combination of public and private provision of education, familial choice, and government regulation of basic educational standards may be the closest approximation of the liberal ideal.

Some may resist the analogy between the public education establishment and religious establishments on the ground that the public school system, rather than attempting to inculcate a particular set of controversial values, is (or, with realistically feasible reform, could be) fair, neutral, and inclusive with respect to the different views that exist in our pluralistic society. The late Justice William J. Brennan observed in *Abington Township v. Schempp*:

> It is implicit in the history and character of American public education that the public schools serve a uniquely *public* function: the training of American citizens in an atmosphere free of parochial, divisive, or separatist influences of any sort—an atmosphere in which children may assimilate a heritage common to all American groups and religions. This is a heritage neither theistic nor atheistic, but simply civic and patriotic.[41]

This notion that public schools are neutral and nonsectarian— "merely civic and patriotic"—while private (especially religious) schools are "parochial, divisive, or separatist"—is the foundational myth of our system of public education.

This premise, however, is false. Any school—at least any school that aspires to prepare children for responsible adulthood—necessarily will have and impart a viewpoint (even if that viewpoint is moral relativism). No such viewpoint is "simply civic and patriotic." Indeed, the claim of neutrality may harbor the most insidious form of ideological hegemony: a hegemony that is invisible because it does not even recognize its own controversial status.

For the most part, defenders of democratically controlled education do not assert that public education is devoid of moral content. From the beginning of public education to this day, one of the principal purposes of public schooling has been to raise morally responsible individuals and citizens. Rather, the claim of neutrality is usually based on the idea that the public schools inculcate *common* values, held by society as a whole, and avoid the teaching of *sectarian* ideas, which are held only by a particular group or faction. Amy Gutmann, for example, writes that "a primary purpose of [public] schools is to cultivate common democratic values among all children, regardless of their academic ability, class, race, religion or sex."[42] The rhetoric of "common" values, however, is not descriptively accurate, and its function is to mask the reality of difference. If the values being cultivated are genuinely *common* they will be taught in all schools, by common consent, without compulsion. The real issue is the inculcation of values held by those who control the public school system, where they *conflict* with the values that would be taught in schools organized by cultural or religious minority groups. If there exists a range of differing, but equally legitimate, ways of understanding the nature of the values appropriate to citizens of this democratic republic, then any attempt to impose one conception of "common democratic values" requires justification. To use the label "common" only obscures the decision that must be made.

A. The History of Common Schools and the Catholic Problem

The history of public education in the United States bears out this analogy between religious establishment and the public school establishment. Our current system is the product of the highly influential Common School Movement, which between about 1830 and the closing decades of the 19th century succeeded in gaining control over the education of the nation from the religious societies that had hitherto been the leading educators. Led by such educational reformers as Horace Mann of Massachusetts, the Common School Movement believed that the states should provide common schools that would educate all children—rich and poor, Protestant and Catholic, native and immigrant—together, through a common "nonsectarian" curriculum. The character of the system they created—and especially its claim to being "nonsectarian"—warrants close attention because analogous issues are with us today.

To the Common School reformers, the principal mission of the school was never merely to teach the "three Rs" but to inculcate the morals and ideals necessary to citizens of a republic. As Noah Webster, author of the most widely used speller of the early 1800s, wrote: "The virtues of men are of more consequence to society than their abilities, and for this reason the heart should be cultivated with more assiduity than the head."[43] Mann described the mission of the common schools as to plant "the germs of morality" in the "moral nature of children."[44] This task of citizenship education became all the more urgent, he thought, as immigrants swelled the population of the large cities. These immigrants, who frequently spoke different languages, had different religions, accepted different cultural and moral standards, and lacked a commitment to American values, were the prime target of Common School reformers. The assimilationist program of the educational reformers went, unselfconsciously, by the label "Americanization."

Common School reformers insisted that the moral values inculcated by the schools must be "nonsectarian."[45] By this, however, they did not mean that the curriculum should be nonreligious. The Bible (King James Version) was an important part of the daily schedule, and other materials were infused with religious and moralistic themes. Common School reformers steadfastly denied any intention of removing religious instruction from the schools. Horace Mann explained that "[m]oral training, or the application of religious principles to the duties of life" is the "inseparable accompaniment" to education.[46]

"Nonsectarian," rather, meant having no connection to any particular religious denomination. Mann explained that the schools should "draw the line between those views of religious truth and of christian faith which are common to all, and may, therefore, with propriety be inculcated in school, and those which, being peculiar to individual sects, are therefore by law excluded."[47] Nondenominational Christianity was assumed to be "nonsectarian." Ohio's first state Superintendent of Common Schools wrote in his first annual report to the legislature: "It can not be too deeply impressed on all minds, that we are a Christian, as well as a republican people; and the utmost care should be taken to inculcate sound principles of Christian morality. No creed or catechism of any sect should be introduced into our schools; there is a broad, common ground, where all Christians and lovers of virtue meet."[48]

From a Catholic or a Jewish perspective, however, "nonsectarianism" was Protestantism in disguise. Educational historian Carl F. Kaestle describes the "ideology" of the Common School Movement as centering on "republicanism, Protestantism, and capitalism."[49] Religious historian Winthrop Hudson calls the early common schools the "new Protestant establishment."[50] The schools used the (Protestant) King James Bible, "without note or comment," and Catholic students were punished for refusing to use what they considered an inauthentic version of the Scriptures. They also used readers, such as McGuffy's, which contained religious and moralistic themes of a Protestant orientation. Catholic leaders complained, unsuccessfully, that the common schools propagated anti-Catholic teaching. A petition from New York Catholics described the texts:

> The term "Popery" is repeatedly found in them. This term is known and employed as one of insult and contempt towards the Catholic religion, and it passes into the minds of children . . . Both the historical and religious portions of the reading lessons are selected from Protestant writers, whose prejudices against the Catholic religion render them unworthy of confidence in the mind of your petitioners, at least so far as their own children are concerned.[51]

They objected to the use of the King James Bible, as well as to the idea that the Bible could be taught and understood independently of the teaching authority of the Catholic Church.

Even some Protestants objected to the reformers' agenda, claiming that common-denominator Christianity amounted to Unitarianism, or what today would be called liberal Protestantism. (Horace Mann happened to be a Unitarian.) One Protestant critic told Mann: "Certain views that you entertain, you call religion, or 'piety.' These you allow to be taught in schools . . . Those which clash with your particular views, you reject as 'dogmatic theology,' or 'sectarianism.'"[52]

The most serious obstacle to the Common School reformers was the existence of what Mann disparagingly called "the rival system of 'Parochial' or 'Sectarian schools.'"[53] By the end of the Civil War, most Protestant denominations (other than Lutheran) had abandoned their efforts to maintain private school systems, in large part because the Protestant character of the public schools made the financial sacrifice unnecessary.[54] By the same token, the Protestant character of the public schools caused the Catholic hierarchy to redouble its efforts to provide Catholic schools for Catholic children. It was during this period that the Catholic Church resolved to provide schools in every American parish, and admonished Catholic parents not to send their children to public schools.[55] The Common School Movement disapproved of these nonpublic schools, arguing that they perpetuated religious division, as well as foreign prejudices and superstition. The "task of absorbing and Americanizing these foreign masses," an opponent of parochial schools testified in Congress, "can only be successfully overcome by a uniform system of American schools, teaching the same political creed." This, he said, would "continue us" as "a united, homogeneous people."[56]

Much of this campaign was conducted in explicitly anti-Catholic terms.[57] Typical was the argument of Horace Bushnell, a prominent advocate of common schools in Connecticut. Bushnell did not hesitate to remind his audience that "[w]e are still, as Americans, a Protestant people." He declared the common school to be "a fundamental institution from the first—in our view a Protestant institution—associated with all our religious convictions, opinions, and the public sentiment of our Protestant society." He warned that the Catholic clergy were "preparing for

an assault upon the common school system." If funds were provided to Catholic schools, Catholic children:

> will be shut up in schools that do not teach them what, as Ameri-
> cans, they most of all need to know, the political geography and
> political history of the world, the rights of humanity, the struggles
> by which those rights are vindicated, and the glorious rewards of
> liberty and social advancement that follow. They will be instructed
> mainly into the foreign prejudices and superstitions of their fa-
> thers, and the state, which proposes to be clear of all sectarian
> affinities in religion, will pay the bills![58]

Note that this argument was not confined to nativists or religious bigots. Bushnell himself was no Elmer Gantry but a representative of enlightened liberal Congregationalism in New England. His equation of Protestantism to republicanism and of
Catholicism to prejudice and superstition was a staple of the
Common School ideology. The tendency to regard Catholicism
as antidemocratic and inconsistent with freedom of thought became especially acute with the publication of the Syllabus of Errors in 1864 and the Vatican decree on papal infallibility in 1870.
These were viewed as evidence that Catholicism was profoundly
illiberal and un-American.[59]

The "School Question" first came to a boil in the 1840s—a
decade when immigration nearly tripled the Catholic population
of the United States. Throughout the North and West, the religious content of public school curriculum and the provision of
public funds for nonpublic schools became a political battleground. The Democratic Party generally supported the rights of
Catholic schoolchildren to be excused from Protestant religious
instruction (or to use their own approved version of the Bible in
lieu of the Protestant King James translation), as well as the claim
of nonpublic schools to a share of the school fund. The increasingly influential Know-Nothing Party took the opposite position,
and the Whigs—seeing a political opportunity—often allied themselves with the Know-Nothings and crushed Democratic efforts.[60]

In Philadelphia in 1844, a decision by the school board to
allow Catholic children to use the Douay translation of the Bible
sparked riots in which two Catholic churches were burned to the
ground and several dozen people killed. In New York, Governor

William Seward (later Abraham Lincoln's Secretary of State), breaking from his party's usual position, proposed that the state extend funding to schools in which pupils would be taught by teachers of their own faith. This prompted vituperative debates at public meetings and in the press, in which Catholics demanded that all parents be able to educate their children in accordance with their own beliefs and anti-Catholic spokesmen insisted that public funds should not be used to teach superstition and disloyalty. After a bitter election in which candidates endorsed by the Catholic hierarchy were defeated, Seward's proposal was voted down, and for the first time public funds were devoted solely to government-run schools.

Similar controversies arose in Massachusetts, Connecticut, Maryland, Ohio, Michigan, Illinois, California, and other states, with the same result. In every state, high-minded reformist rhetoric was mixed with crude attacks on "popery." Protestant and anti-Catholic political forces portrayed Catholicism as antithetical to "Americanism" and Catholics' dissatisfaction with public schools as signs of their disloyalty. "If the children of Papists are really in danger of being corrupted in the Protestant schools of enlightened, free and happy America," a Baptist publication editorialized, "it may be well for their conscientious parents and still more conscientious priests, to return them to the privileges of their ancestral homes."[61]

At the same time that Catholic schools were denied public funding because of their so-called "sectarian" character, Catholic schoolboys were being whipped in the public schools for refusing to read from the Protestant Bible.[62] In 1869, the National Teachers' Association (the predecessor to the National Education Association) adopted two resolutions at its annual convention. One stated that "the appropriation of public funds for the support of sectarian institutions is a violation of the fundamental principles of our American system of education." The other stated that "the Bible should not only be studied, venerated, and honored as a classic for all ages, people and languages . . . but devotionally read, and its precepts inculcated in all the common schools of the land."[63]

After the Civil War, opposition to funding for nonpublic schools became a rallying cry for the Republicans, whose tactic of blaming the Democrats for the Southern rebellion (called "waving the bloody shirt") was wearing thin.[64] In 1875, President Ulysses S. Grant made a speech to the Army of Tennessee, stating: "If we are to have another contest in the near future of our national existence I predict that the dividing line will not be Mason and Dixon's but between patriotism and intelligence on the one side and superstition, ambition and ignorance on the other." "Superstition" and "ignorance" were code words in the anti-Catholic lexicon. Grant urged his listeners to "[e]ncourage free schools and resolve that not one dollar of money appropriated to their support no matter how raised, shall be appropriated to the support of any sectarian school. Resolve that either the State or Nation or both combined shall support institutions of learning, sufficient to afford to every child growing up in the land the opportunity of a good common education, [u]nmixed with sectarian, pagan or atheistical tenets . . . Keep the church and state forever separate."[65]

Republicans in Congress proposed, and nearly passed, the so-called "Blaine Amendment" to the federal constitution, named after presidential aspirant James G. Blaine (who was narrowly defeated after a supporter's indiscreet denunciation of "Rum, Romanism, and Rebellion" inspired a Catholic backlash). The proposed amendment prohibited public support for any school or other institution that is under the control of any religious organization or that teaches "the particular creed or tenets" of any religious denomination. This was not intended to prevent public schools from teaching "nonsectarian" moral and religious principles supposedly common to all denominations. Indeed, the amendment expressly stated that it "shall not be construed to prohibit the reading of the Bible in any school or institution."[66] The amendment thus would have enshrined in the United States Constitution the Common School vision that public schools could teach "nonsectarian" religion, and that no public funds could go to nonpublic schools.

Supporters of the Blaine Amendment made little attempt to hide the connection to anti-Catholicism. Two of the Republican leaders in the Senate read at length from the *Encyclical of Errors* and the 1870 Vatican decree on papal infallibility, explaining that these documents would show "what precisely this issue is."[67]

The amendment was defeated in the Senate, attaining only a 28-16 majority, which was short of the necessary two-thirds. But similar provisions—called "little Blaine Amendments"—were added to the constitutions of about half the states. It is these provisions—not the First Amendment—that pose the greatest legal obstacles to school choice proposals today.

The School Question still did not go away. The continuing tide of immigration in the ensuing decades increased fears that a "common" American heritage would be lost. Nativist feelings rose to their highest peak shortly after the First World War, when candidates affiliated with the Ku Klux Klan gained power in a number of states. In Oregon, voters approved a Klan-inspired referendum requiring all school-age children to attend public schools—an obvious attack on Catholic education. In support of the measure, the Grand Dragon praised public schools as "nonpartisan, non-sectarian, efficient, democratic, for all the children of the people." He objected to private schools on the ground that these schools would prevent the "mongrel hordes" of immigrants from being "Americanized."[68]

The law was challenged in the Supreme Court. The arguments offered by the lawyers defending the law are worthy of attention. They argued that the law was an attempt to cure the "rising tide of religious suspicions in this country," which were caused by "the separation of children along religious lines during the most susceptible years of their lives." They said that "the mingling together, during a portion of their education, of the children of all races and sects, might be the best safeguard against future internal dissentions and consequent weakening of the community against foreign dangers."[69] Note how the themes of religious tolerance, racial and religious integration, and patriotism were weaved together in support of a nativist measure designed to prevent the hated Catholic minority from being able to pass on their religious heritage to their children.

Despite this liberal sugarcoating, the Supreme Court unanimously held the Oregon law unconstitutional. Part of the opinion was devoted to the now-discredited theory that the economic rights of the operators of the private schools were violated.[70] Part was devoted to the constitutional rights of the parents.[71] But the most interesting aspect of the opinion was its institutional dimension.

According to the Court, "[t]he fundamental theory of liberty upon which all governments in this Union repose excludes any general power of the state to standardize its children by forcing them to accept instruction from public teachers only."[72] This was the theme of disestablishment. The real vice of an exclusive system of public education is the extraordinary power it gives to the government to "standardize" the children by inculcating a common set of values. It is essential to a liberal society, the Supreme Court was saying, that such a power to mold young minds not be wielded exclusively by the state.

Civil libertarians recoiled at the overt nativism of the Klan's attack on Catholic schools, but they shared many of the same basic assumptions about Catholic education. Well into this century, respected leaders of the intellectual elite—men such as philosopher John Dewey, journalist Walter Lippmann, and Harvard President James Bryant Conant—argued that Catholicism was a threat to freedom of intellectual inquiry and hence to democracy itself.[73] Dewey, for example, warned that aid to Catholic schools would encourage "a powerful reactionary world organization in the most vital realm of democratic life with the resulting promulgation of principles inimical to democracy."[74] Historian Perry Miller wrote that Catholicism is antagonistic to "free and critical education" and to "the democratic way of life."[75] In *Lemon v. Kurtzman,* Justice William O. Douglas quoted from a notorious anti-Catholic monograph in an opinion holding that aid to parochial schools would violate the Establishment Clause.[76] Among other illuminating statements, the writer claimed that Hitler, Mussolini, and Stalin learned the "secret[s] of [their] success" from the Roman Catholic Church, and that "an undue proportion of the gangsters, racketeers, thieves, and juvenile delinquents who roam our big city streets come . . . from the [Catholic] parochial schools."[77] It is extraordinary to think that, as late as 1971, a Justice of the Supreme Court could rely on such a source in an opinion purporting to interpret and enforce the First Amendment.[78]

B. Secularization and the New Sectarianism

Since the School Prayer Decisions of the early 1960s,[79] the public schools have largely been purged of overt Protestant content. But secularization does not mean neutrality. Over the ensuing decades, the public schools have become instruments for social transformation in such areas as environmental awareness; race and gender egalitarianism; values clarification; drug, tobacco, and substance abuse; multiculturalism; and sexuality. Sociologist James Davison Hunter has observed:

> The older [Protestant-Catholic] struggle faded away, but not because the "School Question" had been resolved. Rather it was because the changing structure of American pluralism made the old antagonism obsolete. Thus, in our own time we see that the institutions of public education continue to mediate cultural conflict, but the character of the "School Question" has altered to conform to the contours of the contemporary culture war. The cast of players has changed completely, yet the stakes have remained the same: power over the public schools.[80]

Although there are regional (and other) variations, evidence suggests that public schools in most parts of the country have embraced a new ideology scarcely less one-sided than the old. In 1985, educational psychologist Paul Vitz conducted a comprehensive study of the ideological orientation of elementary and secondary school curricula for the Department of Education. He concluded:

> public school textbooks commonly exclude the history, heritage, beliefs, and values of millions of Americans. Those who believe in the traditional family are not represented. Those who believe in free enterprise are not represented. Those whose politics are conservative are almost unrepresented. Above all, those who are committed to their religious tradition—at the very least as an important part of the historical record—are not represented.[81]

In history textbooks, Vitz found an aversion to traditional patriotism, an emphasis on left-egalitarian issues, a silence about religious figures, and a hostility toward conservative political causes and leaders. One would think that the legitimate clash of two political parties is a democratic value that would be upheld in American textbooks, but out of dozens of post–World War II historical personages profiled as "role models" in history textbooks, not a single editor found a male Republican or a conservative worthy

of such recognition.[82] Environmental education is particularly
heavy-handed and one-sided. It is not unusual for students to be
mobilized for political advocacy in support of their teachers'
opinions on environmental policy, such as writing letters to
congressmen for credit or participating in demonstrations. Education about family life is almost as one-sided. Vitz's study discovered that not one of the 40 leading elementary social studies
textbooks portrayed a woman in the capacity as housewife, home-
maker, or full-time mother. Interestingly, the books avoided even
the *words* "marriage," "husband," and "wife."[83] Textbooks properly
give attention to the struggles of oppressed groups for dignity and
civil equality, but tend to avoid controversy on other issues of importance to conservatives and traditionalists. For example, only
one prominent health textbook in a 1998 study even mentioned
abortion, the most controversial moral issue of our day, and then
only to say that it was a medically safe alternative to adoption and
that it had sparked "controversy."[84]

One-sidedness is not the exclusive province of the left. In
some parts of the country, an older, more traditionalist and patriotic, ideology still holds sway. In Kansas, for example, the state
board of education voted in 1999 to eliminate evolution from the
required curriculum.[85] In Utah, the legislature voted to prohibit
sex education instruction in birth control methods other than
abstinence, and to require public schools to teach about flag eti-
quette and history.[86] At the national level, the traditional emphasis on capitalist economics seems as strong as ever.[87] The National
Content Standards in Education for economics advocates that
students should be taught only the "majority paradigm" of neo-
classical economics. Including alternative views of the subject
matter, the standards setters say, would risk "confusing and frus-
trating teachers and students who are then left with the responsibility of sorting the qualifications and alternatives without a sufficient foundation to do so."[88]

The ideological slant of public education is particularly notice-
able from the perspective of religious families, especially those
who believe that all of life (moral, intellectual, economic, social)
should be understood in an integrated fashion, as subject to the
sovereignty of God. Secular schools are committed to teaching
the various subjects without the intrusion of religious thinking.

In its parochial school decisions, the Supreme Court frequently refers to the "interjection" of religious doctrine into the curriculum—a revealing choice of words. In the late 1980s, studies by a wide range of researchers and organizations found that religion has been systematically excluded from the public school curriculum, including such subjects as history, social studies, and humanities, where it should be included on pedagogical grounds.[89] A more recent study found that there has been "some improvement" but that "textbooks are still woefully inadequate in their treatment of religion."[90] One can go through elementary and secondary school today and not be aware that religion has played—and still plays—a major role in history, philosophy, science, and the ordinary lives of many millions of Americans. Secular schools may well refrain from overt anti-religious teaching. But the worldview presented to the children will be one in which religion plays no significant role. Such a curriculum may not necessarily produce atheists, but it will tend to produce young adults who think of religion as something separate and distinct from the real world of knowledge, if they think of religion at all.

Against a backdrop of secularized education, religious parents find it difficult to compete. There are only so many hours in the day, and children tend to resist time-consuming efforts to supplement the curriculum. The usual solution is to provide children with a few hours each week of Sunday school, Hebrew school, catechism class, or the equivalent, but this may, ironically, have the effect of underscoring the separation between the academic and the religious spheres. By its nature, education reflects choices about what is objectively knowable (as opposed to what is mere opinion), what is significant and what can be neglected, what positions are worthy of study and what positions may be dismissed as irrelevant or unsupportable. The school speaks with the authority of professionalism, of learning, and of organized society. When it defines the fields of study and specifies the modes of understanding that constitute acceptable scholarly discourse, it necessarily relegates other fields and other modes of understanding to the realm of the unimportant, the subjective, and the dispensable.

James Hunter has commented on the "trail of ironies" produced by the shift of public education from the Protestant hegemony of the past to the secular progressive hegemony of the present. The contending sides have flipped their positions, but the underlying structure of the debate between establishmentarian and dissenter is unchanged. Evangelical Protestants who used to be "the defenders of the public school establishment against the pope's authority in Rome," have "adopted the policy positions of their nineteenth-century Catholic adversaries in the effort to demonopolize, and thereby weaken the power of, the public school establishment." For their part, Hunter comments, "progressivist voices on the contemporary scene defend their own cultural advantage in education in virtually the same manner as the Evangelical Protestants did in the nineteenth century: by appealing to public order and community good."[91] Just as the Common School Movement defended itself against dissenters' charges of sectarianism by claiming to espouse moral and religious principles "common" to all, modern educational progressives claim to be multicultural and inclusive of the views of different groups of Americans. But as in the nineteenth century, there is a selectivity to this inclusiveness and an intolerance masquerading as toleration. Multiculturalism, like common-denominator Christianity, imparts a distinctive ideological position, and it is not noticeably tolerant of dissent.

C. No Help from Constitutional Law

In light of the conflicts over curricular content in the public schools, you might expect to see the emergence of a broad disestablishmentarian principle protecting students against unwelcome indoctrination in public schools. That is what ultimately happened to the Protestant educational hegemony. Through rulings on school prayer, Bible reading, creationism, and other subjects, the courts effectively protected non-Protestants and non-Christians from religious impositions in the schools. In cases like *Lee v. Weisman,*[92] banning prayers at high school graduation ceremonies, the Supreme Court has recognized the coercive impact on public school students when they are forced to choose between acquiescence to a public orthodoxy and becoming a vocal and conspicuous dissenter.

A generation ago it appeared that the Supreme Court might develop a general constitutional doctrine granting a right of dissenters to opt out of ideologically unwelcome exercises in the public schools. In *West Virginia Board of Education v. Barnette*,[93] the Court held that it is unconstitutional for public schools to punish students for refusing to participate in the flag salute. The majority opinion contained the broad declaration:

> If there is any fixed star in our constitutional constellation, it is that no official, high or petty, can prescribe what shall be orthodox in politics, nationalism, religion, or other matters of opinion or force citizens to confess by word or act their faith therein. If there are any circumstances which permit an exception, they do not now occur to us.[94]

In the years that followed, however, exceptions not only occurred but swallowed the rule. For example, in *Mozert v. Hawkins County School Board*,[95] a widely noted appellate decision, the court considered the claims of several fundamentalist families that the reading textbooks used in their children's classrooms were systematically biased against their perspectives on a number of issues. The court held that the families had no legal right to object since their complaint was against "mere exposure" to the offending materials. In another case, a federal appellate court held that no rights were violated when a public school mandated attendance at a sex education assembly during which the speaker, by the court's own description, told the students that they were going to have a "group sexual experience, with audience participation"; used "profane, lewd, and lascivious language to describe body parts and excretory functions"; "advocated and approved oral sex, masturbation, homosexual sexual activity, and condom use during promiscuous premarital sex"; "simulated masturbation"; and informed a male minor that he was not "having enough orgasms.[96] In effect, the Court's condemnation of orthodoxy in "politics, nationalism, . . . or other matters of opinion" was narrowed to the assurance that "the classroom will not purposely be used to advance *religious* views that may conflict with the private beliefs of the student and his or her family."[97] As a constitutional matter, the classroom can be used to advance *nonreligious* views, and students have no legal right to avoid participation in nonreligious educational activities that offend their beliefs.[98] The lack of protection against ideological and other impositions in public education led some disgruntled families to frame their claim as a challenge to the "religion of secular humanism," on the theory that comprehensive moral ideologies not based on God are substitutes for, and equally objectionable to, ideologies based on God. But the courts were not persuaded.[99]

The only constitutional right students or their families have against unwelcome nonreligious indoctrination in the public schools is the exit right recognized in *Pierce v. Society of Sisters*.[100] *Pierce*, however, is at best an uncomfortable compromise. If the government may not use its police power to "standardize" children through compulsory public school education, why can it use its powers of taxation and control over spending to accomplish the same objective? As a practical matter, the *Pierce* exit right can be exercised only by families with the wherewithal to obtain private education or the capacity to engage in home-schooling. One can argue that democratic society has the right to compel all citizens to be educated according to a common curriculum, and one can argue that a liberal society must allow families to control the upbringing of their children. But who would argue that the right of exit from the common schools should be confined to those who can afford it? There may be no constitutional right to funding for educational alternatives, but it would seem consistent with liberal principle to provide it.[101]

IV. PLURALISTIC EDUCATION AS THE BEST MEANS TO INCULCATE DEMOCRATIC VALUES

To review the argument thus far: requiring collective agreement on educational philosophy, like religion, faces two daunting problems. In a pluralistic society, it is difficult to obtain agreement on the content of the "democratic education" that will be supplied, and even if this can be accomplished through an exercise of political will, the results seems inconsistent with our liberal pluralistic premises. These were two of the reasons for disestablishment. But the third reason for disestablishment was that, even assuming the need for inculcation of public virtue through religion, granting churches a legally privileged monopoly status was bad for religion. Disestablishment coupled with free exercise is not only less divisive and more liberal but also more congenial to religious faith. Can the same thing be true for democratic education?

A. *Competition and Quality*

As an initial matter, there is powerful reason to believe that a more pluralistic educational structure would produce better schools, especially for the inner-city poor. Studies in this area are notoriously contested, but the weight of the evidence is that voucher experiments and private school alternatives produce substantial improvements in educational attainment for the children involved, holding constant for income, minority status, family makeup, and other variables.[102] Moreover, most studies show that the quality of *public* schools improves significantly when they are forced to compete with private alternatives.[103] For example, the last three superintendents of the Milwaukee public school system now support the family choice plan precisely because it has been an effective spur to public school reform.[104]

As an economic matter, these results are entirely predictable. When any system has an effective monopoly, it lacks the incentive to improve quality, control cost, and be responsive and accountable to its customers. The economic argument against the public school monopoly is essentially the same as the economic argument against any monopoly.[105] In addition, some political scientists have attributed the poor performance of public schools to their bureaucratic structure, which is an inevitable consequence of democratic control.[106] If democratic control leads to bureaucratic structure and bureaucratic structure is inimical to high-quality education, this suggests a flaw in the argument for democratic control. Finally, from a sociological perspective, researchers suggest that schools more freely chosen by families will be more likely to experience a cooperative union between family and school, which is essential for successful education.[107] At least for children trapped in failing schools in the inner cities, the argument for enabling them to choose alternatives seems powerful.

B. Democratic Values and the Overlapping Consensus

The more fundamental question is whether privately provided education can satisfy the need for inculcation of democratic values. I believe it can. Indeed, just as disestablished churches were better able to provide the moral and spiritual underpinnings required by republican government, disestablished education would have much the same effect.

An effective education in good citizenship must necessarily offer reasons, and must in addition draw upon cultural resources such as stories, songs, and ceremonies. But both the reasons and the cultural resources employed will necessarily resemble those of one moral tradition or community, and thus appear to be parochial or sectarian from other points of view. Accordingly, it is difficult or impossible for a public school to engage in the direct inculcation of democratic virtue without compromising its liberal commitment to neutrality among the different and competing reasonable worldviews of the society. Private schools, by contrast, are free to ground their teachings in deep and coherent—albeit particularistic or sectarian—comprehensive worldviews, and to reinforce those teachings by means of evocative and resonant—albeit non-universalistic—traditions and cultural resources.

Until relatively recently, the common schools were able to communicate an effective brand of democratic values, but that was because they were not squeamish about embracing a particular worldview—the Protestant. It is unlikely that this can be replicated under modern conditions of increased diversity in society and increased assertiveness by minority groups. A modern public school faces two choices: either it adopts a comprehensive doctrine and thus abandons its claim to being a liberal institution, or it avoids comprehensive doctrines and abandons the hope of supplying a morally coherent structure for its teaching of democratic values.

The evidence of failure of the current system to provide an education in morally responsible values is all about us. Studies of high school civics and government courses have repeatedly found that "schools have little if any effect on teaching of the democratic creed or political values in general."[108] As voting

rates, crime rates, drug rates, smoking rates, and sexual promis-
cuity rates demonstrate,[109] the youth of America are not being
sufficiently socialized into good neighbors, good citizens, or
morally upright men and women. These alarming results cannot,
of course, be blamed on the public schools, but they do raise the
question whether public education is capable of dealing with
them. Indeed, despite good intentions, the values actually cultivated among modern students seem almost perverse from a democratic point of view. In all too many schools, the dominant
morality conveyed is materialism and the dominant ideology
taught is critical of traditional American political and cultural institutions. Why is education valuable? Because it helps you get a
job. What do modern students value? Clothes, consumer goods,
popularity. Who is a patriot? Only a chump, or an oppressor.

No one is likely to defend the present state of moral and civic
education in America. Some might say, however, that this means
only that the curriculum and teaching should be improved. If the
courses relevant to civic responsibility are ineffective or counterproductive, let's substitute courses that are effective and well designed. This optimistic response, however, ignores the link between structure and result. What is the reason that public schools
inculcated a sectarian Protestant ideology for their first 100
years, and then collapsed into moral anarchy? It is because democratic institutions are able to present a coherent moral position
under only two conditions: if the society is homogeneous, or if
the dominant faction is willing and able to suppress the dissenters. Nineteenth-century America came closer to being homogeneous, and its educational elite was able to suppress the objections of Catholics, who could be branded as undemocratic and
un-American. As we approach the twenty-first century, America is
far less homogeneous, and the rights revolution and the advent
of multiculturalism have rendered the educational establishment
less capable of silencing dissenters.

Nonpublic schools, by contrast, are in a better position to
teach from a coherent perspective. If schools are institutions of
choice, they can reflect a particular worldview without precipitat-
ing culture wars because it is easier for dissenters to go elsewhere than to fight. This means the schools are less tempted to
water down the moral curriculum for the purpose of avoiding

controversy. Moreover, as institutions of choice, they are likely to experience a greater degree of cooperation between families and schools. One of the clearest findings in the Milwaukee Parental Choice experiment is the greater degree of parents' satisfaction with their children's schools. One suspects that this is not entirely a result of superior performance but must reflect, in part, the human reality that people have a more positive reaction to institutions they have chosen than to institutions they are forced to attend. Sociologist James Coleman's work identified this cooperation between home and school as the principal reason why nonpublic schools are now more successful than public schools—even with children of underprivileged backgrounds and even with significantly less money.[110]

This conception of democratic education through private institutions resembles John Rawls's idea of an "overlapping consensus," which he uses to explain how a society can be pluralistic, democratic, and stable at the same time. According to Rawls, political liberalism represents a consensus regarding political essentials among adherents of different and conflicting comprehensive worldviews. The point to be stressed is that these various groups need not agree on the reasons that support these political arrangements. Indeed, in a pluralistic society no one "comprehensive doctrine" can "secure the basis of social unity, nor can it provide the content of public reason on fundamental political questions." Rather, each of the various worldviews will endorse these political arrangements "from its own point of view."[111]

Rawls's point is consistent with the American experience of disestablishment. The founders recognized that republican government required a citizenry with public virtue, and many of them further recognized that religion was the traditional institution for the inculcation of virtue. But like "democratic values" today, the precise content of religion and morality was a subject of sharp disagreement. The founders concluded that it would be too contentious and too illiberal to attempt to impose any particular thick understanding of religion and morality. The Establishment Clause is the constitutional expression of that conclusion. But this did not mean that the republic would go without institutions for the inculcation of religion and morality; on the contrary, it meant that this function would be performed by groups representing the various "comprehensive doctrines," each from its "own point of view." Allowing the free exercise of religion, it turned out, was a more effective means of achieving the purpose than an established church would have been.

By the same token, the difficulty of imposing any particular version of democratic virtue through the public school establishment does not mean that the nation must go without democratic education. There is every reason to expect that democratic values will be more reliably and effectively conveyed by schools that reflect particular moral and religious worldviews than by schools run by the government.

Skeptics are entitled to ask whether this theory will work in practice. In particular, some might point to the danger that religious and other subcommunities may advocate intolerance toward others, rather than supporting the democratic value of mutual respect. Amy Gutmann, for example, poses the question: "Can a democratic state succeed in forcing parochial schools to teach democratic values in the face of intense religious opposition to these values?"[112] During referendum campaigns on educational choice in Washington and California, teachers' unions ran television commercials depicting voucher-funded kindergartens run by witches' covens.

Much of this fear is based on secularist prejudice: on the assumption that religious citizens and the products of religious education are likely to be less tolerant and democratic than secular citizens and products of secular schools.[113] This stereotype bears little resemblance to reality. Of course, some religions—like some political parties, some newspapers and radio programs, some labor organizations, some universities, and some governments—have espoused undemocratic and intolerant ideas from time to time. But contrary to the secularist stereotype, religion has not, on the whole, been an anti-democratic force in the United States. Indeed, as compared to democratic politics, religion has often been a force for democratic reform, egalitarianism, and justice.

Indeed, as Rawls's theory suggests, religious communities in the United States have been part of the overlapping consensus that supports our democratic institutions. The various religious faiths of this country have adopted and conveyed what may be called a "sacred history" that legitimates and defends American democracy. Not only is this true of mainstream groups like Presbyterians or Baptists, who proudly claim credit for major aspects of American constitutionalism, it is true of religious groups that had every right to be critical of the regime. Black churches maintained faith in the responsiveness of American political institutions even in the depths of Jim Crow;[114] the Catholic Bishops preached that "our country's heroes were the instruments of the God of nations in establishing this home of freedom" even at the height of anti-Catholic bigotry;[115] and the Mormons maintained a similar belief in the providential origin of American constitutional institutions even when they were being driven from their homes and threatened with "extermination" by the Governor of their state.[116]

By most objective measures, religious Americans are more democratically engaged than most of their fellow citizens.[117] Church attendance has a high correlation to voter turnout—far higher than any other institutional affiliation.[118] (Education has less than half this effect,[119] which may suggest—ironically—that churches rather than schools are our prime inculcators of democratic participation.) High school students from families who attend religious services regularly are more likely to be involved in high school activities, which in turn is positively correlated to political activity as an adult.[120] The connection between religiosity and civic involvement is particularly strong among African Americans.[121] These effects are partly attributable to the content of religious teaching and partly to the experience religious participants get in speaking, leadership, and other civil skills.[122] With some exceptions (such as Anabaptists), churches typically teach the sacred character of civil obligations, including voting.[123] An explicit educational objective of Catholic parochial schools is to "form the basic disposition for citizenship in a democratic and pluralistic society."[124]

Religious schools seem to be more successful than public schools in inculcating habits of democratic participation. According to federal Department of Education studies, students in nonpublic schools are more likely to read the newspaper and less likely to watch excessive amounts of television.[125] Students at nonpublic schools are far more likely to engage in community service than students at public schools. Only 9.7 percent of public school students report work on community service, as compared to 22.3 percent of students in Catholic schools and 31.2 percent of students in other private schools.[126] Religion also seems to encourage nonpolitical forms of civic engagement. By far the most common form of voluntary charitable activity in America is under religious auspices.[127] Religiosity also tends to correlate with socially responsible behavior, such as lower drug use, crime, cheating, and adolescent sex.[128]

Participation in religious activity—both worship and social or community action—is significantly less stratified by income, race, or ethnicity than is political activity.[129] African-Americans are significantly more involved in religious activity than are whites, and women more than men.[130] Black churches are typically the most politically engaged.[131] Far from being an anti-democratic or anti-egalitarian force in American life, the predominant effect of religion is the opposite.

It thus appears that, in practice as well in theory, morally coherent subcommunities, such as religious groups and religious schools, may be more effective than government-run schools in inculcating the virtues and values essential for democratic citizenship.

Some nonetheless may fear that private religious schools are likely to preach racial or religious intolerance. But most schools eligible for participation in inner-city voucher programs are Catholic, and the fastest-growing segment of private education is connected to black Protestant churches. These groups have been in the forefront of the fight against racism and bigotry. Defenders of government-controlled schooling therefore put the spotlight on Protestant fundamentalists, whose southern and rural roots make them more suspect. Amy Gutmann, for example, devotes several pages of her book on democratic education to the supposed fact (which she asserts without citation) that "Christian fundamentalism rejects the value of racial nondiscrimination."[132] In this blatant form, the charge is unfounded. While racists certainly can be found among Protestant fundamentalists (as among other segments of our society), the principal institutions of fundamentalist religion and education are (however belatedly) committed to the moral goal of racial harmony. One of the seven principal "promises" of the Promise Keepers, for example, is to work actively for racial reconciliation. Sociologist Peter Skerry conducted a study of Christian schools in the Piedmont region of North Carolina in 1979 and found that "none of the schools I visited displayed the least evidence that racist doctrines are taught."[133] I examined the treatment of the civil rights movement in the American history textbooks published by Bob Jones University for the Christian school market, on the assumption that if opposition to racial nondiscrimination would be found anywhere, it would be found there. In fact, the books express support for the achievements of the civil rights movement, emphasizing its connection to the Christian religion.[134] In its normative discussion of the "rights and wrongs" of civil rights activism, one Bob Jones text praises the racial civil rights movement for addressing "real problems in our society" and helping "to decrease those problems," and reminds students that "[a]s Christians, we should be especially concerned whenever citizens are not treated with justice and truth."[135] The text criticizes "[m]any rights activists" not for their commitment to racial nondiscrimination but for their tendency to place blame on institutions rather than individuals and to emphasize the legal dimension over the need to "change man's heart." The biblical approach, according to the text, is "found when people accept Jesus Christ as their Savior and show Christian love to their neighbors."[136]

Nor are the products of religious schools less tolerant of people of other faiths. A study of Catholic education (in 1966, presumably before the effects of Vatican II had set in) found that Catholics who attended Catholic schools were less likely to espouse anti-Semitic or anti–civil libertarian ideas than Catholics who attended non-Catholic schools.[137] A recent sociological study of middle-class values by Alan Wolfe found a "remarkable" degree of religious toleration among all subjects in the sample, including persons of strong personal religious convictions.[138] Wolfe found that the most religious people in his sample were among the strongest advocates of religious diversity, and understood themselves "as trying to be accommodating to all faiths, not seeking to impose one of them." Indeed, he concluded that "[i]f once in America the question of religious toleration was raised in defense of nonbelievers who dissented from religious orthodoxy, today it is raised by believers who feel excluded from a predominantly secular public world."[139] A disguised bigotry lurks in the assumption that religious conviction breeds intolerance; a secular upbringing can breed its own form of intolerance.

C. *Classroom Diversity*

As has been seen, the argument for collectively controlled education based on the need for democratic content largely disregards the realities of pluralism. It assumes the existence of "common" democratic values, and is willing either to ignore or to disregard the significant differences within the democratic fold. The result is some combination of heightened cultural conflict, majoritarian or elitist hegemony, and mush. There is, however, a second argument for democratically controlled education, which is an explicit response to pluralist realities. The argument is that common schools are worth the increased divisiveness, hegemony, and mush because of the supreme value of having children educated in diverse classrooms, with students of different racial, cultural, socioeconomic, and religious backgrounds. The point of democratic education, according to this version of the theory, is not that the *curriculum* will impart democratic values but that the experience of spending time together with different types of people will teach the valuable democratic skill of getting along in the face of differences.[140] Advocates of this position often oppose educational choice on the ground that it will facilitate "white flight" and further "balkanize" American classrooms.

The problems with this argument are that it imagines a degree of diversity in public school classrooms that does not now exist, that it runs counter to the powerful recent trend toward controlled choice within public school systems, and that it ignores the possibility that a pluralistic system of educational institutions might produce greater—or at least more valuable—diversity within the classroom.

Public schools are currently highly segregated by race and socioeconomic status. The ideal of the common school, in which rich and poor, black and white, and Protestant and Catholic are educated together, is more myth than reality (except perhaps in small-town America, where there is only one school). In 1997, 69 percent of black children and 75 percent of Hispanic children attended schools composed predominantly of nonwhites.[141] The ambitious desegregation efforts of the 1970s have largely come to a halt, but in any event they never crossed the boundaries from urban to suburban districts. The wealthy and the middle classes already choose their schools by choosing where they will live. Studies show a strong correlation between the quality of public education and property values—meaning that families purchase a superior education by paying more for their homes.[142] If that does not work, they can afford to purchase a private alternative.

Indeed, some researchers report that nonpublic schools—especially Catholic schools—more closely resemble the old common school ideal than most urban public schools do.[143] Minority enrollment in private schools roughly doubled between 1970 and 1995.[144] Almost a quarter of the students in Catholic schools are now non-white.[145] Non-Catholic enrollment in Catholic schools has also dramatically increased, especially in urban schools.[146] The vast majority of Catholic schools (4,616 out of 5,591) have students eligible for Title I, which is a reasonable proxy for low income.[147] According to Harvard educational researcher Paul Peterson, "[p]rivate schools . . . are already more racially integrated than public ones."[148]

Moreover, even on the assumption that private schools in urban areas tend to be more white, and of higher income level, than public schools, it is logical to expect that voucher programs, such as those in Milwaukee, Cleveland, and Florida, will *increase* the level of racial and socioeconomic integration. The greatest barrier to increased minority and low-income use of private schools is the fact that they charge tuition. By enabling poorer students to afford to attend private schools, voucher programs can be expected to make private schools, which are already fairly integrated, more so.[149] Data from Milwaukee confirm this expectation.[150] This is why some civil rights advocates have long suggested vouchers as a promising strategy for desegregation.[151]

Although national averages show that public schools still enroll significantly more black and Hispanic students than private schools, Department of Education data indicate that the level of integration *within the classroom* is significantly higher in *private* schools. Indeed, twice as many private school classrooms as public school classrooms (36.6 percent as compared to 18.3 percent) are well integrated (meaning within 10 percent of the national average of minority students). More than half (54.5 percent) of public school classrooms are racially segregated (having more than 90 percent or less than 10 percent minority students), as compared to 41.1 percent of private school classrooms.[152] Perhaps more significantly, these data show that students in nonpublic schools have more interracial friendships and engage in less interracial fighting.[153] Moreover, the educational achievement levels of black and white students are far closer in nonpublic than in public schools.[154] These statistics suggest that integration within nonpublic schools may be more successful and meaningful than in public schools.

It is important to realize that mere contact between people of different races or groups does not necessarily have the effect of lessening prejudice or improving intergroup relations. There have been numerous studies of effects of American school desegregation on prejudice and cross-racial friendships. Sadly, the experience of integrated education has more often *increased* than *decreased* the levels of racial prejudice. As one researcher comments, these studies make "rather pessimistic reading for those of us who have always supported the idea of integrated schools."[155] That is why the relatively greater success in integration in nonpublic schools warrants attention. It is more likely that racial or other mixing will break down barriers where students share other important interests or characteristics.[156] This is more likely to be achieved in a religious school, or in other schools built upon shared interests or affinities.

Finally, with the increasing trend toward magnet schools, charter schools, and other forms of limited choice, the reality of education is increasingly distant from the common school ideal. For sound pedagogical reasons, the one-size-fits-all theory of common schools has been replaced by a system in which the needs and interests of individual children are matched with schools of different themes and emphases: back-to-basics schools, arts-oriented schools, math and science academies, foreign-language-immersion schools, and many other alternatives, including such controversial ideas as Afro-centric schools. While these educational innovations—magnet schools, charter schools, public-school choice—have undoubtedly improved educational quality, they have undermined the argument against private-school choice. Once student selection is based on choice rather than on the common school ideal, what is the rationale for excluding nonpublic schools?

Increasingly, families with determination and organization can find or organize schools that address their pedagogical, methodological, and substantive concerns. The glaring exception to this system, however, is that charter schools and magnet schools, being "public," may not impart a religious philosophy. The movement for choice *within* the public school system has thus exacerbated the secularizing tendency of the public school system and the bias against religious families. During the era of common schools, everyone had to put up with the educational program offered at their local school, and no one had a right to exit with their share of educational funds. Now, under a charter school system, virtually all *except the religious* have the right to form schools that inculcate their own brand of education. That result cannot be defended on any logical ground—unless we assume that religious ideologies, alone among the various worldviews entertained by Americans, are democratically illegitimate. There was a coherent argument for common schools. There is no coherent argument for educational diversity that singles out religion for exclusion.

If our society were serious about restoring the "mixed school" ideal of the common school movement, it would have to change many of its practices. It would have to eliminate neighborhood schools and reverse the Supreme Court's rulings against cross-district desegregation plans. It would have to curtail (or terminate) academic tracking, magnet schools, and charter schools, all of which enable families to sort themselves by ability, interest, or other less attractive characteristics. But there is no movement to do any of these things. Under these circumstances, to deploy the "mixed school" argument against educational pluralism is simple hypocrisy. By refusing to fund nonpublic schools, the system preserves choice for the well-to-do, leaving the poor with fewer choices and the religious with none. It is difficult to see the justice in that.

D. Pragmatic Considerations

It thus appears that the apparent conflict between liberal pluralism and democratic education may be illusory. A pluralist approach to educational institutions, like the pluralist approach to religion adopted 200 years ago, may better achieve the purposes of democratic education as well as better comporting with the disestablishmentarian principles of the regime.

It may be, however, that this is not an issue to be decided on the basis of deductions from principle. A pragmatic choice between these visions of education should be sensitive to the particular social circumstances of the nation.[157] If religious divisions threatened to tear the nation apart, then it might be prudent to encourage forms of education that divided along lines other than religion. If authoritarian religions were so powerful that children had little choice but to conform to religious dictates imposed by their families, it might be consistent with liberalism to encourage forms of education that weakened those ties. But it is hard to argue that the United States today is plagued by young people too closely attached to the faith of their parents. Rather, the most pressing social problem of our time is that parents are increasingly less involved in the lives of their children, who become overly influenced by the culture of their peers, which is largely a product of mass media. The result: crass consumerism, materialism, premature sexualization, rebellion, and nihilism. The public schools, with their thin gruel of liberalism, are largely unable to provide a substitute discipline or a replacement ideology. In this social context, citizens concerned about democratic values should strive to strengthen those institutions that unite parents and children, that provide a coherent moral vision, that combat the materialistic hedonism of our age. In this social context, home schools and religious schools (and other schools provided by morally coherent subcommunities) may be the best democratic schools we have.

Conclusion

It is tempting for a democratic society, like any other, to use primary and secondary education as a means of inculcating the values and virtues appropriate to the society. But democratic majorities should not control everything, and there is something particularly dangerous about allowing democratic governments to control the formation of public opinion. Public opinion should control the government, not the government public opinion. That is the lesson of disestablishment. Just as the establishment of religion foundered on the fact of pluralism, the principle of liberalism, and the realities of effective religious institutions, the public school establishment faces the same problems. In light of our different and deeply held ideas about educational content and method, public schools cannot impose a coherent vision without provoking conflict and inflicting unfairness on the losers. Moreover, even on the assumption that the nation needs to provide education in democratic values to the next generation—an assumption I do not question—it seems doubtful that this can be accomplished as well by a single educational establishment as by a diverse set of pluralistic institutions.

America's experiment with religious disestablishment has worked far better than any of the founders could have expected. It turns out that liberal pluralism is good for religion, just as religion is good for liberal pluralism. After disestablishment, religion continued to provide the moral underpinning for republican society, as well as the democratic impetus to reform movements throughout our history, without the necessity of democratic control. Maybe we are ready for educational disestablishment.

NOTES

The author wishes to thank Peter de Marneffe, Boyd Dyer, Leslie Francis, Steve Gilles, Dan Greenwood, Rick Hills, John McGinnis, James Ryan, and Eugene Volokh for helpful comments on an earlier draft.

1. In other writings, I have explained why the Establishment Clause, properly interpreted, does not prohibit public support for education at religious schools, if it is provided on a neutral basis and the choice of schools is made by individual families. See Michael W. McConnell, "Legal and Constitutional Issues of Vouchers," in C. Eugene Steuerle, et al., eds., *Vouchers and the Provision of Public Services* (Brookings Institution Press, 1999); Michael W. McConnell, "Governments, Families, and Power: A Defense of Educational Choice," 31 *Conn. L. Rev.* 847 (1999); Michael W. McConnell, "Multiculturalism, Majoritarianism, and Educational Choice: What Does Our Constitutional Tradition Have to Say?" 1991 *U. Chi. Legal Forum* 123; see also Michael W. McConnell, "The Selective Funding Problem: Abortions and Religious Schools," 104 *Harv. L. Rev.* 989 (1991).

2. For an example of a thoughtful plan for educational choice, see John E. Coons & Stephen D. Sugarman, *Making School Choice Work for All Families* (San Francisco: Pacific Research Inst. 1999). One essential element, as Coons and Sugarman point out, is that participating private schools "must be protected from new regulations affecting curriculum, hiring, discipline, and other elements of identity." Id. at 87. Educational pluralism would be a mirage if the result were to yoke all schools to a single set of prescriptive standards.

3. It may well be desirable to have a public/private mix in primary and secondary education, similar to the system that prevails for higher education. Indeed, it seems probable that in many parts of the country, the majority of families will choose to use government schools, to the extent those schools are responsive and effective. Moreover, depending on social and demographic circumstances, it may be either wise or necessary for the government to provide public schools as a backstop to the private system, if the private system fails to provide schools that certain children can conscientiously attend. This might occur, for example, in homogeneous communities with small religious minorities.

4. Some conceptions of the good life—such as one based on torturing or enslaving other persons—fall beyond the range of reasonable toleration. But a robust and well-ordered liberal society is generally well advised to operate according to Jefferson's dictum that it is time enough for state intervention when doctrines break out into overt acts against peace and good order. Toleration rather than persecution often is the most effective antidote to noxious views.

5. See Stephen G. Gilles, "On Educating Children: A Parentalist Manifesto," 63 *U. Chi. L. Rev.* 937 (1996); Stephen G. Gilles, "Liberal Parentalism and Children's Educational Rights," 26 *Capital U. L. Rev.* 9 (1997).

6. This is not an argument that the Constitution compels such a result. See McConnell, "The Selective Funding Problem," at 1038, 1043–46.

7. Thomas Hobbes, *Leviathan*, ch. 42–43, at 521–626 [1651] (C. B. Macpherson, ed. 1968).

8. Jean-Jacques Rousseau, *The Social Contract* 132 [1762] (G. D. H. Cole, trans. 1950).

9. Id. at 179–181.

10. Mass. Const. of 1780, Art. III.

11. George Washington, Farewell Address [1796].

12. Lee v. Weisman, 507 U.S. 577, 646 (1992) (Scalia, J., dissenting).

13. Virginia Bill for Establishing Religious Freedom [1779], in P. Kurland & R. Lerner, 5 *The Founders' Constitution* 77 (1987).

14. See James Madison, Federalist No. 10.

15. See generally John Rawls, *Political Liberalism* 29–35, 62, and *passim* (1993); Bruce Ackerman, *Social Justice and the Liberal State* (1980); Ronald Dworkin, *Taking Rights Seriously* 273 (rev. ed. 1978). In its extreme form, this version of liberalism may well be implausible, see Joseph Raz, *The Morality of Freedom* 110–62 (1986); Michael J. Perry, *Morality, Politics, and Law* 57–73 (1988), but it remains true that a liberal society treats as (equally) legitimate a relatively broad range of views regarding the good life. See Michael W. McConnell, "The New Establishmentarianism," *Chi.-Kent L. Rev.* (forthcoming).

16. Adam Smith, *An Inquiry into The Nature and Causes of The Wealth of Nations*, Bk. V., Ch. I, Pt. II, Art. III, at 309–10 [1776] (1976).

17. James Madison, "Memorial and Remonstrance Against Religious Assessments," in Kurland & Lerner, supra, at 82.

18. Alexis de Tocqueville, 1 *Democracy in America* 292, 295–301 (J.P. Mayer, ed. 1969).

19. Ambach v. Norwick, 441 U.S. 68, 76 (1979).

20. Bethel School Dist. v. Fraser, 478 U.S. 675, 681-83 (1986).

21. Amy Gutmann, *Democratic Education* 14 (1987).

22. See Charles Glenn, *The Myth of the Common School* 88–97 (1987).

23. See generally Bernard Bailyn, *Education in the Forming of American Society* (1960).

24. See Carl F. Kaestle, *Pillars of the Republic: Common Schools and American Society, 1780–1860*, at 57, 166–67 (1983); Lloyd P. Jorgenson, *The State and the Non-Public School, 1825–1925*, at 1–19 (1987); Diane Ravitch, *The Great School Wars, New York City, 1805–1973: A History of the Public Schools as Battlefield of Social Change*, at 6–7 (1974). For the most comprehensive study of educational funding schemes in this period, see

Richard J. Gabel, *Public Funds for Church and Private Schools,* 147–470 (1937).

25. Gabel, supra, at 173–79.

26. See Ronald E. Butchart, *Northern Schools, Southern Blacks, and Reconstruction: Freedmen's Education, 1862–1875,* at 4–9, 33–52 (1980); Gabel, supra note 26, at 519. Congress instructed the Freedmen's Bureau to work through private benevolent associations whenever the latter provided suitable teachers. Act of July 16, 1866, § 13.

27. Kaestle, supra.

28. 268 U.S. 510 (1925).

29. For a sociologist's description of the conflict over ideas in education, see James Davison Hunter, *Culture Wars: The Struggle to Define America,* 197–211 (1991).

30. West Virginia Board of Education v. Barnette, 319 U.S. 624, 641 (1943).

31. See Gutmann, supra, at 24 ("The state may not argue simply: 'Because we wish to achieve social harmony, we shall indoctrinate all children to believe that *our* way of life is best.' A reasonable response then would surely be: 'But why should you have the authority to impose *your* way of thinking on the next generation.'").

32. Gutmann, supra, at 39.

33. Public Agenda Online (Gallup Survey conducted May–June, 1999), www.publicagenda.org/issues (Mar. 20, 2000).

34. Center for Educational Reform (International Communications Research survey conducted summer, 1996), www.edreform.com (Mar. 20, 2000).

35. Lowell Rose, et al., 29th Annual Phi Delta Kappa/Gallup Poll of the Public's Attitudes Toward the Public Schools, http://www.pdkintl.org/kappan/kpoll97.htm.

36. Gutmann argues that "secular standards constitute a better basis upon which to build a common education for citizenship than any set of sectarian religious beliefs—better because secular standards are both fairer and a firmer basis for peacefully reconciling our differences." Supra at 103. But religious citizens are unlikely to see it that way. To them, imposition of a secular ideology is just as unfair, just as sectarian, just as divisive. Elsewhere, Gutmann seems to recognize this. See id. at 41 ("To a moralist who believes that a primary purpose of education is to cultivate good character, a view that denies the justice of this educational purpose is just as controversial as a view that offers a direct challenge to the idea that a certain kind of character is good or bad.").

37. See Gutmann, supra, at 61.

38. I wish to stress that my disagreement with Gutmann is not necessarily over the substance of her recommendations for education (though there are important points on which we probably disagree, depending on what precisely she means). It is over the implication that her recommendations are logically entailed by a commitment to democracy, and that they should be given a privileged position over competing democratic visions.

39. This is not to deny that there are some viewpoints that are so inconsistent with the liberal democratic principles of the regime that it would be appropriate to exclude them. But as the McCarthy era taught us, exclusion even of plainly anti-democratic viewpoints has serious costs for our own liberalism, and there should be a heavy presumption that the viewpoints adopted by our fellow citizens are within the range of reasonableness.

40. See Michael Walzer, *On Toleration*, 10–12 (1997); see also John Rawls, *Political Liberalism*, 60–61 (1993).

41. Abington Township v. Schempp, 374 U.S. 203, 241–42 (1963) (Brennan, J., concurring).

42. Gutmann, supra, at 116.

43. Noah Webster, *On the Education of Youth in America*, quoted in Glenn, supra, at 77.

44. Horace Mann, Common School Journal [1838], quoted in id. at 80.

45. See Jorgenson, supra, at 20–21; Glenn, supra, at 152–55.

46. Horace Mann, Ninth Annual Report of the Secretary of the Board 157 (1846), quoted in Glenn, supra, at 165.

47. Quoted in Glenn, supra, at 164.

48. Samuel Lewis, First Annual Report (January 1838), quoted in James W. Fraser, *Between Church and State: Religion and Public Education in a Multicultural America* 38 (1999)

49. Kaestle, supra, at 76. See also Timothy L. Smith, "Protestant Schooling and American Nationality, 1800–1850," 53 *J. Am. Hist.* 679 (1966–67).

50. Winthrop S. Hudson, *The Great Tradition of the American Churches*, 108 (1963).

51. "Petition of the Catholics of New York" (1840), quoted in Fraser, supra, at 55.

52. Quoted in Glenn, supra, at 189.

53. Horace Mann, Twelfth Report, quoted in Fraser, supra, at 45.

54. See Fraser, supra, at 43–44. The attachment of many Lutherans to education and worship in their native language, German, made them the

most resistant of mainstream Protestants to the assimilationist efforts of the Common School Movement. Glenn, supra, at 211–13.

55. See Jorgenson, supra, at 83–85; Fraser, supra, at 57–65.

56. Quoted in Glenn, supra, at 252.

57. See Jorgenson, supra, at 69–110; Francis X. Curran, *The Churches and the Schools: American Protestantism and Popular Elementary Education* (1954).

58. Quoted in Glenn, supra, at 227–29.

59. See Jorgenson, supra, at 129–32; Stephen Macedo, "Transformative Constitutionalism and the Case of Religion: Defending the Moderate Hegemony of Liberalism," 26 *Political Theory* 56, 65–70 (1998). Perhaps the best answer to these accusations may be found in John Henry Newman, "A Letter to His Grace the Duke of Norfolk On Occasion of Mr. Gladstone's Recent Expostulation" (1875).

60. See Jorgenson, supra, at 69–110.

61. Quoted in Jorgenson, supra, at 107. For examples of anti-Catholic rhetoric on the schools issue in the 1870s, see Ward M. McAfee, *Religion, Race, and Reconstruction: The Public Schools in the Politics of the 1870s,* 2–78 (1998).

62. See, e.g., Commonwealth v. Cooke, 7 Amer. L. Reg. 417 (Boston, Mass. Police Ct. 1859) (holding that Catholic schoolboys could be whipped for refusing to recite the Lord's Prayer or the Ten Commandments from Protestant versions). See Jorgenson, supra, at 90–93, for a description of the facts and political context of the case.

63. Quoted in Jorgenson, supra, at 134.

64. See generally McAfee, *Religion, Race, and Reconstruction.*

65. *New York Tribune* (Oct. 1, 1875), quoted in Steven Green, "The Blaine Amendment Reconsidered," 36 *Am. J. Legal Hist.* 38, 47–48 (1992).

66. The text of the amendment can be found at 4 Cong. Rec. 5580 (Aug. 14, 1876).

67. Id. at 5587–88 (Sen. Edmunds).

68. Quoted in Jorgenson, at 211.

69. Pierce v. Society of Sisters, 268 U.S. 510, 525 (1925) (Argument by counsel for the Gov. of Oregon).

70. Id. at 535–36.

71. Id. at 534–35.

72. Id. at 535.

73. See John T. McGreevy, "Thinking on One's Own: Catholicism in the American Intellectual Imagination, 1928–1960," *J. Am. Hist.* 97 (June 1997).

74. John Dewey, Implications of S.2499, in Jo Ann Boydston, ed., 15 *John Dewey: The Later Works, 1925–1953*, at 285 (1989).

75. Perry Miller, Book Review, *New York Herald Tribune*, June 10, 1951, sec. VI, p. 1, quoted in McGreevy, supra, at 125.

76. Lemon v. Kurtzman, 403 U.S. 602, 635 n.20 (1971) (Douglas, J., concurring), quoting Loraine Boettner, *Roman Catholicism* (Presbyterian and Reformed Publishing, 1962).

77. Id. at 363, 370.

78. Stephen Macedo makes the interesting argument that the Protestant hegemony in the last century had the salutary effect of liberalizing Catholicism. See Macedo, supra note 59. He thus suggests that "[c]reating a certain religious homogeneity . . . is crucial and legitimate political work that liberals must hope is performed somehow." Supra at 65. Using government power for the purpose of fostering religious homogeneity is obviously problematical. See Michael W. McConnell, "Religious Freedom at a Crossroads," 59 *U. Chi. L. Rev.* 115 (1992). But even granting Macedo his normative premise, there is another way to read this history. It is significant that the liberalization to which Macedo refers took place only after hostility toward Catholicism had subsided and Catholics came to be recognized as equal citizens (most conspicuously, through the election of a Catholic President, but also through allowing Catholic schools to share in some forms of educational assistance). The Protestant attempt to create religious homogeneity may well have delayed American Catholic assimilation, not least by exposing American "nonsectarianism" as hypocritical. If American schools had allowed Catholic students to read from their own translations of the Bible, to obtain religious instruction in the schools by their own clergy, and to be educated in public schools by teachers of their own faith where possible (as William Seward proposed), the separate Catholic school system would probably never have been created, and both Catholics and Protestants might well have advanced toward mutual toleration a century earlier.

79. Engel v. Vitale, 370 U.S. 421 (1962); Abington School Dist. v. Schempp, 374 U.S. 203 (1963).

80. See Hunter, *Culture Wars*, at 201.

81. Paul C. Vitz, *Censorship: Evidence of Bias in Our Children's Textbooks* 22 (1986). Vitz's original study was published under the title "Religion and Traditional Values in Public School Textbooks" by the National Institute of Education in 1985.

82. Id. at 39–41.

83. Id. at 22.

84. Warren Nord & Charles Haynes, *Taking Religion Seriously Across the Curriculum* 193 (1998).

85. "Kansas Eliminates Evolution from Public School Curriculum," *Washington Post* A13 (Aug. 12, 1999). The decision was reversed in another vote in February, 2001.

86. Dan Harrie & Judie Fahys, "2000 Utah Legislature Calls It A Day," *Salt Lake Tribune* A1 (Mar. 2, 2000). The Governor vetoed the sex education bill.

87. See Samuel Bowles & Herbert Gintis, *Schooling in Capitalist America: Educational Reform and the Contradictions of Economic Life* (1976).

88. National Council of Economics Education, National Content Standards in Education, at viii (1997).

89. O. L. Davis, Jr., et al., *Looking at History: A Review of Major U.S. History Textbooks*, 3-4, 11 (1987); Charles C. Haynes, *A Teacher's Guide: Religious Freedom in America* 6 (1986); Paul C. Vitz, *Religion and Traditional Values in Public School Textbooks: An Empirical Study*, 3-7 (1985); "Educators Urge Turn to Studies About Religion," *New York Times*, July 2, 1987, at A16 (report of the Association for Supervision and Curriculum Development). For a thorough discussion of the problem, see Warren A. Nord, *Religion and American Education: Rethinking a National Dilemma* (1995).

90. Nord & Haynes, *Taking Religion Seriously Across the Curriculum* 77, 78. Oddly, the only reference to religion in any of the proposed national educational standards is in the standard for environmental studies. See National Research Council, *National Science Education Standards* 198 (1996).

91. Hunter, supra note 29, at 224.

92. 505 U.S. 577 (1992).

93. 319 U.S. 624 (1943).

94. Id. at 642.

95. 827 F.2d 1058 (6th Cir. 1987), cert. denied, 484 U.S. 1066 (1988).

96. Brown v. Hot, Sexy and Safer Productions, Inc., 68 F.3d 525 (1st Cir. 1995).

97. Edwards v. Aguillard, 482 U.S. 578, 584 (1987) (emphasis added).

98. For a more complete discussion of the issue, see George Dent, "Religious Children, Secular Schools," 61 *So. Cal. L. Rev.* 863 (1988).

99. Smith v. Board of School Commissioners, 827 F.2d 684 (11th Cir. 1987).

100. 268 U.S. 510 (1925).

101. See McConnell, "The Selective Funding Problem."

102. Helpful overviews of the research literature can be found in Anthony S. Bryck, et al., *Catholic Schools and the Common Good*, 55–78 (1993), and James Coleman, "Schools, Family, and Children" (Ryerson Lecture, University of Chicago 1985). The seminal work is James Coleman, et al., *High School Achievement: Public, Catholic, and Private Schools Compared*, 122–78 (1982). More recently, educational choice experiments have generated data showing that students from comparable backgrounds experience significant gains when they move to nonpublic schools. See Jay P. Greene, et al., "School Choice in Milwaukee: A Randomized Experiment," in *Learning from School Choice*, 345–50 (Paul E. Peterson & Bryan C. Hassel, eds. 1998) (finding that students participating in the program gained 3–5 percentage points in reading and 5–12 percentage points in math over a four-year period, after controlling for other variables, including test scores); Cecelia E. Rouse, "Private School Vouchers and Student Achievement: An Evaluation of the Milwaukee Parental Choice Program," *Q. J. Econ.* 553, 558 (May 1998) (finding that students participating in the program gained between 1.5 and 2.3 percentage points each year, but not finding statistically significant gains in reading); see also Howard L. Fuller, "The Real Evidence: An Honest Research Update on School Choice Experiments," *Wisconsin Interest* 17, 30 (Fall/Winter 1997). Several unpublished studies by John Witte et al., cited in Rouse, supra, found no gains. Rouse explains the differences in methodology that account for these conclusions.

103. See Catherine Minter Hoxby, "Does Competition Among Public Schools Benefit Students and Taxpayers?" (National Bureau of Econ. Research Working Paper No. 4979, 1994); David Osborne, "Healthy Competition," *The New Republic* 31 (Oct. 4, 1999) (citing studies and examples showing that competition from charter schools has forced regular public schools to innovate and reform).

104. Fuller, "The Real Evidence" at 17, 30.

105. See Milton Friedman, *Capitalism & Freedom* 93 (1962); Osborne, supra note 103.

106. See John E. Chubb & Terry M. Moe, *Politics, Markets, and America's Schools* (1990).

107. See James S. Coleman, "Schools, Families, and Children" (Ryerson Lecture, 1985).

108. Robert S. Erikson & Kent L. Tedin, *American Public Opinion* 131 (5th ed. 1995).

109. On political participation rates, see Sidney Verba, Kay Schlozman & Henry Brady, *Voice and Equality: Civic Voluntarism in American Politics* (Harvard 1995); Benjamin Ginsberg & Martin Shefter, *Politics by*

Other Means: The Declining Importance of Elections in America, 2 (1990) (voting rates have declined by 25 percent in the past century). On various measures of antisocial behavior among the young, see Centers for Disease Control, Morbidity and Mortality Weekly Report (Dec. 5, 1997), table 1 (abortion rates); table POP6 (birth rates for teenage mothers); table BEH1 (cigarettes smoking rates); table BEH2 (heavy drinking rates); table BEH4 (violent juvenile crime rate); table BEH3 (illicit drug use). While some of these trends showed signs of improvement in the early 1990s, they accelerated among pre-adolescents. See Kay S. Hymowitz, "Tweens: Ten Going on Sixteen," *City Journal* 26 (Autumn 1998).

110. James S. Coleman, "Changes in the Family and Implications for the Common School," 1991 *U. Chi. Legal F.* 153.

111. Rawls, *Political Liberalism,* 134; see also id. at 147.

112. Gutmann, supra, at 120–21.

113. For a particularly strident example, see James G. Dwyer, *Religious Schools v. Children's Rights* (1998) (combining anti-Catholic and anti-fundamentalist themes).

114. See Peter J. Paris, *The Social Teaching of the Black Churches* 30–31 (1985); Dorothy Roberts, "The Meaning of Blacks' Fidelity to the Constitution," 65 *Fordham L. Rev.* 1761 (1997).

115. Third Plenary Council of Baltimore (Dec. 7, 1884), in 1 Pastoral Letters 216.

116. See The Doctrine and Covenants of The Church of Jesus Christ of Latter-day Saints 101:80 (declaring the Constitution to be of divine origin, through "wise men" whom God "raised up unto this very purpose").

117. I am grateful to Paul Weithman for information and discussion on this issue.

118. Verba, et al., *Voice and Equality,* at 359; Kenneth D. Wald, *Religion and Politics in the United States* 35 (1992). In this context, I use the term "church" to denote any religious worship service or religious organization.

119. Verba, et al., at 358 (the standardized regression coefficient for voting and education is .05, while that for voting and religious attendance is .11).

120. Verba, et al., supra, at 432, 442.

121. Frederick C. Harris, "Something Within: Religion as a Mobilizer of African-American Political Activism," 56 *J. Pol.* 42, 62 (1994); see also Frederick C. Harris, "Religious Institutions and African American Political Mobilization," in Paul Peterson, ed., *Classifying by Race,* 278, 302 (1995) (65 percent of black church members, as compared to 30

percent of white church members, reported that they were encouraged to vote in church).

122. For data regarding both points, see Verba, et al., supra, at 381–84.

123. Theodore F. Macaluso & John Wanat, "Voting Turnout and Religiosity," 12 *Polity* 158, 158–69 (1979).

124. Bryk, et al., *Catholic Schools and the Common Good.*

125. U.S. Dept. of Educ., *Digest of Education Statistics,* Table 146 (1997).

126. Ibid.

127. Verba, et al., supra, at 297; John A. Coleman, "Deprivatizing Religion and Revitalizing Citizenship," in Paul Weithman, ed., *Religion and Contemporary Liberalism* 264 (1997).

128. See David B. Larson & Susan S. Larson, "The Forgotten Factor in Physical and Mental Health: What Does the Research Show?" (National Institute of Healthcare Research 1994); J. Gartner, D.B. Larson, & G. Allen, "Religious Commitment and Mental Health: A Review of the Empirical Literature," 19 *J. of Psychol. & Theology* 6 (1991); R.B. Loch & R.H. Hughes, "Religion and Youth Substance Abuse," 24 *J. Relig. & Health* 197 (1985); N.D. Glenn & C.N. Weaver, "A Multivariate, Multi-Survey Study of Marital Happiness," 40 *J. Marriage & Family* 269 (1978). A recent study by the Urban Institute sought to explain the recent decline in sexual activity among teenaged boys. "One of the things that's shaping some of these attitudes," according to Leighton Nu, the senior research associate on the study, "is related to religiosity. The teen-ager who is more religious felt more strongly about these issues in the 90's." He also said that increasing numbers of teenaged males believe they have a responsibility to provide for a new baby (an increase from 19 percent in 1979 to 59 percent in 1995). "Social movements like the Million Man March, like Promise Keepers, they are really emphasizing men should have a responsibility for the family," Nu explained. See "Number of Abortions, Providers Drops Sharply," *Salt Lake Tribune,* Dec. 11, 1996, at A17.

129. Verba, et al., supra, at 317.

130. Id.

131. Id. at 383–84.

132. Gutmann, supra, at 120.

133. Peter Skerry, "Christian Schools versus the I.R.S.," 61 *The Public Interest,* 18, 29 (1980).

134. See Ralph Larson & Pamela Creason, *The American Republic for Christian Schools,* 549, 570–73, 608–11 (Bob Jones University Press 1993); Mark Sidwell, *Free Indeed: Heroes of Black Christian History,* 5–6 (Bob Jones University Press 1995).

135. Larson & Creason, supra, at 609–10, citing Isaiah 1:16–17 and Jeremiah 22:3.

136. Id. at 610.

137. Anthony M. Greeley & Peter H. Rossi, *The Education of Catholic Americans*, 152–54 (1966).

138. Alan Wolfe, *One Nation, After All*, 61–72 (1998).

139. Id. at 69, 67.

140. See, e.g., Robert Fullinwider, "The State's Interest in Racially Nondiscriminatory Education," in Neal Devins, ed., *Public Values, Private Schools*, 21, 27–30 (1989).

141. Paul Peterson, "A Liberal Case for Vouchers," *The New Republic*, 29, 30 (Oct. 4, 1999).

142. See, e.g., H.S. Rosen and D.J. Fullerton, "A Note on Local Tax Rates, Public Benefit Levels and Property Values," 85 *J. Pol. Econ.* 433 (1977); Wallace E. Oates, "The Effects of Property Taxes and Local Public Spending on Property Values: An Empirical Study of Tax Capitalization and the Tiebout Hypothesis," 77 *J. Pol. Econ.* 957 (1969); M. Edel & E. Sklar, "Taxes, Spending and Property Values," 82 *J. Pol. Econ.* 941 (1984).

143. Coleman, et al., *High School Achievement*, supra, note 102.

144. John Wirt, et al., The Condition of Education 134 (National Center for Educational Statistics, U.S. Dept. of Educ. 1998).

145. Frank X. Savage & Mary Jo Milks, "United States Catholic Elementary and Secondary Schools 1995–96: The Annual Statistical Report on Schools, Enrollment and Staffing" 16 (National Catholic Educational Association 1996).

146. Id. at 18.

147. Id. at 22.

148. Peterson, supra, note 141, at 30.

149. Some critics have suggested that voucher programs will have the effect of "skimming" the best students from the public schools, but the evidence from the current voucher experiments is to the contrary. See Peterson, supra, note 141, at 30. This is, however, an important issue to be considered in voucher design.

150. See Howard Fuller & George Mitchell, "The Impact of School Choice on Racial Desegregation in Milwaukee," *Current Education Issues* (Marquette University Institute for the Transformation of Learning, June 1999).

151. The earliest and best-known advocates of this position are Stephen Sugarman and John Coons. See Stephen D. Sugarman, "Family Choice: The Next Step in the Quest for Equal Educational Opportunity?" 38 *Law & Contemp. Probs.* 513 (1974). See also Kenneth Clark,

"Alternative Public School Systems," *Harvard Educ. Rev.* (Winter 1968). More recently, they have been joined by such public figures as Andrew Young and Floyd Flake.

152. These data come from the National Educational Longitudinal Study, sponsored by the Department of Education, based on surveys conducted in 1992. See Jay P. Greene, "Nation's private schools more integrated and racially tolerant than public ones," Knight-Ridder/Tribune News Service (Oct. 5, 1998). Similar conclusions were reported in James Coleman, et al., *High School Achievement*, at 29–37.

153. Greene, supra, note 152.

154. Coleman, et al. *High School Achievement*, at 143–46.

155. See Rupert Brown, *Prejudice: Its Social Psychology* 237, 248–51 (1995) (citing studies and examples where intergroup contact exacerbated hostility).

156. Id. at 245.

157. See Edmund Burke, Speech on the Petition of the Unitarian Society [1792], in Peter J. Stanlis, *Edmund Burke: Selected Writings and Speeches* 313–317 (1963).

4

PLURALISM AND DEMOCRATIC EDUCATION: STOPPING SHORT BY STOPPING WITH SCHOOLS

NANCY L. ROSENBLUM

"Education Disestablishment" is Michael McConnell's provocative shorthand for the charge that sometimes wittingly, sometimes not; sometimes covertly under the guise of neutrality, sometimes as an official orthodoxy; historically Protestant, capitalist, and nativist, now secular and egalitarian, advocates of common schools have been unfaithful to their own promise of freedom and guilty of the unjustified coercion they pretend to guard against. Strong defenders of the democratic purposes of public schooling go head to head with McConnell on this score, beginning with his claim that the argument for restricting public support for education to common public schools is nearly indistinguishable from the classic argument for an established church. The "public school establishment," he argues, is "inconsistent with disestablishment liberal values."[1]

Instead of analyzing McConnell's negative charge of "education establishment," I want to probe his constructive claims and draw out the case for organizing education along pluralist lines. I will explain why I find his reasons for advocating public funding for private education elusive, and why a similar indeterminacy plagues pluralist positions generally. The question in brief:

Is opposition to "government controlled education" a family quarrel among democratic theorists over the best arrangements for democratic education, as McConnell suggests? Or is it a graver and theoretically more challenging clash between democracy and a regime of pluralism, as his argument implies? Put differently, are democratic values the principal theoretical commitment and what is wanted is a reconstructed balance between the conditions for democratic education and flourishing pluralism? Or is pluralism the foundational value and democracy secondary? Though McConnell contends that "schools have become the primary institutions for the formation of democratic character," it is not clear that producing citizens really is the baseline that justifies and constrains pluralist education.

Against this background of critical analysis, I will go on to support my title claim that the pluralist argument "stops short" by "stopping with schools." To anticipate my argument: to the extent that pluralism is the foundational value, a regime of pluralism justifies more than public support for pluralist schools. It justifies granting groups and sub-communities, religious and secular, a wide range of accommodations and opt-outs from general obligations. It also justifies many forms of public recognition and material support. By stopping with schools, McConnell fails to draw out the full implications of pluralism. He does not fully confront the disjuncture between principled, comprehensive pluralism and strong, democratic public culture. He takes a circumscribed view of the risks of balkanization.

On the other hand, to the extent that democracy figures as the foundational value, a more extensive pluralist case for democratic education can be made, one that relieves schools of much of the burden of democratic education. If civil society is reasonably democratic, a host of formative institutions—voluntary associations, workplaces, public accommodations, and so on—participate in shaping democratic habits and dispositions. Democratic social settings reinforce one another, and a division of educational labor among institutions is possible. But this diffuse and indirect democratic education is conditional on public policy guided by what I have called "the logic of congruence." It requires government to prohibit opt-outs and exemptions for pluralist groups, and it requires government to enforce conformity

to public principles of justice throughout society, except for intimate associations.

The two paths for going beyond schools both draw us onto the
broader terrain of civil society. In other respects, however, they
have divergent implications for democratic education. One face
of pluralism weakens the claim that pluralist education is consistent with democratic education; the other strengthens it. The
second direction is open to pluralists only if they give up the first.
Before returning to these matters, I want to try to decipher the
theoretical commitments that ground McConnell's argument for
pluralist education.

DEMOCRATIC ARGUMENTS FOR PLURALIST EDUCATION

McConnell's subtitle, "Why Democratic Values are Ill-Served by
Democratic Control of Schooling," leads us to expect him to confront opponents of publicly supported pluralist education on
their own terms. We expect him to argue that public funding for
private schools is justified because pluralist education is as good
or better for education in democratic values and practices than
public establishment.

Consider some of the leading propositions in this vein:

When it comes to inculcating substantive values, private
    schools provide the basic requirements of a civic curricu-
    lum—and do a better job of it insofar as they do a better
    job of teaching generally.
Pedagogy is as important for instilling democratic values
    and practices as curriculum, and private schools are as
    likely as public schools to implement participatory activi-
    ties that foster cooperation over competition, delibera-
    tion and so on.[2]
In cultivating democratic dispositions—from tolerance gen-
    erally to comfort with racial integration specifically— pri-
    vate education is better and would be better still if eco-
    nomic barriers were reduced.[3]
In cultivating the competences that undergird the political
    economy of citizenship, perhaps the most important
    thing schools can do to shape citizens is to improve aca-

demic achievement. The potential civic advantages range from defusing the divisive affirmative action debate to cultivating self-esteem.[4] Evidence suggests that in the context of schools, self-esteem has less to do with reinforcing particularistic values and identities, validating family or group norms, or helping students have "a clearer picture of who they are" than with concrete attainments and performance. Christopher Jencks and Meredith Phillips argue that reducing the black/white test score gap:

> is probably both necessary and sufficient for substantially reducing racial inequality in educational attainment and earnings . . . which would in turn help reduce racial differences in crime, health, and family structure.

Again, to the extent that private schools produce better outcomes particularly for the worst off children, democratic education would be served by public support for educational pluralism.[5]

None of these arguments play an important role in "Education Disestablishment." Perhaps McConnell is wise not to marshal social science to try to refute loyalists to public schools in their own terms. This tack is unlikely to be persuasive because it discounts the symbolic significance of public schools in the United States. Most democracies do distribute government funds to support pluralist education. But public institutions have expressive as well as instrumental functions, and in the U.S. this is particularly true of public schools. To say that it is irrational to cling to public schools if the evidence is that private ones do the job as well or better is a slur against prejudice, which is not always irrational or self-serving. Our emotions are informed by reasons, including reasons for seeing a major shift of commitment and resources away from common schools as disloyalty to *the* public institution most closely identified with American democracy and progressive hopes. (It is a historical irony that the development of common schools was inseparable from anti-Catholic and nativist movements, and that separationist constitutional amendments in the states prohibiting public funding of sectarian schools were promoted by "Know-Nothings," among others.)[6]

What would it mean to say that it makes no difference whether we support private rather than public schools so long as they are universally accessible? In some profound way, it would be interpreted by many people as betrayal of public institutions. Indeed, it would be seen as a wholesale disavowal of the capacity of government for positive good—as an end to democratic hope. This may be an inspirational fiction (though I think it has sound basis in the U.S.), but in any case it is unlikely to be exploded by the ambiguous social science evidence we have to date.

That many Americans contending with the worst public schools despair of government's capacity to reform them and are prepared to place their confidence in sectarian groups or educational entrepreneurs is understandable. It means that supporters of school choice have been able to appropriate the arguments traditionally used by supporters of public schools, emphasizing the need to subsidize families who cannot afford to "escape" the system to private schools. However, we simply don't know to what extent this is a reluctant compensatory move or a real erosion of democratic aspirations.

In any case, the symbolic power of commitment to public schools is persuasively countered less by evidence that private schools perform as well or better than public schools when it comes to democratic education than by an equally powerful ideal. Like other education pluralists, McConnell makes the egalitarian case, but his principal argument rests on the ideal of liberty, not equality.

Educational Liberty

In the competition to deliver the bleakest jeremiad of America's decline into "new barbarism," McConnell invokes the specter of government coercion; his lament focuses less on declining civic virtue and schools as restorative seedbeds of democracy than on the loss of personal freedom. Put strongly, "Education Disestablishment" argues that liberty, not democracy, requires publicly funded pluralist education.

McConnell's appeal to liberty is both explicit and implicit in the temper of his piece. Notice his reference to "government" in the singular: should "*the* government itself" control "the development and propagation of ideas, information, opinions, and culture." The phrase "coercive indoctrination" is a staple here, along with the idea that government imposes "one conception of 'common democratic values' *by force*" (italics added). McConnell makes common cause with poststructuralist and multiculturalist reports of disciplinary techniques and insidious ideological hegemony, except that he exonerates the producers and disseminators of academic, scientific, and artistic work. Instead, the onus for "capitulation to the often anti-social values of mass youth culture" is squarely on "government schools." Even though his essay is a brief for public support, not for private opt-outs and exit, government is portrayed as overbearing sovereign, not patron.

McConnell does not articulate the basis for the priority of liberty; still, it is clear enough that "the first freedom" is the ability to act according to conscience. McConnell is concerned with those deep and comprehensive demands of faith that put people in conflict with the obligations of citizenship, even when these obligations are the result of legitimate democratic decisions and within constitutional limits. Since even minimal public requirements for democratic education will implicitly treat some conscientious positions as mistaken, conflict with government is inevitable. This appeal to conscience heightens the specter of government coercion. By invoking liberty of conscience, the contest over public support for private education is heightened in a second respect. "Conscience"—religious (and secular) judgments that "connect to ultimate concerns"—attributes depth and comprehensiveness to pluralist schemes of education. It makes the terminology of "choice" and market analogies applied to schooling seem like a trivialization of what is at stake—personal liberty for nothing less than comprehensive moral values.

I'll leave commentary on McConnell's coercion/orthodoxy argument aside except to say that in public education, the tug-of-war between federal and state, and state and local "control" (itself an abstraction that must be broken down into an array of legal requirements, funding schemes, curricular decisions, classroom organization, assessment, and so on) is part of a larger field of competing authorities that includes professional educators' groups, teachers' unions, textbook publishers, and parents (organized and disorganized). Localism, unionism, and housing patterns dilute unitary government "control." So do the many arrangements for student opt-outs, parental vetoes over aspects of the curriculum, charter schools, and so on. Even if there is one authoritative curriculum in each public school jurisdiction, every parent and student knows that variability from classroom to classroom is the rule. To say nothing of the fact that the substantive content of democratic education is a moving target. "Not every generation but every few years the content of American history books changes appreciably"; the same generation of children in the same school district will have been exposed to vastly different narratives and pictures of national identity.[7] McConnell notes that Kansas recently eliminated evolution from the required curriculum and that Utah prohibits sex education in birth control methods other than abstinence. It is a real question whether the recent push toward national standards and testing will seriously undo local variations. But for now, "government" in the singular is misleading except insofar as the model is confrontation between conscience and coercive sovereign.[8]

Of course, it is an empirical question whether either direct public funding of private schools or vouchers would increase the actual range of educational choices, for whom, and by how much. Nothing in public support for private education indicates the extent of either freedom of choice or pluralism. Certainly nothing in the principled argument for educational pluralism suggests whether choices are among good schools, measured by reasonable standards of educational merit. McConnell is optimistic that "families with determination and organization can find or organize schools that address their pedagogical, methodological, and substantive concerns." Pluralism depends, then, on who has the resources of money, leadership, organizational skill, and motivation to create alternative schools, and how accessible they are to different populations in different areas. Pluralism also depends on whether educational entrepreneurs reflect or create the market for alternative educational forms and goals. Certainly nothing in choice or educational pluralism entails parental involvement in decisions by private school authorities; that is, it says nothing about enhanced parental involvement or control.

Of course, the degree of liberty and of pluralism that results from public funding would also depend on the role of government, above all on the content and enforceability of the curricular goals and pedagogical methods of "democratic education" required of both public and publicly regulated private schools. How much liberty for educational pluralism would McConnell allow? How stringent is his own notion of the requirements of democratic education? Or, to turn things around, how inclusive is his pluralism?

Democracy and the Limits of Pluralist Education

I've said that McConnell frames his objection to "education establishment" in terms of liberty, invoking conscience, and that he does not frame his positive case for educational pluralism by arguing that private schools are as good or better at democratic education than public schools. He asserts more modestly their compatibility with the justifiable democratic goals of education. What, then, does he say in this connection about private schools' responsibility *for* civic education? What does he say about private schools' accountability *to* public authority?

McConnell would limit the use of state funds to choice among accredited schools, that much is clear; he would impose standards to ensure that schools are bona fide educational institutions. So the parameters of "reasonable regulation" encompass ensuring the basic requirements of educational quality and, McConnell adds, "perhaps of minimal civic responsibility." *Perhaps* is not reassuring. McConnell is uncharacteristically unforceful on this key point. He says "I, for one, do not doubt" the need to inculcate the habits of heart and mind of democratic citizenship, but that does not answer the question what, if anything, he would impose "by force" on those who do doubt the need for civic education. Granted that "any attempt to impose one conception of 'common democratic values' by force requires justification," what counts as justification?

He cautions that in practice public education goes beyond some potentially acceptable civic minimum to aim at a contested ideal of what is necessary for the next generation to become responsible citizens. This suggests that public support should not be conditional on private schools supplying anything beyond a "civic minimum." Publicly imposed standards should not be "so prescriptive as to frustrate educational choice."[9]

In this spirit, McConnell rejects regulative principles of nonrepression and nondiscrimination as overly stringent.[10] He does not explicitly endorse any of the usual catalogues of the purposes of democratic education, either: educating future citizens to be free and equal and to relate to one another on terms of mutual respect (along with its practical counterpart—the ability to work together with people different from ourselves); toleration; the ability to be self-supporting; an array of civic competences ranging from basic law-abidingness and the wherewithal to exercise rights to more demanding skills of public deliberation and full-blown civic magnanimity. He rejects "thick" accounts of democratic values teaching, conservative and progressive. Nor does he catalogue unreasonable or impermissible educational practices.

This is a striking lacuna. After all, even "minimal civic responsibility" or teaching the "scant essentials" as a condition of public subsidy is the subject of disagreement. We know that in democracies where the establishment question is resolved in favor of government support for religious schools, the question of the *civic content* of religious education remains unresolved and produces fierce political conflict.

Perhaps McConnell sees the core civic minimum as a contingent and shifting matter, and substitutes a procedural mechanism for a substantive account. Should democratically motivated constraints on choice be democratically decided? If we allow with McConnell that public support for religious as well as secular private schools is constitutionally permissible (which appears to be the direction in which state and federal constitutional law is evolving), still, it is not constitutionally required.[11] This leaves the matter of funding and conditions on funding, floors and ceilings, to the discretion of state legislatures.

Indeed, McConnell trusts that public opinion favors both choice and reducing substantive democratic education to the "scant essentials." There are reasons to think that public opinion, often a shifting tide, is likely to be unstable in the face of actual, comprehensive public funding schemes. Consider: as religious associations shift their goal from securing a right to self-protective exemptions to a right to public recognition and funding, ecumenical cooperation may be replaced by bitter sectarian division. Even citizens who are tolerant of alien faiths are unlikely to want to subsidize the educational missions of strange and despised sects: an expansive network of Muslim schools, or establishments run by the Nation of Islam or the Church of Scientology—whether or not these schools adhere to some civic minimum. It may be that a genuinely comprehensive public funding arrangement for all religious and nonreligious private schools may require only government acknowledgment, not endorsement, of these schools (to borrow the language of First Amendment Establishment Clause doctrine), especially if the funding is indirect via vouchers and individual choice. But it is not likely to be perceived that way, and that is what counts. Public funding, even if it is of "religious schools" in general, is ultimately inseparable from endorsement of the value, if not the truth, of tenets and practices.

We can predict that the instability of public opinion would be amplified in the face of public funding for the wild array of private schools devoted to some secular ideology, schools established by and for ethnic and cultural groups, ideologues of many stripes, vegetarians, weird pedagogic experimentalists, and so on. Public funding amounts to public imprimatur. If McConnell is right that we are "committed above all else to peaceful coexistence" (a point to which I will return), then we cannot be confident that state funding of pluralist education will be less divisive than "education establishment." But by formally multiplying the number of opt-outs, parental vetoes, and forms of school segregation designed to make "peaceful coexistence" easier, an equally likely outcome is competition over pieces of the public pie and hostile balkanization.

Public opinion, and legislation in response to it, may not be decisive in any case, for McConnell would not leave setting the parameters of the civic minimum to "a toss of the majoritarian dice." He looks instead to courts to provide background protection for pluralism and to intervene if the political branches tried to enforce too much (or too little) democratic education as a condition for public support. Since his account of the civic minimum is empty, it is impossible to tell when determining the civic content of publicly funded education should be taken out of the hands of democratic decision makers. Or what sort of democratic education counts as too much and should be judicially disallowed. In constitutional terms, it is difficult to understand what First Amendment precedents would make conditioning public support on anything beyond some civic minimum an impermissible "establishment."

A distinguished First Amendment scholar, McConnell knows that "there is no political establishment clause."[12] Government is constrained as coercive sovereign from censoring or chilling private speech, but not when it acts in its capacity as patron or educator. Government can speak freely. There is no gag rule on democratic authority when it comes to ideology. And government can subsidize speech by private and public agents. There is no prohibition on conditioning public funding on recipients' willingness to deliver government's message, even if this quid pro quo is characterized as professing "civic religion." McConnell does not claim that rulings in First Amendment cases actually prohibit public enforcement of anything beyond some civic minimum either in public schools or as a condition for public support for private schools.

He has, however, offered his own divergent interpretation of constitutionally impermissible (religious) establishment, and we can look there for insight into the parameters of judicially enforced limitations on "forced" democratic education. How thin is McConnell's own democratic establishment? Or, how neutral and inclusive is his pluralism?

Consistent with his view that government is responsible for preserving flourishing pluralism, McConnell rejects separationism and allows for a wide range of state-church partnerships and public support. On this interpretation, an act of government amounts to unconstitutional establishment only if it has the purpose or effect of increasing religious uniformity (or reducing "product differentiation" in religion).[13]

"Uniformity" is an elastic standard.[14] Its utility as a measure of government overstepping its bounds is limited. Besides, it would be difficult to isolate the effects of public policy from other social and cultural forces that influence religious diversity. (We should not mistake subjective feelings of vulnerability to a dominant secular public culture with the objective health, status, or viability of religious groups.) So what does "uniformity" imply for judicial review of conditions on public support for and regulation of pluralist education? In light of experience, any civic minimum will be intolerable to some forms of sectarian education and impose a burden, but it does not follow that enforcing this minimum (or, for that matter, a more stringent standard of democratic education) would increase *religious* uniformity. In light of experience, religious diversity is plainly flourishing here; neither the coercive "establishment" of public schools nor the incentives public policy imposes to attend public over parochial schools have dampened it.[15]

Answers to the questions "What constraints should government impose on pluralist education as a condition for support?" and "Who decides?" depend on broader theoretical commitments. I conclude from this attempt to decipher McConnell's grounds justifying pluralist education that it is difficult to tell whether framing the argument in terms of "good enough" democratic education is more ornamental than structural.

I return to my opening questions, then. Is pluralism the foundational value and democratic ideology just one competing faith among others? If so, McConnell's argument is really a brief for a regime of pluralism (based on conscience). "Our Constitution," he wrote in an earlier essay, is "a multicultural constitution."[16] From this perspective, the chief condition imposed on public support of private schools is that they produce citizens committed to preserving a modus vivendi among pluralist groups. Of course, insofar as virtues like tolerance or nondiscrimination are viewed as necessary for "peaceful coexistence," there will be overlap with the goals of democratic education, but democratic purposes are not decisive. On this view of his position, McConnell offers a comprehensive argument for pluralism that is not sufficiently committed to democracy or democratic education.

Alternatively, McConnell's pluralism is consistent with a deep commitment to liberal democracy. He takes the "liberal" element and its accompanying pluralism seriously, and proposes a different balance between pluralism and democratic education. If this is his view, the parameters of a "good enough" democratic education must be outlined. Otherwise, we cannot tell when democracy has priority over the centrifugal demands of pluralist schools, or why. On this understanding of his priorities, Mc-Connell's argument is vulnerable to the opposite failing: sufficiently firm commitment to democracy may be insufficiently solicitous of pluralism. We simply can't tell.

In either case, McConnell stops short by stopping with schools. I want to draw out the Janus-faced implications of pluralism, beginning with a fuller case for a regime of pluralism.

The Political Logic of a Regime of Pluralism: Opt-outs and Separationism

If McConnell's foundational value is pluralism, the logic of the argument pushes well beyond education. Recall that Mc-Connell's principled case for public support for educational pluralism is based on the claims of conscience. He does make common cause with secularists, arguing that public support should be impartial not only among religious schools but also among all private schools. His argument for public funding is inclusive; it extends to religious, moral, ideological, or pedagogical differences. Doubtless, emerging constitutional doctrine on separationism contributes to this ecumenical stance. (Public support is permissible if a program offers benefits to a broad array of recipients, secular as well as religious, and if aid is indirect, via individual choice.) In any case, it is hard to resist the conclusion that secular private schools are the incidental beneficiaries of a position based on the claims of "communities of conscience." Only religious schools face a presumptive Establishment Clause constitutional bar to public support. Only believers are "second class citizens," whose beliefs and wishes are excluded by that bar from having weight in democratic decisions at the outset.[17] Religious schools would be the principal beneficiary of public support.

McConnell invokes "disestablishment" in his title to point up constitutional protection against government coercion. But consistent with his view that "the moral-cultural role of primary and secondary schools today, closely resembles that of churches at the time of the founding," the positive thrust of his argument for pluralism tracks the Free Exercise Clause.[18] McConnell reads the Free Exercise Clause generously. It often requires and almost always permits exemptions on religious grounds from burdensome general obligations—exit rights and opt-outs from the countless regulations imposed by the welfare state (for example, the Amish should not have to pay social security taxes if they care for their own). It often requires and almost always permits positive rights to "accommodation" to relieve groups of the burden of government-created obstacles to the exercise of faith (for example, the obstacle imposed when public resources are controlled in a way that "induces the families of America to accept instruction from government employees").[19]

The practical implications of this theory of accommodation are far-reaching. It means that Title VII anti-discrimination law is not enforced against the Mormon Church when it fires a janitor in a gymnasium open to the public for failing to conform to temple rules.[20] It means that landlords can refuse to rent to unmarried couples if it offends their faith and that employers must accommodate the conscientious needs of employees unless they impose "undue hardship" on business, and so on. A regime of pluralism also requires substantive public support for the real conditions of diversity, including the distribution of public benefits.

This constitutional argument for opt-outs, exemptions, and entitlements is plainly magnified if it extends beyond religious communities of conscience to other groups with strongly held secular ideologies, counterparts of religious faith; it is magnified immeasurably if it extends to pluralism based on "values" or "culture" or "identity" broadly. (Though as a matter of constitutional law, exemptions and accommodation require that a liberty claim has its basis in the exercise of religion. Secular conscience has been afforded equal status with religious conscience—explicitly by analogy to religious conscience—only in the matter of exemption from military service.)[21] McConnell's conscientious case for public support for private schools carries over into other forms of public support for pluralism. Implicitly, the argument could be extended to secular conscientious claims for exemption from general obligations.

In short, if McConnell's is a comprehensive, principled pluralist position, its political logic extends far beyond education, and principled pluralism can lead to "runaway" exemptions and accommodation.[22] Justice Scalia warned that constitutionally mandated First Amendment exemptions from facially neutral laws courted anarchy and created "a system in which each conscience is a law unto itself."[23] Accommodation that is not constitutionally mandated—generous accommodation by legislatures—would have the same result. It would be hyperbolic to say that in urging courts as a constitutional matter and legislatures as a discretionary matter to accommodate religion, or pluralism more broadly, McConnell flirts with anarchy. "Anarchist" and "libertarian" are particularly misleading labels since he wants government subsidies, not self-sufficiency and disengagement.

Still, assuming McConnell proposes a political theory of a regime of pluralism, how inclusive is his pluralism? What risks of balkanization is he prepared to acknowledge? How much dilution of democratic public culture would he tolerate? A great deal, if the baseline constraint is not a secular liberal democratic order but "peaceful coexistence."

Focusing on education, the centrifugal force of publicly supported private schools is an important empirical question. There are three reasons to agree with McConnell's claim that the practical consequences of pluralist education in the U.S. are not likely to be anarchy or political disintegration.

For one thing, he points to the happy accident that the "sacred history" of religious faiths here "legitimates and defends American democracy." He is sanguine that with liberty and public funding for their schools, pluralist groups will flourish and bring their comprehensive doctrines and worldviews to bear in an uninhibited fashion, thickening the democratic minimum with their own moral and sentimental education. Of course, not all tenets and practices reinforce *democracy* specifically in contrast to social order generally. And some are interpreted as revolutionary or separatist. Recall that religious exemptions and accommodation are needed precisely because of recurrent conflicts between the obligations of citizenship and the demands of faith. Overall, however, there is sociological support for the view that in the U.S. pluralism is not disintegrative; studies report just how marginalized antidemocratic and antiliberal sentiments are in middle-class America, and how broad the consensual center, particularly as regards religion and public life.[24]

McConnell is also confident that public support for pluralist education would provide motivation for commitment to democracy.

He is certainly right that public benefits are incentives to identify with democratic public life. Cooperation is tied to the perception of stakeholding. This is particularly important because Mc-Connell is unable to argue that all pluralist groups recognize the motivational force of liberal democratic principles per se. Public recognition and material distributions are the practical motivation for pluralist commitments to democratic society.

Finally, de facto compatibility between pluralist education and democracy finds support in the observation that it is not necessary for everyone to exhibit civic virtue. It is a real question, after all, how many people must be good democratic citizens, how consistently, and in what contexts, to provide the underpinnings for institutions to work. Citizens must be normally law-abiding, pay taxes, and perform a limited set of public services when called. But active political participation and civic mobilization are neither universal nor constant. Under what circumstances we judge participation to be imperative and apathy crippling (in the face of severe injustice, say) depends in part on the stringency of democratic theory and in part on perceptions of contemporary threats to democratic public life. Civic engagement in the U.S. is typically limited and episodic, yet social scientists nevertheless agree that America is a stable and legitimate democracy.

In fact, McConnell's main argument for the stability of democracy here turns the threat of divisive conflict upside down: disallowing public support for private schools would enflame dissidents. The "winners" in conflicts over education get it for free, which "will breed further alienation and division—and probably make out-groups more antagonistic toward the mainstream values of the community" (at 98).

Whether or not a public policy of pluralist education is tenable from the standpoint of political stability and legitimacy says little about what justifies a regime of pluralism over strong democracy, of course. And if pluralist education is *not* a tenable way to produce sufficient commitment to democratic institutions and exhibitions of democratic virtues, or if the goal of democratic education is not just stability and legitimacy but some more demanding exhibition of civic identity and virtue, which side of the fence does McConnell come down on? Does he articulate, justify, and enforce his own "good enough" democratic establishment as a condition for public support of private schools? Or does he articulate a principled argument for pluralism enhanced by public support even if it dilutes democratic aspirations and weakens public political culture? Is the limiting consideration compatibility with democratic education and civic identity, with a reasonably strong secular civil order? Or compatibility with a regime of pluralism, so long as it produces peaceful coexistence?

McConnell stops short of explicitly adopting the bolder pluralist case. But it is latent in his views: "I believe that our constitution recognizes the legitimacy of a belief in powers higher than the state . . . that judgments about the dictates of the higher power can be made only by individuals and communities of believers, and not by the state. The First Amendment thus understood undermines any claim by the state to ultimate normative authority," even in civil matters.[25] It is latent, if not in the intent of his position, then in its effects. If not in its effects, that owes to the unique and contingent constellation of American pluralism.

STOPPING SHORT BY STOPPING WITH SCHOOLS

There is another direction open to those whose principal theoretical commitment in educational matters is to democracy but who want to strike a different balance between democracy and pluralism. We can argue that pluralist education is consistent with democratic education, and with a (bare) civic minimum, if we don't look on *schools* as the sole educational contexts but rather at the effects of a wide range of institutions in civil society. With rare exceptions, schools are not isolated from the flow of social life; certainly students are not.

Both McConnell and his adversaries in this debate over education assume the primacy of early years. They assume the impressionability of children and the irreversibility of what is learned in childhood. They also assume the unique formative power of schools: "schools have become the primary institutions for the formation of democratic character," McConnell insists. They undervalue democratic education outside schools, in civil society generally, lifelong. If we think that other formative contexts are as strong or stronger when it comes to instilling certain civic dispositions and practices, or that compensation and reparation are possible—that democratic education missed in childhood can be made up—then our perspective on the question of pluralist schooling will shift.

Americans should be particularly open to the idea of ongoing moral development, including democratic education. In the U.S., being "born again" is commonplace, support groups promising moral transformation are big business (they enroll something on the order of four out of ten adults), and the current generation of people in their 60s and 70s is not only the most privileged generation of elderly in history, a cultural avant-garde with its own institutions and customs, but also the most mobile, independent, and powerful, with a feared political lobby. Despite evidence of transformation over the life cycle, the propensity to fix on early experiences as decisive holds sway.

Nothing is more important for our topic (or less studied by political and legal theorists) than comprehending the stages of moral development and the educational goals appropriate to them. That should help set parameters to the core of civic education for children in schools. It should also help identify the elements of civic education appropriate for adults. Nothing is more important than a realistic assessment of the comparative advantages of various institutions when it comes to democratic education; nothing, that is, except understanding the many points in life at which individuals can be educated, even transformed.

In this context, two suggestions stand out. First, we should take care to identify the dispositions and competences that are irrevocably lost if they are not formed in childhood. What aspects of education, including civic education, cannot be compensated for in adulthood? Second, we should ascertain which of these aspects children can learn best or only at school.

There are good reasons to take some of the burden of democratic education off schooling and to acknowledge a division of educational labor. We know little about what habits spill over outside the orchestrated educational environments of schools. Even when schools are dedicated to democratic education and have exemplary curricula, say, or are well integrated racially or religiously. We know little about what school experiences produce sturdy norms, whether or when the lessons in school effectively inform adult experiences, and whether they survive contradictory adult experiences. Moreover, we do know that a great deal of moral and civic education of children goes on outside schools. William Damon reports two findings. First, basic moral education—the truly irreplaceable foundation of moral sense and practice—is provided by parental authority. Second, much of what we call civic education—cooperation and reciprocity, for example—is learned mainly among peers in informal settings without adult intervention.[26]

We also know that a lot of civic education goes on among adults in the associations of civil society, which have formative effects on members' dispositions and practices. William Galston points out that racial attitudes in the U.S. have improved despite the fact that most schools, public and private, remain segregated. These changes owe in large part to experiences with diverse people in the workplace and public institutions, and in part because of other practical incarnations of public principles of justice and other forms of moral persuasion. Racial and gender integration in civil society is the result of public policy prohibiting discrimination in employment, for example, and compelling restricted membership groups to admit unwanted members. Public principles of justice are enforced in public accommodations, workplaces, housing, and social groups that are said to provide important resources and opportunities. These policies conform to what I have called "the logic of congruence"—legal enforcement of public norms throughout society. They aim not only at insuring fair opportunity but also at shaping dispositions. Democratic education operates as an explicit justification of public policy in court opinions and legislative records; government as sovereign enforcer of equal opportunity shares center stage with government as educator.

In *Membership and Morals: The Personal Uses of Pluralism in America,* I argued that the "logic of congruence" can be taken too far when it is applied "all the way down." There is a danger that enforcement of public norms directly or as a condition of public recognition and support alters the membership practices and forms of authority, internal lives and purposes of voluntary associations. But this caution is not meant to question the perfectly justifiable application of due process and anti-discrimination law in many arenas of civil society, nor the fact that these practices are at least as important for democratic education as schools.

When it comes to democratic education, the tendency of legal and political theorists is to stop with children and schools. In fact, however, the question of publicly supported pluralist education in schools is inseparable from a realistic account of the division of educational labor and of the force of democratic education beyond schools. Compatibility between pluralist schooling and democratic education depends on the fact that formative public and quasi-public institutions are regulated so that they are reasonably congruent with liberal democratic practices. It depends on the fact that the educational as well as instrumental impact of fair housing laws and Title VII is strong and widespread, if not universal. Whether this face of pluralism is open to McConnell and other advocates of a regime of pluralism depends on his theoretical commitments. It is not available to him if he concludes that the same liberty and free exercise argument he uses to justify pluralist education also justifies religious or conscientious exemptions for pluralist groups from the public norms that regulate other domains of social life. For if a regime of pluralism prevails, diluting civic obligations and detracting from the number of institutions that conform to public norms of justice and cultivate democratic dispositions, then the case for common schools and for robust constraints on private schools holds.

CONCLUSION: DEMOCRATIC EDUCATION AND PUBLIC SCHOOLS

The more severe our goals for democratic education, the greater the focus will be on common schools and stringent public control of private schools. The more demanding we are in our assessment of the requisites of citizenship, the stronger the argument for democratic control. If we accept a minimalist notion of democratic education, and if we take a cold-eyed view of what is best accomplished in schools and what dispositions can be shaped in other settings, then the case for pluralist schools is significantly advanced.

Even so, two things continue to seriously undercut arguments for publicly supported pluralist education. One is if civil society is both pluralist and segmented, so that the vast majority of citizens are not members of voluntary associations or employed in workplaces governed by public democratic norms. If men and women are not normally exposed to democratic practices, if myriad settings do not call on them to exhibit democratic dispositions in everyday life, the onus returns to schools.

The other countervailing consideration is aspirational. Public schools are an American heritage. There can be little doubt that both vouchers and public funding for private schools would undermine public schools—confirming their inadequacy in practice and substituting an array of alternative educational ideals. To my mind, "common schools," or "education establishment," are inseparable from progressive democratic aspirations here. There may be alternative means of democratic education, and good reasons not to put the whole burden on schools—not to stop short when we consider democratic education. But there are no alternative institutions as repositories of these wishes.

Nor is any other institution as powerful in drawing attention to the demands of democratic citizenship. For better or worse, disagreement about the relation between government and schooling is our form of collective self-exploration. It is the occasion for the dialogues (civil and uncivil), political battles, federal and state legislation, and litigation by which we construct and deconstruct our civic identity and our particular, pluralist identities. It is where we are most engaged—most passionate and most participatory—in "revising America." Which is why the dispositive argument is not simply the instrumental business of schools; I've argued that democratic education does not stop with schools. Rather, it is the aspirational side of this peculiar institution—the way Americans associate progressive democracy with public schools, and the ritualistic way we engage in collective self-definition in the context of public schools.

NOTES

1. Though McConnell does not argue that educational disestablishment is compelled by the Constitution.

2. Joseph Coleman, "Civic Pedagogies and Liberal-Democratic Curricula," *Ethics* 108 (July 1998): 746–761.

3. Jay P. Greene, "Civic Values in Public and Private Schools" forthcoming, Paul E. Peterson, editor, *Lessons from School Choice* (Washington, D.C.: Brookings Institution). In this connection McConnell does present evidence that religious Americans are more politically engaged than Americans overall, cf. pp. 55–56.

4. Christopher Jencks and Meredith Phillips, "America's Next Achievement Test: Closing the Black-White Test Score Gap," *The American Prospect* (September–October 1998): 44–53. The argument is that self-esteem is tied less to pluralism than to "having a clearer picture of who they are" and environments that reinforce identity of family or group than performance. The authors are strong supporters of reformed public schools.

5. See counterarguments cited in Gutmann, "Civic Minimalism, Cosmopolitanism, and Patriotism," in this volume, note 24.

6. Among the many pieces on this is Joseph P. Viteritti, "Blaine's Wake: Schools Choice, The First Amendment, and State Constitutional Law," 21 *Harvard Journal for Law and Public Policy* 657 (1998).

7. Frances Fitzgerald, *America Revised: History Schoolbooks in the Twentieth Century* (Boston: Little Brown, 1979).

8. Of particular interest are the divergent separationist doctrines among state constitutions. See Viteritti.

9. McConnell prefers standardized testing to ensure positive results rather than particular requirements regarding curricular materials, staff, or plant, in "Multiculturalism, Majoritarianism, and Educational Choice: What Does Our Constitutional Tradition Have to Say?" *The University of Chicago Legal Forum* (1991): 123–151 at 126 note 3.

10. "Multiculturalism and Choice" at 127. Though he would have laws prohibiting racial discrimination in private education to continue to apply.

11. Recent state and federal supreme court cases indicate that the matter is in flux. The emerging criteria for permissible aid appear to be whether aid is organized to flow through private parental choice and not directly to schools, and whether public support for religious education is part of a neutral system of support for choice among private schools generally. Another consideration may be whether subsidies are also available to students in public schools. The background condition is private conformity to state educational requirements.

12. Kathleen Sullivan, "Religion and Liberal Democracy," in *The Bill of Rights in the Modern State,* ed. Geoffrey Stone, Richard Epstein, and Cass Sunstein (Chicago: University of Chicago Press, 1992), p. 206.

13. Michael W. McConnell and Richard A. Posner, "An Economic Approach to Issues of Religious Freedom," 56 *University of Chicago Law Review* 1 (1989) at 57.

14. For a discussion of the use of the standard of "viability" in religion cases, see Nancy L. Rosenblum, "Amos: Religious Autonomy and the Moral Uses of Pluralism," in Rosenblum, editor, *Obligations of Citizenship and Demands of Faith* (Princeton: Princeton University Press, 2000).

15. See McConnell and Posner, "An Economic Approach," for an illuminating discussion of the vexing question of government neutrality (modeled on tax neutrality in public finance), and how public support for education can be provided without distorting the relative demand for religious or nonreligious education.

16. "Multiculturalism and Choice" at 132.

17. Michael McConnell, "Believers as Second Class Citizens," in Rosenblum, ed., *Obligations of Citizenship and Demands of Faith*.

18. "Multiculturalism and Choice" at 134.

19. This runs directly counter to the Court's decision in *Employment Division v. Smith*, 110 S.Ct. 1595 (1990).

20. Rosenblum, "Amos," in Rosenblum, ed., *Obligations of Citizenship and Demands of Faith*.

21. Even there secular pacifists are not treated identically with Quakers. For a comprehensive discussion of how courts define religion and its analogues, see Kent Greenawalt, "Five Questions about Religion Judges Are Afraid to Ask," in Rosenblum, ed., *Obligations of Citizenship and Demands of Faith*.

22. The phrase is Amy Gutmann's in "Religion and State in the United States: A Defense of Two-Way Protection," in Rosenblum, ed., *Obligations of Citizenship and Demands of State*, p. 149.

23. *Employment Division v. Smith* at 1605–6.

24. Alan Wolfe, *One Nation, After All* (New York: Viking, 1998)

25. Michael McConnell, "Accommodation of Religion: An Update and a Response to Critics," 60 *George Washington Law Review* 685 (1992) at739.

26. William Damon, *The Moral Child: Nurturing Children's Natural Moral Growth* (New York: Free Press, 1988).

5

CAN PUBLICLY FUNDED SCHOOLS LEGITIMATELY TEACH VALUES IN A CONSTITUTIONAL DEMOCRACY? A REPLY TO McCONNELL AND EISGRUBER

AMY GUTMANN

Can publicly funded schools legitimately teach values in a constitutional democracy? Michael McConnell argues that they cannot unless parents consent to the values that they teach. Parents should choose what values are taught to their children in schools that are publicly funded through vouchers. He argues that democratic values would be ill served by anything greater than a "minimal" degree of public control or regulation of publicly funded schooling. The "core idea" of McConnell's defense of school vouchers is that "families [i.e. parents] be permitted to choose among a range of educational options . . . using their fair share of educational funding to pay for the schooling they choose." Public funds for schooling, on this voucher view, are fairly distributed when parents control the use of public funds and the funds are not tied to anything more than the most minimal degree of public control of schools. On this view, democratic citizens are expected to fund schools but are prohibited from requiring anything more than "minimal" standards on schools.

Why is the only fair way of educating children in a constitutional democracy to give parents maximal control over what publicly funded schools teach? McConnell's major argument against anything other than maximizing parental choice through vouchers is that "educational pluralism would be a mirage if the result were to yoke all schools to a single set of prescriptive standards." On closer inspection, this argument against anything other than vouchers is little more than misleading rhetoric. The conception of democratic education opposed by McConnell explicitly opposes centralized public control, also explicitly opposes the imposition of a comprehensive set of prescriptive standards on all schools, and defends a mixed system of private and public schooling. Democratic education defends decentralized public control of publicly funded schools constrained by constitutional standards of non-repression and non-discrimination. *Pace* McConnell, decentralized and constitutionally constrained public control is quite compatible with educational pluralism. But it is also misleading to suggest (as McConnell does) that educational pluralism, however desirable, is the fundamental value or aim of publicly funded schooling.

Let's more carefully consider the claim that decentralized public control of publicly funded schools that are constitutionally constrained not to indoctrinate, discriminate, or prohibit private schooling makes educational pluralism a mirage. If every democratic majority required the schools that they publicly fund to teach literacy, numeracy, and toleration, and to practice racial, religious, and gender non-discrimination in admissions, educational pluralism would still result even within the publicly funded system. (Many private schools, which are not publicly funded, would teach religion, creating even more diversity within the mixed school system of a democracy.) Public schools would be different in the many ways that are consistent with teaching literacy, numeracy, toleration, and practicing racial, religious, and gender non-discrimination, and private schools would add to these differences in other ways, including the teaching of a particular religion (but not at public expense). Educational pluralism is not a mirage unless it is supposed that public regulation of schools means that all schools must abide by a single *comprehensive* set of prescriptive standards. But no one who defends democratic education argues for a *comprehensive* set of prescriptive standards that would make all schools the same.

No one who defends democratic education aims to maximize diversity among schools either. Is maximization of educational diversity the aim of voucher plans of the sort that McConnell would defend? How could maximization be the fundamental aim of publicly funded schooling? Most voucher proponents like McConnell distrust public standards beyond the minimum that they take to be right (and therefore required of all voucher schools). They therefore reject requirements like that of racial integration, whereby children from different backgrounds learn together as preparation for associating together as democratic citizens. McConnell opposes a public requirement that voucher schools practice racial, religious, or gender non-discrimination. Yet voucher schools would be publicly funded and accredited institutions. But if they do not have to serve some public purpose, such as ensuring that all children receive an education adequate for becoming free and equal citizens, it is a mystery why the public should fund them. Voucher proponents think that the public purposes of publicly funded schools must be minimal and whenever those purposes are controversial—as are many curricular standards along with race, gender, and religious non-discrimination—they would not publicly enforce those standards on schools but defer to parental choice in a marketplace of voucher funded schools.

According to McConnell and other voucher advocates, our present school system—in which only public schools are fully funded (while private schools are subsidized by tax exemption and smaller subsidies)—is unfair to parents who send their children to private schools. But is it unfair to parents who prefer sending their children to a private school that the public does not fund schools that teach Christianity, Judaism, Islam, or atheism as the truth, and give preference to children of parents who have the true religious faith or eschew all faith? (Many private schools do none of the above, but voucher proponents oppose the idea that public funding may justifiably be made conditional on private schools abiding by public standards of non-discrimination.) In a constitutional democracy that protects both religious freedom and the disestablishment of any and all religions, private religious schools (or schools that teach atheism) are permitted to discriminate on grounds of religion precisely because they are not publicly funded. Otherwise the state would be funding the teaching of religion (and atheism) and schools that practice discrimination in their admissions on grounds of religion (and atheism). Publicly funded schools, by contrast, must not teach religion or atheism and must not discriminate in admissions on the basis of religion or its lack thereof. Existing school systems in the United States are indeed unfair, but their unfairness is not the result of the public's refusal to fund any school preferred by any parent.

The unfairness of the status quo system of elementary and secondary schooling in the United States resides not in the absence of vouchers but in the presence of poverty and a school system that disadvantages the children of poor parents, who deserve better and are entitled to more. It is not only unfair but also unjust that some adults who are willing and able to work cannot find decent-paying jobs (which cover child care), cannot afford to live in safe neighborhoods, or in neighborhoods that provide good public schools for their children. A potentially far more effective proposal than educational vouchers, and one that is fully defensible on liberal democratic grounds, would be for our democracy to support a real safety net for everyone, including decent-paying work, good child care, public schools, and health care. When democracy falls short of supporting a real safety net, the question arises as to whether it should support vouchers as a second-best response to the far broader problem of unfairness that cannot be resolved as long as some people are poor through no fault of their own.

One problem with defending vouchers as a second-best response to the problem of unfairness to poor children born of poverty is that the logic of voucher proposals—and the aim of many proponents—is equal public financing of private and public schools, not a guarantee of good schooling for poor children. Voucher advocates like McConnell argue that it is unfair that *any* parents—even the richest—should have to pay more to send their children to private schools than they would to send their child to a comparably costly public school. The argument is that parents whose preferences tend toward private schools are double-taxed. The underlying idea of fairness here is that (in any given school district) the same tax dollars should follow all children—not just poor or otherwise disadvantaged children—to private or public schools. The publicly funded private schools, however, would not be publicly governed or subject to public standards (other than the most minimal ones), while the public schools would be. The logic of vouchers is to subsidize the choice of all parents, whether financially needy or not, to send their children to any school, whether that school teaches a high level of literacy or numeracy, or racial, religious, or gender discrimination, or not. If public funding of schools for rich and poor parents alike is the voucher proponents' aim, then the controversy is not about achieving parity between rich and poor but, rather, about whether private schools, in fairness to the rich more than the poor, must be publicly funded.

Should private schools be publicly funded? John Chubb and Terry Moe, two of the most prominent academic defenders of vouchers, put the positive case most straightforwardly: "Choice *is* a panacea." A voucher plan, they argue, "has the capacity *all by itself* to bring about the kind of transformation that, for years, reformers have been seeking to engineer in myriad other ways." Vouchers uniquely have this capacity, they say, because competition in a free market is the only way of really improving the quality of just about anything people want in the world, and parents want better schools for their children. They don't want to depend on state bureaucracies, which are surely not the best way of satisfying consumer demand. A case in point, which I had the pleasure of sampling, was the difference between the old state-run restaurants and the new private ones in Prague, shortly after the collapse of communism. (The latter all publicly displayed signs that proclaimed the same name: "Private Restaurant.") Little doubt about it: Market choice in restaurants *is* a panacea for improving the quality of cuisine—or at least close enough to a panacea not to quibble. Most arguments for disestablishing schooling—by which voucher advocates mean minimizing all political controls whether they be federal and state constitutional constraints or local public oversight—trade on this analogy between disestablishment of state control over the economy and disestablishment of state control over schooling.

Is there no significant difference between the challenge of improving schools in Chicago and improving restaurants in post-communist Prague? Not according to the fundamentals of the libertarian philosophy of Milton Friedman, who can be credited with getting the voucher ball rolling in this country. In *Capitalism and Freedom*, Friedman compared schools and restaurants. Beyond funding school vouchers, the sole role of government in education, he argued, should be to inspect schools to assure that they meet minimal curricular standards "much as it now inspects restaurants to assure that they maintain minimum sanitary standards." The analogy with restaurants, which drives the market model, reveals more than most people who defend vouchers acknowledge, at least publicly. If the public's interest in schools is analogous to its interest in restaurants, then citizens have no obligation to pay for other people's children to attend schools any more than we have a public obligation to pick up other people's restaurant tabs. At least as troubling from the perspective of a constitutional democracy, the analogy suggests that the public has no obligation to ensure that schools are desegregated or that they teach to high standards, rather than just minimal ones. We do not have a public obligation to dine at a communal table together or to eat good food.

Unlike restaurants, primary and secondary schools serve public purposes as well as private ones and fulfill public obligations to children. Citizens should ensure that all children—regardless of their socioeconomic status, gender, race, ethnicity, or religion—receive an education that prepares them for effectively exercising their rights and responsibilities as future citizens. Ardent advocates of parental choice and market control downplay the public purposes of schooling, and their downplaying is not accidental. It coincides with their elevation of consumer sovereignty to a voracious value: the market should deliver whatever the consumers of its goods want. The problems with applying the market model to vouchers, however, are enormous. First, the market model is based on consumer sovereignty, but parents are not the consumers of education. Children are. But not even the most ardent advocates of the market model want to argue that children's preferences are the ones that should be counted. Second, the market model is based on the idea that "he who pays the piper picks the tune." Democratic citizens, not parents, pay the piper. If the tune that democratic citizens pick is that schools should serve public purposes, then the market model completely collapses into a defense of democratic control over publicly funded schooling. Ironically, if the market model takes any side in this controversy, it supports public control over schools. But its applicability is extremely attenuated when the education and well-being of children are concerned.

Nothing I have said in criticism of the philosophy behind vouchers is a defense of the status quo school system that is now in place in the United States or a defense of public control of schools regardless of whether that control is consistent with providing a good education to all children. The question that needs to be answered by anyone who is critical of the status quo—which everyone has reason to be—is how a democratic society can deliver on its promise to provide all children with an education adequate to enjoying the freedoms and opportunities of a free and equal citizen. The admirable impetus behind means-tested voucher programs is a commitment to finding some way to deliver a decent education to the most disadvantaged students when public schools are failing them. The problem is that the results of the few voucher programs in existence lend no support to the claim that school choice by itself is a good way of significantly improving the education of a sizable proportion of students at risk, let alone a panacea. The results after three years of the private-public school voucher experiment in Milwaukee, which targets the least advantaged students in the city, show modest improvements in the mathematics test scores of voucher school students but no improvement in their English test scores over non-voucher-school students. These educational improvements are more likely attributable to smaller class size than to competition or private control of schools, according to the analysis of economist Cecilia Rouse. This finding is reinforced by the Project STAR experiment in Tennessee, where 11,600 students were randomly assigned to either small or regular-size classes within public schools. The analysis of this experiment by Alan B. Krueger and Diane M. Whitmore found that small class size significantly increased educational achievement, especially among disadvantaged minority students, and narrowed the black-white gap in college-test taking by 54 percent. These preliminary findings offer another reason to doubt the claim that parental choice in schooling is the key to improving schooling, let alone the panacea.

Is increasing parental choice important at all? The perspective of *Democratic Education* along with the best empirical evidence we now have suggests that it is, but that it is not anything close to a panacea. The most defensible way of increasing competition among schools is to give parents good choices for their children among public schools. To give parents good choices, some new public schools need to be created and old schools reformed, often by breaking them up into smaller, more educationally responsive units with smaller class sizes. To create smaller class sizes, more classrooms need to be built and more high-quality teachers who know their subject matter need to be hired. There is no good evidence that private schools—any more than public ones—can teach well without highly qualified teachers and small class size. The need for these reforms as a means of providing not just more but better choices for parents is therefore independent of whether schools are privately or publicly controlled.

There is also something to be said on behalf of a voucher plan that serves some disadvantaged students better than the status quo. Nobody can tell an African-American inner-city parent who wants the chance to send her child to a better public school that her reasons are selfish, sectarian, or illegitimate. Her reasons are at least as good as the ones that lead her middle-class counterpart to move into a better school district, often in the suburbs. But no good evidence exists to support the claim that private school choice is the best available means for improving schools for children at risk. Acting together to change public school systems, citizens have found effective ways of improving public schools *and* of giving parents choice among them, as demonstrated for example by the school system of Cambridge, Massachusetts, which years ago instituted a very effective program of public school choice. The most defensible system of public school choice would not limit the choices open to parents of disadvantaged inner-city students to schools in the inner city. The boundaries between city and contiguous suburbs are otherwise porous, and suburbanites draw heavily and asymmetrically upon the city's resources.

But public school choice is not an adequate antidote to what is ailing status quo systems of schooling in the United States. There is in fact no single antidote for ailing schools. Rather there are many means to improving schools, no one of which is sufficient (and there are even more means of creating and maintaining bad schools). Pursuing many means together—what some have called "systemic reform"—is far more promising than relying on a single remedy, whether it be public or private school choice. Some of the most promising, mutually reinforcing means include decreasing class size, increasing pre-school programs, setting universally high standards, engaging students in cooperative learning exercises, empowering principals and teachers to innovate, increasing social services offered to students and their families, and increasing incentives for the ablest college students to enter the teaching profession, and in particular to teach in inner-city schools. The list could be longer, but it cannot be formulaic. When it comes to the nitty-gritty questions of how to improve the status quo in the direction of educating all children so that they can enjoy the liberties and opportunities of citizenship in a democratic society, there is no mantra—whether of parental choice or democratic control—that will substitute for our asking how well schools are educating children. Schools educate not only by what and how they teach but also by whom they teach together in classrooms. We therefore need to ask: Do schools educate children from many backgrounds together in classrooms to a high level of literacy, numeracy, economic opportunity, and mutual respect for one another as equal citizens?

The privatizing impulse behind vouchers threatens to push democratic politics toward even less public concern about educating the children in our society who are most at risk of being left far behind, and toward a narrowing of our vision of a good education for all children. The narrowing of the vision is inevitable if good schools become identified with whatever market choice produces by way of association among children within schools. Association among children of different backgrounds within schools is an important part of the promise of a democratic education. Reasonable hope for improving schools rests on employing the link between public funding and public oversight as a means of fulfilling a democratic obligation to all children to offer a high-quality, socially integrated education. The political will of citizens is necessary to improve schools. This is another reason why we should be wary of perspectives that threaten to erode public support for public schools by considering schooling a private concern of parents (as if children were their parents' property). Or that present themselves as simple substitutes for the hard work of judging schools on their educational merits.

The voucher perspective is plagued by all of these problems. No one can honestly offer most inner-city parents hope for their children without also offering them better public schools with smaller classes, stronger principals, more dedicated teachers, more challenging curricula, and whatever else it takes to create a good school. Good schools must be created before parents can choose them. There is no evidence that vouchers will produce good schools for the majority of children who need them most.

Voucher proponents fall back on the argument that their proposals avoid the need to reach public agreement on what constitutes a good education, and therefore are more consistent with a pluralist perspective on public policy. Is this so? For it to be so, voucher proponents would need to deny that a constitutional democracy depends on public action to create good schools for all children, and also to deny that the passage of voucher proposals requires public action. It is therefore all the more misleading to suggest that only a public school system depends on public agreement on what constitutes a good use of public funds. Voucher systems also depend on public agreement, but they are distinctive in insisting that public funds not be tied to public standards, except the most minimal standards of literacy and numeracy. The minimal standards are left largely undefined—perhaps because to define them would immediately make it clear that requiring any specific set of minimal standards (and prohibiting any additional requirements) is no less controversial and no less in need of a public defense than a non-minimalist perspective of what democracies should afford all children by way of schooling.

Advocates of vouchers also misleadingly suggest that what is at stake in accepting or rejecting a voucher plan is educational pluralism versus educational monism. This claim is misleading in many ways. First, the public value of *educational* pluralism is surely not diversity for its own sake. *Educational* pluralism in schools will be of *educational* value—and worthy of public funding—if and only if the schools teach students well, and are therefore worthy of public support. What is at issue between voucher advocates and their critics, therefore, is whether unregulated schools would be worthy of public funding and accreditation simply by virtue of the fact that they are chosen by parents. What is not at issue is the idea—supported by both sides—that some substantial degree of diversity among schools is valuable to support educational innovation and to satisfy the diverse educational needs of students. Second, the distinctive problem that voucher advocates face, ironically, is that they cannot consistently say that educational diversity is a public value for these reasons unless individual parents find it so for these reasons. Voucher advocates engage in double-talk when they at once deny that there are any controversial public values that need to be acted upon in education and they claim that diversity is the paramount public value. Third, they also undermine any credible sense in which diversity in education is a value if they fail to provide any standards for what counts as "educational" pluralism, as distinct from whatever schools any unregulated market will support.

Democratic Education defends the kind of educational pluralism that takes education seriously. Maximizing diversity with minimal regard for educational content is not the aim of any defensible alternative to the status quo of schooling in the United States, nor is maximizing diversity among schools a defensible primary aim of publicly funded schooling in any democracy. It's possible that more diversity in schools could be achieved, for example, by lifting any restrictions on whether publicly funded schools discriminate on grounds of race, religion, and gender. Greater pluralism of this kind is surely not what democracies today should seek because it would come at a perilously high cost for democracy, the cost of disestablishing non-discrimination as a democratic standard for publicly funded schooling. We could achieve even greater pluralism at the cost of disestablishing publicly funded schooling altogether. This reductio ad absurdum is where we would be led if we followed the logic of McConnell's rhetorical criticisms of the educational philosophies that he opposes. He writes that people who defend democratic control of education think they "know what principles are best for democracy," and concludes that to avoid such arrogance "maybe we are ready for educational disestablishment." The logic of his accusation is that citizens should not publicly defend the principles that they believe are best for democracy.

But McConnell of course thinks that he knows what degree of democratic control over schools is best for democracy. Oddly enough, only the principles that he thinks are best for democracy—voucher principles—escape being tarred by his rhetorical brush of accusing those with whom he disagrees of arrogantly knowing what principles are best for democracy. If this is more than misleading rhetoric designed to make everyone who defends standards other than McConnell's seem arrogant, then it can only be an argument whose logic would prevent everyone—including McConnell—from saying that they think they know what is better or worse with regard to education in a democracy. If taken seriously, the logic of denying that anyone knows (with any degree of likelihood) what is better or worse with regard to schooling would disestablish publicly funded schooling for all children in a constitutional democracy. The logic of McConnell's argument turns out to be the following: Citizens would be arrogant to think that they can know what is better and worse with regard to schooling. They therefore would be either foolish or frivolous to support public funding of schooling. The defense of *public* funding of schooling is after all not that it is good for me or my child, but that it is good for all children because they are all future democratic citizens who should be able to benefit from an education that enables them to enjoy the rights and to bear the responsibilities of living in a constitutional democracy as free and equal individuals.

Christopher Eisgruber asks how liberal democracies can teach values. Unlike McConnell, Eisgruber is not skeptical—or even selectively skeptical—that there are better and worse ways of answering such questions. Instead, he offers a distinctive and quite constructive argument that is worthy of more attention than anyone has yet given it, especially in the specific context of considering the desiderata of democratic education. Eisgruber's argument is in the spirit of seeking an economy of moral disagreement among people who disagree on some basic principles. The spirit of civic magnanimity that he pursues in the context of democratic education is sorely needed—and too often lacking—in the day-to-day workings of American democracy. It is also often lacking in intellectual disputes where theorists sharpen their differences in intellectual debate rather than explore common ground, which is what Eisgruber explores in his commentary on the *Mozert* case. In the course of doing so, however, Eisgruber sharpens his differences with those of us who think that basic principles—and not only or even primarily pragmatic considerations—divide people in specific public controversies over teaching values, such as the *Mozert* case.

Sharpening differences when they are real is an invaluable part of intellectual engagement. I will therefore do so in reply. But nothing I say by way of criticism undermines the important contribution Eisgruber makes by asking whether there is neglected common ground to be found between people who disagree on basic principles. He often succeeds in showing that there is, or at least that there can be. But he also at least as often overestimates the common ground. He gives a pragmatic liberal perspective more credit in claiming common ground than is warranted by any facts that he cites (or than I can produce in his favor). Controversial claims on behalf of his liberal perspective therefore do more work than he admits. His criticism of invoking principles of democratic education in controversies like *Mozert*—even if they are right, they are unnecessarily divisive since everyone can converge on pragmatic liberal considerations—does not succeed.

Eisgruber's major claim is that to answer the question "How can liberal democracies teach values?" we need not resolve the debate between incompatible and controversial philosophical positions like "civic minimalism" and "democratic education." Instead, he argues that answering this question "turns upon pragmatic questions about how to ensure that school bureaucrats will faithfully serve goals which are shared by civic minimalists and defenders of democratic education alike." The arguments and evidence Eisgruber offers support only a more modest claim, which is that pragmatic claims (that are non-philosophical and can be agreed upon by both sides to the dispute) are relevant to settling the dispute. He falls far short of actually showing that pragmatic claims can settle even the *Mozert* case, which he uses to illustrate the force of his argument. He fails for two reasons. First, interpretations of facts are often as controversial as interpretations of values, and therefore pragmatism that focuses on facts rather than values cannot promise to resolve disputes among people who also disagree on basic values. Second, several of the "facts" that Eisgruber cites as pragmatic considerations—such as what teaching literacy entails—are actually philosophical in just the sense that Eisgruber wants to avoid, but cannot. Eisgruber's claims about literacy are no less controversial to the civic minimalist side in the *Mozert* case than the explicitly philosophical principles that I offer.

Eisgruber's account of how to teach values in a liberal democracy would not be problematic were it not for the fact that he defends it as an alternative to a philosophical account, and therefore as a way of avoiding the kinds of controversial claims that he is in fact making, for example, on behalf of what teaching literacy entails. Eisgruber says he is speaking only pragmatically. But he is speaking philosophically while denying that he is. He therefore claims that his position transcends the philosophical dispute between civic minimalists and defenders of democratic education. But it actually takes the side of defenders of democratic education while denying that it is taking a philosophical side in the dispute.

Let's revisit the *Mozert* case with Eisgruber's pragmatic claims in mind. One assigned story in the required reading text for third graders in Hawkins County schools reads in part: "Jim cooks. Jim has fun." Eisgruber writes:

> Apparently, both the parents and the school district assumed that "Jim Cooks" is a radically subversive story. They took for granted that the story had the power to disrupt or transform students' views about gender roles. But that shared premise seems fanciful. Is there really some sub-culture within the United States in which men never cook?

Eisgruber's questionable claims here (and elsewhere) make his conclusion that the case can be resolved on pragmatic grounds seem far easier than the facts of the case permit. First, the school district did not claim that "Jim Cooks" is a radically subversive

story. It claimed quite the reverse, that it was eminently reasonable for public schools to expect children to read a story about
boys cooking since reading the story is not tantamount to indoctrinating boys into cooking, let alone into reversing the gender
roles prescribed in the Bible. Similarly, the school district argued
that it was reasonable to expect children to read the many other
kinds of stories to which the *Mozert* parents objected. These included an excerpt from Anne Frank's diary in which she writes
that perhaps non-orthodox belief in God is better than no belief
at all, and a passage describing a central idea of the Renaissance
as belief in the dignity and worth of human beings. In all these
(and other) excerpts, one of the school district's strongest positions was that it was not indoctrinating children into believing
what the *Mozert* parents claimed the stories indoctrinated their
children into believing. The Mozert parents insisted that their
children not be assigned any stories to which they objected *without an explicit disclaimer attached to the story that what it said was
false and what the parents believed was true.* It is far harder to find
common ground here that is acceptable to both sides than Eisgruber suggests. This is not to say that it is harder to find a publicly
justifiable position here, but a publicly justifiable position
should not be confused with one that would in fact satisfy the
claims of both sides. When Eisgruber asks, "Is there really some
sub-culture within the United States in which men never cook?"
I wonder whether the answer is as obviously "no" as he seems to
think it is.

Eisgruber then suggests that civic minimalists could not object
to assignment of the following passage to public school children:
"Ruth is a famous judge. Martin is her husband. Martin likes to
cook. Martin cooks often." But civic minimalists object to the assignment of "Jim Cooks" not in their own name but in the name
of parents like Robert Mozert who sincerely say that it violates
their religious principles to assign texts that portray people in incorrect gender roles without telling their children that these are
incorrect gender roles. That objection applies as much to Martin
and Ruth Bader Ginsberg as it does to Jim. The objection may
seem wild and crazy to many of us, but that doesn't make it any
less real. To counter the objection, we cannot help but rely upon
a position that takes philosophical sides in this dispute. Nor can

we help but rely on matters of empirical judgment. The dispute in this sense is *both* pragmatic and philosophical, but that does not make it any easier to resolve in a way that is consistent with the philosophical claims of both sides.

A second argument that Eisgruber offers in defense of convergence between defenders of civic minimalism and democratic education is that surely school districts do not need to assign particular works of fiction such as "Jim Cooks" to introduce children to the idea that boys and girls in a liberal democracy are not required by the liberal democracy to occupy specific, biblically assigned gender roles. As Eisgruber writes: "it is discomforting to think that democratic citizenship depends crucially upon whether states can force particular fictions upon children." But the school district did not at any stage argue—nor would it be plausible to argue—that it had to assign these specific texts. It argued something far more defensible and far ranging in its applicability. It argued that if the Court compelled school districts to tailor reading assignments and classroom arrangements to every parents' sincere religious convictions, which is the constitutional principle at stake in the *Mozert* case, it could not teach boys and girls from the same texts and in the same classroom regardless of their religious backgrounds. Convergence is also absent here between the defenders of civic minimalism and democratic education. Civic minimalists want public schools to be forced by courts to tailor their curricula and their classroom practices to parental preferences. The more difficult courts make it for public schooling to continue, the better, because this could be another way to open the door to the creation of a voucher program, which many civic minimalists claim is not only constitutionally permissible but constitutionally required on grounds of the religious freedom of parents, which they assume give parents near-exclusive educational authority over their children.

A third argument in defense of convergence is that even defenders of democratic education would decide the *Mozert* case against the school district if it refused to assign different basic reading texts "out of sheer bureaucratic indifference or even discriminatory animus." In other words, were the facts different in the *Mozert* case, then defenders of democratic education and civic minimalists could converge. I agree. Why? Because defenders of

democratic education recognize the desirability in a liberal constitutional democracy for "a [judicial] doctrine which protects individuals against the irresponsible exercise of power by citizens
and school officials but which simultaneously respects the discretion of citizens and responsible officials to make the ultimate
judgment about contestable pedagogical issues." Under the
counterfactual conditions that Eisgruber imagines, in which the
school district refuses to assign alternative texts out of sheer arbi-
trariness or discriminatory animus, "a judge could subscribe to
the position that Gutmann calls democratic education (or any
other position which likewise affirms the authority of the community to teach civic values) and simultaneously rule in Robert Mozert's favor." I concur that convergence is possible, but notice how
narrowly circumscribed the circumstances are under which convergence would actually occur.

It is telling that although Eisgruber chooses the *Mozert* case to
illustrate the possibility of convergence, the circumstances of
convergence do not actually obtain even in this narrowly circumscribed case, the very one that he chooses to pursue the logic of
convergence. Eisgruber's analysis of the actual *Mozert* case does
not support his conclusion that "the crucial issues in *Mozert* are
not issues about the scope of parental autonomy or community
authority but, rather, more pragmatic issues about whether and
how judges can improve the quality of decision making by school
officials." Quite the contrary, the *Mozert* case illustrates that civic
minimalism and democratic education diverge on important *actual* cases (as *Democratic Education* suggests). Although *Democratic
Education* does not suggest that these two conceptions could
never converge in their conclusions, it does demonstrate why
they diverged in the *Mozert* case, which is a seminal case for civic
education precisely because the *Mozert* parents pose such a broad
challenge to the assignment by public schools of even basic reading texts to their children. Combining the basic principles of
democratic education with the actual circumstances of the *Mozert*
case yields the opposite conclusion from that reached by civic
minimalists, and it reaches the opposite conclusion because civic
minimalists cede decision-making authority to parents rather
than to public schools even in cases where public schools are not
acting arbitrarily or with discriminatory animus. Upon closer

analysis, Eisgruber's arguments undermine his claim that the crucial issues in *Mozert* are not about the scope of parental autonomy or community authority but, rather, are pragmatic, where pragmatic means non-philosophical (or not dependent on philosophical differences as between claims about parental or community authority). Given the actual circumstances of the case, a crucial issue turns out to be precisely the scope of parental autonomy versus community authority.

A central problem with Eisgruber's argument is that though he speaks as if his pragmatic approach does not depend on any controversial philosophical position, upon closer analysis, it does. (This is not to say that the philosophical position *should* be controversial, only that it *is*.) For liberals, to teach literacy without teaching critical reading and thinking skills is to indoctrinate. But literacy is often understood, as it is by one side in the *Mozert* case, in a far more minimal sense that does not require the teaching of critical reading and thinking skills. People who are literate in this more minimal sense can read and interpret what they have read as they were taught to do so (say, by rote or by the word of a religious authority that is not to be questioned). These competing understandings of literacy are all morally loaded, as any understanding will be. Eisgruber should therefore recognize that the liberal perspective that he is defending is not distinctively "pragmatic" (as contrasted to controversially philosophical). And there is nothing wrong—or in any way less worthy of public defense—with its being so! Many seminal public controversies and court cases, like *Mozert*, pit people against each other who disagree about understandings as basic as what counts as literacy. When a view that people take for granted is challenged at its foundation, as it is in the *Mozert* case, commentators cannot avoid invoking claims that are controversial among at least some parties to the dispute. This does not make our claims any less justifiable on democratic grounds than they would be simply by virtue of being less controversial.

Eisgruber raises a related point that is well worth pursuing about how to teach liberal democratic values, which is independent of his claims about pragmatic convergence. Any conception of democratic education needs "a supplemental theory about how and when judges should intervene to protect individuals against abuses of discretion by school officials." He suggests that "[t]he content of that supplemental theory will depend upon whether one trusts judges to do a good job ferreting out bad behavior by bureaucrats. People who agree about the merits of democratic education (or civic minimalism) can disagree quite sharply about that question of judicial competence." The supplemental theory will be largely empirical, since it will depend in good part on a comparative evaluation of judicial competence in such cases compared to the competence of alternative decision-making authorities. We should recognize that what constitutes "competence," however, is not a purely empirical question. In the absence of more systematic evidence, let alone a real "theory" of comparative judicial competence, neither theorists nor actual decision makers can be expected to rely heavily on this consideration in coming to conclusions about controversial cases. But the more that we learn about comparative judicial competence in different kinds of cases, the more defensible our conclusions about judicial intervention can be.

I have saved for last by far the most pointed question that Eisgruber asks of a defender of democratic education. "Is it reasonable to believe," he asks, "that the liberal democratic state's capacity to teach values will depend upon whether it has the authority to assign particular texts?" This question is ambiguous between two importantly different interpretations (which any person who is well educated by Eisgruber's standards should be able to discern). On the first interpretation, the question asks whether the capacity to teach values in a public school setting requires the authority to assign one and only one particular set of texts. The answer to this question is clearly no. (And that's the answer Eisgruber is seeking.) On the second interpretation, however, the question asks whether the capacity to teach values in a public school setting requires the authority to assign some particular set of texts, i.e. the authority to pick some reasonable set of texts and not be required by another authority to substitute other texts whenever any parent objects on conscientious grounds to the selected texts. The answer to this question is no less clearly yes.

What follows is that while it does not matter whether a public school is free to assign the particular story "Jim Cooks," it does matter that it is free to assign some set of textbooks to be read by all children in a particular classroom. Treating children as equals in the classroom means, among other things, not segregating them by their parents' religious beliefs. Yet that is precisely what would need to be done if public schools were denied the constitutional authority to assign (non-repressive and non-discriminatory) reading texts to a class of children. And if public schools are denied this authority, by what principle would they not also be denied the authority to teach boys and girls together as equals, or children of different colors, or sexual orientations, or religions together as equals if their parents objected on grounds of sincere conviction? By a similar argument to the one that claims that no particular texts are necessary to teach values, one can argue that no single pedagogical method—including that of racial, gender, and religious integration—is absolutely necessary to teach liberal democratic values. Some children who are taught in segregated classrooms turn out to be as tolerant as some who are taught in integrated classrooms. There are (almost) always at least two ways of teaching a single value (and many more ways of not doing so). The claim that most liberal democratic values are better taught by classroom practices than by textbooks is probably true, but the extent and limits of public authority over both classroom practices and textbooks stand or fall on the same sorts of arguments. And those arguments, as it turns out, often cannot bypass basic principles.

PART II

NEUTRALITY, INDIVIDUAL AUTONOMY, AND EDUCATIONAL REFORM

6

CIVIC EDUCATION AND ETHICAL SUBSERVIENCE: FROM *MOZERT* TO *SANTA FE* AND BEYOND

JOHN TOMASI

How Spillovers Threaten Legitimacy

Liberal regimes shape the ethical outlooks of their citizens, deeply and relentlessly influencing even their most personal commitments over time. This idea, much resisted by liberals only a decade ago, has become a mantra of contemporary political theory. Rawls describes his political liberalism as committed to neutrality of aim but abandons any ambition to neutrality of effect as sociologically "impracticable." Galston likens the ethical culture generated by liberal politics to a broad current in a river, a current which allows human vessels considerable freedom of movement but encourages them all in a certain individualizing direction nonetheless. Macedo describes the cultural spillovers from liberal public norms as a system of unequal psychological taxation, with citizens of faith typically paying at the higher rates.[1]

But in the headlong rush of contemporary liberals to "come clean" about the unavoidable, albeit unintended, cultural side effects of liberal politics, a crucial liberal commitment is in danger of being lost. This is the commitment to legitimacy.

There is currently much debate as to the nature of political legitimacy, in particular regarding the role of its attitudinal component, legitimacy's relation (if any) to the idea of political obligation, about whether legitimacy is a property of governments or of states, and even about the relation of legitimacy to the ideal of political justification itself.[2] For my purposes, it is enough to bypass those disputes about the precise nature of the liberal legitimacy requirement and proceed instead from a definition about the conditions of its fulfillment. Let's say that a liberal state is *just* insofar as democratic self-rule honors basic rights and realizes a fair distribution of benefits and burdens among citizens. A liberal state is *legitimate*, by contrast, insofar as the authority of the state elicits the free assent of many citizens for the right reasons.[3] Liberals, through their concern for legitimacy, are concerned that assent to the (just) political order be given as *widely* as possible among the citizenry and as *freely* as possible.

Unintended cultural spillovers may cause problems for this legitimacy condition. Of course, the valence of spillovers is indeterminate and, in a diverse society, spillovers may well pose different kinds of threats with respect to different kinds of citizens. But the crucial point is that spillovers may threaten legitimacy on both dimensions I just mentioned—regarding the breadth, and the freedom, of assent.

First, the threat of spillovers may *alienate* certain groups of citizens, especially otherwise admissible groups on the society's cultural margins. The bare threat of spillover effects—absent any liberal account of how unavoidable spillovers might be counteracted and absorbed—may disaffect people who might otherwise have signed on.[4] The fewer the citizens who can be brought on freely, the larger the class of those labeled "politically unreasonable" and thus the less stable the arrangement as a whole. Even within the domain of the politically reasonable, the problem of unaddressed spillovers may weaken citizens' allegiance to the regime, decreasing the depth by which they affirm the regime as their own, again with instability the result.

Second is a threat to legitimacy from a different direction: spillovers threaten to *colonize* mainstream reasonable citizens. The fact of unintended spillovers can weaken the sense in which people's assent (and that eventually to be given by their children) can be said to be given freely. If liberal political institutions do gradually though unintentionally remake even the nonpublic aspects of the liberal social world in their own image, people may well give their assent to liberal political arrangements with ever more enthusiasm. But that does not necessarily show that they are giving their assent in the way that legitimacy requires—that is, as freely as possible.

In both kinds of cases, of alienation and of colonization, the impossibility of achieving complete neutrality of effect sets a kind of floor as to how completely these concerns about spillovers can be answered. Regarding the threat of alienation: some reasonable groups will always lose out, and this prospect may always dissuade some from freely entering and weaken the commitment of some others. Regarding colonization: young people's development of their sense of justice can never be completely free, if such an ideal is even logically coherent. Complete neutrality of effect is indeed impracticable. But those admissions do not excuse liberals from seeking out ways to *minimize* the unintended effects of political spillovers so far as liberal justice allows. This is a requirement of legitimacy.

In this essay I wish to focus on perhaps the most important area of spillover concern: unintended spillovers from liberal programs of civic education.[5] Of the two threats to legitimacy I just mentioned, for reasons of space I shall concentrate on the threat of alienation. Most debates about civic education focus on the requirements of liberal justice, and especially the question of whether those requirements vary on ethical and political understandings of liberalism. Even those few theorists, Harry Brighouse prominent among them, who have considered questions of legitimacy have done so only in terms of concerns about legitimacy that arise directly from the programs of civic education that liberals, variously, intentionally pursue—that is, threats to legitimacy from the educational effects that liberals, as such, intend. My approach is different. I wish to explore the implications of the requirement that liberals seek methods to counteract or minimize threats to legitimacy that arise *indirectly*—that is, through the wider effects of their educational regimes which liberals, as such, do not intend. In the realm of schooling, liberals must become aggressive *tax flatteners*—even while acknowledging that their world may never be one of completely flat taxes.

THE DERIVATIVE PARADIGM

Most debates about liberal civic education proceed from the assumption that civic education concerns fitting children for the role they are to play as *public* persons. In particular, the requirements of civic education are understood to be largely derivative from the requirements of the shared public project of pursuing justice. Children are to be fitted to participate in a social project which honors basic rights and seeks to realize a fair distribution of burdens and benefits among their fellow citizens. This approach sees a list of so-called "liberal virtues" as derivable in advance from established liberal public values. I shall call this the derivative paradigm. Within it, debates about civic education are typically limited to conflicting accounts of what precisely is involved in teaching children about what rights they have and about the moral ideas on which those rights are grounded.

With the terms of debate set up this way, civic education has proven one of the most hotly contested terrains on which proponents of political liberalism have sought to differentiate their view from the various forms of ethical or comprehensive liberalism they seek to displace. Political liberals claim that civic education reveals the great practical divergence between comprehensive and political liberalisms. According to Rawls, "The [comprehensive] liberalisms of Kant and Mill may lead to requirements designed to foster the values of autonomy and individuality as ideals to govern much if not all of life." But political liberalism requires merely the skills needed for people to understand and reason about shared political values. Compared to the civic education requirements of comprehensive liberalism, Rawls concludes, "political liberalism has a different aim and requires far less" (1993 199).

This claim is controversial. Amy Gutmann argues that the civic educational requirements of the most plausible versions of political and of comprehensive liberalism in practice converge: "most (if not all) of the same skills that are necessary and sufficient for educating children for citizenship in a liberal democracy are those that are necessary and sufficient for educating children to deliberate about their way of life, more generally (and less politically) speaking."[6]

Eamonn Callan makes a similar argument and draws an even more dramatic conclusion.[7] Among the ideas that a political liberal education must include is a recognition of the "burdens of judgment." But, Callan argues, "the psychological attributes that constitute an active acceptance of the burdens of judgment, such as the capacity and inclination to subject received ethical ideas to critical scrutiny, also constitute a recognizable ideal of ethical autonomy" (21).[8] The requirements of civic education, far from showing how political and comprehensive conceptions of liberalism diverge, reveal that political liberalism is merely a species of comprehensive liberalism. "The partition Rawls labors to erect between ethical and political liberalism has collapsed" (22).

I think Gutmann and Callan have a point.[9] So long as we think of citizenship within the derivative paradigm, the practical implications of political and of comprehensive civic education do show that those two metatheoretical views converge in significant ways. But what if we conceive of civic education as bound to take up problems not only about justice but also about legitimacy—including the unintended threats of citizen alienation that I earlier described? I wish to propose an approach to civic education which includes these broader, legitimacy-directed issues. I shall call this a "substantive" approach in order to distinguish it from the familiar justice-based, derivative approach. If we think of liberal citizenship in a broader, more substantive way, then civic education may indeed demonstrate the great divergence between comprehensive and political liberalism after all. This is not because political liberal civic education typically requires less than do forms of ethical liberalism (as the early pioneers of political liberalism suggest). It is because education for political liberal citizenship requires *far more*.

From the substantive perspective, education for liberal citizenship involves teaching children not merely the skills and attitudes needed for them to grasp the impersonal perspective of justice and its attendant political ideas. Education must also prepare each citizen to play her socially constructive role in making her society maximally just *and legitimate*. A liberal society succeeds in the latter goal when it is organized in ways that make it maximally worthy of citizens' long-term devotion, given the public constraints of justice. To play their roles well in that project, political liberal citizens need to appreciate the *fit* between the norms of public reason and whatever politically reasonable views of moral personality they happen to affirm. In doing this they must develop skills beyond those needed to see how their nonpublic views support their public ones. They also need to consider how their affirmation of the public norms, if once they give it, can lend support to the particular nonpublic view each holds dear. For this, each of them needs the information and skills required for the art of living their nonpublic lives in a way that is rewarding to each over time, given the particular characteristics of the political institutions that frame their social world.

Political liberals have abandoned the philosophical hope of producing uniformity of opinion about the nature of (nonpublic) moral personality. So the fit political liberals want children to consider is that between public reason and the more local, internal understandings of value particular to the various politically reasonable narrative traditions each citizen will inhabit—without assuming that those nonpublic narratives must necessarily all be written with the pen of individual autonomy or critical self-reflection. Each person who grows up in a liberal society needs to be told not merely that she has rights, or merely given some account of the grounding of those rights. Much more, her program of civic education must explicitly invite her to consider the *meaning* of her rights within the context of her own life, and to consider the strand of her full set of interests that the imperatives picked out from that perspective protect. She needs to be encouraged to consider those other aspects of her self and her interests that her own rights—if exercised obtusely or without skill—can erode or corrupt from her own eudaemonistic perspective.

What would it mean, in a diverse society, to educate people about the meaning of their political autonomy? Such a civic education program might begin by telling future citizens that they are entering a highly risky form of human living-together. In a successful liberal society, people are bound together as citizens through the way they interpret and exercise their individual freedoms and not just through their performance of public duties.

The success of the liberal social project is measured ultimately through the internal evaluations of each person concerning the quality and value of the life he leads given his commitment to social justice. Those evaluations of quality and value are determined directly by the degree of skill, or lack thereof, with which each individual person (along with the others around him) manipulates the binding mechanism that liberal societies entrust to each of their members. That binding mechanism—the system of ligaments that holds a liberal society together and allows it to function—is found in the flexibility in the exercise of every rights claim that abstract principles of justice pick out. Rights and the other claims set out by public reason are not merely protective devices but communicative ones. They can be used to communicate good will, one's understanding of degrees of commitment so far achieved, and the nature of one's hope for eudaemonistic connections yet to come. In liberal societies, it is through their rights as much as or more than through their duties that people build their social worlds.[10] Future citizens, as such, need to be told explicitly about this distinctively liberal mechanism of social construction. They need to be brought to understand that the success of the experiment that a free society represents depends ultimately *on each of them*, and on the attitudes each develops regarding the claims that the political conception of justice sets out.

But liberal civic education, from the substantive perspective, would require more even than teaching children about the abstract mechanism by which interpersonal virtues are constructed in their societies. Education for citizenship must also help them understand why virtues constructed that way are worth having at all. On its most plausible version, the civic education regime of any free society must primarily be a matter of providing information and developing skills by which citizens can best realize the motivational norms they develop outside the state-schooling system. But just as education into the particular terms and ideals of derivative citizenship can satisfy people's desires to act from their sense of justice, so too the further education into the art of exercising one's rights is aimed at satisfying people's further and equally deep desire toward ethical individuation.

People who grow up in a well-functioning liberal society can be expected to want not merely to be just, foundational as their commitment to that aspect of social construction may be. They also want—and very much—to make an interpersonal success of their own lives on their own non-public terms, just as they have already observed other people they admire doing in the course of their lives. Satisfying this desire, in a free society, requires that they develop the dispositions and habits of mind that enable them to live a life of meaning and integrity (each according to the forms of nonpublic reasoning most salient to her) given the public commitments they share. Teaching those virtues necessarily involves discussion in schools about the value of the non-public norms by which citizens actually steer when deciding how to exercise their various claims of right. It requires lessons crafted with an eye toward the challenge each citizen must face of skillfully negotiating the interface of public values and those nonpublic normative concepts with which he himself most closely identifies. It is along that interface that every citizen must take up the project of constructing a personal life of value and integrity within a diverse society committed to a single political conception of justice. The political stability of their society depends ultimately on how well they see themselves as equipped to succeed in that project, each by his own politically reasonable eudaemonistic light.

This means that civic education, for political liberals, must address issues that lie deep in the moral worlds of individual citizens. Designing a program of civic education within a free society is not like tearing a page out of a cookbook and then simply drawing up lessons designed to encourage whatever traits one finds on the list. Teaching good citizenship is more like teaching a craft, with the dispositions requisite of people as citizens borne immanent in the actions and attitudes of the real people who carry out their various social roles well.

When we prepare children for citizenship in a liberal society, we immediately find ourselves engaged with questions about the various ways individuals understand themselves, the forms of relation each has to others, and even the various understandings about the sources of reasons held by various formally admissible citizen types. Of course, such education must always take care to respect the architecture of public reason. No liberal program of civic education can mandate determinate *answers* to any of those eudaemonistic questions—whether uniform or global, or even in any highly localized way. But within that constraint, a liberal educational regime must see to it that its citizens are prepared to take up the crucial and unavoidable question of how each of them, as persons who care deeply about justice, can negotiate the interface of public and nonpublic value.

The substantive account of liberal civic education requires more than the derivative one because it aims higher. Citizens need to be encouraged in the dispositions that they must have for their society not merely to be just, but for their society—once just—to flourish or be healthy in a legitimacy enhancing way.

RELIGIOUS SCHOOLING AND ETHICAL CITIZENSHIP

Political liberals who operate within the derivative paradigm might well object to all of this. Orthodox political liberals typically abdicate responsibility for any and all unintended effects of liberal politics. They admit that the prospect of such effects may alienate some otherwise admissible citizens. But they emphasize that such effects are not intended by political liberalism. So long as the burdens caused by these effects do not become so great that they themselves constitute an injustice, they constitute no violation of the liberal commitment to neutrality of aim. Since such spillovers can never be wholly eliminated, this orthodox line continues, it is enough simply to acknowledge their possible existence and then leave it at that. But if this denial of theoretical responsibility for unintended effects is plausible anywhere, the state-based education of children is one place where it clearly is not.

The idea that the political liberal's commitment to the political ideal of mutual respect requires that nonpublic eudaemonistic discussions be kept out of civics lessons finds an analog in the more familiar (though equally dubious) idea that the American commitment to the First Amendment requires that religious perspectives be kept out of the classroom. Many religious scholars argue that keeping discussion about religion out of the classroom does not necessarily make for classrooms that are more neutral between religions, or between religious and secular perspectives. On the contrary, since public schools are committed to providing children with the secular skills and perspectives they need to function in modern society, the concomitant omission of discussion of religious perspectives and attitudes can give children the false impression that religion is dead. Religious ways of thinking—whether concerning the place of mankind in the universe, responses to particular moral dilemmas, or the solution to broad social problems—were something the students' grandparents or parents may have relied upon, but those approaches are insignificant or irrelevant in the world in which the state is now preparing them to play their parts.

Some religious advocates who have this concern make politically controversial demands, such as the inclusion of religious practice within the public schools. But many others simply ask for a more balanced approach, one that does not infringe on the rights of other children but also does not unintentionally send a negative message about religion. Such scholars argue that *Abington Township School District v. Schempp*, the famous case which disallowed devotional Bible study in public schools, is often misread in this respect. Justice Clark's majority opinion forbade only the advocacy of religion in schools, not all teaching about it.[11] Warren Nord, for example, uses this reading of *Abington* to argue for a form of liberal education which includes religious and traditionalist elements along with the more familiar secular and critical ones. "Liberal education has both a conservative and a liberating task: it should provide students with a ballast of historical identities and values at the same time that it gives them an understanding of alternatives and provides critical distance on the particularities of their respective inheritances." Nord continues:

> The essential tension of a liberal education, properly understood, lies in its commitment to initiating students into the communities of memory which tentatively define them, and, at the same time, nurturing critical reflection by initiating them into an ongoing conversation that enables them to understand and appreciate alternative ways of living and thinking. The error of traditional education was its emphasis on the former; the error of much modern education is its unsystematic and uncritical acceptance of the latter.[12]

The analogous problem with liberal civic education is that by teaching children the rights-based forms of thinking and interest identification central to liberal politics, liberal civic education unintentionally encourages that form of thinking in all domains of reason, including ones where such ways of thinking are transformative beyond what liberal politics strictly requires. Such lessons may thus unintentionally operate to undercut the ethical worldviews that many politically reasonable citizens—and citizens of faith in particular—hold dear. Insofar as citizens perceive this justice-generated cultural current as a threat to their own view, this weakens the form of affirmation that each of them can in good conscience give to those liberal political values themselves.

The solution to this problem in the case of general education is to seek out a more balanced approach, one that educates students honestly into the role of religious belief in their society's history and culture and yet does so without falling into proselytization. This is a difficult balancing act to be sure. But any general education worthy of a free and diverse society must insist upon performing it. Is there an analogous—and politically acceptable—remedy to the problem of spillovers within the sphere of strictly civic education?

Some classic accounts of civic education suggest that there might be. Aristotle, for example, argued that in the real world of imperfect regimes, programs of civic education should always be designed relative to whatever imperfections each type of regime tended inadvertently to foster. Civic education was centrally about *counteracting* the tendency of regimes to produce citizens marked by the regime's characteristic imperfections. As Peter Berkowitz has rightly emphasized, Aristotle saw civic education as concerning "education in virtues that serve as a counterpoise to the characteristic bad habits and reckless tendencies that regimes tend to foster in their citizens."[13] For Aristotle, as Berkowitz writes, "One task of education, then, is to form citizens who in some measure oppose the mold of the regime. Political education or education relative to the regime is typically an urgent matter because regimes more readily and distinctly imprint citizens with the regime's characteristic vices than with the virtues necessary to its preservation."[14]

There is an insight here for political liberals. The rejection of any commitment to neutrality of effect does not excuse political liberals from seeking out politically permissible means of *diminishing* those unintended effects. A substantive conception of civic education like that I have described might provide political liberal regimes with their own internal corrective. So long as the corrective is designed in a way that fully respects the architecture of public reason, the political liberal commitment to legitimacy requires that they seek to include self-corrective educational measures. If we adopt this substantive perspective toward civic education, some familiar disputes may come out in unexpected new ways.

BACK TO TENNESSEE

Consider, for example, the controversy over *Mozert v. Hawkins*—that brightly polished touchstone of civic education theory. In this case, a group of Christian parents in Tennessee objected to an English textbook mandated by a county school board. The parents objected to the textbook because it encouraged their children to make critical judgments for themselves in areas where the Bible provides the answer. Thus, complainants objected to a story about a Catholic Indian settlement on grounds that it promoted Catholicism; to a science fiction story as advocating the occult; to biographies extolling the accomplishments of women who pursued careers outside the home (and even to a story of a boy making toast for a girl); to many passages about the Renaissance, including one describing Leonardo da Vinci as the human with the creative mind that "came closest to the divine touch." Indeed, one of the complainants, Mrs. Vicki Frost, testified that she had spent some 200 hours studying the mandated civics reader and could distinguish seventeen discrete categories of objectionable materials. In her lengthy testimony Mrs. Frost provided the court with numerous examples, many cross-referenced, of each.[15]

Most liberal theorists applaud the Court of Appeals' decision to reject the *Mozert* complainants' plea for exemptions or other special accommodations regarding that text. Deferring to the demands of the *Mozert* parents, such as classroom exceptions, would effectively mean giving up on civic education beyond teaching literacy and numeracy. Some, such as Gutmann, also draw a metatheoretical lesson from the *Mozert* case.[16] Political liberals claim to advocate a form of civic education that encourages critical and reflective skills only about politically relevant issues, and not as a general world outlook. But, Gutmann says, because the skills and dispositions conducive to political deliberation cannot help but spill over into nonpublic domains of reason, the form of civic education required by political liberalism does not offer any more accommodation to the kinds of diversity represented by the *Mozert* case than does comprehensive liberalism. "The only discernible difference turns out to be different theoretical rationales for denying the parents' claims." Thus, "Comprehensive and political liberalism come down on the same side, once again, in this case."[17]

If Gutmann, and the court majority, are correct in understanding the uncompromising and politically unreasonable nature of the *Mozert* parents' position, then the conclusion Gutmann draws about the convergence of political and comprehensive responses to the *Mozert* case must also be correct. For on that reading, the *Mozert* parents are politically unreasonable—they affirm a religion that requires that they deny even the very general political ideals of reciprocity and equal political respect.[18] Comprehensive and political liberal positions do indeed converge regarding the treatment of such politically unreasonable citizens (even though their rationales may differ). However, that is not the only plausible reading of the *Mozert* parents' position.

The case record states clearly that the Tennessee parents did not consistently object to the mere exposure of their children to the ideas in the reader. Nor even did the parents consistently object to their children acquiring critical skills like those needed for political purposes from the reader. Rather, the *Mozert* complainants objected consistently only to the repetitiveness and the depth of the exposure. They saw the overall effect of the reader, whether intended or not, as denigrating to the faith-based form of reasoning on which their nonpublic worldview depends. For example, the court record indicates that even Vicki Frost was willing to have her child read science fiction, study Renaissance philosophy, and learn about other religious faiths, provided that the presentation was not so "profound" that it "deeply undermined her religious beliefs."[19] Mrs. Frost, on this reading of the case record, produced her long list to the court not so much to show precisely how many discrete objections she had but rather to show the repetitive and unbalanced presentation of the reader as a whole.[20] What's more, the complainants indicated that—despite even their objections about repetitiveness and depth—they were willing to have their children use the reader, provided that the lessons made explicit and clear to the children that they were not being encouraged to view any of these philosophies or religions as true. Significantly, the *Mozert* parents sought only measures to protect their own children's faith: they never sought to use the state apparatus to impose their religion on other people's children. For all these reasons, it is at least plausible to view the *Mozert* parents not as politically unreasonable outcasts but as exactly those kinds of citizens which political liberalism was devised to accommodate: the formally admissible "citizens of faith" of Rawls or the "reasonable Romantics" of Charles Larmore.[21] If we think of *Mozert* this way, the case may reveal what is distinctive about political liberal civic education after all.

Political liberal civic education must take as its task not only the preparation of students for liberal *politics* but also their preparation for *life* within a society that is bounded by that particular view of politics. Because education for substantive citizenship aims for more in this way, this form of education has not one but two reasons for requiring students to learn about diverse ways of life, such as the stories that civics reader depicted. First, the point derivative theorists emphasize, political liberals need to teach students about other ways of life that are pursued by their reasonable fellow citizens because political liberals want them to learn to respect others as political equals, and thus to understand why the liberal posture of state neutrality is morally required in a society such as theirs. If they learn to respect others as their equals for political purposes, then they can recognize their own support for state neutrality as the appropriate institutional expression of their (freely formed) desire to act from their sense of justice.

However, the civic importance of these lessons in diversity do not stop there. Political liberals must also be concerned that they not send a distorted or misleading message about *nonpublic value* as they go about preparing students for public life. Political liberals are concerned to prepare citizens to play their roles in making their society flourish or do well as a political liberal society, that is, in a society where a certain kind of moral union has been achieved among people who continue to affirm as true a variety of incompatible (but politically reasonable) moral, religious, and philosophical outlooks. The stories about other people are thus significant to children's education not just to teach them equal respect. These stories also serve the crucial purpose of providing examples of how people holding different views of life, and even different views of the nature of reason itself, have each found ways to reintegrate their capacity for public reason (and the skills that entails) with the nonpublic commitments that give point to their lives.

On this view, political liberals teach students about their fellow citizens not simply to detach them politically from the traditions of their parents or communities (so that they may come to appreciate the norm of equal respect). Political liberals teach them detailed stories about others in order to show them how others who have come to affirm the norm of equal respect have then gone on to find ways to live lives of meaning and integrity given their own background and set of life experiences (for example, how they have achieved a level of individuation that allows them to affirm their own nonpublic view as true). In a well-functioning liberal society, as I have suggested, people can accomplish this integration only by the way they come to understand the particular *meaning* of those public norms and rights to them, and by the way they practice the interpersonal art that the exercise of those norms and rights makes unavoidable.

Notice that a substantive conception of civic education such as this might in practice generate very different requirements if built atop an ethical rather than a political justificatory foundation. For ethical liberalisms, in their various ways, typically affirm only a narrower view about the forms of human reasoning that are morally (and thus politically) appropriate. Even if ethical liberals affirm the idea that children should be taught to reintegrate their political understanding into their own nonpublic lives for eudaemonistic reasons, still they typically affirm only some autonomous form of reasoning as appropriate for achieving that reintegration. By contrast, political liberals are committed to affirming as reasonable, and as *equally* reasonable from a political perspective, not only forms of reintegration that match some

philosophical ideal of moral autonomy (such as that inspired by
the work of Mill or Kant) but also those that come from more embedded, traditionalist ways of understanding reasons for action
and attitude (the "reasonable Romantics," or citizens of faith).

This has an important consequence. If the *Mozert* parents can
plausibly be understood as affirming a doctrine that lies within
the boundaries of the politically reasonable, then political liberals—but not most ethical ones—may have reason to *support*
some central demands of the Tennessee parents. One way to
read the original request of those fundamentalist parents, after
all, was simply that their children's program of civic education
include a component concerning how they might *reintegrate* the
lessons of public reason into the deep nonpublic self-understandings of their own group. To take one kind of example, before the appellate court decision against the parents the schools
had reached an accommodation with the parents of two children (whose parents could not afford private schooling) by
"specifically not[ing] on worksheets that the student was not required to believe the stories."[22] This seems to me an eminently
political liberal solution. Of course, respect for the architecture
of public reason would forbid certain ways of conveying that lesson about nonpublic reintegration and thus certain formulations of riders such as those in the Tennessee case.[23] The reintegrative component could not assert that any one religious view
in fact was universally true and that others were universally false.
That would indeed have the state be teaching a religion as part
of its education of citizens.[24] But the reintegrative component
surely could include exercises that encouraged students to consider what attitudes, beliefs and even *what forms of reasoning,*
might be most appropriate for them given their own histories
and expectations. Rather than indoctrination, this is merely a
matter of calling children's attention to premises from their
own lives, premises from which they might draw their own conclusions about what forms of reasoning and ways of assessing
value are most significant for them.

This substantive approach would in no way mean denying that
children need to gain a "lively" understanding of the burdens of
judgment, nor that children might *ipso facto* be led to consider
how those burdens apply to their own sets of beliefs and tradi-

tions (the points Callan emphasizes). Rather, on this reading, people such as the *Mozert* parents are simply asking that the lessons concerning the burdens of judgment be *carried through* in an even handed way. To do that, the civics lessons must be carried through in a way consistent with the motivational foundations of political liberalism and not of some closet preference for the ethical liberal life view.

It is precisely because of how the burdens of judgment apply to each child's own beliefs—the way the boundaries of the integrity of each of are shaped by his particular experiences, the whole course of his life up to now—that each does in fact have reason to give some special weight and consideration to the traditions, and even to the forms of reasoning, that have already played a prominent role in the story of his life. A political liberal education, from the substantive perspective, should include a broad-minded component that brings that fact to children's attention. Ethical liberal forms of civic education, by contrast, typically are committed to a reintegrative component that draws much narrower boundaries about the acceptable forms of reintegrative reason. *Mozert v. Hawkins* demonstrates vividly how the civic educational requirements of ethical and of political liberalism diverge—both in theory and in practice.

SANTA FE INDEPENDENT SCHOOL DISTRICT AND BEYOND

Civic education, for political liberals most of all, must be concerned about the eventual *ethical situatedness* of developing citizens rather than simply about the (first-level) *political liberation* of them. Depending on their own backgrounds and the shape of their lives up to then, some reasonable citizens may find it most satisfying to individuate in the direction of highly individualistic, reflective forms of integrative reason that liberals have traditionally affirmed. Other citizens now deemed politically reasonable may do better to individuate via more embedded forms of reason such as those based on received authority (the Bible, the Koran, or the Church). The form of integration of what I take to be the great sweep of citizens in the mainstream may well involve a complex and uneven mixture of reason elements from each side.

But the only form of liberation that can be encouraged intentionally under a liberal form of civic education after the politicization of justice is one that gives foundational weight to citizens' *political* autonomy. When considering rival systems of encouraging political autonomy within public schools, political liberals are bound to prefer systems with the lesser rather than the greater unintended (nonpublic autonomy-promoting) effects. In a diverse society, there is no other path toward the kind of broad ethical satisfaction of citizens on which state legitimacy in the end depends. The challenge for political liberals is to devise reintegrative forms of schooling that prepare students to live lives of integrity affirming their own (diverse and incompatible) doctrines as true, even once recognizing a common moral foundation for the political standing of diverse others.

I am not suggesting that children of Catholics, for example, must learn to be Catholic in their public school civics classes. Nor, certainly, am I suggesting that each child is to be assigned to whatever particular ethical orientation it is determined in advance is irrevocably appropriate to him. Liberal civic education always centers on the affirmation of strong political freedoms and on discussions about the importance of such freedoms in each person's construction of her or his own life. But since children of Catholics, for example, are to learn about their rights and about the standing of all citizens as political equals, they must also be helped to understand what it means to be a Catholic within the liberal social world they are about to enter. Being a committed Catholic in a world where individual freedoms are strongly protected (for example, a world where no-fault divorce laws, physician-assisted suicide, and wide reproductive rights are politically affirmed) is different from what it would mean to be a committed Catholic in some social world where no such freedoms were recognized—just as affirming the Bible as the true word of God must be different in a world where the broad facts of evolutionary theory are scientifically accepted than in a world where those facts are not. Children need to be taught how it is that the liberal social world makes itself available to people with a worldview such as the one they have so far grown up in—always taking care to avoid proselytization, whether on a general or an individual basis. The emphasis on political freedoms, central to any politically acceptable scheme on the substantive perspective, must be used within classrooms to prevent the fall into proselytizing excesses. Within the classroom, discussions about political freedoms are the balancing weights that make this tightrope walk possible. It is the liberal concern for legitimacy that forces them determinedly to attempt it.

A complete schedule of political liberal civic education must do more than address children's latent capacity for a sense of justice. Civic education must also address young people's freely formed and very deep desire for ethical individuation. This desire for ethical individuation does not spring from nowhere nor does it emerge with no form. It comes from, and is formed by, each child's own history, the whole story of her life up till then. In a well-ordered liberal society, that story always includes both public and nonpublic normative components—with the child's sense of justice providing a kind of scaffolding for her desire for ethical individuation.

People with an ethical liberal orientation typically argue that parents do not "own" their children but rather children own, or at least are on their way toward owning, themselves. While the notion of ownership in this context is famously obscure, such people typically argue for an activist tutorial state, encouraging students to adopt the thickly autonomous worldview they themselves affirm. But political liberals, by their own view, are required to abandon all such ambitions. The political liberal state cannot aim to promote any particular view or approach to questions of nonpublic value, whether that of strong individual autonomy, of deference to traditions of authority, or of some complex and uneven mixture of these two extremes. The politicization of justice thus opens a yawning reintegrative gap—a gap, that is, about the form of reasoning by which individual children should most appropriately learn to interpret and exercise their political autonomy. Political liberals, but not ethical ones, are bound to defer to the wishes of parents when reintegrative questions arise for developing children. There is no one else, from the political liberal perspective, with the standing to fill that gap.

To put the point dramatically, political liberals are committed to a form of "ethical subservience" on the part of the publicly funded school system to children's (politically reasonable) parents when it comes to reintegrative questions. This does not mean denying rights but, rather, assiduously getting the state out of the business of influencing children—intentionally or not—about the *meaning* and *appropriate use* of the freedoms and liberties they have as citizens. The alternatives, after all, are either (1) to advocate some ethical ideal of autonomy as a good for all children, or (2) simply to tell students about all their rights and their groundings, then halt the lesson and send them out to play. Political liberals, as such, are bound to eschew the first path. But insofar as theorists such as Gutmann and Callan are right that the latter approach in practice amounts to much the same thing as the former one, that approach levies a disproportionate psychological tax on worldviews that political liberals claim to deem reasonable. Political liberals are bound to search for politically acceptable methods that might save them from pointing all their young citizens down that path too.

What methods might be available to political liberals who wish to try a different way? The guiding idea would be to find ways of teaching students about the political norms of their society that did not unintentionally disrupt students from the ethical worldviews of their parents, at least not beyond what an appreciation of their own nascent political autonomy requires (which is already a very significant, and politically appropriate, check on the parents). The "subservience" political liberals owe to politically reasonable parents, of course, is owed just as much to people wishing to pass on their autonomous life ideal as it is to people wishing to transmit their faith-based one. (From the perspective of the citizens of faith, notice, proponents of "children's ethical autonomy" are foisting their own worldview upon their children just as much as anyone else). The views of Millian individualists and of Larmore's reasonable Romantics are equally reasonable from the political liberal perspective. The political liberal state, to be true to its own ideals, must be equally solicitous of every politically reasonable parent's concern about the practical standing of their own reintegrative ideal within the social world.

The distinction between curriculum (roughly, the books and other course content) and pedagogy (classroom design, lesson plans, and other aspects of delivering the lessons) opens a whole range of options here. Joseph Coleman has argued brilliantly that liberals might employ progressive pedagogues to teach many public values, thus allowing them to bypass the familiar debates of curricular content.[25] Political liberals have every reason to encourage innovations in the pedagogical area.

While treating public values as foundational, political liberals are committed to classrooms that are aggressively concerned to make room for the diverse nonpublic views held by their citizenry. Their schools are vibrant places, full of the color, warmth, and variety found in the society which they are to serve. In the early grades, for example, parents might be invited into the schools on a regular basis, to speak to the children about their personal views about work, family, and religion. In later grades, the children themselves might be given chances to express the nonpublic views they have come to affirm—whether or not those nonpublic views happen to be deemed "religious" in an orthodox sense. Thus children in public schools might be allowed to take turns "solemnizing" important moments of the school calendar, by talking about the personal meaning of those events to them: convocation, graduation, the start of classes each day, perhaps even football games and other extracurricular events.

In *Santa Fe Independent School District v. Doe*, for example, the U.S. Supreme Court held that a school policy allowing student-led, student-initiated prayer at football games violates the Establishment Clause. Certainly, any policy that allows some children to express their personal views in such a powerful forum must receive serious scrutiny: no student, or group of students, should be able to dominate such fora, imposing just their own interpretation of proper "solemnization." Still, this is a worrying decision. From the broader perspective I have been defending, our approach should be seek out ways to accommodate such student initiatives whenever possible. Justice Sandra Day O'Connor voted with the majority in the *Santa Fe* case, but there was wisdom in her eloquent dissent in *City of Boerne v. Flores*, the 1997 case which struck down the Religious Freedom Restoration Act. As Justice O'Connor wrote in that earlier case, "Our nation's founders conceived of a republic receptive to voluntary religious expression, not of a secular society in which religious expression is tolerated only when it does not conflict with a generally applicable law." The motivational springboard for political liberalism was the hope of devising a form of association which could be a home not just to Millian individualists but to citizens of faith as well. In her dissent in *Boerne v. Flores*, O'Connor attributes to the founders what I see as the quintessence of the political liberal view.[26]

The aim of any such policies, of course, is not that of allowing some particular faction of parents, or aggressive children, to proselytize other children within the public schools—whether in a religious or secular direction. The idea, crucially distinct, is to give all parents and students a chance to *bear witness* to their own deep beliefs, wherever the issue of rights and liberties are raised. Civics lessons, for political liberals, must be a particularly dynamic and relevant part of each child's school day. Civics lessons, in a diverse society, should be studded with enriching examples of how the political freedoms shared by all citizens can be used in the construction of various personal lives worth living.

This political liberal concern for reintegration has further implications as well. Because of their concern for reintegrative autonomy, political liberals may have a unique class of reasons, not shared by ethical liberals, for acceding to parental demands for school vouchers and a greater range of school choice. The school system required by political liberalism, after all, must prepare children for the roles they will play in a society where citizens not only respect one another as free and equal but do so *while* continuing to affirm a diverse and irreconcilable range of views—religious, moral and philosophical—as true. Parents may reasonably be concerned about the "substantive civics" lessons their children pick up not just in their classes but from their wider school environment—lessons about value transmitted by their peers' clothing, manners, and topics of conversation; by their attitudes toward authority figures, athletic events, and voluntary organizations. While a degree of such informal exposure can be crucial to children's learning to respect other children with views unlike their own, the informal assimilative pressures in large common schools typically go well beyond any such requirement. These concerns, always present, may be exacerbated as political liberals respond to their fellow citizens' reasonable concerns about reintegration.

For example, the measures adopted in response to the reintegrative concerns of reasonable parents, while justified from the political liberal perspective, may *themselves* generate assimilative pressures that would cause additional worries for many parents—especially in schools with large, diverse student bodies. Political liberals who recognize that neutrality of effect is "impracticable" recognize that school classrooms and the wider school environment are always ethically charged, like it or not, and charged in ways that extend far beyond what is politically relevant or required. Because engagement with those reintegrative questions about life and value are unavoidable once the issue of political norms has been broached, political liberals must seek to level the playing field within the domain of the politically reasonable however they might.[27] This means allowing *all* reasonable reintegrative ideals a more equitable share of influence in classrooms and hallways and on athletic fields. In a school environment that is ethically charged in this more open and evenhanded way, it would be no surprise to hear parents—Millian and Catholic alike—demanding that their children be given school options that promise a total experience less likely to unsettle their children from the reasonable worldview they themselves hope their children will come to affirm as true.

The political liberal drive toward division and subservience is not unqualified, of course. All students are to be prepared for full political autonomy, and reintegrative ideals which parents hope to encourage in students (whether by informal notes on worksheets or by whole school designs) must always be done in a way compatible with each student's coming to appreciate her or his full range of rights and the political ideas of person and society on which they are grounded. Further, political liberals, while deferring to the demands of all reasonable parents regarding reintegrative questions, must always insist that *all* school environments—public, semipublic, private and home ones alike—include a mandatory component that ensures that the requirements of the derivative model of civic education are fully met there. Even the most broad-minded political liberals cannot tolerate those whose worldviews lead them to seek to exempt their children from that component of their civic education.[28] Such a demand is a flat denial of the political values on which political liberalism is founded. It is an opting out, a kind of secession from equal political membership, that cannot even masquerade as a form of "reintegration."[29]

Still, civic education is one of the most dramatic places where the broader legitimacy-directed components of liberalism touch down and make a distinct institutional impression. The substantive perspective reveals that political liberals must say something positive here to their young citizens, and what they must say diverges from the positive things that most ethical liberals may say. They must say: "Become just, but do so in a way that makes sense of the importance that your own particular history up to now has to you. Your citizenship, in a liberal society, involves not just your performance of your political duties but the way you build your life. We explicitly encourage each of you to build that life, not *in spite of* your awareness of rights and of the public perspective of evaluation from which principles of justice are affirmed, but *through your use of* those rights and that shared perspective their political primacy implies. We must prepare each of you to lead a life of meaning and integrity within the particular kind of social world you are now entering—a world where human lives must be built on the interface of people's public and nonpublic identity components. Citizenship, in a free society, is not merely a list of skills but a craft: the craft of living well. It is therefore as political liberals that we respectfully play our part in preparing you all to be good people. We must prepare you, that is, for the crucial human task of finding personal meaning in your political autonomy. For it is on your capacity to be good people in that special politically structured sense that the legitimacy of any political liberal polity ultimately depends."

NOTES

I thank Michael McConnell, Amy Gutmann, Dennis Thompson, Eamonn Callan, Joseph Coleman and Steve Macedo, each of whom kindly sent me written suggestions. I presented an early version of this essay at APSA in Atlanta in 1999, on a panel with Bill Galston, Eamonn Callan and Rob Reich. I profited from the many challenges put to me by the audience that day, and especially from the suggestions of Susan Okin, Sandy Levinson and Paul Weithman. I develop the argument presented here in my book *Liberalism Beyond Justice: Citizens, Society and the Boundaries of Political Theory*, Princeton University Press, 2001.

1. See respectively Rawls *Political Liberalism* Columbia University Press 1993 193–4; Galston *Liberal Purposes* 1991 296 and "Two Concepts of Liberalism" *Ethics* 105 (April 1995); Macedo "Transformative Constitutionalism" *Political Theory* Feb. 1998: 56–80 and *Diversity and Distrust: Civic Education in a Multicultural Democracy* Harvard University Press 2000.

2. An excellent canvassing of these difficulties is A. John Simmons "Justification and Legitimacy" *Ethics* 109 (July 1999). I think Simmons is right to criticize some, Harry Brighouse in particular, for overstating the distance between the justice requirement and the legitimacy requirement, at least within a Rawlsian political liberal schema. Though, as will soon be clear, this does not mean that I necessarily endorse the "Lockean" interpretation of the relation between justification and legitimacy for which Simmons himself argues, nor that I think the attitudinal component of legitimacy can be downplayed as much as Simmons suggests.

3. That is roughly Eamonn Callan's formulation of the distinction (working draft of paper prepared for APSA 1999). But I think it picks up most other recent formulations as well (including Simmons's, though with some tweaking on the attitudinal question).

4. Consider, for example, the logically admissible but sociologically doomed citizens of faith that Rawls describes [*Political Liberalism* (New York: Columbia University Press 1993) 196–7].

5. I said before that spillovers may pose different kinds of threats to legitimacy with respect to different kinds of citizens. So too spillovers may come from many different sources within the liberal social world— legislative, judicial, and educational just for starters. The liberal commitment to legitimacy requires that liberals seek to counteract unintended spillovers from all sources.

6. "Civic Education and Social Diversity" *Ethics* 105 (April 1995) 573.

7. "Political Liberalism and Political Education" *The Review of Politics* 1996, 10–14, and *Creating Citizens: Political Education in a Liberal Democracy* (New York: Oxford University Press 1997).

8. The only way to maintain a distinction between citizens' public and nonpublic self-understandings would be for political liberals to recommend what Callan says would be an integrity-destroying form of compartmentalization (1996 12–13). One political liberal who grasps this horn is Norman Daniels *Justice and Justification* (Cambridge 1996) 168–74.

9. Though Callan, it seems to me, overstates his case when he calls this a conceptual convergence. There is at least a logical difference between recognizing the consequences of the burdens of judgment when applied to one's own doctrine for political purposes and recognizing

those consequences as part of one's own nonpublic moral evaluation of one's own view. The truly worrying convergence here, I believe, is one of practical effect.

10. See my "Individual Rights and Community Virtues" *Ethics* 1991 and "Community in the Minimal State" *Critical Review* 1995.

11. Harvey Cox writes, "[T]o teach nothing about religion is, in effect, to teach something wrong about it: that it is unimportant and unworthy of serious study." Cox continues, "This form of exclusion discriminates against those Americans for whom religion has been particularly integral—for example, African-Americans, whose struggle against slavery and segregation was inspired, to a great extent, by their religion, and Catholic immigrants, whose faith helped them survive prejudice." He concludes, "What excluding religion from the classroom produces is simply bad education" (New York Times October 16 1998, A23).

12. Nord *Religion & American Education: Rethinking a National Dilemma* (Chapel Hill: University of North Carolina Press 1995) 202–3. Nord says, "A good liberal education should map out the cultural space in which we find ourselves. It should help us fill in our identities, locating us in the stories, the communities of memory, into which we are born. It should root us in the past" (233). See also Cox 1998.

13. *Virtue and the Making of Modern Liberalism* Princeton 1999 11.

14. Berkowitz continues: "Education relative to the regime, which Aristotle argued is the preserver of regimes, must in significant measure cut against the dominant tendency of the regime, which is to form citizens with immoderate enthusiasm for its guiding principle. For the guiding principle ceases to become an effective guide if it is allowed to become the regime's sole guide" (176–7).

15. For detail, see Mozert v. Hawkins County, 827 F.2nd 1058 (6th Cir. 1987); and especially Stephen Bates *Battleground: One Mother's Crusade, the Religious Right, and the Struggle for Control of Our Classrooms* Poseidon Press 1993.

16. See also the discussions in Amy Gutmann and Dennis Thompson *Democracy and Disagreement* Harvard 1996 63–69, Callan *Creating Citizens* 157–61, Macedo *Diversity and Distrust* 174–187, Meira Levinson *The Demands of Liberal Education* (New York: Oxford University Press 1999) 53–4.

17. Gutmann 1995 573.

18. As Gutmann describes the *Mozert* complainants, "Their religious convictions . . . command them not to expose their children to knowledge about other ways of life unless the exposure is accompanied by a statement that their way of life is true and all the others are false and inferior" (1995 571).

19. *Mozert* at III.A.[1].

20. For example, an expert witness for the *Mozert* parents in a lower court testified that he found "markedly little reference to religion, particularly Christianity, and also remarkably little to Judaism" in the Holt series (*Mozert* III.A.[1]).

21. See Larmore *The Morals of Modernity* Cambridge 1996 127–133. To be clear, my position is merely that there is enough indeterminacy in the court record, and surrounding documents, to make this alternative reading plausible. The plaintiffs were a diverse group. They had many internal disagreements not only on religious matters but on legal ones, and certainly not all of the demands voiced on their behalf were politically reasonable. Still, even a concurring judge, Circuit Judge Boggs, expressed a concern for the sort of indeterminacy I have in mind. Boggs writes: "A reasonable reading of the plaintiffs' testimony shows they object to the overall effect of the Holt series, not simply to any exposure to any idea opposing theirs. . . . By focusing narrowly on references that make plaintiffs appear so extreme that they could never be accommodated, the court simply leaves resolution of the underlying issues here to another case, when we have plaintiffs with a more sophisticated understanding of our own and Supreme Court precedent, and a more careful and articulate presentation of their own beliefs." Boggs reported his own profound sense of sadness about this case, quoting hopefully from the poet Edwin Markham: "He drew a circle that shut me out— / Heretic, Rebel, a thing to flout. / But Love and I had the wit to win: / We drew a circle that took him in!" (Mozert at Boggs I, II). As we shall see, I believe that political liberals must show that same wit to win—though some of them may be discomfited by doing so.

22. *Mozert* at [1]I.B.

23. The parents did not consistently formulate their request in a politically acceptable way. For example, one formulation from the case record states that they demanded "a statement that the other views are incorrect and the plaintiff's views are the correct ones." The record is ambiguous as to whether the parents would be willing to accept an interpretation of that as meaning "the truth *for our children*," or whether they would accept only the (politically unreasonable) interpretation of "the truth for all students, period."

24. The grounds for this prohibition are especially clear if that reintegrative lesson was to be delivered to a classroom of children with diverse beliefs. But it would also forbid this sort of conclusory truth teaching even in private riders to be written only on worksheets by parental request. Calling children's attention to premises from their own lives (from which children might draw their own conclusions about truth) is a

different matter entirely. The substantive approach would allow, indeed encourage, that, both as a general lesson and as part of specific parental request—insofar as the pedagogical and curricular constraints of real public classrooms would allow (and within the constraint of respect for the architecture of public reason).

25. Joseph Coleman "Civic Pedogogies and Liberal Democratic Curricula" *Ethics* 108/4 (1998) 746–761.

26. For a defense of the principles underlying the Religious Freedom Restoration Act, see my book *Liberalism Beyond Justice*.

27. This is why I say that political liberals must be aggressive *tax flatteners*, even though it is sociologically impracticable for them to be strict flat taxers. (And this remains true even in the case of those citizens who are not owed those flattened taxes as a matter of formal "right.")

28. For a different view, see the fascinating discussion by Shelley Burtt "In Defense of Yoder: Parental Authority and the Public Schools" *NOMOS XXXVIII: Political Order*, ed. Ian Shapiro and Russell Hardin (New York: New York University Press, 1996) and "Religious Parents, Secular Schools: A Liberal Defense of an Illiberal Education" *Review of Politics* 56 (Winter 1994).

29. This political liberal drive toward ethical inclusion and so toward school division would be subject to other constraints as well. Most obviously, political liberals cannot advocate vouchers or choice under models that result in injustices to other students on other dimensions, e.g. models which leave some classes of student at unjustly poor schools, or models which produce so much local homogeneity that in practice they render the teaching of mutual respect an empty sham.

7

LIBERALISM, NEUTRALITY, AND EDUCATION

PETER DE MARNEFFE

Liberalism and the Problem of Education

The education of children seems to pose a problem for liberalism. Liberalism, on at least one interpretation, is committed to the principle that the government ought to remain neutral toward different conceptions of how it is best for people to lead their lives.[1] Yet any public educational policy must, it seems, take a stand on what kinds of life are best. This is because any morally defensible system of education must, it seems, seek to provide children with the best education it can, and any conception of what education is best must, it seems, be based on a view of what kinds of life are most worthwhile. So, it seems, either the government must not seek to provide children with the best education it can or it must violate the principle of neutrality.

A natural response to this dilemma is to hold that a liberal regime should not *provide* education to children. Instead, it should provide parents with vouchers that may be used to pay for schooling at private schools. This alone does not eliminate the difficulty. A morally defensible voucher system will limit the application of vouchers to accredited schools, and standards of accreditation strong enough to protect the legitimate interests of children in receiving a good education will, it seems, inevitably express a view on what kinds of life are best, thus also violating the principle of neutrality.

At this point some may wish to deny that liberalism is committed to neutrality. Liberalism, they may say, is based instead on an abstract view about how it is best to live—one that gives a central place to critical reflection and the active creation of the kind of person one wishes to be and the kind of life one wishes to lead.[2] Since individuals might affirm many different particular conceptions of how it is best to live upon critical reflection and pursue many different conceptions in creating themselves, this abstract conception of the best life is neutral among many particular conceptions of how it is best to live. Still, it contradicts the principle of neutrality by implying that lives not characterized by a high degree of critical reflection or self-conscious self-creation are less worthy of pursuit than those that are.

If liberalism were properly based on this abstract conception of how it is best to live, this would seem to solve the problem of liberalism and education: a liberal regime should seek to provide all children with an education that encourages critical reflection and self-conscious self-creation. There are, however, at least four objections to this "perfectionist" interpretation of liberalism.[3] First, it seems false that lives of critical reflection and self-conscious self-creation *are* the only good lives, or the best lives for everyone. Lives closely ordered by religious doctrines that require a high degree of deference to tradition are also good, and may be the best kind of life for some people, given their temperament and circumstances. Second, even if lives of active reflection and self-creation were the best lives for everyone, an educational system based on this conception of the good life would seem unfair and disrespectful to those who reject this conception in favor of a more traditional, less reflective or self-creative conception.[4] Third, it seems that liberal institutions are less likely to be stable over time if generally understood to be based on this perfectionist conception of how it is best to live, since those who reject this conception will then be less likely to support these institutions as a matter of principle.[5] Finally, if, as I will argue below, it is possible to identify and justify the moral rights we have without presupposing the correctness of any such conception of how it is best to live, then it is false, as a matter of moral theory, that liberalism, understood as a conception of what rights there are, *is* based upon this abstract conception of how it is best to live.

The idea that liberalism is essentially committed to neutrality is in fact a recent one, and there are other ways in which liberalism might be understood. Traditionally, liberalism has been defined by an ideal of limited representative government in which coercive government power, even though it is exercised by representatives of the people, is limited by a constitution, or system of fundamental law, that effectively protects certain important liberties, such as freedom of political speech and freedom of worship, from unjustifiable government interference. More recently, liberalism has been identified with the principle that socially created resources and opportunities ought to be distributed fairly among all members of society. On neither of these interpretations is liberalism essentially committed to neutrality.

While it is not necessary to define liberalism by a commitment to neutrality, the idea of neutrality contains important thoughts. It contains the thought, for example, that the government should not prohibit the expression of a belief about the ultimate nature of reality or about how it is best to live solely for the reason that this belief is false—regardless of the further negative consequences of expressing this belief. It also contains the thought that the government should not prohibit an activity or way of life solely for the reason that it is intrinsically worthless—regardless of the further negative consequences for anyone of engaging in this activity or pursuing this way of life. Liberalism seems committed to both these thoughts. Moreover, they seem correct. So it seems hasty to abandon the idea of neutrality altogether. But if we remain committed to the idea of neutrality, how are we to understand this idea in a way that is compatible with the justification of a morally adequate educational system for children?

For reasons I will shortly explain, I believe the principle of neutrality is best understood as a constraint on the reasons that can justify coercive government policies. It states that certain reasons—such as that a belief about how it is best to live is false or that an activity or way of life is intrinsically worthless—cannot alone justify the government in depriving individuals of opportunities and resources. Since it is possible to defend a morally adequate educational system without reference to these reasons, the conflict between neutrality and the education of children is merely apparent.

An important consequence of this interpretation is that the principle of neutrality has surprisingly little bearing on the issue of education. It does not warrant a system of vouchers. It does not even prohibit prayer in public school. This is because, as a constraint on the reasons that can justify coercive government policies, the principle of neutrality does not tell us how to weigh the reasons for and against educational policy that it allows as legitimate, and so does not alone rule out any policy for which there is some legitimate reason. If we wish to evaluate educational policies from the liberal point of view, we must therefore go beyond the principle of neutrality to a more general theory of rights.

In this essay I sketch a theory of rights and outline how it bears on the issue of education. According to this theory, the government violates a person's rights when it adopts a policy that imposes a burden on that person and this burden is substantially worse than any burden someone would bear in the absence of this policy. To determine whether an educational policy, such as school prayer, violates a person's moral rights, we must therefore consider whether it imposes a burden on her that is substantially worse than any burden someone would bear in the absence of this policy.

The aim of this essay is not, however, to offer a complete account of rights in education. It is rather to make a methodological point about how to evaluate educational policies from the liberal point of view. For reasons that will become increasingly clear, it is misguided, in my opinion, to evaluate educational policies by considering which are "most neutral." Educational policy ought to be evaluated instead by carefully considering the burdens that individuals bear under various policy alternatives. It is this attention to the relative weight of burdens on individuals, and not neutrality, that respect for individuals' moral rights fundamentally requires.

THE PRINCIPLE OF NEUTRALITY

Liberalism has recently been identified with the principle of neutrality because this principle seems to provide the basis of a number of specific rights, such as freedom of worship and sexual free-

dom, to which liberalism seems committed. Since, it seems, the
government would fail to be neutral toward different conceptions of how it is best to live if it were to prohibit certain forms of
worship or certain forms of consensual sexual conduct between
adults, the principle of neutrality seems to explain why we have a
right to freedom of worship and sexual freedom.

Despite this appeal, the principle of neutrality is problematic.
It suggests it is wrong for the government to adopt any policy that
intentionally favors some ways of life over others. Some perfectly
permissible policies, however, would seem to have this intent.
Thus, when the government requires those caught driving drunk
to attend meetings of Alcoholics Anonymous, it intends to encourage them not to drink and so to live and act differently. This
does not render this policy impermissible.

For this reason, the principle of neutrality is best understood
as a constraint upon the *reasons* that can justify coercive government policies, and not as a constraint upon their intent.[6] It
should be understood to imply that certain reasons cannot justify
certain government policies, and not that any government policy
is wrong that aims to encourage people to live in one way as opposed to another. Thus, while the government would violate the
principle of neutrality if it were to send drunk drivers to Alcoholics Anonymous for the reason that drinking is inherently
worthless, it would not violate this principle if it were to send
them to Alcoholics Anonymous for the reason that those who
drink less as a result will pose less of a threat to others and themselves when they drive—even if the *aim* of this policy *is* to encourage them to live and act in one way as opposed to another.

A complete account of the principle of neutrality along these
lines would require a complete list of all the specific reasons that
it identifies as insufficient to justify coercive government policies.
It would require an explanation of why the justification of government policies by these reasons constitutes a failure to be neutral in the relevant sense, whereas the justification of government
policies by other reasons does not. And it would require an account of why all these reasons are morally insufficient to justify
coercive government policies. Since my concern here is to make
a methodological point about the evaluation of educational policy, I will not undertake to provide a complete account of the

principle of neutrality here. I will simply claim that neutrality *must* be interpreted along these lines, as identifying certain reasons as illegitimate justifications for coercive government policies, if neutrality is to be justified as a valid principle that represents a feasible political ideal.

If this is the correct interpretation, then public educational policy raises difficulties for neutrality only if any morally adequate educational policy must be justified by reference to the reasons that the principle of neutrality rules out as illegitimate. Offhand, there is no reason to think this is the case. Thus consider the reasons already mentioned—that a belief about the ultimate nature of reality or about the best way to live is false or that an activity or way of life is intrinsically worthless. There is no reason to think that any morally adequate public educational policy must be justified by reference to these reasons. So the education of children presents no obvious difficulties for the principle of neutrality so understood.

This interpretation makes the principle of neutrality a more permissive constraint on policy than might have been thought. Thus suppose, for the sake of argument, that when children recite a non-denominational prayer at the beginning of school each day, concentration and discipline, cooperativeness and respect for others, are markedly improved, and that the government adopts this policy solely for this reason. Assuming that the principle of neutrality does not rule out facts about what will improve concentration and discipline in school as reasons for school policy, a policy of school prayer justified solely by these reasons would not violate the principle of neutrality.

This consequence will suggest to some that I have misinterpreted this principle—since, in encouraging religiosity and in being biased against atheism, a policy of school prayer will strike some as a paradigm violation of neutrality. If, however, the principle of neutrality were understood to prohibit policies regardless of the reasons for and against them, it would appear to be unjustifiable. So suppose that *violence* in schools would be substantially reduced if children were to recite a non-denominational prayer each morning, and that this policy would not, as a matter of fact, subject the children of atheists or non-Christians to persecution or harassment. If the principle of neutrality were to prohibit this policy nonetheless, it would appear to be indefensible. For this reason it is best to understand the principle of neutrality as ruling out *certain reasons* for government policy—that children will go to Hell without school prayer, for example—and not as ruling out policies for which there is perfectly good reason because they appear in some way to be non-neutral.

Rights and Burdens

Because liberalism has recently been identified with the principle of neutrality, it is natural to evaluate educational policies by asking which are "most neutral." This method is flawed if the principle of neutrality is properly understood in the way I have just proposed. This is because the principle of neutrality, as a constraint on reasons, cannot alone tell us how to weigh the competing reasons that it allows as legitimate, and so cannot tell us which educational policies are best, morally speaking.

To illustrate this point further, consider the dilemma faced by the Supreme Court in *Wisconsin v. Yoder*.[7] The legal issue in this case was whether the state of Wisconsin violated the constitutional rights of Yoder, a member of the Old Order Amish, in requiring him to send his children to public high school. While the government has a duty to protect the legitimate interests of children in education, this law arguably violated Yoder's constitutional right to the "free exercise of religion." How, then, should this dilemma be resolved? Intuitively, it seems that the principle of neutrality favors Yoder. This is because, in requiring all children to receive formal secondary school education, the government's educational policy would seem to be biased against traditional ways of life like that of the Amish. If, however, the reason for requiring Amish parents to send their children to public high school was simply to ensure that Amish children are adequately prepared to lead independent lives outside the Amish community, this policy did not violate the principle of neutrality, for this is not a reason that any defensible principle of neutrality would rule out as illegitimate. The principle of neutrality alone cannot tell us how this dilemma should be resolved, then, because it alone does not tell us how to balance the legitimate reasons there are for Amish parents and Amish children to want conflicting things. If we wish to evaluate this policy "from the liberal point of view" we must therefore go beyond the principle of neutrality to some more fundamental method of evaluation.

Underlying the liberal concern that government policies be neutral is the more general concern that government policies not violate individuals' moral rights. Once we see that the principle of neutrality alone cannot resolve moral dilemmas in the area of education, it therefore makes sense to explore how educational policy might be evaluated more directly by considering what educational policies are compatible with a due respect for individuals' moral rights. To this form of evaluation I now turn.

The idea that we have moral rights rests, I believe, fundamentally upon individualism, understood as a form of moral reasoning. According to this form of moral reasoning, the government should not observe a principle or adopt a policy that burdens an individual unless someone would bear a burden that is at least roughly as bad when the government does not observe this principle or does not adopt this policy. The government should not burden a person by prohibiting him from worshipping in accordance with his conscience, for example, unless toleration of this form of worship places a burden on someone that is at least as bad—as might be the case, for example, if this form of worship were to involve human sacrifice. This form of reasoning about government policy is individualistic in requiring us always to make one-to-one comparisons of the burdens that individuals bear as the result of various government policies, and in forbidding us from evaluating government policies solely by considering their net aggregate benefit, or net benefit summed over individuals. Thus, according to individualism, it would be impermissible for the government to establish and maintain a system of slavery even if this system would maximize social welfare in the aggregate, for this system would impose a burden on the individual slave that is substantially worse than any burden someone would bear in the absence of this policy.

Individualism tells us how to reason about rights, but not what rights *are*. Rights, in my view, are valid moral principles that state that certain reasons cannot justify individuals in acting towards others in certain ways. Rights against the *government*, then, are valid moral principles that state that certain reasons cannot justify the government in adopting certain policies. The right of free speech, for instance, is a set of valid moral principles that includes, among others, the principle that the government is not justified in prohibiting a person from publicly expressing his political opinions solely by the reason that someone would be upset by hearing them. What makes a specific principle of this kind morally valid is that it is grounded in some way upon individualism.

There are two ways in which a specific right might be grounded on individualism, the direct way and the indirect way. According to the direct way, the principle is valid that a certain reason, R, cannot justify the government in adopting a certain policy, C, if C places a burden on someone, and this burden is substantially worse than the burden anyone would bear in the absence of C that is identified by R. The principle is valid, for example, that it is wrong for the government to prohibit a person from expressing his political opinions solely for the reason that they are upsetting because it is a substantially greater burden to be prohibited from expressing one's political opinions than it is to be at a greater risk of being upset by the expression of opinions one disagrees with. According to the indirect way, in contrast, the principle, P, is valid that a certain reason, R, cannot justify the government in adopting a certain policy if someone would bear a burden when the government does not observe this principle, P, and this burden is substantially worse than any burden someone would bear when the government does observe P. Thus, according to the indirect method, the principle is valid that it is wrong for the government to prohibit the expression of political opinions for the reason that they are upsetting, not because every particular policy of this kind is unjustifiably burdensome but because a failure by the government to observe this general principle would itself impose a burden on someone that is substantially worse than any burden someone would bear as the result of the government observing this principle—in failing to secure good conditions for political deliberation, for example. Both direct and indirect methods have advantages. I adopt the direct method here because it is simpler to apply to particular cases and adequate to the point I wish to make about education and neutrality.

If the direct method of grounding specific moral rights on individualism is sound, we can evaluate whether or not a government policy violates an individual's moral rights by judging whether or not it satisfies the *burdens principle*. This principle is that it is wrong for the government to enact a policy that imposes a burden on someone if this burden is substantially worse than any burden someone would bear in the absence of this policy. The government places a burden on someone, I suppose, when its policies place her in a situation that there is good reason for her to want not to be in. The weight of this burden is determined by the weight of the reasons there are for her to want not to be in this situation. To determine whether a policy satisfies the burdens principle, we thus make a judgment about the relative weight of the reasons individuals have to want not to be in the relevant situations. We are justified in holding a judgment of this kind if it withstands our critical scrutiny, or remains stable upon critical reflection when we are thinking clearly and are adequately informed.

To illustrate this method of reasoning about rights, consider whether the government violates the rights of children if it requires them to recite a non-denominational prayer at the beginning of school each morning. Suppose that this policy makes the children of atheists feel like outsiders, and puts them in the unhappy position of having either to dissemble or risk harassment. These are good reasons for them to want the government not to adopt this policy, and the government therefore places a burden on them if it does so. Suppose, then, for the sake of argument, that this practice does *not*, as a matter of fact, substantially improve concentration and discipline, cooperativeness and respect for others, and that the only good reasons there are for other children to want the government to adopt this policy is that it gives them a good feeling in the morning. Since this reason to want this policy is substantially weaker than the reasons of the children of atheists not to want it, this policy would violate the moral rights of the children of atheists, on these assumptions, in imposing a substantially greater burden on them than the burden other children would bear in its absence.

One objection to this method of reasoning about rights is that it makes talk of rights eliminable in principle, since we might evaluate policies simply by making judgments about the relative weight of burdens without any reference to rights. Moral rights, it might be said, should be taken instead as primitives in our moral reasoning, and not as things that can be reduced to or replaced by something else. But if the moral principles that constitute rights were not grounded on defensible judgments about the relative weight of burdens on individuals, the judgment that a policy violates an individual's moral rights would seem arbitrary and indefensible, floating free of the sorts of considerations that might justify it. And if, as I have suggested, the fundamental moral insight underlying our talk of rights is that government policies must be evaluated individualistically, or one-to-one, and not merely by aggregative reasoning, the burdens principle captures what is most important in our talk of rights, even if it does make explicit reference to "rights" eliminable.

Another objection to the method of reasoning about rights represented by the burdens principle is that it makes what rights there are depend too much upon the facts. Thus suppose that a policy of school prayer *did* improve concentration and discipline substantially, and *did not* make the children of atheists feel like outsiders, or force them to dissemble or risk harassment. Then the claim that this policy violates their rights would not be warranted by this method of reasoning. This, it might be argued, misconstrues the character of rights: rights are abstract principles that regulate the permissibility of policies in abstraction from the consequences of particular policies, and so which imply that school prayer is wrong regardless of its consequences.

I believe, however, that our judgments about whether or not a policy violates an individual's moral rights must be sensitive to the facts about its actual consequences because our moral reasoning about the justifiability of a government policy is always sensitive to these facts. Thus suppose, again, that a policy of school prayer would substantially reduce violence in schools without imposing a substantial risk on anyone of persecution or harassment. This fact would clearly be relevant to our moral evaluation of this policy. If it were not relevant to our reasoning about rights, a strange gap would then exist between our reasoning about whether or not a policy is morally justifiable and about whether or not it violates a person's moral rights, raising doubt about the relevance of rights to our moral evaluation of government policy.

There are, as I have already noted, two ways in which our reasoning about rights might be sensitive to empirical consequences, the direct way and the indirect way. Some may believe the indirect way is superior precisely because it makes our judgments about whether a policy violates a person's rights less directly sensitive to the particular consequences of this policy. My aim here is not to defend the direct method as superior to the indirect method. It is only to outline a method of evaluating educational policy from the liberal point of view that goes beyond the idea of neutrality. For this purpose it suffices to say that our reasoning about what rights there are must be sensitive *in some way* to the facts. The only question is *how*. According to individualism—in either form—our reasoning about rights should be sensitive to the facts by making one-to-one comparisons of the burdens individuals bear in the relevant alternative situations. It is this individualistic, non-aggregative, form of reasoning, and not insensitivity to the facts, that shows our respect for individuals' moral rights.

Neutrality and the Weighing of Burdens

The justification of a morally adequate educational system is compatible with the principle of neutrality, I have now argued, because a morally adequate educational policy can be fully justified without reference to any of the reasons the principle of neutrality rules out. A consequence of this defense of neutrality is that in many cases this principle gives us little guidance to what educational policies are actually best. To arrive at a judgment of what educational policies are best from the liberal point of view, we must therefore turn to a more general theory of rights. I have now sketched such a theory.

At this point, however, it may be objected that the problem of education and neutrality simply reappears, albeit in a different form. If we take seriously the idea that individuals have moral rights, then an educational policy can be fully justified only by showing that it is compatible with these rights. This can be shown, in my view, only by making a judgment about the relative weight of burdens. Suppose, then, that any judgment about the relative weight of burdens in the area of education must presuppose that some ways of life are better than others, as some may suspect. If so, then the full justification of any educational policy would appear to violate the principle of neutrality after all.

Here it is helpful to distinguish two different principles of neutrality that have been endorsed by liberal theories of rights. First, there is the principle of *legislative neutrality*, which regulates the justification of coercive government policies by ruling out some reasons for these policies as illegitimate. This is the principle of neutrality that Ronald Dworkin endorses in arguing, for example, that it is wrong for the government to prohibit pornography solely for the reason that the kind of sexual conduct depicted in it is not the most admirable.[8] Second, there is the principle of *justificatory neutrality*, which regulates government policy in a different way, by requiring that coercive government policies obey principles of political morality, such as the principle of legislative neutrality, that can themselves be fully justified without presupposing any particular way of life is best. This is the principle of neutrality that John Rawls endorses in arguing that the government should obey only those principles of political morality that would be chosen behind a "veil of ignorance," which prevents individuals from choosing principles of justice on the basis of their particular conceptions of how it is best to live.[9] In arguing that a morally adequate educational policy can be justified compatible with the principle of neutrality, I have so far argued only that this is compatible with *legislative* neutrality. It is still an open question whether the justification of a morally adequate educational system can satisfy the principle of *justificatory* neutrality.[10]

Education may seem to pose a special problem for justificatory neutrality. It can seem that the burdens individuals bear under various government policies may be understood in general in terms of the degree to which they satisfy or frustrate considered and informed preferences. The burden that a person bears when prohibited by law from worshipping according to his conscience, for example, may be understood in terms of the strength of his considered and informed preference to worship in this way. Since children do not have the adult capacity to reflect on their preferences, their interests in education are not plausibly understood in terms of *their* considered and informed preferences; nor are these interests plausibly understood in terms of the considered and informed preferences of their parents or other adults, since the interests of adults in education may conflict with those of children. It therefore seems that in order to identify the important interests of children in education we must go beyond preferences to a list of objective educational goods. But, then, how are we to arrive at such a list without making a judgment about how it is best to live?

The puzzle here presupposes that burdens on individuals are properly identified in general by reference to preferences. Preferences, however, are the wrong basis for identifying burdens, for at least two reasons. First, the fact that someone lacks a preference for something does not show that he does not bear a substantial burden in not having it. Thus, someone may not care, as a matter of fact, whether his choices are informed, and so have no preference for the social conditions necessary for making informed choices. He would still bear a substantial burden if the government were to suppress information necessary for his making informed choices, and one that ought to be taken into account in assessing whether or not this policy violates his moral rights. Second, the fact that someone has a strong preference to do something does not show that he bears a substantial burden in not having the opportunity to do it. Thus while someone may have a strong preference to discriminate against others on the basis of race, it does not follow from this that he bears a substantial burden if he does not enjoy the legal opportunity to do so.

For these reasons, judgments about the relative weight of burdens are properly based on judgments about the relative weight of the *reasons* there are for individuals to want things, and not on judgments about the degree to which their *preferences* are satisfied. This may prompt the objection that the account of rights offered by the burdens principle is circular, since it does not reduce claims about rights to non-moral descriptive judgments about degrees of preference satisfaction. The aim of this account, however, is to identify how we are to think about whether or not a government policy violates a person's rights; it is not to show that we can do this without making normative judgments about the relative weight of the reasons there are for individuals to want things.

Once burdens are identified in general by the good reasons there are for individuals to want things, education no longer poses a *special* problem for justificatory neutrality. This is because the burdens that children bear under various educational policies may be identified by the good reasons there are for them to want various things from their education in the same general way that the burdens adults bear under various coercive policies may be identified by the good reasons there are for them to want liberty and other social goods. But if education poses no *special* problem for justificatory neutrality, perhaps the principle of justificatory neutrality still faces a *general* problem.

In judging how burdensome on someone a government policy is, we must consider three things. First, how this policy actually affects the situation of that individual as a matter of empirical fact. Second, what good reasons there are for that individual to want not to be in that situation. Third, how much weight these reasons have relative to the good reasons there are for other individuals to want not to be in the situation they will be in if the government does not adopt this policy. In order to make judgments of the first kind about the empirical effects of government policy, it is not necessary to judge that some ways of life are better than others. Nor, it seems, is it necessary to judge that some ways of life are better than others in order to make judgments of the second kind about the good reasons there are for individuals to want things. It may well seem impossible, though, to make judgments of the third kind about the relative weight of reasons without judging that some ways of life are better than others. How, after all, are we to make judgments about the relative moral weight of individuals' reasons to want things without making judgments about the relative moral worth of their goals? And how are we to make judgments about the relative moral worth of their goals without making a judgment about the relative worth of different ways of life?

It is an error, though, to believe that we must presuppose that some particular way of life is best in order to make defensible judgments about the relative weight of the reasons there are for individuals to want things. Thus suppose we defend laws that prohibit theft by arguing that the reasons there are for individuals to want their possessions to be secured by the law have greater moral weight than the reasons there are for individuals to want to be legally free to take anything they want when they want it. In making this judgment, we are not presupposing that any particular way of life is best. We are not presupposing, for example, that the life of a person who has more possessions is better than the life of a person who has fewer. We are not presupposing that middle-class suburban family life is better than that of an unattached wanderer. We are presupposing only that it is more important, other things being equal, for one's possessions to be legally secure than to have free legal access to all possessions. This judgment *does* express a view about "the good"—that it is *better*, other things being equal, to have legally secure possessions than to have unlimited legal access to things—but it does not express any particular view about how it is best for individuals to lead their lives. This judgment does not fail, then, to be neutral in the relevant sense among different conceptions of how it is best to live.

The sense that judgments about the relative weight of reasons to want things must presuppose some view about what kinds of life are best arises, I think, from puzzlement about what else they could be grounded on. How are we to make such judgments if not by consulting our views about the good life? But it is our capacity to recognize and weigh reasons—to want things, to believe things, to feel things, to do things—that is prior to our capacity to make judgments about how it is best to live, and not the other way around. If it were not possible for us to recognize and weigh reasons it would not be possible for us to make rational judgments about how it is best to live. Our capacity to recognize and weigh reasons is what makes us rational. Our capacity for rationality is not something that needs to be understood or explained in terms of some *further* cognitive capacity.

If it is possible for us to recognize and weigh reasons to want things without presupposing any particular view of how it is best to live, it is possible for us to identify and weigh the important interests children have in education without presupposing such a view. Thus consider some of the things that there is good reason for children to want from their education. There is good reason for children to want an education that develops and exercises their capacities to reason; that inculcates certain virtues, like self-discipline, respect for others, and cooperativeness; that develops the knowledge and skills necessary to be economically self-sufficient as an adult; that develops the understanding and the moral motivation necessary to meet the reasonable demands of citizenship and to perform other important duties, like those of parenting; that puts them in a good position to continue to grow intellectually and emotionally, by developing the ability to form and pursue new interests and to form and consider new ideas as they grow older; that does not put them at a substantial risk of harm or abuse; that is fun and stimulating, or at least not boring and dispiriting. To say there is good reason for every child to want an education that has these properties is not say that any particular way of life is best for everyone. An educational system justified by reference to these interests can therefore satisfy the principle of justificatory neutrality.

To bring this point to bear on a specific case, suppose we come to the conclusion that Amish parents should be required to send their children to public high school because the education they receive within the Amish community fails to develop the knowledge and skills necessary to be economically self-sufficient outside the Amish community. Not only would this policy not violate the principle of legislative neutrality—because this reason for government policy is not ruled out as illegitimate by this principle—it would not violate the principle of justificatory neutrality either. This is because the judgment that this reason has greater moral weight than the reasons there are for Amish parents to want not to send their children to public high school does not rest upon or imply the judgment that the Amish way of life is less worthy of pursuit than others. It implies only that the education that children receive within the Amish community is inadequate because it does not adequately prepare Amish children for economic self-sufficiency should they decide to leave the Amish community as adults.

Of course, the Wisconsin law that required Amish parents to send their children to public high school might still have violated their moral rights. Thus suppose that Amish parents sincerely believe that the education they provide within the Amish community is better for their children than the education they would receive in public high school; better for their continuing relationship with their children; better for their community; and better, perhaps, for the human race as a whole. Given these sincere beliefs, there is good reason for Amish parents to want not to be required to send their children to public high school, and the government imposes a genuine burden on them if it requires them to do so. The Wisconsin law would have violated the moral rights of Amish parents, then, if an Amish education protects the important interests of Amish children and others in education as well as a public high school education does—as the Supreme Court supposed in deciding this case in favor of Yoder.[11] This is because, on these assumptions, this policy imposes a substantially heavier burden on Amish parents than their children or others bear in the absence of this policy.

VOUCHERS

One way to address the apparent conflict between education and neutrality is to advocate a system of vouchers. Indeed, it might be argued, a system of vouchers is *required* by the principle of neutrality because the government cannot *provide* education without implicitly endorsing or promoting some particular conception of how it is best to live. It should now be clear why I do not think this argument in favor of vouchers is compelling. Assuming that local governments design their educational curricula on the basis of reasons that the principle of legislative neutrality allows as legitimate, a public educational system is neutral in the relevant sense.

At the outset I responded to the voucher proposal in a different way, by pointing out that it alone fails to solve the problem of neutrality, since standards of accreditation strong enough to protect the legitimate interests of children in receiving a good education will express a view about the good life in roughly the same way that the public school curriculum now does. It should now be clear why I think this argument against a voucher system is also uncompelling. If a public school curriculum can be developed by reference to the good reasons there are for children to want certain things from their education, and these reasons can be identified without presupposing that any particular way to live is best, then standards of accreditation for private schools can be developed in the same way. The principle of neutrality neither requires nor forbids either educational system, then, and the choice between them must therefore be made on other grounds.

The main argument for a voucher system is that by creating a market in education, schools will be forced by competition either to provide the best possible education for the dollar or to go out of business as a result of consumer dissatisfaction, thereby improving the quality of education for all over time. The main objection to a voucher system is that, as a matter of political reality, vouchers will never be funded at a high enough rate to pay for quality education for those who have no other funds available to spend on their children's education, and that a voucher system will therefore inevitably worsen the educational prospects for less advantaged children, by enabling more affluent children to attend other schools and so by directing resources away from the education of the less advantaged. Suppose, though, for the sake of argument, that vouchers were funded at a high enough rate to improve the educational system for all in the way the argument for them supposes they would. Would there be any compelling objection against them?

Some Americans would no doubt feel offended by the prospect of their tax dollars paying for religious education of which they disapprove. But if vouchers were applicable to a wide variety of schools, religious and non-religious alike, there would be no good reason for anyone to feel resentful or alienated at having to contribute to this system. Whatever feelings of offense this system might generate would therefore not be good reasons against it— any more than feelings of offense are good reasons against teaching tolerance of homosexuality.

Another objection to the voucher system is that it would remove the content of education from the control of elected officials, and so diminish the influence that citizens have over how the next generation of citizens will be educated. The amount of control that any non-official enjoys when school curricula are subject to legislative discretion is so slight, however, as to be virtually negligible. Indeed, given a choice between this form of indirect political control over the education of children in general and greater direct control over the education of one's own children, it seems any rational parent would choose the latter. This distribution of control may seem to leave those without children with an inadequate opportunity to influence the education of future generations, but there are other, more effective, ways to influence their education open to those who care most, such as teaching.

At this point some may argue that a voucher system is objectionable precisely because it would give parents *too much* control: by giving so much discretion to parents it would fail to insulate children adequately from their parents' values and so threaten their development of mental independence. The development of mental independence—or the capacity for independent reflection and criticism—is an inevitable part of normal cognitive development, though, which is not so easily stifled. Scary images of indoctrination, like scary images of addiction, exaggerate the degree to which humans are like automata. To be sure, some people do temporarily abdicate their claim to reflect and criticize—when they join cults, for example—but this abdication is generally voluntary, and is not easily brought about by coercion. Thus even under the most mentally oppressive regimes, such as China during the Cultural Revolution, normal humans develop the ability to recognize and criticize dishonesty, hypocrisy, and incompetence. Of course, it may still be argued that the interests of children in developing mental independence will not be adequately protected unless they are sent to public secular school. But, given the natural tendency of normal cognitive development, these interests would, to the contrary, seem to be adequately protected by any private education that satisfies reasonable standards of accreditation.[12]

Parents do not *own* their children; but they do have special obligations to promote their welfare as they reasonably understand it. Assuming, then, that a voucher system would improve the opportunities of parents conscientiously to discharge these special duties, this is something to be said in its favor. Private schools in general may not welcome direct parental participation in the formation of curricula any more than public schools now do; indeed private schools may now welcome parent participation even less. But a voucher system would give parents greater control over *which* schools their children attend, and so make it easier for them to discharge their special obligations to their children in a way that seems right to them. And given the value to some parents of more active participation, it is reasonable to assume that a market in vouchers would provide private schools that encourage parent participation in the formation of curricula, and that those parents to whom participation is especially important would therefore find adequate opportunities to participate.

Aside from the values of direct control over or active participation in the education of one's children, the opportunity to participate with other members of one's political community in the education of the next generation of citizens also has value. Some citizens may lose this opportunity under a voucher system, since under this system members of the same political community will be more likely to send their children to different schools. Other common political concerns will remain, however, and the opportunity to deliberate about these concerns will remain available to those who value political participation most highly.

On the assumption that a voucher system would result in a substantially better education for all children whose parents cannot already easily afford private school, there is, I conclude, no compelling argument against it. It is also true that, on the contrary assumption, there is no compelling argument *for* it. The current system of public schooling gives parents less control over the education of their children, but it does not prevent them from conscientiously seeking to promote the welfare of their children as they reasonably understand it. It allows parents to augment their children's public education, by religious or musical instruction, for example, or simply by spending more time with them on reading and writing. And parents may exit the public school system altogether, if they wish, in favor of private schools or home schooling.

Whether or not we should adopt a system of vouchers depends almost completely, then, on whether or not this system would actually improve education, particularly for the least advantaged children. This serves to underscore the general methodological point I have wanted to make here about liberalism and education. When we reason about educational policy from the liberal point of view we should seek, not to maximize neutrality, but to minimize the burdens that individuals actually bear. It is this practical concern with the relative weight of burdens on individuals, and not neutrality, that taking rights seriously involves.

NOTES

1. See, for example, Ronald Dworkin, "Liberalism," in *A Matter of Principle* (Cambridge, Mass.: Harvard University Press, 1985).

2. For this version of liberalism, see John Stuart Mill's discussion of individuality in *On Liberty*, ed. by Elizabeth Rapaport (Indianapolis: Hackett Publishing Co., 1978), Chapter III.

3. Joseph Raz was the first, to my knowledge, to use the phrase "perfectionist liberalism" to describe a liberalism based not on the value of neutrality but on the positive values of personal autonomy and value pluralism. See "Liberalism, Skepticism, and Democracy," *Iowa Law Review* 74 (May 1989), p. 781. The version of "perfectionist liberalism" sketched here is different from Raz's in placing special value not on personal autonomy or value pluralism but on lives that are led through reflective self-creation.

4. Amy Gutmann makes a similar objection to the liberal approach to education she calls "the state of individuals" in *Democratic Education* (Princeton: Princeton University Press, 1987), p. 36.

5. This is a central theme of John Rawls's *Political Liberalism* (New York: Columbia University Press, 1996). I think he would also endorse the second and fourth criticisms of a perfectionist liberalism mentioned in this paragraph.

6. Bruce Ackerman adopts a similar interpretation of neutrality in *Social Justice in the Liberal State* (New Haven: Yale University Press, 1980), Chapter One, maintaining (p. 11) that the principle of neutrality prohibits the government from adopting coercive policies *for certain reasons*: any reason that presupposes that some conception of how it is best to live is better than another, or that some person is superior to another.

7. 406 U.S. 205 (1972).

8. See Ronald Dworkin, "Do We Have a Right to Pornography?" in *A Matter of Principle*.

9. See John Rawls, *A Theory of Justice* (Cambridge: The Belknap Press of Harvard University Press, 1971).

10. In "Liberalism, Liberty, and Neutrality," *Philosophy and Public Affairs* 19 (Summer 1990): 253–274, I draw a related distinction between neutrality of grounds (justificatory neutrality) and concrete neutrality (legislative neutrality). The central claim of that article is that legislative neutrality does not follow from justificatory neutrality. I might have

pointed out also that legislative neutrality does not presuppose justificatory neutrality. Thus Ronald Dworkin, who still endorses legislative neutrality, now explicitly bases this principle on an abstract conception of how it is best to live which he refers to as the "challenge view," and so rejects the principle of justificatory neutrality. See Ronald Dworkin, "Foundations of Liberal Equality," in Stephen Darwall, ed., *Equal Freedom* (Ann Arbor: University of Michigan Press, 1995).

11. See 406 U.S. 224–227.

12. Richard Arneson and Ian Shapiro have criticized the Supreme Court's decision in *Wisconsin v. Yoder* for failing to protect the important interests Amish children have, as citizens of a democracy, in developing the disposition and ability to question authority. This disposition and ability is developed in later adolescence, they suppose, and is likely to be underdeveloped in a traditional society like that of Old Order Amish where questioning authority is not encouraged. A similar point might be made here against any private school that does not encourage students to question authority. In response I would argue that the interest in developing the ability to question authority, *beyond* the ability to think intelligently about moral issues and to disagree with others about them, and *beyond* the ability to recognize dishonesty and incompetence, which will develop normally with any adequate education, is not as weighty as Arneson and Shapiro suppose. See Richard Arneson and Ian Shapiro, "Democratic Autonomy and Religious Freedom: A Critique of *Wisconsin v. Yoder*," in Ian Shapiro, *Democracy's Place* (Ithaca: Cornell University Press, 1996).

8

SCHOOL VOUCHERS, SEPARATION OF CHURCH AND STATE, AND PERSONAL AUTONOMY

HARRY BRIGHOUSE

See p. 13

The most powerful and fastest spreading school reform idea in the U.S. today is school choice—the idea that parents should have a great deal more say than they have traditionally over where their children attend school. School choice, understood in this vague way, is relatively uncontroversial: both major parties, as well as both the main teacher's unions are on record as supporting choice plans within public school districts, open enrollment programs between school districts, and also legislation establishing Charter schools, schools which are funded by school districts and states but free of many of the regulatory burdens placed on government schools. Far more controversial are school voucher schemes—schemes in which the government pays tax-funded vouchers to parents which can be used to pay for children to attend private schools.

The model of the voucher program is the Milwaukee Private Choice Program (MPCP). It was initiated in Spring 1990 and has undergone several changes: I shall describe its shape as of Fall 1999.[1] Students may attend private schools in the Milwaukee Public Schools area. Vouchers are available only to children who come from households with household income at 1.75 times the federal poverty level or below, and who have not attended a private school in the previous year (though, of course, after the first year, participation in the program in the previous year does not disqualify students from participation). Transportation costs are not the responsibility of the schools, but in some cases the MPS will assist in transportation. Schools may not charge parents any additional fees for attendance, but they can charge reasonable fees for extra-curricular activities, towels, school uniforms, etc. The "voucher" comes in the form of a check, payable to the parents, which is sent directly to the choice school four times a year and must be signed over by the parents to the choice school. Schools may have no more than 65 percent of their students as participants in the program. The 1997–98 value of the voucher was $4,894, which was the state equalization aid per-pupil which would otherwise have been sent directly to the Milwaukee Public School District: the total amount sent to the choice schools is deducted from the grant made to MPS. Choice schools are subject to strict non-discrimination requirements: they must not discriminate on the basis of race, special educational needs, past academic performance, or past behavior. If a school is oversubscribed it must select from the choice pool randomly, with the small exception that it may prefer a student whose sibling already attends the school. Although there is no discrimination against children with special educational needs, schools are required to provide only the special services that they can provide with "minor adjustments," and parents are directed to discuss this matter with the schools they are applying to.

At first the program was restricted to secular private schools. A series of changes passed in 1995 included extending the program to include religious schools. This measure was blocked by court action until June 1998, when the Wisconsin Supreme Court found that it did not violate the separation of church and state and that the measure could go ahead pending further appeal: the U.S. Supreme Court refused to hear a further appeal in November 1998, so the change is now permanent. One crucial element of regulation on religious schools is that they are not permitted to require that Choice children participate in any form of religious service if the children's parents object. In 1998–99, 87 schools with 6,200 students participated. Thirty secular schools enrolled about 2,200 students, while 57 religious schools enrolled about 4,000 students. Around $28.6 million in state aid was therefore diverted from MPS to the participating choice schools.

Only two other schemes currently use state funds for private religious schools: the Cleveland Scholarship and Training Program and the Florida A-Plus Plan for Education. The legal status of these programs is unclear. Opponents of vouchers have filed First Amendment suits against the schemes, with varying success. In November 1998 the Supreme Court refused to hear an appeal against a circuit court decision in favor of the participation of religious schools in MPCP. But in August 1999 the Cleveland scheme was suspended on the orders of U.S. District Judge Solomon Oliver, pending the full consideration of its merits, because in his judgment it probably violates the Establishment Clause of the First Amendment of the U.S. Constitution. The eventual outcome of the legal battles is anyone's guess. *The Economist* newspaper, a fervent supporter of vouchers, has even expressed the hope that the Court finds against vouchers for religious schools, arguing that:

> advocates of vouchers—which include this newspaper—had better settle for second best: a swift ruling, in line with its previous position, that vouchers cannot be used in religious schools. And then vouchers will be free to help improve the public schools.
>
> The alternative is worse: that, embroiled in religious controversy, voucher schemes could become so contentious that they might disappear. . . . by restricting vouchers to secular schools, the Court would at least encourage the creation of a thriving market in secular education, public and private, which could attract more of the corporations and philanthropists who are already interested in the field.[2]

Vouchers are opposed on non-separationist grounds too. It is sometimes argued that introducing markets into the provision of education commodifies education in a way that is destructive to the practice; that markets violate the principle that public education should be regulated democratically by the community; and that vouchers will lead to a two-tier system in public schooling, to the detriment of the principle of educational equality.[3] However, the structure of the American legal system ensures that separation of church and state will continue to be the main grounds of opposition to vouchers.

In this chapter I shall argue that the liberal state's obligation of neutrality with regard to religion is not violated by its paying for children to attend schools that are run by religious groups. I have no view as to the actual state of the law with regard to these matters: my argument is philosophical, in that it describes what the state of the law should be, not what it is. I shall also argue, though, that the state has an obligation to ensure that every child has a full opportunity to become personally autonomous. This obligation has wide-ranging policy implications. In particular, it cuts against the differential regulation of public and private schools with respect to religious instruction. If all children are owed this obligation, they are owed it regardless of whether it is the state, their parents, or a religious foundation that pays for their education, and regardless of whether they attend privately-run or government-run schools. I want to emphasize that the argument I make does not support the extension of vouchers: I am quite sympathetic to opponents of vouchers on other grounds. But the central public argument being made against voucher schemes is deeply flawed.

The Separationist Case against Vouchers

Separationist opponents of vouchers appeal to the current understanding of the Establishment Clause articulated in *Lemon* in 1971. This test forbids government actions that either (1) have no secular purpose; (2) have a "primary effect" of advancing religion; or (3) foster an "excessive entanglement" between government and religion. Obviously, vouchers for religious schools do serve a secular purpose, so the second or third prongs must be the offenders. Opponents can cite the failure of the state to monitor properly its requirement that religious schools receiving vouchers not provide religious education or require religious worship for voucher children whose parents object; and can claim that vouchers lead to excessive entanglement. Sandra Feldman, the President of the AFT (the second largest teachers' union) has argued that vouchers cut against the independence of private religious schools, because the government will inevitably begin to regulate them if it funds them:

> For religious schools, public scrutiny and accountability raise issues of religious freedom; the deep infusion of religion throughout their curriculum and lessons is essential to them, as is their freedom to require children to attend religious services. They don't want state interference in any of that. Yet, accountability to the broader public must go along with public funding.[4]

The regulation claim is borne out by opinion polls, which show that although vouchers are increasingly popular, both opponents and supporters of vouchers believe that the government should regulate those schools that it funds.

Michael McConnell has pointed out that the current understanding of the *Lemon* decision makes the law "a mess." Because the Court understands the second prong to require monitoring and regulation of religious organizations receiving aid, and understands the third prong to forbid the same, the law is hard to interpret:

> With doctrine in such chaos, the Warren and Burger Courts were free to reach almost any result in almost any case. Thus, as of today, it is constitutional for a state to hire a Presbyterian minister to lead the legislature in daily prayers, but unconstitutional for a state to set aside a moment of silence in the schools for children to pray if they want to. It is unconstitutional for a state to require employers to accommodate their employees' work schedules to their Sabbath observances, but constitutionally mandatory for a state to require employers to pay workers compensation when the resulting inconsistency between work and Sabbath leads to discharge. It is constitutional for the government to give money to religiously-affiliated organizations to teach adolescents about proper sexual behavior, but not to teach them science or history. It is constitutional for the government to provide religious school pupils with books, but not with maps; with bus rides to religious schools, but not from school to a museum on a field trip; with cash to pay for state-mandated standardized tests, but not to pay for safety-related maintenance.[5]

But, chaos aside, it is hard to see how the vouchers violate any prong of the *Lemon* test, at least on any natural (as opposed to legal) understanding of it. Provision of the vouchers is neutral with respect to religion: Muslim, Orthodox Jewish, Methodist, Communist, or Wiccan schools that meet the regulations would be eligible for the vouchers. The subsidy is a subsidy for schools, not for churches. The Federal government already indirectly subsidizes churches to the tune of billions of dollars a year by providing them with charitable status. According to *The Economist,* in 1995 about 57 percent of the $144 billion made in contributions to tax-deductible charities in the U.S. went to churches.[6] Assuming an implausibly low average marginal tax rate of 20 percent, and that each contribution would have been diminished by the amount that was saved via the tax deduction, the Federal government indirectly subsidized churches to the tune of about $16.5 billion, even without counting the state and local tax exemptions churches often receive (they are frequently exempt, for example, from real estate taxes). If the Federal government is allowed to subsidize churches, the sole purpose of which is the promotion of religion, it is hard to see why the local government should not be allowed to subsidize schools, the primary purpose of which is usually providing an education.

The subsidies provided by tax deductions are admittedly indirect. But there is no difference from the *moral* point of view between a direct and an indirect subsidy. Indirect subsidies exercised through permitting tax deductions will doubtless be used in a different way from direct subsidies, and will have different outcomes in terms of what gets supported. It is also worth noting that indirect subsidies through tax deductions tend to help the wealthy pursue their religious goals, whereas vouchers tend to help the poor. Tax deductions benefit only those wealthy enough to pay taxes, whereas vouchers are given equally to all—or, in the cases of the Cleveland and Milwaukee programs, they go only to the poor.[7] But the morally significant feature is that funds which would otherwise have gone to some other public purpose are being diverted to churches. Whatever the legal issues, it would be *morally* inconsistent for the Court to rule out vouchers for private religious schools, on the grounds of the separation of church and state, while permitting indirect subsidies to churches.

Perhaps the tax deductions for contributions to churches violate the separation of church and state too. I doubt this. The

moral (as opposed to legal) issue that should concern us must be
the underlying purpose of separation of church and state: if this
purpose is not violated by a policy, then the policy should not be
objectionable on separationist grounds.

But what is the purpose of separation? Of course, different defenders may have different purposes for it, but the central purpose for a liberal defender of separation is to prevent the state
from putting its authority behind some sectarian way of life and
thereby setting itself against the moral convictions of its reasonable citizens. But if this is the purpose, then as long as all bona
fide religious and non-religious groups that meet reasonable regulations are included in a financial scheme, the spirit of
church/state separation is intact. While it is true that charitable
status in the U.S. is widely misused, this is because it is overly lax,
allowing subsidies to sectarian political organizations such as the
Heritage Foundation and the National Organization for Women,
not because it is overly restrictive. The policy does not discriminate among religions, or between religious and non- and anti-religious organizations. So the purpose of separation is not threatened by the tax-deduction policy.

Does the voucher constitute an unacceptable entanglement?
Well, it is true that voucher schemes, in order to be acceptable to
the public, will involve the government in considerable monitoring and regulation. Priscilla Pardini, in an organ not known for
its friendliness to sectarian religious education, argues as follows:

> John Allen, opinion editor of the St Louis-based National Catholic
> Reporter, predicts that the kind of minimal government oversight
> currently enjoyed by Milwaukee's religious voucher schools will be
> short-lived. "The core reality here is that public money inevitably
> and necessarily means there has to be some element of public ac-
> countability" . . . While no-one knows for certain what form such
> controls would take, some envision a scenario that would give gov-
> ernment agencies the right to dictate that religious schools shape
> their curriculum and personnel policies so as to conform to secu-
> lar law. Some possible questions: Should religious voucher schools
> be forbidden to teach creationism? Told that they cannot teach
> that homosexuality is wrong? Ordered to enroll a pregnant un-
> married student?[8]

The fear is simply that the religious character of private religious schools will be compromised by the monitoring and regulation which will inevitably accompany public funding in the long term. It is hard to accept this objection. Religious schools face a choice about whether to temper their religious mission with a secular mission when they accept public funding: and even if regulations are imposed after the fact they have the choice to opt out. They are simply being presented with a new option: more financial security in return for fulfilling a secular function, or refusing that security and refusing the secular function. Furthermore, if the Court stipulates that voluntary acceptance of monitoring and regulation constitutes unacceptable entanglement, it thereby establishes the curious situation in which it is acceptable for a scheme to require that a school shed its religious character in order to receive funding, but not for a scheme to require that a school accept monitoring and regulation while maintaining its religious character.

Now, it is true that once vouchers are available the position of all schools is changed, even those that reject vouchers, because their relative market position is altered. Prior to the introduction of vouchers parents face the following choice: subsidized secular schools or non-subsidized sectarian schools. In the voucher scheme they face three options: subsidized secular schools, subsidized religious schools which fulfill prescribed secular functions (whatever functions are prerequisites of receiving funding from the state), or non-subsidized religious schools which fail to fulfill those prescribed secular functions.[9] It is a fair bet that a good number of parents who absent vouchers choose non-subsidized religious schools which do not fulfill a secular function will, in the presence of vouchers choose a subsidized religious school which does fulfill that function. So non-subsidized religious schools are threatened by vouchers.

But it is still hard to sympathize. The mechanism through which they will suffer is not deliberate government action but the exercise of parental choice in the presence of an expanded range of options. If, as defenders of religious schools often suggest, parental choice is the core value in the exercise of religious freedom, then vouchers expand that, and religious schools that refuse to adopt legitimate secular purposes have no more to complain about than under the conditions where the state subsidizes (whether through vouchers or simply through standard public schooling) only secular schools.[10]

These considerations might be thought, though, to support a different objection. The desired neutrality of the state with respect to religions is undermined by requirements that voucher schools fulfill certain secular purposes. Some religions will naturally benefit from such requirements, because they will not have to compromise their fundamental values in order to obey the requirements. Unitarian schools, liberal Episcopalian schools, Jesuit schools, and Reform Lutheran schools will cheerfully take the vouchers without having to alter their curriculums or practices at all, while fundamentalist schools of various kinds, and Roman Catholic schools run by some non-Jesuit Orders, will suffer. So the state will, through its regulation, favor some religious views over others.

The response to this objection is simple. The regulation will, indeed, be non-neutral in *effect*. But it will not be non-neutral in *intent*. The secular purposes embodied in legitimate regulation are arrived at without regard to religious considerations. Take Pardini's examples: forbidding schools to teach creationism (as a true theory of natural history) and that homosexuality is wrong, and requiring that they not discriminate against pregnant teens. These are legitimate public purposes susceptible of public justification in child-centered terms. For example, every child has a right to an education, and being pregnant neither ill-suits one to receiving an education nor inhibits the education of one's classmates: to demand of institutions which want to participate in the social mission of guaranteeing the right to education that they abide by this rule is not unreasonable nor is it motivated by prejudice against any particular religion. Similarly, all children have an interest in being able to make responsible use of the sexual freedom they will be accorded as adults. A rule requiring that participants in the public project of education respect this interest by refraining from teaching that some legally permitted sexual choices are wrong is not motivated by prejudice against any particular religion.

Neutrality of effect is simply not a defensible constraint on government action. So many government actions will have non-neutral effects on religious pursuits that to embrace this constraint would entirely paralyze the government. The very project of public education undermines some religious movements which can flourish only with widespread illiteracy and ignorance; the practice of allowing religious organizations access to the airwaves benefits fundamentalist Christianity (which has no objections to using modern technology) more than it does the Old Order Mennonism which balks at using broadcast media to spread the faith. If neutrality is a constraint at all, it is in the form of neutrality of intent, which is observed when vouchers for religious schools are accompanied by legitimate public regulation.

Just to emphasize, again, I am arguing that on a commonsense understanding of what constitutes unacceptable entanglement, vouchers accompanied by regulation will not constitute that. What constitutes unacceptable entanglement in the legal sense of that term I am not qualified to comment on, though it might not be unreasonable to hope that common sense enters the deliberations of lawmakers somewhat.

Finally, on this point, the mere fact that the state provides the funds cannot constitute entanglement. Although the state does pay money directly to the school, it does so only after the school has been chosen by the qualifying parent. This no more entangles it in religious matters than does the fact that retired persons donate some of their social security payments to a church or, again, that it provides indirect subsidies to churches with charitable status.

It may appear that I have missed the *real* point of separationist objections to vouchers. If opponents hope to defeat vouchers, they have to resort to arguments which have some chance of legal success, and separationist arguments are the only ones that have a chance. The reason they have a chance is that the Supreme Court's understanding of the Establishment Clause is sufficiently complex for it to be an open question how it will respond to the issue. The Supreme Court, furthermore, gives lexical priority to Establishment Clause concerns (however they are understood) over any other interests involved. As James Dwyer says:

From a child-centered perspective, it is very puzzling to read judicial analyses of state aid to religious schools that begin with pronouncements that the purpose of the aid is to advance children's educational interests, that this aim is of tremendous importance, and that the aid in fact has that effect, but then to conclude that the aid is nevertheless impermissible, simply because it also advances religion in some way, which might be comparatively insignificant—for example by simply creating an impression of church-state coziness in the minds of (perhaps irrational) bystanders.[11]

Because it is not clear how things will turn out and because the Supreme Court assigns an implausible lexical priority to separation, making separationist arguments is the most rational strategy for opponents of vouchers. But the real, underlying, concern is not with separation but with the interests of children (which are, as Dwyer points out, given short shrift, legally). The real fear is that, with religious fundamentalism of various kinds so politically strong in the United States, the introduction of vouchers for religious schools will result in more children being subjected to indoctrination in the religious views of their parents, and in a public culture in which the values of toleration and civic respect are less secure than now.[12]

I have a great deal of sympathy with the version of this argument that appeals to the effects on the children of religious parents. One of the central reasons that it is so important that the state refrain from putting its authority behind controversial conceptions of the good life, which is the motivating principle behind separation, is that citizens should be presumed to be, and enabled to be, autonomous with respect to their religious views. The interest in autonomy that adults have supports the idea that when they are children they have an interest in their prospective autonomy, which interest plausibly merits protection by the state.

Evaluating the objection, though, is difficult. In the U.S. today private religious schools tend to have low tuition costs, and are virtually unregulated by the states. Home schooling is unregulated in most states: parents who home school need no qualifications, and do not need to demonstrate that their children will be exposed to views other than their own. There is already a great deal of scope for parents to have their children indoctrinated in their religious views, and it is hard to believe that vouchers for religious schools will increase this significantly, especially when the schemes are targeted and regulated as are the existing schemes in the U.S.

But there is something right about the objection. It is perhaps cynical to compare a reform only with the status quo: it should also be compared with alternative reforms. And the underlying premise: that all children have a right to a real opportunity to become autonomous with respect to their religious beliefs is, in my view, correct. In the next section I shall defend this premise. In the final section I shall explore its consequences for the voucher debate.

WHY ALL CHILDREN SHOULD HAVE THE OPPORTUNITY TO BECOME AUTONOMOUS

For the autonomy objection to work against vouchers for religious private schools, it must be asserted not only that every child should have a real opportunity to become an autonomous person but also that the state must, as a matter of justice, guarantee this opportunity. How could such an argument work? Proponents of what I shall call an autonomy-facilitating education are sometimes accused of believing that autonomy is an essential ingredient of a good life. Such accusations sting because the claim seems straightforwardly untrue, at least if autonomy is understood as requiring actual reflection on one's ends. Consider two people, both of whom live exactly as Mother Teresa is popularly supposed to have lived. One returns to her pallet every night and thinks carefully about what sort of life she should be living, seriously entertains alternatives, and each night settles on the decision to continue living her life as she has been living it. The other lives identically, except that at the end of each day she goes to sleep, oblivious of the possibility that there are other options for her, and unthinkingly prepared for the new day. While it may be plausible that the autonomous Mother Teresa lives a better life, it is completely implausible that, by virtue of her lack of thought, the thoughtless Mother Teresa's life has no value at all. It seems possible for someone to live a good life without exercising much rational reflection, and even without having an opportunity to live any other way than he does.

But the argument that children must have a real opportunity to become autonomous does not rest on any such premise. The foundational premise is that everyone should have a realistic opportunity to live well. Living well has at least two components: someone lives well only if she lives a life the content of which is actually good, and in addition she endorses the content of that life from the inside.[13] I do not want to offer a list of which ways of life are good and which are not; nor do I have some simple criteria for distinguishing good from bad ways of life: this is clearly contested ground. But I should say a word more about what it means to endorse a way of life from the inside. Endorsement does not, in my view, require autonomous and critical reflection, as it is normally understood. People can know that their way of life suits them well without knowing or thinking much about alternatives. What it does require, at least, is that they not experience their way of life as being at odds with their most fundamental experienced interests and desires.

Both components are essential (though they may not be jointly sufficient). Some ways of life are not good, and children whose parents pass them down cannot live them well even if the children endorse them: those children have no opportunity to live well unless they are able to find good ways of life. Other ways of life are, of course, good. But some children whose parents try to pass those ways of life down cannot endorse them from the inside: although the ways of life are good, these people cannot live them well. They have opportunities to live well only if they can exit into other good ways of life which they are able to endorse from the inside. How able they are to exit into a good way of life depends, partly, on whether they possess epistemically reliable ways of evaluating different ways of life.

Why should it be that some people are unable to live some good ways of life from the inside? The answer to this can be seen by noting two things: first that there is a plurality of individual constitutions, and second that there are limits to the plasticity of human personalities. People's personalities differ as to how exuberant or morose they are; how calculating or spontaneous; how much they need the company and regard of others; how much they find their fulfilment in their work and how much in their personal relationships. Some of these differences are, no doubt, socially constructed, and some lie within the control of the individual. But not all. Some people just could not be fulfilled without their work (or some work); others could not be fulfilled without having children. It is not possible for us to design children's upbringings to get a desired personality type: whether this is because genes matter too much, or because we cannot know enough about the effects of the environment to design it correctly is not really important.

The plurality of personal constitutions is important: some persons' constitutions will allow them to live some ways of life from the inside, but not other ways of life. The starkest case I can think of concerns people who experience their sexuality as fixed and unadaptable. A homosexual who experiences his homosexuality as unchangeable simply cannot live, from the inside, a way of life which requires heterosexual marriage and child rearing of fully respected adults. Trapped in such a way of life he will be alienated from it: it may be a very good way of life, but it is not one that *he* can endorse from the inside, and is therefore not one that *he* can live well. Similarly, some religious ways of life which impose on women the duties of fidelity in marriage and modesty conflict with the natures of some women who are raised in those religions. Take the character Sonia Horowitz in the film *A Price Above Rubies*. She is an orthodox Jew who marries a young scholar as a teenager. He becomes much revered for his scholarly and spiritual life, but as he develops it he neglects her both emotionally and sexually. Now, there may well be some women who could be comfortable living modestly as the wife of a saint for their whole lives, and there is nothing to suggest that there would be anything wrong with their lives. But for Sonia, with her particular constitution, it would be impossible to continue such a life and endorse it from within, even if she were unaware of alternatives.

Different ways of life elevate different virtues, and some children are ill constituted to develop the particular virtues their parents' way of life endorses. Some children will, of course, be well constituted to the ways of life into which they are inducted by their parents. But neither the state nor their parents can identify these children in advance. So to guarantee that all children have the opportunity to live well the state must ensure that all children have a real opportunity to enter good ways of life other than those into which their parents seek to induct them.

What does it take to provide a child with the opportunity to enter other ways of life than her parents'? Liberals are properly reluctant to have the state comment on the substantive ends of citizens, and they tend to focus on the provision of resources and liberties to citizens. But if someone has all the resources and liberties that justice requires but has, as an avoidable result of the design of social institutions, hardly any opportunity to live well, she has not been treated justly. One purpose of delivering the resources and liberties that justice requires is that they enable people to live well by their own judgement. But to live well one needs more: one needs also some sense of what constitutes living well. So providing the opportunity to enter ways of life requires that the state educate children in the skills of rational reflection and comparison usually associated with autonomy.

Were learning how to live well an entirely mysterious matter, or if equipping people with the skills associated with learning how to live well conflicted with other elements of justice, it might be conceded that justice requires only the delivery of external resources and conditions. But the basic methods of rational evaluation are reliable aids to uncovering how to live well, and they are the only such aids that can be identified and taught. This is especially important in modern conditions, with "fast changing technologies and free movement of labour [which calls for] an ability to cope with changing technological, economic and social conditions, for an ability to adjust, to acquire new skills, to move from one subculture to another, to come to terms with new scientific and moral views."[14] Without the autonomy-related skills we are easily lost in the moral (and economic) complexity of modernity. This does not imply that no one will hit upon, or at least approach, good ways of life without their aid, nor that rational deliberation is infallible. As in other areas of knowledge, inspired guesses, trusting the reliable communication of another, and manipulation by reliable others can help us find out how to live well. And rational deliberation confronts barriers. But in the absence of fortunate guesses and well-informed parents, children will be much better able to enter alternative good ways of life if they are well informed about alternatives and are able rationally to compare them.[15]

The conception of autonomy I am invoking may seem rather abstract. Rational reflection does not suffice to weigh different alternatives of how to live, or different immediate choices about what to do, in the way that propositional logic suffices when evaluating the validity of arguments. However, no other (known) device is so reliable in this area of human understanding. Rational reflection can help us to detect inconsistencies and fallacious argumentation, and to uncover misuse of evidence. It helps us to see whether a choice coheres with our given preferences, including our higher-order preferences. It helps us therefore in determining the relative plausibility of different positions on the grounds of both evidence and coherence.

These facts support a strong presumption that children should have the opportunity to learn the skills associated with autonomy and that parental preference is not sufficient reason to deny them that opportunity. In waiving the opportunity parents would be depriving their children of skills which are of great value in working out how to live well. Does the argument, though, support intervention in the school curriculum? It is important to see that the primary question here concerns the institutional distribution of authority over children. The instrumental argument suggests that the state (as an agent on behalf of society) has the authority to provide children the opportunity to be autonomous. Whether this requires intervention in schooling, and what form that intervention should take, will depend on the character of non-educational institutions and facts about developmental psychology.

If, for example, a robust public culture provided abundant opportunities to develop the relevant skills, and parents could not shield their children from those aspects of the public culture, then perhaps no intervention would be needed. I assume that this is false in most liberal democracies; and many parents who might exempt their children from autonomy-facilitating education at school also refrain from teaching them the relevant skills at home.[16] I do not mean to suggest for a moment that there is, in liberal democracies, a public culture conducive to autonomy, which religious parents revile and protect their children from. In fact the mainstream public culture in most liberal democracies is grossly commercial, and dominated by agencies the aims of which are precisely to *undermine* children's autonomy at least with respect to how they spend all their leisure time and all their disposable income. The problem is partly that these aspects of the public culture are those from which it is most difficult to shield children: the failures of religious parents to shield their children from public culture by no means necessarily enhance their autonomy.

Some may still be unpersuaded that *justice* requires that all children have the opportunity to become autonomous. It might be a very good thing for children to learn the relevant skills, but that does not suffice to show that justice requires it. The connection with justice can be shown by considering an argument *against* requiring autonomy-facilitating education recently offered by Francis Schrag. Considering Schrag's argument is particularly helpful because it shares some of my own argument's key premises.

Schrag takes it for granted that what matters fundamentally is that children have real opportunities for living well, and he posits the Berlinian claim that there are plural and conflicting (good) values. There are, in other words, many diverse ways of life which human beings are capable of living well. He claims furthermore (consistently with the claims I have made) that some deeply religious ways of life are good, or, as he puts it "choiceworthy," quoting the articulate and well-considered testimony of an Orthodox Jewish woman, Lisa Aiken, who was brought up in mainstream secular America but converted as an adult to Orthodox Judaism. We know the following about her:

1. She was not brought up in the Orthodox community and hence her socialization did not confine her to the Orthodox world-view.
2. Her conversion was—at least according to her testimony—neither a coerced nor a sudden transformation that bypassed her rational processes.
3. She is able to articulate the features of the life she's chosen that make it fulfilling.[17]

Her testimony is thus powerful evidence that this deeply religious way of life can be chosen autonomously and is hence capable of being lived well. But, as I have suggested earlier, it would be implausible to think that the goodness of her way of life depends on its being chosen autonomously. Her testimony is ultimately evidence that the way of life can be lived well even when it is not chosen autonomously: that is, even when it is lived by someone who was brought up in the faith without ever having been taught about other options. Surely, then, we do not need to teach children the skills needed to make comparative evaluations between their parents' and other ways of life in order to give them a real opportunity to live well.

Notice that Schrag's argument does not rely on any claim about parental rights or obligations to respect parental authority. His central moral premises are just the same as those of the instrumental argument: that there are plural and conflicting ways of life and that children are owed real opportunities to live well.

However, there is a problem with his argument, which highlights the connection between justice and autonomy-facilitating education. I have already accepted value pluralism and that lives can be lived well without being autonomously chosen. But Schrag (like others who seek to accommodate the demands of religious parents) neglects the observation I have already made that people have different personalities, characters, or internal constitutions that suit them differently well to different ways of life and these differences do not correlate perfectly with the demands of their parents' or their communities' religious commitments.

If what I have called constitution pluralism is true, and religious parents are permitted to exempt their children from autonomy facilitation, then whereas some children will have great opportunities for living well (those in mainstream communities who get autonomy-facilitating education, and those growing up in religious communities whose constitutions suit them to the given ways of life), others will have few or none. This constitutes a strong prima facie injustice.

The key to seeing why justice is involved here, then, is to think about the requirement of equal opportunity. Equality of opportunity impugns unequal life prospects when they arise from unequal circumstances, but not when they arise from conscious choices. But unequal prospects are faced by children who learn the skills associated with autonomy and those who do not, and those inequalities are the result of their circumstances rather than their choices (and, in the case of children, it is not clear that the principle of equal opportunity even permits inequalities arising from choices). And in my argument I have used the even weaker notion that we owe others merely some significant (rather than strictly equal) opportunity to live a good life.

AUTONOMY, CURRICULUM, AND VOUCHERS

The argument for mandating autonomy-facilitating education suggests that schools, whether public or private, should ensure that the following elements are included in their curriculums:

- The traditional academic content–based curriculum. Proponents of teaching critical thinking skills and autonomy in the curriculum often sound as if they are opposing the traditional emphasis on teaching "facts" and "content" in the curriculum. But there is no real conflict here: an autonomous life cannot be led without the information about the world in which it is led, and the critical thinking skills involved in autonomy can neither be developed nor exercised without the ease of access to a considerable amount of information which is provided only by having learned and internalized it. It is true that there is far more information available than any child can expect to learn, and that it is crucial that children learn how to get access to information, but the idea that they might develop the more complex skills of reasoning about information without having a good deal of it instantly available is silly.

- How to identify various sorts of fallacious arguments, and how to distinguish among them, as well as between them and non-fallacious arguments. The autonomous person needs to be able to distinguish between appeals to authority and appeals to evidence, between inductive and deductive arguments, as well as to identify ad hominem arguments and other misleading rhetorical devices.

- Exposure to a range of religious, non-religious, and antireligious ethical views in some detail, as well as the kinds of reasoning deployed within those views, and the attitudes of proponents toward non-believers, heretics, and the secular world.

- Information about the diverse ways (including non-reason-based ways) in which secular and religious thinkers have dealt with moral conflict and religious disagreements, and with tensions in their own views; and about how individuals have described (and to the extent possible how they have experienced) conversion experiences, losses of faith, and reasoned abandonment of ethical positions.

These last two elements are particularly important, since autonomy with respect to one's religious and moral commitments requires exposure to alternative views. It also requires that this exposure be done in a controlled and non-pressured way, but also in a way that reflects the reality of the lives lived according to these commitments. Exposure to moral views would be done best by allowing proponents of views to address children in the controlled environment of the classroom. While the instrumental argument is connected to the liberal humanism which is anathema to many religious sectarians, the implementation of autonomy-facilitating education would probably require a nuanced attitude to the exposure of children to religion in schools. A child cannot be autonomous either in her acceptance or in her rejection of a religious view unless she experiences serious advocacy. As John Stuart Mill argues, concerning the exposure of adults to free speech:

> Nor is it enough that he should hear the arguments of adversaries from his own teachers, presented as they state them, and accompanied by what they offer as refutations. That is not the way to do justice to the arguments, or bring them into real contact with his own mind. He must be able to hear them from persons who actually believe them; who defend them in earnest and do their very utmost for them.[18]

Neutral, antiseptic textbooks describing each view and serially explaining its advantages and defects may contribute little to autonomy facilitation—they certainly would not suffice. Autonomy, though susceptible of an abstract description, cannot be practiced outside the specific situation of individual lives; education should reflect this.

Does the requirement that all children be exposed to such a curriculum impugn vouchers for private religious schools? The question is difficult to answer. Of course, few private religious schools adhere to the stringent standards suggested. But many public schools are equally neglectful of their students' interest in autonomy, though in different ways. Religious and moral matters are often thoroughly neglected, or treated as if ways of life are to be chosen among arbitrarily: as if lifestyles are mere matters of preference rather than matters to be rationally and carefully considered. A motivating fear for many religious parents is not that their children will be exposed to objectionable views at school but that there will be no counterweight of exposure to religious views; or that when there is exposure to religious views it will be inaccurate and dismissive. I believe this fear is reasonable, and when it is realized the autonomy of the children thus exposed is compromised. Many urban schools operate in circumstances in which attention to the curricular requirements of autonomy facilitation is something of a luxury anyway—their students lack the freedom from material need and the circumstantial security required for rational reflection among different ways of life. The autonomy objection impugns the practices of many of our public schools just as well as it does most of the private schools that receive vouchers.

Opponents of vouchers who press the autonomy objection are, furthermore, in a difficult moral position unless they are also willing (as few of them are) to advocate that all schools be required to adopt an autonomy-facilitating curriculum regardless of whether they receive public funding. After all, the argument supports that all children receive such an education, regardless of whether their parents approve.

So while it is possible to use the autonomy objection to oppose vouchers, it is just as natural to, instead, use it to suggest that all schools receiving vouchers, and all other government-funded schools, implement an autonomy-facilitating curriculum. It may be that few religious schools will want to accept that bargain: so that religious schools will be excluded de facto, although not de jure. I have already argued in section one that religious schools embodying public regulation will exert a considerable pull on religious parents: many will prefer to spend less money on a school with a muted religious character than more money on a school with an unbridled religious character. In the next section I want to explain why autonomy-facilitating education should be preferred to autonomy-promoting education, and shall suggest that it may be less troubling for religious parents than the more demanding policy.

AUTONOMY-FACILITATING VERSUS AUTONOMY-PROMOTING EDUCATION

In the previous section I described the curricular requirements of an autonomy-facilitating education. But the argument that all children should have a real opportunity to become autonomous also supports a different policy goal, which may, in certain circumstances, conflict with mandating an autonomy-facilitating education. Currently, in the United States, deeply religious communities feel alienated from the mainstream culture of their society. This alienation is, in some ways, admirable: many Christians believe that the odds are stacked against their faith, and against their children, by a culture which is ostentatiously materialistic, and in which even human relationships (especially sexual ones) are treated as commodities. In her account of the life of a Conservative Christian family which home schools its children Margaret Talbot describes the magazines available for teenagers: "It has its own magazines for every demographic niche, including Hopscotch and Boy's Quest for kids 6–13, which promise 'no teen themes, no boyfriends, girlfriends, makeup, fashion or violence and NO ADVERTISING.'"[19] Religious parents fear that schools which do not incorporate strong moral values, and which treat spirituality as just another lifestyle option, one which may not even be presented to children by sincere believers, endanger their children's prospects for a balanced and satisfying life. The alienation is also partly artificial. The inaccessibility of political elites and the lack of transparency of many public institutions enable political entrepreneurs such as the Christian Coalition to foster a sense of alienation by promoting false but (in context) believable myths about the hostility of "the Establishment" to religious belief in general and Christianity in particular.[20] Furthermore, attempts to insulate children from mainstream culture, which can never be fully successful, may make matters even worse, by depriving those children of the resources coolly to evaluate the alternatives to their parents' faiths; and this may lead to even worse consequences for some of the children.

This illustrates that there are other barriers to the exercise of autonomy than not having the appropriate skills. One central problem is that the boundaries between deeply religious and secular, or non-deeply-religious ways of life are relatively impermeable. The proponent of autonomy-facilitating education who is motivated by the argument I have presented must also be concerned, as far as possible, to make more permeable the barriers between different ways of life, to facilitate movement between them that is based more on assessment of their relative merits for the individual concerned than on the personal costs incurred by moving. This is a concern not only because we want good secular ways of life to be realistically available to children raised in religious ways of life but also because we want good religious ways of life to be realistically available to children raised in but alienated from secular ways of life.

Yet mandating autonomy-facilitating education may make this more fundamental goal harder to achieve. Even the current restrictions on teaching religion in public schools contribute to an air of distrust among religious parents, which is, as I suggested earlier, readily exploited by religious entrepreneurs who spread scare stories about children not being allowed to read the Bible during personal reading time and children not being allowed to pray in public schools. These restrictions contribute to the sense of alienation, which in turn contributes to the hardening of the barriers between religious and secular ways of life. Wouldn't autonomy-facilitating education simply exacerbate this problem?

I think there is a real possibility that it would, so my recommendation of autonomy-facilitating education is tempered by that fact. But I would also like to speculate that the proposals I have made have advantages in this respect over alternative civic-oriented education proposals. Take, for example, Amy Gutmann's recommendations for a civic education curriculum. Gutmann's civic education includes education for autonomy but also substantive teaching of values. She suggests that the need for a common civic education flows from the "democratic ideal of sharing political sovereignty as citizens."[21] The ideal of sharing political sovereignty requires both behavior which is in accordance with political authority and critical thinking about authority. Democratic civic education aims at inculcating in children the habits and values which the good democratic citizen will possess:

> Deliberative citizens are committed, at least partly through the inculcation of habit, to living up to the routine demands of democratic life, at the same time as they are committed to questioning those demands whenever they appear to threaten the foundational ideals of democratic sovereignty, such as respect for persons.[22]

In order to produce such citizens the state should educate children in a way that predisposes "children to accept ways of life that are consistent with sharing the rights and responsibilities in a democratic society"[23] as well as foundational democratic values.

The skills associated with autonomy are acquired by children via their learning of the requirements for effective participation in political debate. Gutmann argues that *mutual civic respect* must be taught to secure the "minimal conditions of reasonable public judgment."[24] Mutual civic respect is contrasted with mere tolerance: when we are merely tolerant we refrain from coercing those with whom we disagree, but when we accord them civic respect we take them—and their ideas—seriously. The idea is that in order to take adherents of other beliefs—and their beliefs—seriously, children must learn skills such as how rationally to evaluate different moral claims. The basic idea is that unless citizens know what other citizens believe and are able to evaluate their arguments, their abilities to press their own interests effectively in democratic processes, and to assess the arguments pressed by others, are both hampered.

But the skills involved in "political reflection cannot be neatly differentiated from the skills involved in evaluating one's own way of life."[25] "Most (if not all) of the same skills and virtues that are necessary and sufficient for educating children for citizenship in a liberal democracy are those that are necessary and sufficient for educating children to deliberate about their own ways of life, more generally (and less politically) speaking."[26] Education for autonomy is, then, a by-product of what is needed to teach civic respect, which in turn is an element of civic education. There are obvious similarities between my proposals and Gutmann's but also interesting divergences. Under my recommendations children are taught that diversity is a fact, but they are not taught that it is desirable. Correlatively they are not taught sympathetically to address views about the good life other than their own; only about such views, and how to engage them seriously. They are taught neither Gutmann's virtue of civic respect nor even the weaker value of tolerance.[27] Though not value-free, my recommendations favor knowledge and skills over virtue.[28] This is because the recommendation is for autonomy-facilitating rather than autonomy-promoting education. The argument claims that equipping people with the skills needed rationally to reflect on alternative choices about how to live is a crucial component of providing them with substantive freedom and real opportunities, by enabling them to make better rather than worse choices about how to live their lives. The education does not try to ensure that students employ autonomy in their lives, any more than Latin classes are aimed at ensuring that students employ Latin in their lives. Rather it aims to enable them to live autonomously should they wish to, just as we aim to enable them to criticize poetry, do algebra, etc. without trying to ensure that they do so. The argument suggests that, other things being equal, people's lives go better when they deploy the skills associated with autonomy, but it does not yield any obligation to persuade people to deploy these skills: autonomy must be facilitated, not necessarily promoted.

Autonomy-facilitating education differs from autonomy-promoting education on two dimensions. The justificatory strategy is different. While traditional arguments for civic education (like Gutmann's) appeal to the civic responsibilities of future citizens, and comprehensive versions of liberalism appeal to the intrinsically superior value of autonomous over non-autonomous living, my argument emphasizes the instrumental value of the skills associated with autonomy for the individuals acquiring them in their quest to live well. The content is also at least somewhat different, in a way that fits with the justificatory strategy: the education aims

to be "character-neutral," in that it seeks to provide certain critical skills without aiming to inculcate the inclination to use them,
and minimal inculcation of substantive controversial values. I
must emphasize, though, that although the methods recom-
mended will be more somber than evangelizing, it may be hard
to distinguish autonomy-facilitating from autonomy-promoting
education in practice, because the skills cannot be learned without being exercised and because it may be hard to teach the skills
without also communicating that they are worth using. For this
reason, although the difference in justificatory strategies may be
significant, the practical differences may be negligible, thus lacking the cushioning effect on religious parents that might be
hoped for.

Why refrain from the focus on civic virtue that animates Gutmann's proposals (and which is also found in the work of Eamonn Callan and Stephen Macedo)?[29] I shall leave a full explanation of this to another piece, but I can make three relevant comments.[30] First I doubt that Gutmann is working with a correct
view of civic virtue. Her view relies on an overdemanding charac-
terization of democratic participation; and while autonomy is no
doubt *a* virtue, one which yields civic benefits, there are others
which may be equally beneficial and which are incompatible with
autonomy at least in the individuals who carry them. For example, the disinclination of the Amish to engage with the surrounding society politically is a great virtue given the kinds of issues
they would be liable to push if they were to engage. Second, Gutmann argues from the need to fix a threshold level of civic stability of a certain sort. But civic stability can be achieved without
everyone having all the civic virtues—all that is needed is that
enough people have enough of the virtues to yield a threshold
level of stability. So even if this view of civic virtue is correct the
motive of providing civic stability does not support autonomy-
promoting education for all children—a (possibly high) degree
of exemptionism is quite compatible with the underlying motive.
And there are opportunity costs, rightly cited by defenders of "diversity," to teaching them to more people than are necessary.
Similar opportunity costs may well attend universal autonomy-facilitating education. But whereas they cannot be justified by the
need for civic stability (since educating more than the necessary

threshold number in the virtues yields no more gain in stability), they can be justified by appeal to the contribution of autonomy facilitation to the good of the individuals who receive it. The third criticism raises a feature of my view that I ought to highlight briefly. My argument is entirely child-centered. It focuses entirely on the good that autonomy facilitation does for the individual child who learns it, and not at all on the benefits this yields for society or civic stability. As I have indicated I suspect that civic stability is—in our modern democracies which are already pretty stable—too easily achieved to justify autonomy-facilitating or autonomy-promoting education for each child. But it is also because children rightly have a unique place in or thinking about education. Children are not yet participating citizens, they do not yet have conceptions of how to live that can properly be thought of as their own, and their capabilities to engage in citizenship and to develop and pursue conceptions of the good which *are* their own are entirely in the hands of others. And unlike some other persons who are similarly vulnerable and dependent (such as some of the very elderly, and some of the mentally ill or disabled) they do actually have the capacity to develop that capability. The prospective capability is in the hands of others who have already developed it. I think these facts support giving children's interests a certain sort of priority in the design of educational institutions. Now, the argument I have given for autonomy-facilitating education for all depends on the premise that all should have a real opportunity to live well: that is, to live a good life from the inside. The main reason I am reluctant to endorse autonomy-promotion, then, is this: I think that living well—living a life that is good, from the inside—is possible in a way of life that does not deploy the skills associated with autonomy. My argument does not make autonomy a necessary part of living a good life, or of living well, and this is because it seems to me that many good lives are lived "from the inside" by people who do not choose them autonomously, and who do not exercise autonomy within those lives. Some personal constitutions may be very ill-suited to living autonomously, and by trying to inculcate autonomous character into those people we may jeopardize their opportunities to live well. We may, admittedly, jeopardize their opportunities by providing them with an autonomy-facilitating education, but if there is any difference in the two practices, we can hope that we shall not be jeopardizing them as much.

It should be clear, then, why I think my recommendations are less vulnerable to the charge that they will exacerbate the alienation of deeply religious parents from mainstream society than, say, Gutmann's. In refraining from teaching substantive civic values, autonomy-facilitating education refrains from putting Mammon before God. While religious parents may remain distrustful of the authorities, autonomy-facilitating education does not actually teach values that contradict their own. Furthermore, in insisting that children are exposed in school to a wide array of religious and non-religious views, and that they encounter actual believers of these views, my recommendations address the reasonable fear of many religious parents that views like their own will be either ignored or, worse, ridiculed in the schools. The aim of this policy is not to disarm religious parents; it is to provide an autonomy-facilitating education for children, including children from secular home backgrounds. But disarming religious parents may be a welcome side effect which will improve the general cultural ethos surrounding questions of religion, making it politically easier to implement autonomy-facilitating education.

Notice that I am not claiming that there would be no resistance to these kinds of measures from religious parents, just that there is liable to be less than to the civic-virtue and autonomy-promoting versions. Even this claim depends a great deal on the details of the policies involved, and on the manner in which they are carried out. When the details are fully worked out it may turn out that autonomy-facilitating and autonomy-promoting education resemble each other a great deal, and that in fact both are more liable to defuse conflict than the vague relativism disguised as tolerance of diversity that pervades a great deal of education policy making. On the other hand, the reverse may turn out to be the case. If so, I am wrong that conflict can be diminished: but I would stand by the claim that autonomy-facilitating education should be a condition on any school, religious or otherwise, receiving public funds.

CONCLUDING COMMENTS

I have tried to show that vouchers for religious schools should not be resisted on separationist grounds. I also believe, though I have not shown, that resistance on those grounds contributes to a political dynamic which is deeply damaging to the aim of a tolerant secular polity and, more importantly, to the goal of ensuring that every child has a real opportunity to become an autonomous person. That said, voucher schools, like public schools, should be required to implement an autonomy-facilitating education, and assurances should be given to deeply religious parents that religious ways of life will be among those that their and other people's children will be exposed to in an environment that encourages serious engagement with and reflection on those ways of life.

NOTES

This paper draws on, and develops arguments from, my book *School Choice and Social Justice* (Oxford University Press, 2000), especially Chapter 4. Thanks to Steve Macedo and John Holzwarth for comments on previous drafts.

1. Details of the scheme can be gathered from the Wisconsin Department of Public Instruction. Its web site contains the instructions for parents and answers many questions about the details of the scheme. See http://www.dpi.state.wi.us

2. "America's Voucher Battle," *The Economist,* Sept 4, 1999.

3. See John McMurtry, "Education and the Market Model," *Journal of Philosophy of Education* 25 (199): 209–217; Michael Strain, "Autonomy, Schools and the Constitutive Role of Community," *British Journal of Educational Studies* 43 (1995): 4–19; Stuart Ranson, "Markets or Democracy for Education," *British Journal of Educational Studies* 41 (1993): 333–352 for some of these objections. I reject all but the equality objection in *School Choice and Social Justice* chapter 3.

4. Sandra Feldman, "A commentary on public education and other critical issues: First Choice," *The New York Times,* October 3, 1999 (advertisement).

5. Michael W. McConnell, "Religious Freedom at the Crossroads," *University of Chicago Law Review,* vol. 59 (1992): 115–194 at 119.

6. "Tax-exempt and loving it," *The Economist*, January 4–10, 1997, p. 17.

7. MPCP currently grants vouchers only to households which are at 175 percent of the official poverty line or below.

8. Priscilla Pardini, "Church/State Complexities," *Rethinking Schools* 14, no 2 (1999).

9. I should note here that almost all schools presumably fulfill some secular functions to some degree—they teach children to read and write, basic numeracy, socialize them to some extent, etc. The functions I refer to here are those functions—whatever they are—that opponents of funding of religious schools believe all schools should fulfill in order to receive funding. As will become obvious, I believe facilitating the child's autonomy to be one of these functions.

10. Lisa Borchardt has pointed out to me that this claim needs qualification. It may depend on the working of the particular market whether parental choice is "truly" expanded. If in many regional markets there is not a critical mass of parents who want for their children a school which rejects the secular regulation, then all such parents will effectively lose their preferred option. However under a voucher scheme with all religious schools ineligible for subsidies, unless there is a critical mass of parents whose first preference is a religious school which already fulfills the secular requirements that would be imposed on all schools participating in a voucher scheme, *those* parents' first choice is not available to *them*. This is because many parents whose children attend such religious schools for secular reasons absent the voucher may, once a voucher is introduced, defect to subsidized secular schools, which would suddenly have a competitive advantage over all religious schools.

11. James G. Dwyer, *Vouchers Without Strings? A Child-centered Assessment of State Aid to Religious Schools* (unpublished manuscript, on file with author).

12. Another quite independent fear, is that vouchers and choice will violate the ideal of educational equality. I discuss this in *School Choice and Social Justice* chapters 6,7,9.

13. See Will Kymlicka, *Multicultural Citizenship* (Oxford: Oxford University Press, 1995), pp. 80–84 for an elaboration of the idea of living a life from the inside.

14. Joseph Raz, *The Morality of Freedom* (Oxford: Oxford University Press, 1987), pp. 369–370.

15. See the valuable discussion in *The Morality of Freedom*, pp. 370–378.

16. See Stephen Bates, *Battleground: One Mother's Crusade, The Religious Right, and the Struggle for Control of Our Classrooms* (New York: Simon & Schuster 1993) for an account of *Mozert v. Hawkins*, in which parents

demanded that textbooks teaching, among other things, that a central ideal of the Renaissance was a belief in the equal worth of all human beings, be removed from the school. The *Mozert* parents, like the Amish parents in *Wisconsin v. Yoder*, took the prospective autonomy of their children as a threat to their continued adherence to their religion.

17. Francis Schrag, "Diversity, Schooling and the Liberal State," *Studies in Philosophy and Education* 17 (1998): 29–46 at 43.

18. J. S. Mill, *On Liberty* (New York: Norton, 1975), p. 36.

19. Margaret Talbot, "A Mighty Fortress," *New York Times Magazine*, Feb. 27, 2000, p. 40. Caps in the original.

20. Given the apparent transparency of American public life I should say a word or two to justify the non-transparency claim. It is partly a matter of inadequate education—citizens are not well equipped to understand information in the public domain, and are not helped a great deal by the broadcast media. But it is also partly a matter of institutional design: American voters face many levels of elected government (at least 12 in my own state of Wisconsin), and however clear it may be to constitutional experts what the division of power is between them, it is far from clear to voters. Matters are not helped by the absence of organized political parties, which in most democracies convey a great deal of information to voters, nor by the campaign funding system which allows massive influence overall, which is nevertheless hard to measure in particular instances, to a diverse array of "special interest" groups.

21. Amy Gutmann, *Democratic Education* (Princeton: Princeton University Press, 1987), p. 51.

22. Ibid., p. 52.

23. Ibid., p. 42.

24. Amy Gutmann, "Civic Education and Social Diversity," *Ethics*, 105 (1995): 557–579 at 578.

25. Ibid., 578.

26. Ibid., 573.

27. There may be reasons that children should be taught these virtues. The instrumental argument does not provide them.

28. Although I have focused on the "skills associated with autonomy" I am skeptical that any cognitive skills can be taught independent of teaching knowledge. See E. D. Hirsch, Jr., *The Schools We Need and Why We Don't Have Them* (New York: Doubleday, 1996), chapter 2.

29. See Eamonn Callan, *Creating Citizens* (Oxford: Oxford University Press, 1997), and Stephen Macedo, *Diversity and Distrust* (Cambridge: Harvard University Press, 2000).

30. See also my "Civic Education and Liberal Legitimacy," *Ethics*.

9

TESTING THE BOUNDARIES OF PARENTAL AUTHORITY OVER EDUCATION: THE CASE OF HOMESCHOOLING

ROB REICH

When political theorists write about the boundaries of parental and state authority over education, they often write about two United States court cases—the Supreme Court's 1972 decision in *Wisconsin v. Yoder* and the Sixth Circuit Court's 1987 decision in *Mozert v. Hawkins County Board of Education.*[1] Such a staple of discussion are these two cases that it seems scarcely an article or book on the topic of liberalism and civic education in the past decade has failed to address at least one of the cases in some detail.[2]

The unusual focus on these two cases is understandable, for they help to illustrate a number of central tensions in liberal theory generally, and a number of tensions in the demands of liberal civic education more specifically. The *Yoder* case, in which Amish parents were granted an exemption from compulsory attendance laws, raises a number of difficult questions about the scope of religious liberty (whether the religious freedom of parents extends to the control of the upbringing of their children), about the significance of claims that a cultural group's very existence may be threatened by state regulations, and about how much schooling is necessary to develop the bare essentials of citizenship. The *Mozert* case, in which

Christian Fundamentalist parents were not granted an exemption from state requirements that in public schools children were to read from textbooks exposing them to a diversity of value orientations, raises questions about how the clash between religious conviction and secular authority should be resolved within public schools, about whether exposure to value diversity constitutes an indoctrination in secular humanism, and about the limits of state authority in prescribing curricular materials for students. Both cases highlight questions about whether parents possess actual *rights* to direct the upbringing of their children and about how a liberal state should strike the proper balance among parents' interests, state interests, and children's interests in education. These assorted questions are obviously of deep importance and warrant repeated analysis and scrutiny.

But the unusual attention devoted to these cases is in my opinion excessive. Though examinations of *Yoder* and *Mozert* continue to yield fresh insights and arguments, I believe that the cases attract the energy and attention of theorists to an unfortunate and disproportionately high degree. If theorists really want a test case to examine the limits of parents' authority over the education of their children, to consider the proper balance of parents', the state's, and children's interests in education, they should stop fixating on *Yoder* and *Mozert*. They should instead be looking at a burgeoning and, compared to the number of Amish defectors or Christian Fundamentalists challenging public school curricula, far more prevalent educational phenomenon: homeschooling.

Homeschooling is the education of children under the supervision of their parents within the home, apart from any campus-based school. As such, homeschooling represents the paradigmatic example of the realization of complete parental authority over the educational environment of their children. In no other setting are parents as able to direct in all aspects the education of their children, for in homeschools they are responsible not only for determining what their children shall learn but when, how, and with whom they shall learn. If it is permissible for parents to homeschool their children, then we will have gone a long way toward identifying the wide scope of parental authority over the education of their children, or put conversely, toward severely limiting the role of the state in educational supervision. The issues raised in *Yoder* and *Mozert* are still worthy of continuing attention, but it is homeschooling that illustrates in its purest form the instantiation of parents' authority over the education of their children, and therefore it provides the ideal test case of the boundaries of this authority.

In this chapter, I take up the question of homeschooling, offering, in effect, a brief for its worthiness of study. In the first section, I look at the recent history of homeschooling in the United States, showing that beyond its interest in purely theoretical terms, the actual practice of homeschooling also provides powerful reasons to focus theoretical (and policy) attention on it. In section two, I canvass a trilogy of interests in education—the parents', the state's, and the child's—as a prelude to considering the justifiability of homeschooling. On the basis of these three interests, I draw the conclusion that at a bare minimum one function of any school environment must be to expose children to and engage students with values and beliefs other than those of their parents. I argue therefore that while the state should not ban homeschooling it must nevertheless regulate its practice. I conclude in the final section by briefly offering a few suggestions about the best means to exercise regulatory authority and by considering some problems with regulation.

I. The History and Current Practice of Homeschooling

Schooling in the home is the oldest form of education. Traditionally, and across cultures, children have been taught at home by their parents or, sometimes, by tutors. This was also true of the United States in the late 1700s and early 1800s. But with the advent of publicly funded common schools in the mid-nineteenth century and the widespread passage of compulsory education laws in the early twentieth century, homeschooling practically disappeared.[3] In the early 1970s, the number of children schooled at home was estimated to be around 10,000, and in 1983 around 60,000.[4] Parents who schooled their children at home were often prosecuted under compulsory attendance laws, and several states explicitly forbade homeschooling. Only since 1993 has homeschooling been legal in all fifty states.

During the 1990s, however, homeschooling exploded in popularity. Because many states do not collect data on homeschooling, and because parents sometimes resist the monitoring efforts of the state, accurate data do not exist.[5] But even conservative estimates of homeschooling pin the current number of students at 350,000 in 1990, 750,000 in 1996, and 1.3 million in 1998.[6] Growth has been exponential and, according to recent news reports, has accelerated due to fears of school safety following the shooting deaths of students on the grounds of Columbine High School in April 1999.[7] Homeschooling is no longer a fringe phenomenon in American education.

To put these figures in perspective, it is helpful to compare the number of homeschooled students to the population of students enrolled in regular schools, public, private, or religious. If we take the conservative estimate of 1.3 million homeschooled students, we find that this figure is greater than the combined number of students enrolled in schools in Wyoming, Alaska, Delaware, North Dakota, Vermont, South Dakota, Montana, Rhode Island, New Hampshire, and Hawaii, the bottom ten states in school enrollment.[8] That is to say, there are more students schooled at home than who attend school in all ten of these states combined! Or thinking of the *Mozert* case, the 1.3 million figure is almost double the number of students enrolled in conservative Christian schools, 737,000 in 1998.[9] As if to symbolize the mainstream acceptance of homeschooling, the U.S. newsmagazine *Newsweek* devoted a cover story to the topic in 1998, giving explicit instructions to parents on how to begin homeschooling, and the United States Senate passed a resolution declaring September 19, 1999, "National Home Education Week."[10] When we consider the relative popularity of homeschooling, compared to the numbers of Amish children or Christian Fundamentalists, it seems all the more important for political theorists and educational policymakers to devote serious attention to the phenomenon.

Why do parents homeschool, who is choosing to homeschool, and what explains the rapid growth of the past decade? The scattered studies of homeschooling reveal a host of motivations on the part of parents to remove their children from school in order to teach them at home, ranging from a desire for pedagogical innovation, a rejection of the secular ethos of public schools, a belief that the special needs of some physically or mentally handicapped children are better served at home, to a fear for the safety of children in schools. But researchers tend to agree that, as one historical survey concluded, whereas homeschools of the 1970s "reflected a liberal, humanistic, pedagogical orientation," the vast majority of homeschools in the 1980s and 1990s "became grounds of and for ideological, conservative, religious expressions of educational matters."[11] Today, it appears that the reason most, but not all, parents choose to educate their children at home is because they believe that their children's moral and spiritual needs will not be met in campus-based schools; like the *Yoder* and *Mozert* parents, most homeschooling parents have religious objections to placing their children in a public, and even private, school environment.[12]

Two factors are primarily responsible for fueling the expansion of homeschooling. First, the *Yoder* decision inspired many homeschool advocates to press their claims in state legislatures and courts, a strategy which has yielded significant victories.[13] Homeschooling is now legal in all fifty states and at least thirty-seven states have explicit homeschooling statutes. Second, over the past few years the Internet has provided the means to create homeschooling networks, distribute curricular materials, and offer legal advice.[14] Moreover, with its growing popularity has come mainstream acceptability; this in turn has made homeschooling yet more popular.

Though homeschooling is legal everywhere, states still possess the authority to regulate its practice. Even in *Yoder*, the case granting parents the widest exemption from state regulations, the Court went to great lengths to indicate the singularity of the case, emphasizing that "[n]othing we hold is intended to undermine the general applicability of the state's compulsory school-attendance statutes or to limit the power of the state to promulgate reasonable standards . . ."[15] But how states exercise their regulatory authority varies widely. Some states require homeschooling parents to register with their local school districts, others establish minimal academic qualifications for parents who will offer instruction, and still others mandate that parents submit portfolios of student work to school district administrators or that children take and score at an acceptable level on standardized tests.

In many or even most states, however, it appears that regulations go utterly unenforced. In California for example, a state without any statute explicitly permitting homeschooling and whose laws make it on paper among the most difficult places to establish a homeschool, parents must either qualify their homeschool as a private school, offer instruction by a certified private tutor, enroll in an independent study program at home, using the public school curriculum, or enroll in a private school satellite program and take independent home study. Yet, according to a recent news report, "[M]ost families do not report to the state at all, and many school districts turn a blind eye toward prosecuting parents for violating the compulsory public school attendance law."[16] At a more general level, James Dwyer argued recently that despite possessing the authority, "states and the federal government have effectively relinquished all authority to oversee private schooling . . . [I]n contrast to the extensive regulatory scheme governing public schools in most states, there are virtually no constraints today on what religious schools teach or how they treat their students."[17] What Dwyer says of private and religious schooling applies equally well to homeschooling.

Even in states where regulations are enforced, the rules are in practice often so minimal or full of loopholes that homeschools can be established and maintained with great ease and with barely any state monitoring. According to the Home School Legal Defense Association, forty-one states do not require homeschool parents to meet any specific qualifications and only twenty-five states insist on standardized testing and evaluation.[18] In Virginia, for example, parents who intend to homeschool need only notify the local school superintendent, possess a baccalaureate degree, and submit a brief description of the curriculum they will use. And if the parents have sincere religious objections to these requirements, they are entitled to an exemption. In other words, parents with sincere religious beliefs in Virginia may legally remove their children from school and teach them at home without any state requirements or oversight of their homeschool whatsoever.[19] Similar religious exemptions exist in other states.

For both theoretical and practical reasons, then, homeschooling is an ideal test case for political theorists arguing about the boundaries of parental and state authority over children's education. From a strictly theoretical point of view, the very structure of homeschooling raises questions about whether the interests of the state in education can be met in a setting where parents control both the academic program and social interactions of children and can, if they so desire, effectively shield children from exposure to anything that offends the values and beliefs of the parents. From a strictly practical point of view, the actual practice of homeschooling reveals first that it is a widespread and growing phenomenon; second, that state regulations for establishing homeschools are often minimal and, even when in place, often go unenforced; and third, that the majority of parents who choose to homeschool have conservative religious motivations, similar to the sort of parent in a case like *Yoder* or *Mozert*.

But while the *Yoder* and *Mozert* cases raise questions about the extent of parental authority over the education of the children, it is homeschooling that throws these questions into sharpest relief. At bottom, *Yoder* asks whether parents of a self-segregated religious order may exempt their children from compulsory attendance laws *after eight years of regular school attendance.*[20] The Amish exemption applies only to the final two years of required attendance. At bottom, *Mozert* asks whether state authorities have the power to require students *in public schools* to read from specified texts that might expose a child to values other than or in opposition to those held by the child's parents. The *Mozert* parents were always free to withdraw their children from public schools and send them to a religious school in which the curriculum adhered to their own beliefs.[21] The case of homeschooling raises the stakes over parental authority considerably: should parents have the authority to educate their children of any and all ages apart from any formal, institutional setting, public or private, where in current practice the regulations are minimal, often unenforced, and sometimes non-existent? Seen in this light, the control that homeschooling parents seek to exert over the educational environment of their children is markedly greater than that sought by the *Yoder* parents or *Mozert* parents. And for this reason, homeschooling is a ripe topic for study.

II. A TRILOGY OF INTERESTS: PARENTS, THE STATE, AND THE CHILD

As it currently stands in the United States, more than one million children are homeschooled by their parents, learning in an educational environment that is more often than not wholly or nearly unregulated by any state or federal authority. These children receive an education in which their parents have exclusive or nearly exclusive control and authority. From the perspective of the liberal state, is this a problem? What are the boundaries of parental and state authority in educational provision?

To answer these questions, it is necessary to indicate who has an interest in education and to spell out what these interests are. And the first comment to be made here is that it is not only parents and the state who have an interest in education. Children, who are themselves subject to the education, and therefore are the party most directly affected by educational decision making, also have an interest, one that may possibly conflict with their parents or with the state. To decide, therefore, what the boundaries of parental and state authority in educational provision may be, we must consider the interests of the parents, the state, and the child.

Before spelling out these three interests, two preliminary comments are in order. First, it is not my purpose here to argue whether or not parents (or the state or children) have *rights* rather than mere interests. I want to sidestep the issue of whether parents possess rights over their children, whether they are merely trustees of their children's interests, or whether parents merely have a rebuttable privilege to direct the upbringing of children. Suffice it to note that while American legal doctrine often uses the language of rights to describe the relationship of parents to their children, it is a hotly contested claim, both legally and philosophically, one that I cannot aim to resolve here.[22] For my purposes, it is enough to survey the interests of each party in order to argue about how homeschooling might or might not serve to meet these interests. The question I seek ultimately to answer is what the outer limits of sole parental authority over education may be in meeting these interests.

Second, it is beyond the scope of the chapter to spell out a full-blown theory of parents', the state's, and children's interests in education, to provide a complete account of the nature of parental authority over children generally, or to settle the proper balance of authority in a liberal state amongst this trilogy of interests. I aim more specifically to consider, given a general understanding of the interests at stake, what the limits of parental control over educational provision may be. Thus, I limit myself here to sketching a general view of what these interests are and then asking the question, can the interests of the state and children be met when, as in the case of homeschooling, parents have complete control over the provision of education?

Parents' Interests in Education

Parents obviously have very strong interests in the education of their children.[23] In the abstract, these interests are twofold, grounded in the independent and self-regarding interests of the parents themselves and grounded in the other-regarding claim that since children are dependent for their well-being on others, parents are best situated to promote their welfare. Let us consider each in turn.

It may seem odd on the face of it to think that parents have independent interests in exerting authority over the education of children. After all, we are rightly suspicious of parents who seek to use their children as vehicles for the realization of their own goals or who seek to raise children as if they were nothing more than lumps of clay to be molded into figurines of the parents' liking. Children are not mere extensions of the parent; children are not their parents' property. But we can acknowledge this truth while also giving due to what Eamonn Callan calls the "expressive significance" of child rearing. We can bring this notion into view by considering that parenting is for many people a central source of meaning in their lives. As Callan puts it, "Success or failure in the task [of parenting], as measured by whatever standards we take to be relevant, is likely to affect profoundly our overall sense of how well or badly our lives have gone."[24] Raising a child is never merely a service rendered unto another person but is the collective sharing of a life. If we think in commonsensical terms that adults often have children in order to fulfill their goal to have a family, and to live life as part of a family, the sense in which child rearing is something in the self-regarding interest of parents becomes clearer.

Of course, the parents' interest in exerting authority over the educational provision of their children is also grounded in the interest of the children themselves. Children are dependent beings, not yet capable of meeting their own needs or acting in their own interest. Parents, it is generally understood, are best situated (better situated than the state and the children themselves) to act in the best interests of their children, or, in an alternate formulation, to promote their general welfare. In modern society, the welfare of a child depends in part on being educated. Therefore, as the guardian of their children's best interests or welfare, parents have an interest in the education that their children receive.

There is a problem with the "best interests" or "general welfare" standard, however. Despite the fact that the "best interest of the child" is the coin of the realm in legal decision making about children—judges routinely make rulings on the basis of the best interests of the child—it is not of logical necessity that a child's *parents* are the agents who will act on these best interests. Others—grandparents, aunts and uncles, or state officials—might be better able to promote the welfare of the child. And of course, when parents are clearly negligent or harmful to their children, the state intervenes and awards guardianship to a relative or foster care family or, in the most dire situation, to the state itself (at a state orphanage, for example). Who is to say, then, that parents are best suited to pursue the best interests of children?

But the best answer to this question is to consider the possible alternatives, all of which appear to be worse.[25] The more telling problem with the "best interests of the child standard" is that the best interests of a child do not admit of an objective answer. How does one define "best interests"? The answer depends very much, it seems, on a particular view of the good life. Secular parents (or state authorities), for example, may define the best interests of a child in a very different manner than deeply religious parents. This fact obviously cuts to the heart of the conflict in the *Yoder* and *Mozert* cases. But we need not view this only as an issue of religious difference to see it as a problem. People may differ drastically on their interpretation of best interests in purely philosophical terms. Given plural conceptions of the good life, there will be no readily identifiable consensus about the best interests of the child in all cases.

In light of this fact, one response is to suggest that parents are best situated not to realize the best interests of their children, for that is an inevitably contestable standard, but rather to meet the basic developmental needs of their children, the content of which appears to admit of a more objective answer. The basic developmental needs of the child include shelter, food, protection, and, not least, nurture, affection, and love. These it would seem the parents surely are in the best position to provide, at least in comparison to the state and the children themselves. The problem here, however, is that when the needs of children are reduced to such an elementary and unobjectionable level, they do not yield any corresponding interest in control over educational provision. Whereas the "best interest" standard clearly implicates some parental interest in having a say in or perhaps even directing the educational environment of children, the lesser "basic developmental need" standard has no such implication. Shelter, food, protection, and love are responsibilities of a child's primary caregiver; not, or at least not to a large degree, of a child's teacher. Thus, we can identify an interesting dynamic. The greater substance one packs into the notion of a child's needs and interests, the greater claim one has to influence the education of the child but the less likely that there will be objective agreement about what these needs and interests are. Conversely, the less substance one packs into the notion of a child's needs and interests, the more likely one will be able to secure objective agreement about them, but only at the cost of failing to justify an interest in educational provision.[26]

Despite these difficulties, it remains clear that parents have substantial interests in the education of their children. To say that the best interests standard is contestable is of course not to say that this conclusion obviates parental interests. Even when there is violent disagreement about what constitutes the best interests of the child, the very fact of disagreement does not void the parental interest. To the contrary, we can conclude one of two things. Either the best interest standard should not be used when making decisions about educational authority, in which case the parents' claims must rest heavily on the weight of their expressive, self-regarding interests.[27] Or, to the extent that the best interest standard is employed, we cannot interpret "best interests" only from the perspective of the parents. When conflicts about the education of children arise, parents cannot wield a trump card based solely on their understanding of their child's best interests.

To summarize, then, parents possess interests in educational provision because they have personal or expressive interests in raising their children. Parents also possess interests in educational provision because they can claim, absent a showing of obvious incompetence, to seek to promote the interests of the child, as they understand them. But when these interests are defined beyond meeting elementary needs such as food, shelter, and love, or more obviously when these interests are defined as a child's best interests, the definition will depend on one's conception of good. Thus, even before we have considered the state's interests and the child's interests, we can conclude that while parents clearly have substantial interests in the education of their children, it appears highly unlikely that they will be so weighty as to justify a claim that parents should command complete authority over the education of their children. But to substantiate such a conclusion, we need to consider what the state's interests and child's interests are.

States' Interests in Education

Like parents, the state also has very strong interests in the education of children. And also like parents, these interests are twofold. First, the state has an interest in educating children to become able citizens. Second, the state has an interest in performing a backstop role to the parents in assuring the healthy development of children into independently functioning adults. Both of these interests serve to justify some role for the state in exercising educational authority over its youngest citizens.

The civic interest of the state in providing and regulating education for children is familiar, and in American legal doctrine, well established. As many commentators have pointed out, the original justification for setting up publicly funded common schools, and later for passing compulsory attendance laws, was civic. Schools would be the vehicles for turning children into able and participating citizens.[28] The Supreme Court has often recognized the importance of schooling for developing citizens. Even in the *Yoder* case, for example, the Court acknowledged that the state possesses a fundamental interest in educating for citizenship: "There is no doubt as to the power of a State, having a high responsibility for education of its citizens, to impose reasonable regulations for the control and duration of basic education. Providing public schools ranks at the very apex of the function of a State."[29] Similarly, in its landmark *Brown v. Board of Education* decision the Court found, "Today, education is perhaps the most important function of state and local governments."[30]

The state may possess an interest in education for citizenship, but the scope of civic education is a matter of intense debate. In recent years, political theorists have interpreted the demands of civic education in very different ways. On the more demanding end of the spectrum, some argue that the state must teach children not only basic literacy but knowledge of public policy issues, the conclusions of contemporary science, a foundation in world and national history, the structure and operation of federal, state, and local government, and a broad palette of critical thinking and empathy skills necessary to facilitate democratic deliberation amidst a multiplicity of competing interests and among diverse races, religions, and worldviews.[31] Others indicate that the state's civic interest in education lies more generally in assuring that children will have the opportunity to participate in public institutions and come to possess a number of political virtues, such as tolerance, civility, and a sense of fairness.[32] And on the less demanding side of the spectrum, some argue that civic requirements are more minimal, encompassing the teaching of tolerance and, as one theorist puts it, "social rationality."[33]

My point here, however, is not to argue exactly how wide or narrow the scope of civic education should be. Like the best interests of the child standard, the demands of civic education are contestable. And to be sure, the degree of state authority over education may vary with respect to how broad these demands are. I cannot settle the debate here. My point is simply *that* the state has legitimate interests in educational authority based on providing children with the capacities to become able citizens.

Beyond providing an education for citizenship, the state also has an interest in education because it must perform a backstop role to parents in ensuring that their children develop into independently functioning adults. By "independently functioning adults," I mean persons who are self-sufficient, productive members of society, who are able to navigate and participate in the familiar social and economic institutions of society. Educational attainment and academic achievement have become increasingly important in modern society. We would rightly consider a child unfairly deprived if he or she were denied the opportunity to receive an education. While compulsory attendance laws arose in part to ensure that children received a civic education and to complement child labor restrictions, it is no exaggeration to claim that today educational attainment is essential simply to becoming an independent adult who is able to find a place in the workforce. These educational outcomes, it should be emphasized, are different from the exercise of citizenship, having to do more minimally with the capacity to lead a normal life amidst the main social and economic institutions of society.

Now while educational attainment may be necessary to developing into normal adulthood, we cannot conclude from this fact that the state must control and regulate all educational provision. On the contrary, since parents almost always share this interest in educational attainment and wish for their children to develop into independent and normal adults in the sense indicated above, and since parents are better situated than the state to know their children's particular learning needs and capacities, the state properly exercises authority over the aspects of education necessary to becoming an independently functioning adult in a backstop role. That is to say, the state rightly provides and regulates publicly funded schools for those parents who wish to send their children to them. The state also rightly legislates that children shall attend schools until a specified age. But, with respect to the education necessary to develop into independent adulthood, the state rightly interferes with parents' educational choices only when they are plainly negligent or abusive, and thereby impede the development of their children into normal, healthy adults.

To summarize, the state possesses two distinct interests in the education of children: first, that children become able citizens; and second, that children develop into independently functioning adults. On this analysis, the parents and the state share the second interest but not necessarily the first. State interests are likely to clash with parents' interests only where civic education is concerned.[34] Parents and the state may clash, for example, on their respective interpretation of what civic education requires, or in some cases parents may reject aspects of civic education altogether. As the *Yoder* and *Mozert* cases show, conflicts between parents and the state with respect to how children should be educated to become citizens are by no means uncommon.

Such conflicts lead to a set of very difficult questions. Should the state's interest in developing citizenship trump parents' interests in education when parents do not share the state's civic goals for their children? Can the state sometimes tolerate, if the stability of the state is not threatened, parents who will not provide an education that develops requisite citizenship capacities? Must children attend public schools in order for civic education to be most effective? What are the empirical findings on effective civic education?[35]

At the very least, the possibility that parents' interests and the state's interests may clash leads to questions about how such interests might best be balanced, how such usually overlapping but occasionally competing interests may yield a just distribution of educational authority. But to seek an answer is as yet premature; we have yet to consider the independent interests of children.

Child's Interests in Education

I consider this much to be uncontroversial: both parents and the state have clear interests in education that lead to legitimate claims to exert authority over educational provision. Typically, American social and legal institutions consider these to be the only interests at stake.[36] But as the subjects of the educational process, children have independent interests in education as well. As with parents and the state, I shall claim that these interests are twofold. First, children have an interest in developing into independently functioning adults, in the sense indicated earlier. Second, children have an interest in becoming autonomous, at least to a minimal degree.

Two prefatory comments. First, though the content of these interests may overlap with those of either the parents or the state, they are nevertheless *independent* interests. Children have an interest, separate from what their parents or the state may wish, in becoming independent adults and becoming minimally autonomous. In certain circumstances, these interests may place them in conflict with their parents or with the state. Children's interests in education potentially conflict with their parents' interests when, for example, parents seek through the educational environment (and elsewhere) to satisfy an expressive interest in molding their children into certain persons without regard to the will of the children themselves. Think for example of the parent who wishes to make a martyr of his or her child; or in a less extreme example, of the parent who forces a child to quit, against his or her will, all forms of educational activity except those which forward the parent's expressive interest in raising, say, a virtuoso pianist. Children's interests in education may conflict with the state's interests in cases, for example, like *Tinker v. Des Moines Independent Community School District*, where the right of students to express themselves politically in schools clashed with the power of the state to control the educational environment of the school.[37] Because of the possibility of conflict, it is important to identify children's interests as distinct and not to subsume them under those of their parents or of the state.

Second, the fact that children are needy and dependent justifies a certain amount of parental and state paternalism with respect to educational provision, and also often necessitates that someone other than the child be able to represent his or her interests. Acknowledging the fact that children have independent interests in education does not mean that children are best suited to supervise the promotion of these interests; nor does it mean that they are able, especially at young ages, even to articulate them. But the problem of children's neediness and dependence, and the problem of who shall represent children's interests, does not invalidate the interests. It merely points to the need for debate about when paternalism over children is no longer justified and when, developmentally, children might capably represent themselves, especially in cases where interests conflict.

Turning then to delineating the child's interests in education, the first interest should seem obvious: a child has an interest in education because education is necessary to developing into an independently functioning adult. I understand "independently functioning adult" in the same way as in the previous section: a person who is self-supporting, capable of participating in the main social and economic institutions of society, and able to find a place in the workforce. A child rightly expects to grow into an independent being who makes choices about his or her life's course. Presumably, the child's parents as well as the state wish for this too. Except in the most unusual circumstances, all three—parent, state, and child—would seem to share this interest. This much, I hope, is uncontroversial.

It is the second interest of children—becoming autonomous—that may seem controversial. The value of or need to lead an autonomous life, some have argued, is open to debate, and liberal states overstep their bounds when they consciously seek to foster autonomy in all of their citizens. William Galston, for example, argues that liberalism properly values diversity over autonomy and that the state should permit wide, though not unlimited, tolerance of parents who do not wish to lead autonomous lives nor want their children to lead autonomous lives.[38] In a similar vein, John Rawls argues that because strong conceptions of autonomy ultimately describe comprehensive modes of life— lives, for example, permeated by heightened self-scrutiny—a liberal state can legitimately foster autonomy only in political life.[39]

In order to make my case as plausible as possible to skeptics of autonomy, I want to defend a very minimal conception of autonomy.[40] When I say, therefore, that a child has an interest in becoming minimally autonomous, I understand autonomy to mean something akin to self-governance. Minimally autonomous persons possess the capacity to develop and pursue their own interests and are able, if they so choose, to participate ably as equal citizens in democratic deliberation about the exercise of political power. This definition is not so minimal, I am sure, that it will convince all skeptics of autonomy to accept it. But neither does it approach the robust conceptions of autonomy rejected by these same critics. The achievement of minimal autonomy, for example, does not require a Socratic "commitment to sustained rational examination of self, others, and social practices," as Galston puts it.[41] Nor does it demand that a person lead "a mode of life and reflection that critically examines our deepest ends and ideals," as Rawls puts it.[42] Nor even does it demand what many have read into Justice William Douglas's noted dissent in the *Yoder* case: that children be "masters of their own destiny," able to chart their own path in life from a wide array of options.[43]

The achievement of minimal autonomy construed as self-governance requires far less. It refers simply to the capacity of the child to develop into an independent adult who can seek and promote his or her own interests, as he or she understands them, and who can participate, if he or she chooses, in political dialogue with others. This conception requires, to be sure, significant development of one's rational capacities, an ability to articulate and defend one's political positions, and a willingness to treat civilly those with whom one disagrees. But nothing in this conception implies that children must lead Socratic lives of sustained critical reflection or that they be weaned away from the lives of their parents in order for them to choose a way of life for themselves. A person need not subject his or her interests to Socratic critical scrutiny on a regular basis to be considered minimally autonomous; a person need not have the widest possible array of life choices to be considered minimally autonomous.

Defined in this restricted fashion, I submit that children have an interest in becoming minimally autonomous. To put more substance behind the ideal of minimal autonomy, and to appreciate just how minimally I conceive it, consider why children have an interest in becoming minimally autonomous. On my view, there are two reasons, one rooted in the terrain of one's private or personal life and one rooted in the terrain of one's public or civic life.

Children have a private interest in becoming minimally autonomous because the achievement of a minimal degree of autonomy precludes the possibility that they will be, in Eamonn Callan's words, "ethically servile."[44] Servility is a condition that implies a dutiful slavishness or submissiveness to others, an unwillingness or incapacity to make decisions or judgments for oneself. Because children are not the property of their parents or of the state, because they possess human dignity as independent beings, children cannot be educated so as to be made servile to their caretakers. Neither parents nor the state can justly attempt to imprint indelibly upon a child a set of values and beliefs, as if it were an inheritance one should never be able to question, as if the child must always defer and be obedient. To do so would in effect render the child servile. In developing through education a basic capacity for critical deliberation, in exposing a child to and engaging a child with diverse values and beliefs, a child learns to think for him or herself enough to surpass the threshold of ethical servility. Understood in this way, the degree of autonomy necessary to escape ethical servility is extremely minimal. Rare is the existence of a servile child.

Children also have a civic interest in becoming minimally autonomous because the achievement of a minimal degree of autonomy is necessary to participate ably in shared political decision making, if a citizen opts for such participation. Liberal states guarantee the equality of citizens under the law and the right to participate, as equals, in decision making about the use of state power. Though citizens are not obligated to participate, the right to participate is guaranteed. As I indicated earlier, the scope of what citizenship entails is a matter of great debate. But on any view of able citizenship, a citizen must be able, it seems to me, to respect others as political equals, to forward and defend his or her own political values and beliefs, and to consider sympathetically the reasoned arguments of other citizens. These capacities require that one be able to make political choices from an array of possibilities, and to reason about these choices. The capacity for such behavior, I submit, involves the exercise of at least some degree of autonomy.

In addition, the political autonomy of citizens is necessary to the very legitimacy of the state.[45] For the exercise of the state's power to be legitimate, citizens must freely consent to the principles of justice on which the state is founded.[46] Consent cannot be coerced; it must be the product of a person's own deliberation. On any reasonable understanding of informed deliberation, we have to acknowledge that people must possess certain critical thinking and reflective skills that are tantamount to minimal autonomy.

Therefore, because in a liberal state all citizens possess the right to participate in civic affairs, and because the state seeks to gain the consent of each citizen for its legitimacy, and because such participation and consent require the achievement of minimal autonomy, I conclude that children have a civic interest in receiving an education that fosters minimal autonomy.

To summarize, a child has two interests in education, the first to become an independently functioning adult and the second to become minimally autonomous. A child shares an interest in becoming an independent adult with parents and the state. A child's interest in becoming minimally autonomous may not be shared, however. But so long as autonomy is not defined as a robust ideal that requires the subjection of all values to ongoing critical scrutiny, the personal and civic reasons for achieving a minimal degree of autonomy are substantive and independent, and must be counted in any decision calculus when determining the balance of authority over children's education.

Implications of the Trilogy of Interests

What can we conclude from this general survey of the interests of the parents, the state, and the child in education? One thing is immediately obvious: all three parties have an interest in education because each wishes for the child to become an independent, self-sufficient adult. Indeed, many view the primary function of education to be the sufficient provision of capabilities, encouragement of talents, and fostering of scholastic achievement so as to allow children to develop into adults who will be able to function on their own in society—able, that is, to secure work, care for themselves, and seek and develop their own interests. In fact, a harmony among parents, the state, and children may in practice very often extend across all interests. The parents' self-regarding expressive interests may coincide with the state's interest in developing the capacity for children to exercise the rights of citizenship; the child's interest in becoming minimally autonomous may coincide with the parents' expressive interests and the state's interest in citizenship.

But this harmony of shared interests is not inevitable. As we have seen, the interest of the state in fostering citizenship may not be shared by the parents. Similarly, a child's interest in becoming minimally autonomous, for both the private reason of surpassing ethical servility and the civic reason of making possible free consent to the principles of justice of the state, and more broadly, of participating in shared political decision making, may not be shared by parents or by the state. Parents or perhaps repressive states may wish for children to be non-autonomous in some respects.

How do these interests translate into arguments for educational authority and control? From the trilogy of interests and the fact that they can come into conflict, I conclude that no one of these interests can trump the others and justify sole authority for any party over educational provision. Neither parents, nor the state, nor children themselves should unilaterally and without a countervailing balance direct and control the educational environment of children. Given the triad of interest holders, and the significance of their respective interests, a theory of educational authority that claimed only the interests of one party mattered could potentially establish a kind of parental despotism, state authoritarianism, or child despotism.[47] Any defensible theory of educational authority, then, will strike some balance among the three parties.

How should the balance of educational authority be struck? However interesting and necessary such an undertaking, determining the proper distribution of power among parents, the state, and children is not my task here.[48] I want instead to use this general survey of the range of interests in education and redirect our attention to the phenomenon of homeschooling. I aim in the next section to consider whether homeschooling—the educational arrangement which, as I showed earlier, in both theory and practice tilts most heavily in the direction of parental interests and authority—permits the realization of both the state's and the child's interests in education. If under a scheme of complete parental authority the interests of the state and the child in education can be met, then homeschooling should be a legitimate educational practice. But if not, then not.

III. HOMESCHOOLING AND INTERESTS IN EDUCATION

The question, therefore, under consideration is: When parental authority over the educational environment of their children is complete, as in homeschooling, can the state's and the child's interests in education be met?

The answer to the question is clearly yes. Parents who homeschool their children, apart from any state regulation or authority, can realize the state's and the child's interests in education. In fact, some evidence suggests that in some circumstances, parents who homeschool their children may be better at achieving the state's and the child's educational interests than public or private schools! In a recent news article on homeschooling in California, one child appears to suggest that the reason she wishes to be homeschooled is because the development of her autonomy is threatened in campus-based school settings. Speaking of her former school, she reported: "I didn't want to be there. All the kids are just like sheep, and they don't have any independence."[49] The coercive power of peer pressure may in some cases be too much for children to resist. Moreover, recent studies of homeschooled children show that they often outperform their public and private school counterparts in scholastic achievement.[50] It appears possible, therefore, that with respect to the child's interest in developing autonomy and to the shared interest in academic achievement, homeschools can sometimes be more effective than traditional campus-based schools.

There is also a very practical reason that homeschooling should be a legitimate and important educational alternative. Some children, in particular those with severe or rare physical or mental disabilities, may have such specific learning needs or require such a tailored learning environment that public or private schools simply cannot accommodate them. In this circumstance, justice and practicality require that the state permit parents to teach such children at home. Beyond the problem of severely disabled or impaired students, some families live in such rural or sparsely populated regions that the nearest school, public or private, may be many miles away. It may be cost-ineffective to build a public school for a small number of families living a great distance from other public schools. Instead, the state may find that homeschooling such children is simply the only option available.

On account of the fact that homeschools can feasibly realize the state's and the child's interests in education, and because homeschooling may in some circumstances be the only practical educational option, it would be unjust for the state to ban homeschooling. Educating children at home under the direction and authority of their parents must be a legitimate form of schooling.

However, homeschools can also fail at realizing the state's and the child's interests in education. Because some homeschools promote the autonomy of children and some conduce to high academic achievement does not imply that all do so. That they sometimes succeed or are sometimes practically necessary does not imply that the state can grant educational authority to parents whenever they express a desire to homeschool. On my account of the trilogy of interests in education, parental authority must end when its exercise compromises the development of children into independently functioning adults or when it disables or retards the development of minimal autonomy in children. This marks the outer boundary of parental authority over education.

Parents compromise the development of their children into healthy, independent adults when they are negligent or abusive, preventing children from becoming independent, self-sufficient beings who can participate in the main social and economic institutions of society. One imagines cases of malnourishment, physical or mental abuse, or sheer neglect. In such circumstances, the intervention of the state on behalf of children is not controversial. The state acts in its backstop role. If parental authority over education does not conduce to the self-sufficiency and independence of children, the state must step in and ensure such outcomes.

The problem with homeschooling and parental authority over education arises not out of conflicts over whether children should become independently functioning adults. The problem arises over the development of autonomy in children. Even when this is defined minimally, some parents may object to the idea that their children should receive an education that promotes their critical thinking and capacities for reflection on their own and others' ends. Being minimally autonomous, I claim, is in the interest of the child for personal and civic reasons. The fact that autonomy is necessary for citizenship makes education for autonomy an interest of the state as well. Thus, when parents reject the facilitation of autonomy in their children, they find themselves in conflict with the interests both of the child and of the state.

We must therefore ask the question What does it take, educationally, to become autonomous? Under what circumstances might homeschooling environments disable or retard the development of autonomy? We might imagine that the question admits of an empirical answer. Given a definition of minimal autonomy, some test or evaluation might be concocted to measure its development. The test could then be administered to homeschooled children. Were they not to achieve to some determined threshold, state intervention would be justified.

The creation of such a test may be desirable, but it seems highly unlikely. The empirical measurement of autonomy, especially in children, seems to me an exceptionally difficult quest. I wish to approach the question somewhat more abstractly. What structural aspects of the educational environment might promote or retard autonomy? What features of schooling are essential to fostering autonomy?

Meira Levinson suggests a bold answer:

> . . . it is difficult for children to achieve autonomy solely within the bounds of their families and home communities—or even within the bounds of schools whose norms are constituted by those from the child's home community. If we take the requirements of autonomy seriously, we see the need for a place separate from the environment in which children are raised . . . [51]

Levinson argues, in other words, that children must attend institutional schools in order to achieve autonomy. In her view, "even the most well-intentioned and resource-laden parents" cannot accomplish what a school can with respect to fostering the development of autonomy.[52] On these grounds, Levinson would presumably rule out homeschooling as an educational alternative.

As I have suggested, banning homeschooling would be unjust. Levinson underestimates the capacities and indeed the intention of some parents to provide an education for autonomy within a homeschool setting. Additionally, an unfortunate implication of her argument seems to be that, prior to the advent of institutional schools, no one was autonomous.

If education for autonomy does not require the banning of homeschooling, what then does it require? Recall the two reasons that children have an interest in becoming minimally autonomous. The first is to surpass ethical servility; the second is to enable the exercise of citizenship and make possible the legitimacy of the state. Now, the degree of autonomy necessary to avoid servility is quite minimal; the slightest bit of autonomy militates against servility. The degree of autonomy necessary to enable the exercise of citizenship is greater but hard to define precisely and also dependent on one's definition of citizenship. I suggested earlier that any reasonable definition of citizenship would include the ability to forward and defend one's own political values and beliefs and to be able to consider the reasoned arguments of others. What, we may now ask, are the structural aspects of schooling that are essential to achieving autonomy to this requisite degree?

I submit that even in a minimal construal of autonomy, it must be the function of the school setting to expose children to and engage children with values and beliefs other than those of their parents.[53] To achieve minimal autonomy requires that a child know that there are ways of life other than that into which he or she has been born. Minimal autonomy requires, especially for its civic importance, that a child be able to examine his or her own political values and beliefs, and those of others, with a critical eye. It requires that the child be able to think independently. If this is all true, then at a bare minimum, the structure of schooling cannot simply replicate in every particularity the values and beliefs of a child's home.

Clearly, not all homeschooling arrangements are troublesome in this regard. But if there is any educational environment that might potentially be able to replicate the values and beliefs of a child's home, homeschooling is it. In homeschools, parents are able, after all, to control not only the curriculum but also the social environment of their child. Parents can severely limit social interaction and thereby curtail the opportunities that their child will have to encounter other children from different backgrounds. These informal opportunities to engage with difference are likely just as effective in facilitating the development of autonomy as the formal curriculum. Moreover, we know empirically that the majority of homeschooling parents are motivated by a desire to control the moral and spiritual upbringing of their children. Some of these parents are eager to prevent their children from being exposed to anything contrary to the moral and spiritual values they wish their children to learn.

To be sure, exposing children to and engaging children with diverse values and beliefs is potentially threatening to some parents. As bell hooks has written of her own childhood:

> School was the place of ecstasy—pleasure and danger. To be changed by ideas was pure pleasure. But to learn ideas that ran counter to values and beliefs learned at home was to place oneself at risk, to enter the danger zone. Home was the place where I was forced to conform to someone else's image of who and what I should be. School was the place where I could forget that self and, through ideas, reinvent myself.[54]

But in the interests of children, these are risks that must be accepted, for parents cannot be entitled as a matter of justice to ensure that their child grows up to become exactly the kind of person they want him or her to be. To prevent the risk is to ask that the child become ethically servile to the parent.

The state must therefore ensure that all children, regardless of the environment in which they are schooled, receive an education that exposes them to and engages them with values and beliefs other than those they find at home. It does not require that children engage always with values and beliefs that conflict with those of the home, nor does it require that children receive maximal exposure in order to provide them with maximal options in life. A helpful illustration of this difference is provided by Justice White in his concurring opinion in *Yoder*. Noting that while many Amish children may desire to continue living a rural existence within the Amish order, White wrote memorably that:

Others, however, may wish to become nuclear physicists, ballet dancers, computer programmers, or historians, and for these occupations formal training will be necessary . . . A State has a legitimate interest not only in seeking to develop the latent talents of its children but also in seeking to prepare them for the life style that they may later choose, or at least to provide them with an option other than the life they have led in the past.[55]

The achievement of minimal autonomy does demand that a child be capable of pursuing any life path imaginable. No one can be guaranteed the right to a future so open that he or she may choose any occupation or endorse any possible value or belief; neither the state nor parents owe it to children as a matter of justice to make it possible that they can choose lives of absolutely any sort. This asks too much of minimal autonomy. It is instead Justice White's final clause that I wish to highlight: children must achieve the minimal degree of autonomy necessary to provide them with options other than that into which they have been born. Children are owed as a matter of justice the capacity to choose to lead lives—to adopt values and beliefs, pursue an occupation, endorse new traditions—that are different from those of their parents. Because the child cannot him or herself ensure the acquisition of such capacities, the state must ensure it for the child. The state must guarantee that children are educated for minimal autonomy. Thus, on this analysis, the state must not forbid homeschooling but regulate it so as to ensure the interests of the state and the child are met.

Where in this analysis, one might ask, can or should children themselves exercise authority over their own education? Do their independent interests in education yield a claim to controlling their own education? More specifically, should children have a say in whether or not they are homeschooled? This is a difficult question, for while very young children clearly are incapable of exercising educational authority it is nevertheless true that older children are capable of making informed and reasonable choices about their education. If children were to decide unilaterally, a six-year-old might elect to attend a private school or homeschool (or no school at all) rather than a public school.

But the preference of such a young child cannot be decisive, else children would not need guardians at all. But if a seventeen-year-old were to decide that he or she wanted to attend a public school rather than be homeschooled (or rather than attend a private school), the preference should weigh much more heavily, if not be entirely decisive.

A recent case in Virginia raises the question of what the state should do when older children wish to attend public school and their parents wish to homeschool them.[56] Jennifer Sengpiehl had been homeschooled for many years when in her teenage years she began to ask her parents to permit her to attend the local public school. Her parents refused and continued to educate her at home, at which point Jennifer's behavior began to deteriorate. In an attempt to teach her a lesson about obedience, her parents called the police after she had vandalized her bedroom and brandished a knife at her father. The involvement of the police led to a juvenile court date, where unexpectedly the judge ruled that Jennifer should attend a public school. Because the court records of juveniles are sealed, it is impossible to know the details in order to make an informed judgment in Jennifer's case about how continued homeschooling or public schooling would or would not meet the parents', the state's, and the child's interests in education. But the question remains: Should we accept as just the prevailing legal presumption that parental preferences about schooling are determinative, absent a showing of negligence or abuse?

In my view, parental preferences should not be determinative. If the state has reason to believe that the child's future achievement of minimal autonomy will be compromised by an education conducted solely under the direction of parents in the home, or when the child is older and expresses a desire himself or herself not to be homeschooled, there is an exceptionally strong case for the state to intervene and end the homeschooling arrangement. Determining when the preferences of children should be given due weight in such conflicts is admittedly a difficult matter, highly dependent on each particular case. Clearly, the age of the child will make a large difference. The older the child, the more likely that the child's preferences will be autonomous and therefore worthy of respect. The younger the child, the less likely the preferences are autonomous and therefore the less weight such preferences should be given. In either case, I believe the state should provide a forum where children's educational preferences should be heard and duly considered when they are contrary to the preferences of the parents. And even in cases when children are too young and cannot articulate or represent their own interests in education or their preferences of an educational environment, when the state believes that the interest of the child in becoming minimally autonomous is threatened, intervention is justified. Contrary to much current practice in the United States, the state must therefore regulate and monitor homeschooling, and enforce its regulations.

IV. CONCLUSION: THE PROBLEMS OF REGULATING HOMESCHOOLING

In conclusion, I want to explore briefly the kinds of regulations the state might promulgate and some likely problems with such regulations. Over the past decade, as I noted in the first section, the regulations on homeschooling have eased dramatically and, where they exist, are often unenforced. Whereas some states once forbade homeschooling, its practice is legal now everywhere, with actual regulations varying significantly from state to state. Such regulations have included requirements that parents be certified teachers or have a college degree, that parents submit a curricular plan to local educational authorities for review, that parents administer standardized tests to their children in order to gauge their academic progress, that school officials make periodic visits to homeschools to evaluate the educational progress of children, that parents keep attendance records and meet a minimum number of days in school or hours spent learning, and that parents submit regular reports to local educational authorities. The fact that regulations have diminished and in some cases disappeared, and the increasing prevalence of wholly unregulated homeschools, is cause for concern. The state must indeed regulate homeschools in order to assure that its and the child's interests in education are met and in order to perform its backstop role in assuring the development of children into independently functioning adults.

What regulations are most appropriate to this task? Regulations are properly a matter of democratic politics, not deduction from theory, but at a bare minimum, I imagine the following will be necessary. First, the state must require that any homeschooling parents register their homeschools with local educational authorities, who in turn should be required to collect this information and report to the state. Such action will allow states to collect more accurate data on homeschooling, help make decisions about how to distribute resources for homeschoolers, and enable simplified communication between school leaders and homeschooling parents. At the moment, since many parents have never notified districts of their homeschooling intentions and arrangements, states have few means to regulate such parents. By requiring registration with local officials, the state can more effectively distinguish between truants and homeschooled children.

Second, the burden of proof that homeschools will satisfy the state's and the child's interest in education must rest with the parents who express the desire to homeschool. Parents must demonstrate to relevant education officials that their particular homeschooling arrangements are up to determined educational standards. Aligning the burden with parents is important, because if the homeschooling arrangements were presumed to be satisfactory unless the state were to show otherwise, the state would have to resort to difficult and intrusive means to make such a case. Especially in light of the number of homeschooled students today, school officials cannot be expected personally or closely to monitor the activities of all homeschools.

Third, because the state must ensure that the school environment provides exposure to and engagement with values and beliefs other than those of a child's parents, the state should require parents to use curricula that provide such exposure and engagement. I imagine that parents could satisfy such a regulation in a variety of ways: they could submit their curriculum for review to local school officials, they could choose curricular materials from a state-approved list, they could allow their children to take periodic assessments that would measure their success in examining and reflecting upon diverse worldviews. Surely other methods are possible.

And fourth, the state should require homeschooled children to take annual standardized tests to measure academic progress. If a child repeatedly fails to make academic progress relative to his or her peers in public or private schools, the state should intervene and compel school attendance.

This short list of regulations is tentative and provisional, for I am myself unsure about the most effective way to craft regulations pursuant to meeting the state's and the child's interests. It is far easier to point out the problems with regulating homeschooling. Foremost among these is that religiously motivated homeschooling parents may simply reject the very notion of submitting to a secular authority over matters concerning the upbringing of their children. It is not that deeply religious parents refuse to acknowledge the power of the state generally, for such a position in a liberal democracy would be clearly untenable. Rather, the problem arises when secular state authority is exercised over the rearing of children. Conflict between the state and religious parents on this score may be endemic and inevitable. On my view, even given the deep importance of religious freedom, the state cannot relinquish its regulatory role in education because parents invoke their religious beliefs as a bulwark against secular authority.

Another problem with regulating homeschooling is what Cass Sunstein labels the overregulation-underregulation paradox.[57] The idea is that aggressive statutory controls designed to maintain strict compliance often result in practice in under-enforcement or minimal regulations. When regulations are many and elaborate, they often require significant spending, time, and human resources in order to enforce them. I can imagine this paradox at work in homeschooling regulations quite easily. Given the numbers of homeschoolers, local school authorities need to devote their time and energy to tracking parents and children who have opted out of the public school system. To the already harried educators, spending significant time or devoting significant resources to tracking homeschools may seem wasteful. After all, by removing their children from public schools, parents in effect reduce the public system's funding. Moreover, the very idea of making periodic home visits or meeting with parents to assess curricular materials and monitor educational progress can be unseemly. Being a truant officer/homeschool monitor is surely among the more thankless jobs in society.

The overregulation-underregulation paradox can be mitigated by placing the burden of proof on parents to demonstrate that homeschools will meet the educational interests of the state and the child. But it does not remove it entirely. It appears, therefore, sensible to keep regulations strict but minimal and as nonintrusive as possible.

In the past few years, another and very different regulatory problem has arisen. Some parents who homeschool their children wish to avail themselves and their children of the resources of the local public school—extracurricular activities and sports teams, the library, computers, and internet facilities, guidance from schoolteachers on curricular matters, and in some cases select academic offerings.[58] Most state laws currently make it difficult for parents to claim such resources as a right; homeschoolers are assumed to have exited the public school system and thereby forgone the resources it has to offer. As the number of homeschooled children continue to grow, this is likely to become a new frontier in homeschool legal battles. I can only note here that while the administrative burden placed on public school teachers and leaders to allow homeschool parents selectively to choose the resources that the public school has to offer is undoubtedly a large burden, to the extent that bringing children back within a campus-based school environment conduces to meeting the interests of the state and the child in education—especially to the extent that it brings children into social and intellectual contact with other children of diverse backgrounds—it may be a burden worth assuming.

NOTES

1. *Wisconsin v. Yoder* (1972), 406 U.S. 205; *Mozert v. Hawkins County Board of Education* (1987), 827 F.2nd 1058.

2. For some of the more prominent examples, see Meira Levinson, *The Demands of Liberal Education* (Oxford: Oxford University Press, 1999); Eamonn Callan, *Creating Citizens* (Oxford: Clarendon Press, 1997); Will Kymlicka, *Multicultural Citizenship* (Oxford: Clarendon Press,

1995); Jeff Spinner, *The Boundaries of Liberal Citizenship* (Baltimore: The Johns Hopkins University Press, 1994); Nomi Stolzenberg, "'He Drew A Circle That Shut Me Out': Assimilation, Indoctrination and the Paradox of Liberal Education," *Harvard Law Review* 106 (1993): 581–667; Amy Gutmann, "Civic Education and Social Diversity," *Ethics* 105 (1995): 557–79; Stephen Macedo, "Liberal Civic Education and Religious Fundamentalism: The Case of God v. John Rawls?" *Ethics* 105 (1995): 468–96; William Galston, "Two Concepts of Liberalism," *Ethics* 105 (1995): 516–534; Shelley Burtt, "In Defense of *Yoder*: Parental Authority and the Public Schools," in *NOMOS XXXVIII: Political Order*, eds. Ian Shapiro and Russell Hardin (New York: New York University Press, 1996), pp. 412–437; Richard Arneson and Ian Shapiro, "Democratic Autonomy and Religious Freedom: A Critique of *Wisconsin v. Yoder*," in *NOMOS XXXVIII: Political Order*, eds. Ian Shapiro and Russell Hardin (New York: New York University Press, 1996), pp. 365–411.

3. For a history of the rise of common schools and the spread of compulsory attendance laws, see David Tyack, *The One Best System: A History of American Urban Education* (Cambridge: Harvard University Press, 1974).

4. See Patricia Lines, "Homeschoolers: Estimating Numbers and Growth," U.S. Department of Education, Office of Educational Research and Improvement, 1998, p. 1; J. Gary Knowles, Stacey E. Marlow, and James Muchmore, "From Pedagogy to Ideology: Origins and Phases of Home Education in the United States, 1970–1990," *The American Journal of Education*, February 1992, p. 196.

5. Lines notes that "[m]any families do not file papers, although it is required . . . Some families are homeschooling under a state constitutional or statutory provision that excuses religious-based homeschoolers from filing requirements" (Lines 1998, p. 2).

6. Lines, who offers the most conservative estimate, uses current rates of growth to suggest a number of 1,000,000 in 1997. A cover story in *Newsweek* in 1998 claimed that up to 1.5 million children were being homeschooled. And the National Home Education Research Institute, an advocacy group, offers a high estimate of 1.7 million children in 1999.

7. Mindy Sink, "Shootings Intensify Interest in Home Schooling," *The New York Times*, August 11, 1999, p. B7; Lynn Schnaiberg, "Home Schooling Queries Spike After Shootings," *Education Week*, June 9, 1999, p. 3.

8. *Digest of Educational Statistics, 1998*, U.S. Department of Education, National Center for Educational Statistics (1999), p. 24.

9. "Private School Survey, 1997–98," U.S. Department of Education, National Center for Educational Statistics (1999), p. 12. The categorization

"conservative Christian" is not mine but the Department of Education's.

10. Barbara Kantrowitz and Pat Wingert, "Learning at Home: Does It Pass the Test?" *Newsweek*, October 5, 1998: 64–70; United States Senate Resolution 183, 106th United States Congress (1999). Echoing contested language first found in the *Pierce v. Society of Sisters* case (1925), the Senate declared in the resolution that the "United States recognizes the fundamental right of parents to direct the education and upbringing of their children."

11. Knowles, Marlowe, and Muchmore, "From Pedagogy to Ideology," p. 227.

12. See, for example, Cheryl Lange and Kristin Kline Liu, "Homeschooling: Parents' Reasons for Transfer and the Implications for Educational Policy," Research Report No. 29, University of Minnesota, College of Education and Human Development, 1999. For the most extensive survey on homeschooling parents, see Lawrence Rudner, "Scholastic Achievement and Demographic Characteristics of Home School Students in 1998," *Educational Policy Analysis Archives*, Vol. 7, No. 8, 1999.

13. Knowles, Marlowe, and Muchmore, "From Pedagogy to Ideology," pp. 211–2; see also James Tobak and Perry Zirkel, "Home Instruction: An Analysis of the Statutes and Case Law," *University of Dayton Law Review*, Vol. 8, No. 1, 1982: 1–60.

14. See, for example, Dana Hull, "Home Schooling's High-Tech Wave," *San Jose Mercury News*, October 24, 1999, p. A1.

15. *Wisconsin v. Yoder* (1972), 406 U.S. 205 at 236. The Court also stated, "There is no doubt as to the power of a State, having a high responsibility for education of its citizens, to impose reasonable regulations for the control and duration of basic education."

16. Hull, "Home Schooling's High-Tech Wave," p. A20. For another example of non-enforcement, see Jeff Archer, "Woman in Maryland Home-School Case Acquitted," *Education Week*, October 30, 1996.

17. James Dwyer, *Religious Schools v. Children's Rights* (Ithaca, NY: Cornell University Press, 1998), p. 2; see also p. 10.

18. Christopher Klicka, *Homeschooling in the United States: A Legal Analysis* (Purcerville, VA: Home School Legal Defense Association, 1999). A note of caution: because the HSLDA is an advocacy group, the legal analysis likely interprets state laws in the light most favorable to homeschoolers.

19. Ibid, p. v, pp. 105–106. See the Virginia Home School Statute, 22.1-254.1.

20. The importance of the limited exemption in the Court's ruling was reflected in Justice White's concurring opinion: "This would be a

very different case for me if respondents' claim were that their religion forbade their children from attending any school at any time and from complying in any way with the educational standards set by the State" (406 U.S. 205 at 238).

21. Indeed, one of the reasons to be concerned about the actual outcome of *Mozert* is that, from a strictly practical standpoint, the likely result of the decision is to hasten the exit of Christian Fundamentalists in Tennessee from public schools into private schools or homeschools. If exposure to value diversity is an important element of the civic education required in public schools, the long-term consequence of *Mozert* is almost certain to result in the children of fundamentalist believers receiving less exposure. On this reasoning, it might have been better to permit the exemption the *Mozert* parents requested on the grounds that at least their children would receive the benefits of the public school environment for the remainder of the school day.

22. In *Pierce v. Society of Sisters,* for example, the Court established the principle that a law compelling parents to send their children to public schools "interferes with the liberty of parents and guardians to direct the upbringing and education of children under their control" (*Pierce v. Society of Sisters,* 268 U.S. 510 (1925) at 534–35). Similarly, in *Yoder* the Court opined, "[T]his case involves the fundamental interest of parents, as contrasted with that of the State, to guide the religious future and education of their children. The history and culture of Western civilization reflect a strong tradition of parental concern for the nurture and upbringing of their children. This primary role of the parents in the upbringing of their children is now established beyond debate as an enduring American tradition" (*Wisconsin v. Yoder,* 406 U.S. 205 at 232). On the other hand, Yael Tamir has argued that there can be no right to educate, only a right to be educated (Yael Tamir, "Whose Education Is It Anyway?" *Journal of Philosophy of Education,* Vol. 24, No. 7, 1990: 161–170). Or see James Dwyer's argument "Why Parents' Rights Are Wrong" (Dwyer, *Religious Schools,* pp. 62–101).

23. By using the term "parents," I do not mean to privilege biological parents over other kinds of parents. A more general, and for my purposes synonymous term, would be "guardians."

24. Callan, *Creating Citizens,* p. 142. Callan's point in the book, however, is not to make parent-centered claims about education.

25. There are some plausible alternatives, of course, most famously the communal child rearing described in Plato's *Republic* or, more contemporarily, the communal parenting on kibbutzim. But such possibilities are highly unlikely ever to be implemented on a wide scale in modern society.

26. In a defense of the decision in *Yoder,* Shelley Burtt has argued that parents' authority over their children's education cannot be justified in the free exercise claims of the parents nor in the satisfaction of parental conceptions of the good life. Instead, Burtt argues, parents are best situated to meet the "developmental needs" of their children. Burtt defines "developmental needs" as including emotional, physical, and cognitive needs, as well as moral, spiritual, and cultural needs. With the addition of these latter three needs, however, Burtt sets a standard that is contestable, which in turn undermines, on my view, his claim that parents are entitled to state deference in determining the educational environment of their children (Burtt, "In Defense of *Yoder*").

27. This approach is taken, for example, by Jon Elster in *Solomonic Judgments: Studies in the Limitations of Rationality* (Cambridge: Cambridge University Press, 1989), pp. 134ff.

28. Of course, this rationale has sometimes been taken too far, justifying for example the deeply jingoistic Americanization programs in schools of the early twentieth century and the atrocities visited upon Native American children in the name of civilizing them through schooling.

29. *Wisconsin v. Yoder,* 406 U.S. 205 at 213.

30. *Brown v. Board of Education* (1954) 347 U.S. 483 at 493.

31. See, for example, Arneson and Shapiro, "Democratic Autonomy and Religious Freedom," pp. 376ff.

32. See, for example, John Rawls, *Political Liberalism* (New York: Columbia University Press, 1993), pp. 194–200; Stephen Macedo, *Liberal Virtues* (Oxford: Clarendon Press, 1990); and Macedo, "Liberal Civic Education," pp. 486ff.

33. Galston, "Two Concepts of Liberalism," p. 525, p. 528.

34. It is tempting to think that when clashes occur between parents and the state with respect to ensuring the development of children into independent adults, it is because the state is acting in its backstop role, intervening in the face of negligent or abusive parents. But it is far more likely that such clashes will take the form of parents alleging that the state is negligent and abusive in providing schools of sufficient quality so as to assure that their children will be educated enough to become successful adults. It is not only the state that seeks to hold parents responsible for helping to develop their children into healthy adults; parents also seek to hold the state responsible for providing good schools in the service of the same goal.

35. On this latter question, the available empirical evidence seems to indicate that Catholic schools, for example, can be very successful, perhaps more successful than public schools, in developing citizenship. See

Anthony Bryk, *Catholic Schools and the Common Good* (Cambridge: Harvard University Press, 1993).

36. As many commentators have noted, United States courts have rarely recognized independent interests, much less rights, of children. (See, among others, Hillary Rodham, "Children Under the Law," *Harvard Educational Review*, Vol. 43, No. 4, 1973: 1–28.) In a more general vein, Ian Shapiro writes about the waning authority of religious leaders over children, concluding, "States and parents have thus emerged as the two principal sources of authority over dependent children. Partly competing, partly mutually reinforcing, they structure the basic terms of children's existence into adolescence and beyond" (*Democratic Justice* (New Haven: Yale University Press, 1999), p. 67).

37. 393 U.S. 503 (1969).

38. Galston writes, for example, "Autonomy is one possible mode of existence in liberal societies—one among many others; its practice must be respected and safeguarded; but the devotees of autonomy must recognize the need for respectful coexistence with individuals and groups that do not give autonomy pride of place" (Galston, "Two Concepts of Liberalism," p. 525).

39. Rawls writes, "The liberalisms of Kant and Mill may lead to requirements designed to foster the values of autonomy and individuality as ideals to govern much if not all of life. But political liberalism has a different aim and requires far less" (Rawls, *Political Liberalism*, p. 199; see also p. xliv).

40. I have elsewhere argued for a somewhat more robust understanding of autonomy. Rob Reich, *Liberalism, Multiculturalism, and Education*, Ph.D. Dissertation, Stanford University, 1998, chs. 4–5.

41. Galston, "Two Concepts of Liberalism," p. 521.

42. Rawls, *Political Liberalism*, p. xliv.

43. *Wisconsin v. Yoder* 406 U.S. 205 at 245. For theorists who support the notion that autonomy involves maximizing options, see Elster, *Solomonic Judgments*, p. 137; Joel Feinberg, "The Child's Right to an Open Future," in *Whose Child? Children's Rights, Parental Authority, and State Power*, ed. William Aiken and Hugh LaFollette (Totowa, NJ: Littlefield, Adams, 1980), pp. 134–5.

44. Callan, *Creating Citizens*, p. 152.

45. Rawls provides a much more detailed argument about the importance of political autonomy in *Political Liberalism*. See esp. pp. 77–8, pp. 199–200.

46. For the importance of autonomy to liberal legitimacy, see Harry Brighouse, "Civic Education and Liberal Legitimacy," *Ethics* 108 (1998): 727–53.

47. For a similar argument just with respect to the parents and the child, see Callan, *Creating Citizens*, p. 145.

48. A number of recent arguments answer the balancing question very differently. For a view that gives predominant weight to children's interests and wholly cancels parental interests, see Dwyer, *Religious Schools v. Children's Rights*. Dwyer argues here that religious and private schools should be heavily regulated because without such regulation they frequently harm children. For a view that divides educational authority between parents and the state, see Shapiro, "Governing Children," in *Democratic Justice*, 64–109. Shapiro argues here that parents should be responsible for the education of children for their best interests, as the parents understand them, and that the state should be responsible for the education of children for their basic interests, which include security, nutrition, health, and citizenship. In the event of conflicts, the state's basic interests trump the parents' assertion of best interests. And for a view that gives almost exclusive authority to parents, see Stephen Gilles, "On Educating Children: A Parentalist Manifesto," 63 *University of Chicago Law Review* 937 (1996): 937–1034. Gilles argues here that ". . . the deference we extend to parental educational choices should approach (though not necessarily equal) the deference we give to the self-regarding choices of adult individuals" (p. 939). In addition, Amy Gutmann's recently reissued *Democratic Education* addresses this question of educational authority directly, arguing that such authority "must be shared among parents, citizens, and professional educators . . ." (*Democratic Education* (Princeton: Princeton University Press, 1999), p. 42).

49. Hull, "Homeschooling's High-Tech Wave," p. A20. Hull quotes another student who says, "School isn't about learning. It's about writing 'Metallica' on your notebook and wearing the right clothes and trying to be popular" (p. A1).

50. Rudner, "Scholastic Achievement and Demographic Characteristics of Home School Students in 1998."

51. Levinson, *The Demands of Liberal Education*, p. 58.

52. Ibid, p. 61.

53. Both Levinson and Callan reach similar conclusions. Callan writes, for example, "The essential demand is that schooling properly involves at some stage sympathetic and critical engagement with beliefs and ways of life at odds with the culture of the family or religious or ethnic group into which the child is born" (*Creating Citizens*, p. 133).

54. bell hooks, *Teaching to Transgress* (New York: Routledge, 1994), p. 3.

55. *Wisconsin v. Yoder*, 406 U.S. 205 at 240.

56. Mark Walsh, "Court Sends Girl to Public School Against Parents' Wishes," *Education Week*, November 25, 1998; Maria Glod, "An Education

in the Courts; Couple Fights Order on Teen's Schooling," *The Washington Post,* November 7, 1998, p. B1.

57. Cass Sunstein, "Paradoxes of the Regulatory State," in *Free Markets and Social Justice* (Oxford: Oxford University Press, 1997): 271–297.

58. Comment, "The Latest Home Education Challenge: The Relationship Between Home Schools and Public Schools," *North Carolina Law Review* 74 (1996): 1913–1977.

10

CHANGING THE CONVERSATION
ABOUT CHILDREN'S EDUCATION

JAMES G. DWYER

The conversation political theorists have carried on in recent decades concerning children's education has been dominated by a debate between proponents of "civic education" and defenders of pluralism. The first part of this paper explains why this debate is misguided. What we should be debating is what sort of education best promotes the welfare of children. The adult-centered thinking about child rearing that characterizes the prevailing discourse is morally problematic and plagued by conceptual errors, because it fails to give full effect to the moral implications of children's distinct personhood. Thus, it is not adequate simply to broaden the existing conversation to welcome child-centered perspectives, as this volume shows is now happening. Everyone who presumes to reach ultimate conclusions about education policy, or about policy concerning other aspects of child rearing, should adopt such a perspective.

The second part of this paper illustrates how shifting from an adult-centered to a child-centered approach to child-rearing issues can lead to dramatically different outcomes. It outlines an analysis of the school voucher question. Discussion of vouchers among political theorists and legal scholars has focused primarily on the rights of parents, the rights of secularist taxpayers, and the rights of the liberal state, with attention also increasingly paid to the developmental needs of children in bad public schools. This discussion has yielded conclusions ranging from the position that parents have a right to state support for their unfettered choice of schools to the position that no public funds should go to private schools under any circumstances. In between these extremes are those who hold that it is permissible for the state to provide limited financial support for private schooling, to enable children in the worst public schools to transfer, so long as the private schools abide by certain minimal regulations.[1]

In contrast, I conclude from a child-centered analysis that it is *mandatory* for the state to provide funding for private schools, religious and non-religious, and that the strongest theoretical argument for vouchers actually rests on the rights of children already attending private schools. At the same time, I conclude that the state must attach *extensive* regulations to such funding, regulations that would substantially control the content and methods of instruction in private schools, including religious schools, and thereby transform the nature of private schooling in this country. A focus on the developmental interests and life opportunities of children, rather than on sustaining liberal institutions or protecting parental control over belief formation, dictates a very different balance of state authority and private authority than either liberal statists or the champions of pluralism endorse.

I. WHY A NEW CONVERSATION?

Discussion of education policy by political theorists in recent years has principally focused on the problem of stability, on what a liberal society must command by way of children's education to ensure that succeeding generations support the institutions of a just liberal society. Readers familiar with the work of John Rawls will understand this is as the concern of the latter parts of *A Theory of Justice*. In recent years, this concern has often been expressed in terms of fostering civic virtues and creating the right kind of future citizens. The principal counterpoise to this aim among political theorists has been a concern with violating rights of parents and of non-liberal cultural minorities whose adult members wish to pass on their beliefs to their children and thereby preserve their way of life. Eamonn Callan captures the essence of this two-sided struggle when he writes:

> If the role of the state in education is to keep faith with its constitutive morality, a path must be found between the horns of a dilemma. The need to perpetuate fidelity to liberal democratic institutions and values from one generation to another suggests that there are some inescapably shared educational aims, even if the pursuit of these conflicts with the convictions of some citizens. Yet if repression is to be avoided, the state must give parents substantial latitude to instill in their children whatever religious faith or conception of the good they espouse. Similarly, the state must permit communities of like-minded citizens to create educational institutions that reflect their distinctive way of life, even if that entails some alienation from the political culture of the larger society.[2]

Thus, the philosophical debate over educational authority has by and large treated children's schooling as an instrument for serving ends of society as a whole and ends of parents and adult members of religious groups. The participants in this debate divide into liberal statists who give primacy to creating the right kind of future citizens, and conservatives who give primacy to protecting the power of parents and minority cultural communities to create the kind of future persons they want. Theorists on both sides take note of children's interests as individual persons whose lives are at stake, but typically as an afterthought or as a secondary concern; most commonly, they simply assert that their positions are not inconsistent with children's welfare. By no means are children's interests and rights driving the theories.[3]

A. The Liberal Statist View

Amy Gutmann's *Democratic Education* exemplifies the liberal statist view. In that influential work, Gutmann argues that the liberal state can justifiably demand of all parents that they allow their children to be taught certain virtues, such as mutual respect, necessary to preserve liberal democratic society. One could certainly argue for teaching virtues on the basis of children's welfare; instilling respect for other persons, for example, promotes children's ability to interact harmoniously and constructively with a wide range of people throughout their lives. However, in *Democratic Education*, Gutmann does not approach questions of school curriculum by asking what best serves the interests of children or what children are entitled to as a matter of justice. Rather she asks how children's education can serve the interests of liberal society as a whole and the "right" of adult citizens to participate in "conscious social reproduction."[4] To be sure, how society as a whole fares is important to the welfare of today's children as well as today's adults, so children presumably benefit in some way from policies that aim at the good of society as a whole. The problem is that in the liberal statist approach to education, children's welfare has no special place, is not the focus of moral attention, and is satisfied *only* to the extent of sharing with all other citizens in the good of a stable liberal society. Whether promoting particular liberal aims for society as a whole, or promoting liberal aims by particular means, *is* entirely consistent with children's educational interests, and if not whether those societal aims could be served by some other means, and whether children's interests require *more* by way of education than liberal societal aims require are questions left unexamined.

Gutmann explicitly rejects in *Democratic Education* an approach to education policy whereby the state would impose on all schools requirements designed to give each child the best possible education, so that children in school today might have the happiest, most fulfilling lives possible.[5] Of course, there are often substantial difficulties involved in determining what is best in terms of education for children,[6] as well as practical difficulties in implementing any education policy that some parents and cultural communities oppose. Gutmann discusses those difficulties,[7] but ultimately they are not why she would not require that all children receive an education comporting with the best current understanding of what is a good education. Rather, she objects that this approach would violate "the right of citizens to deliberate collectively about how to educate future citizens."[8] The overriding point of *Democratic Education* is that adult rights to control the lives of children are not distributed broadly enough; not only adults-as-parents but also adults-as-citizens deserve such rights.

Gutmann's citizen right of participation in social reproduction is not inherently inconsistent with the conclusions a child-centered approach would generate, but it is also not inherently consistent with a child-centered approach. It might be that children's welfare in general is best served by a decision-making process for education policy that relies substantially on democratic deliberation. Gutmann does suggest that democratic deliberation about education policy is likely to increase our understanding of education and lead to more enlightened education policies.[9] But her project is not one of showing that to be the case, as a child-centered argument for democratic control would strive to do, nor is it necessary to her position that this supposition be true. Her ultimate standard of acceptable decision-making procedures is whether they treat fairly the groups of adults who disagree[10] and whether they gratify the desires of adults as parents *and* as citizens to shape the future of our society, to participate in social reproduction.[11]

Thus, if any of Gutmann's conclusions in *Democratic Education* are in fact consistent with children's welfare on the whole, it is coincidental rather than compelled by her approach. In fact, there is reason to believe that the decision-making procedure Gutmann recommends would sometimes generate outcomes contrary to children's welfare, and that Gutmann views that as entirely appropriate. This would appear to be a necessary implication of her position that, even if the wisest educational authority knew what is good for children, that authority should not be able to act to ensure that good for them:

> without taking our good, both as parents and as citizens, into account . . . [W]e shall want some assurance from even the wisest educational authority that our good as parents and as citizens, and not just the good of our children, will be considered in designing the educational system for our society.[12]

Gutmann's more recent work continues the theme of citizens' rights vs. parents' rights.[13] She takes on "civic minimalists," champions of plenary parental control over education, arguing against their position in part because they deny adult citizens their right to a substantial measure of control.[14] However, Gutmann focuses more now on the content of education, rather than just the procedures of decision making. The content she would prescribe for children's education, sometimes characterized as "civic education," is "an education adequate to exercising their basic rights and responsibilities as free and equal citizens." It would be easy to mistake this prescription as one grounded in the rights of individual children, but it is not. It is a prescription grounded in the abstract "democratic ideal" of a universal "commitment to treating adults as free and equal beings."[15] In other words, a political theory of democracy dictates that all or nearly all adult citizens must possess certain skills and virtues, including the capacity to deliberate rationally and to respect the equal citizenship of others, in order for our liberal society to persist. Children's education is primarily about fostering those virtues, for that purpose.

Gutmann does refer explicitly to rights of children in her recent work. Students' rights, to some uncertain degree, constrain both parental authority and the discretion of adult citizen majorities in connection with schooling. In addition, Gutmann acknowledges that children have an independent interest in living fulfilling lives, and offers assurance that an education designed to further the democratic ideal will incidentally also further that interest of children.[16] But children's rights and welfare are still not driving the theory, and there is no analysis of what the content of children's rights should be. Therefore, there is no reason to believe that the policies embodied in the concept of democratic education do coincide with the policies a child welfare approach would dictate. The particular rights Gutmann identifies appear, from a child welfare perspective, important but incomplete and unexplained. She specifically identifies only rights against repression and discrimination,[17] and it is not clear that these rights dictate anything by way of curriculum.

In addition, there are several indications that Gutmann's theory remains predominantly adult-centric. For example, in responding to civic minimalism she argues for giving local majorities *discretion* to mandate certain practices in the interests of children.[18] Thus, for example, whether schools in our still-pervasively-sexist society affirmatively promote gender equality would be a matter of discretion for local polities, dependent on how adult citizens in any given locale choose to exercise their right of participation in social reproduction.[19] From a child-centered perspective, one would instead address that issue first by asking whether girls (and boys) in all schools have a right to instruction that promotes gender equality.

When Gutmann discusses funding and regulation of private schools, her views likewise reflect a focus on the claims of parents and citizen majorities rather than on doing justice for children. When discussing school vouchers, her analysis is couched in terms of subsidizing parental choice: "Democratic education calls for the choice of an effective school for every parent whose child is not now receiving an adequate education in a neighborhood public school."[20] Why should the transfer of children from bad schools to good schools turn on parental choice? If subsidized transfers to private schools do become necessary, why not do it on the basis of random selection among all students, not just those whose parents apply for vouchers, or on the basis of individual educational need or ability to benefit from the transfer?[21] Operating from a child-centered perspective, one would not simply assume that only children whose parents affirmatively seek a better education for them should receive one. Similarly, when discussing children already enrolled in private schools, Gutmann writes that it is not unfair to their parents that the state make them bear the cost of their (the parents') choice.[22] From a child-centered perspective, one would instead ask whether it is fair *to those children*—many of whose schools are resource poor and many of whom miss out on educational experiences outside of school because of tuition costs—that they do not share in the benefit of state funding for education.

Finally, when discussing imposition of educational standards on schools, Gutmann at times seems to assume that only public schools and publicly subsidized private schools should be subject to such standards, as if it is only fair to parents to regulate the schools they choose when the state is giving them financial support.[23] Do the children attending private schools that are not receiving public subsidies have no claim to state protection of their educational interests? From a child-centered perspective, one might well conclude that the state has an obligation to regulate those schools as well, because doing so is necessary to protect those children's developmental interests.

In sum, there is no necessary or inherent conflict between the liberal statist approach and a child-centered approach to state education policy, but there is also no necessary or inherent identity between the sets of policies the two approaches yield. There is, in theory, a single standpoint—that of the state—from which all issues are assessed and, again in theory, it is possible that the state could, though focused on serving democratic ideals, reach decisions on all child-rearing matters that are consistent with the welfare of children. The problem is that nothing in the liberal statist approach, as represented by Gutmann and others, guarantees decision making consistent with the welfare of children. Liberal statists advance certain aims for education, such as instilling liberal virtues, that might well benefit today's children, as individuals and as members of a society that benefits from stable liberal institutions. But liberal statists have little to say about children's other, unique interests as developing individuals, which are quite important and which might conflict with particular means of pursuing liberal statist aims.

Further, in addition to identifying particular aims for schooling, "democratic education" specifies, to some degree, decision-making procedures regarding education policy, but there is no reason to think those procedures will always, or even more often than not, produce decisions conducive to children's welfare. It imposes no substantive criteria for majoritarian deliberation about education, and there is certainly reason for concern that local adult majorities will reason on the basis of, and vote so as to promote, interests other than those of children.[24] Finally, liberal statists typically posit as the principal, and sometimes only, constraint on majoritarian decision making, the supposed rights of parents and cultural communities—that is, the competing claims of other adults.[25] And liberal statists frequently make concessions to those adult rights that potentially sacrifice the welfare of children.[26]

B. The Conservative View

The conservative view is even more troubling from a child welfare perspective, because it *does* entail an inherent conflict between children's welfare, as the state—which ultimately must create an education policy—sees it, and adult interests. William

Galston is among those who give priority of place to pluralism and parental and community rights, as against the state's views regarding better and worse forms of education. In reasoning about conflicts over schooling, Galston takes as his point of departure the need "to take deep diversity seriously as an abiding fact of social life."[27] Diversity is not simply to be accepted out of necessity, though; it is to be valued, because it protects personal liberty, the ability of individuals to live their lives by their own lights.[28]

Galston accordingly posits that parents have a right to presumptive authority over their children's education. This right is predicated not on an assumption that it is in children's interest for parents to have that right but, rather, on parents' desire to pass on their way of life to their children.[29] This right is limited only by the bedrock needs of the liberal polity—specifically, by society's need for citizens to be self-sufficient, rather than social burdens, and in possession of the minimum liberal virtues—specifically, respect for the law, "willingness to coexist peacefully with ways of life very different from one's own," and "the minimal conditions of reasonable public judgment."[30] For the liberal state to require anything beyond these "functional needs of its sociopolitical institutions" would constitute an unwarranted infringement of the right of parents.[31] Thus, for conservative theorists, as for the liberal statists, two values really matter in resolving parent-state conflicts over education—stability and diversity, or in other words, social reproduction and individual or community reproduction. Education is not principally, or at all, about promoting the welfare of individual children. Only after general societal aims and the desires of current adults have been balanced is there any consideration of the rights and individual interests of today's children, and then only to say that the conclusions reached are consistent with, or at least not terribly at odds with, children's welfare.[32]

On the topic of school reform and vouchers, conservative theorists are naturally inclined to emphasize parental choice even more so than the liberal statists. They tend to support school voucher schemes that contain only the barest of regulatory conditions, and are particularly reluctant to accept any conditions that would influence the content of instruction. In the conservative view, such conditions would threaten free exercise rights, by coercing religious organizations to sacrifice to some degree their religious mission, and would threaten equal protection rights, by disadvantaging some religious denominations relative to others in seeking public subsidy.[33]

C. The Argument for a Child-Centered Approach

What is wrong with the prevailing discourse as I have described it? Why should the conversation among political theorists be any different? After all, adults do have interests at stake; we want the future of our society and the future of our own offspring to reflect our vision of the good life. And children's education is a particularly propitious means of accomplishing this end, even if it is not the only means. Why not approach education policy with these ends foremost in our minds?

The most straightforward response is to point out the obvious fact that among all the interests potentially affected by children's schooling, none are more important than those belonging to the children themselves. In fact, they are the only persons who have immediately at stake interests that are truly fundamental.[34] Schooling is about shaping minds, fostering skills, providing socializing activities, and generally preparing young people for adult life. The minds that are being shaped belong to the children, not to us adults. The skills reside in them and largely determine their life prospects, not ours. They are the ones being socialized, not us. And they are the ones who will live the adult lives. Ordinarily when we debate policies concerning the fundamental welfare of some group of individuals, those individuals— *their* rights, *their* interests, *their* claim to justice—are the focus of moral inquiry. The interests of other persons—and typically other persons do have interests at stake as well—are at best of secondary importance, and consideration of them might even be ruled out.

This is especially important when the persons whose fundamental welfare is at stake are non-autonomous. Making decisions about the lives of such persons on the basis of societal aims or the rights of their caretakers is fraught with danger, because of their inability to protect their own interests and because of the historical tendency to undervalue or altogether ignore their interests.

Our current practice with respect to non-autonomous adults is scrupulously to guard against this danger; the law mandates that decisions about their lives be based solely on their interests and rights, even though it is often quite difficult to define their interests and rights.[35] Even in regard to adults who have never been autonomous, we believe that ordering their lives so as to further the interests of other people, or to advance general societal aims,[36] would be immoral and incompatible with a proper respect for their personhood.

Why is it, then, that political theorists do not give priority of place to the welfare of children when discussing child rearing? It is not that they deny the personhood of children or explicitly assert that children's welfare does not matter. Rather, the reason is undoubtedly at least partly that their basic theories were developed historically in contexts involving only competent, self-determining adults, and have historically been applied almost exclusively to real-world contexts that involved only—or were treated as involving only—such adults (e.g., property rights, wealth distribution, freedom of speech, punishment of crime). The principal theories in the tradition of political philosophy depend to a significant degree on the premise that all the individuals about whom the theories must concern themselves are autonomous adult individuals. Thinking about non-autonomous persons is unfamiliar terrain for most theorists, and most are likely to find unattractive the prospect of revamping wholesale their intellectual apparatus. In addition, many are undoubtedly, and understandably, squeamish about discussing individuals' interests rather than, and independent of, individuals' choices. Determining the interests of children and other non-autonomous persons is particularly difficult.

For these reasons, it seems, political theorists ignore or bracket child welfare questions when initially formulating a position on education or other child-rearing issues, preferring instead to conceptualize the issues as involving simply a conflict between adults—parents on the one hand, and other adult citizens (represented by the state) on the other. But these explanations do not amount to a justification. It does require a substantial effort to rethink one's basic theoretical approach, in order to address properly the lives of non-autonomous persons, but it is an effort that must be undertaken. Reasoning about what is better or worse for persons who cannot determine that for themselves *is* a complicated matter, but that does not mean that legislatures and courts can have no confidence in any judgments they reach. The difficulty hardly justifies abandoning the welfare of dependent persons as the primary aim of decision making about their lives. As noted above, that is generally understood with respect to non-autonomous adults. It is equally true of children.

Eamonn Callan directly responds to the position that a child-centered approach is the only proper approach to defining the bounds of state and parental authority over child rearing.[37] He rejects the position for three reasons: First, child rearing is of tremendous personal importance to most parents, a "cardinal source of self-fulfillment,"[38] so they have interests at stake sufficient to generate rights, including a right to make bad choices for their children.[39] Second, parents expect a reward from their child-rearing labors that includes realization of certain educational ends in the lives of their children.[40] Parents "do not experience the rearing of a child merely as unilateral service on behalf of a separate human life."[41] And third, although Callan stops short of saying that children are not in fact separate persons, he finds moral purchase in the supposition that "we are tempted to think of the child's life as a virtual extension of our own,"[42] and he quotes Robert Nozick for the proposition that one's children "'form part of one's substance'" and "'are organs of you.'"[43] Accordingly, he treats child rearing as a component of adults' "personal sovereignty."[44]

These reasons do not do the work Callan assumes they do. The first reason fails because it is not the case that we are entitled to whatever is of tremendous subjective importance to us. Many things can and do constitute a cardinal source of fulfillment for people—marrying a particular person, controlling the behavior of one's spouse, pursuing a particular career, securing political office, preventing pregnant women from having abortions, etc.[45] In none of these other cases does the subjective importance of a preference or aim itself give rise to any entitlement. Moreover, I suspect few if any parents would say that their own interests, objectively speaking, in connection with their children's education are more important than their children's interests, so it would be peculiar for the law to presume that the parents' interests are more important. In addition, it is deeply problematic to attribute to anyone a right—an *entitlement*—to direct the life of another human being.[46] With non-autonomous persons, some one or more persons must as a practical matter direct their lives, but they should be viewed as doing so in the role of a fiduciary, effectuating rights of the non-autonomous persons, as construed by the state. That is in fact how the legal system treats caretakers for incompetent adults, even when the caretakers are ideologically opposed to the standards of care or decision making that the state imposes.[47]

The second reason fails in part because it is simply unsupported; Callan cites no evidence as to what parents expect. Personally, I view my parenting as "unilateral service on behalf of a separate human life," rather than as an investment of labor for which I demand a return, and consider myself quite ordinary in viewing the matter that way. Deeming control over a child's life as payback for parenting labor makes a virtue of self-centeredness. This is not to say that parents must be martyrs and sacrifice all their own, *self*-determining interests for the sake of their children. We parents reasonably expect to reserve a fair portion of our time and family resources for our own projects, and we have a right simply as persons, rather than as parents, not to be unduly harassed by state actors in our daily lives.[48] But control over children's education is not about balancing parents' self-determining interests against children's welfare. Nor is it about state officials intruding into the home or seeking to control parent-child interactions. It is about parents' desire to determine how their child's life will go, and to have their own views of a child's interests trump the state's views in setting education policy. There is a child-centered case to be made for parents' views trumping in some instances, and in fact Callan offers one,[49] but Callan has not shown that a child-centered approach should not also be used to determine when parents' views should *not* trump.

Callan's third reason for rejecting a child-centered approach fails for similar reasons. Some people might be tempted to view their children as mere extensions of themselves, but many might not, and one might reasonably believe that any such temptation should be resisted rather than protected with a legal right. If

Callan can make the case that children actually *are* extensions or organs of their parents, so that control over my children's lives really is a matter of my *personal* sovereignty, that would be quite significant. But he has not made that case.

In fact, theorists on both sides of the civic virtue/pluralism debate purport to accept the separate personhood of children. The problem is that they do not fully realize the implications of that moral assumption. In addition to the general lack of attention to children's individual interests described above, this problem is often manifest in writing rendered incoherent by an unacknowledged eliding of the distinction between parent and child. Many theorists, in constructing their core arguments, implicitly and mistakenly treat parent and child as a single entity or as having a complete identity of interests. Ignoring the separateness of children allows them to view conflicts over education as involving only two parties—parents and the state, so that questions of children's welfare never come up. The situation can then be analyzed in familiar and simpler ways, as just another type of conflict between (competent adult) individuals and the state.[50] The result, however, is conceptual confusion. Avoiding such confusion is another reason to abandon adult-centered thinking about state education policy.

Sometimes the elision of parent-child separateness is manifest in an ontologizing of families. Theorists will speak of "families" having rights or claims, and of families choosing a form of education,[51] even though it is plainly the case that parents typically do the choosing, with little or no consultation of children, especially when choices turn on basic values or ideology.[52] Speaking of family rights and family decisions creates an artificial simplification, one that allows theorists to apply standard "autonomous individual vs. the state" forms of reasoning where they really do not fit. It allows them to ignore the fact that child-rearing policy is a matter of the state supervising what some private individuals (parents) do to other private individuals (children), and not a matter of the state restricting self-determining behavior.

At other times, the separate personhood of children is masked by simply speaking very abstractly about rights, freedoms, and choices, without identifying any entity as the holder or source of the rights, freedoms, or choices. Callan, for example, argues as follows against the view that children might be owed as a matter of justice an education that maximizes their development of autonomy:

> Acknowledgment of the great variety of lives that people permissibly lead under free institutions is fundamental to our pre-reflective understanding of liberal politics. But we cannot square that acknowledgment with a reading of personal sovereignty that protects only lives that aim to meet the maximal demands of autonomous reflection and choice. I think the point of trying to understand rights in relation to the "adequate" rather than the maximal development of the moral powers is to seek a reasonable threshold that would be responsive to the range of lives that a free people could accept as worthy of political protection.[53]

Once one recognizes that the lives in question when discussing primary and secondary education are lives of persons who are currently children, this passage appears incomprehensible. A child does not yet have a life that can sensibly be said to aim or not aim at meeting demands respecting autonomy. The question education policy raises is not whether society should "protect" already formed lives that are relatively non-autonomous but, rather, whether society should foster for today's children lives that are relatively more autonomous. Callan in this passage must really have in mind protecting parents, some of whom do not value autonomy. Yet it is not clear that education policy today has anything to do with the autonomy of any current adults.[54]

Similarly, Galston, in arguing against moral autonomy as an aim of public schooling, asserts that "liberal freedom entails the right to live unexamined as well as examined lives."[55] Galston would likely incur little objection to an assertion that current adults, including parents, who are living unexamined lives have a right to be left alone, to be free of efforts to force them to examine their lives. But that assertion would be irrelevant to a discussion of children's schooling. What Galston needs to assert, if he wants to say something relevant to education policy, is that today's children have a right to live unexamined lives. That would be a very peculiar, and arguably incoherent, assertion. Galston makes his claim about unexamined lives appear coherent and plausible by omitting the subject of his statement, glossing over the fact that it is the lives of today's children, not the lives of today's parents, that are under discussion.

A legitimate political theory of children's education must recognize and give full effect to the distinct personhood of children. Children must not be subsumed under the identity of parents, and it should not be assumed that children's interests coincide with those of parents. In addition, child-rearing issues such as education should not be treated as tangential to theories of justice. Child-rearing institutions should be treated as part of the basic structure of society whose features are to be mapped out in accordance with basic principles of justice. A child-centered approach would place children alongside adults when asking in the first instance what kind of liberties and other goods people should generally receive as a matter of justice.[56] This would give rise to some unfamiliar questions that go to the heart of family structure and the state's relationship to the family.

For example, we should ask whether the liberty or power parents and citizens today seek in connection with education is *of a kind* that the basic theory supports. A child-centered approach would recognize that it is a conceptual mistake simply to assimilate the claims of parents and citizens regarding education to rights, such as freedom of religion and the right to political participation, whose core content has to do with self-determination. A parent's power to govern his child's life is a *very* different thing from his freedom to govern his own life; a parent's control over his child's education is very different from his control over what he himself reads or writes or where he goes to church. Any participation a citizen is allowed in the political process to determine how the next generation lives must rest on a very different moral foundation from her participation in a process to determine, for example, what legal restrictions are placed on use of her property or operation of her business. Individuals properly possess rights to direct their own lives and to protect their property interests. But if as a general matter we believe it neither necessary nor appropriate to attribute to anyone a right to determine how *other* persons live, a proper respect for the personhood of children demands that we not attribute such rights in connection with child rearing, absent a convincing demonstration, grounded in sound general principles, that child rearing should be treated anomalously. To be sure, some adults must make decisions for children, but a child-centered approach would assume that, as is the case with non-autonomous adults, decision makers and caretakers for children are to be viewed as acting in a fiduciary, rather than proprietary, role, absent a convincing argument to the contrary.[57]

In addition, a child-centered approach would directly address the questions of what liberties and other goods the basic theory says children must receive, and what procedural mechanisms or allocations of paternalistic authority are most conducive to securing those goods for children.[58] In answering these questions, a child-centered approach would certainly take into account that children are members of families and cultural communities. Children's relationships to others would not, however, be assumed to give the others a claim on children's minds. Rather, children's relationships and the inevitable influence they have on children's minds would simply form the backdrop against which state authorities must decide how to give content and effect to children's rights, how to further children's developmental interests. In making such decisions, state authorities should appreciate the unique aspects of children's lives, but should also be mindful of general moral and legal principles that presumptively apply to children—principles regarding the respect individuals are owed simply as persons, as well as principles regarding proper treatment of less than fully autonomous persons.

Until political theorists give full effect to the separate personhood of children, return to their basic theories to address questions about child rearing, and reason about child-rearing policy on the basis of sound general principles, their reasoning about parent-state conflicts over education cannot be anything but ad hoc. At its worst, such ad hoc reasoning produces unthinking philosophical treatment of children and children's lives in ways we would clearly deem morally unacceptable for other groups of persons. Galston at one point implicitly treats children's lives as a commodity to be bargained with; he suggests that the liberal state allow parents in nonliberal religious groups to put their children in the kind of schools the parents want, because this will give the parents "redress for various types of informal establishment and cultural hegemony."[59] It is as if to say, "We are sorry that your conception of the good is disadvantaged in the liberal public square, so we are offering you as compensation the freedom to do (almost) whatever you want with your children." If the topic were spousal abuse, and a conflict arose between liberalism and religious beliefs that support physical chastisement of wives, would anyone think about the conflict in the same way? I am fairly certain Galston would not recommend exempting men in certain religious communities from domestic violence laws as a way of compensating them for their beliefs being disfavored in the political realm. Why is it morally appropriate to bargain away children's lives but not the lives of any other persons?

The tendency unreflectively to treat child rearing in anomalous ways is hardly confined to conservatives. Peter de Marneffe has presented an argument for deciding the content of children's education in such a way as to ensure competing groups of adult citizens an equal opportunity to lobby children for their future votes on contested political issues.[60] In deciding whether to allow children access to sexually explicit materials, public officials should, according to de Marneffe, take into account that excluding sexually explicit materials from schools and libraries is unfair to adult citizens who favor sexual freedom and who want to persuade others to think similarly. Those adults have a right to freedom of expression that should give them equal access to children as future voters. It is difficult to imagine anyone making an analogous argument that, for example, habilitation decisions for mentally disabled adults should be made in such a way as to give other citizens an equal opportunity to influence the disabled adults' voting. Such an instrumental view of the lives of vulnerable persons is inconsistent with basic moral and legal principles.[61]

In both examples just given, theorists treat children instrumentally, rather than as ends in themselves. That is the basic problem with so much of the political theorizing about education today. Just because it is possible to use children's education to serve collective ends, or the ends of individual adults, does not mean that it is appropriate to do so. And it certainly does not mean that it is appropriate to make those ends the primary focus of one's theory. Both the liberal statist and the conservative approaches to children's education are so at odds with our moral intuitions and practices in cases involving other groups of less able persons, that their proponents should be expected to offer an extensive justification for approaching child rearing in such an anomalous way. Yet they offer none.

In sum, then, prevailing approaches to education policy among political theorists are fundamentally flawed, off-track from the outset because of false premises and conceptual confusion. They acknowledge at some point that children are persons, distinct from their parents, but their theories do not sufficiently reflect that moral fact. Any adequate approach to education policy must begin with a basic theory that takes children's distinct personhood and individual interests fully into account, and should arrive at conclusions regarding rights and duties by reasoning from general principles, principles concerning what a proper respect for individuals qua persons entails and concerning proper treatment of non-autonomous persons. Such an approach would, in my view,[62] dictate a "child-centered" analysis of contemporary education reform issues such as school vouchers— an approach that begins with a focus on children's developmental interests and assigns those interests trumping power over conflicting adult interests, in recognition of the plain fact that children have more important interests at stake in connection with their education than does any group of adults, and in fact are the only persons whose affected interests are "fundamental" in the true sense of that word.[63]

This is not to say, of course, that the task of deciding what kind of education is most conducive to children's well-being is easy or simple. As noted above, there are difficulties both in specifying what the aims should be—for example, to maximize happiness, to promote autonomy, to protect identification with family and community of upbringing, and/or something else—and in figuring out the best means of accomplishing the selected aims. But the difficulty of a task does not make it the wrong one, nor lessen its importance. It simply demands that greater attention be paid to it.

We can begin by discussing what are the better and worse ways to think about what is best for children and how to achieve it. There might be no way that is entirely unproblematic; all may have some weaknesses. But an eclectic approach, looking at the question from a number of different perspectives, might lead to a convergence on one set of answers, or at least narrow the options. For example, reasoning from Rawls's original position, taking fully into account that everyone is a child at the outset of life, could yield some conclusions about what people are owed as a matter of justice as children, and these conclusions might converge with conclusions reached by taking a retrospective assent approach—that is, asking what people upon reaching adulthood could, or typically do, regret or resent in their upbringing. Looking at the matter from still other perspectives might lend further support for, or might cut against, these initial conclusions.

Consider an educational policy of developing critical thinking skills. Would persons in the original position, considering that they will be a child at the outset of their lives and that their parents might hold to any conceivable conception of a good way of life, want to ensure that their education includes this regardless of their family circumstances? If so, is this desire outweighed by consideration of the possibility that they will become parents themselves as adults and might place great importance on their child's adhering to the same worldview? After thinking through those questions, we might ask whether anyone, as an adult, ever regrets or resents not having had an early education that fostered critical thinking skills.[64] And then whether anyone, as an adult, ever regrets or resents *having had* an early education that promoted critical thinking skills.

While there are weaknesses in both of these approaches,[65] I believe they are useful in generating insights, and the fact that they converge—or so I have argued elsewhere[66]—on a conclusion in favor of a policy of promoting critical thinking in all children, might give us some confidence that we are approaching a single best answer. We might additionally canvass the empirical literature on the extent to which people experience happiness or a sense of fulfillment in different sorts of lives—lives that appear to involve critical thinking and those that do not. We might also draw from any work that has been done in moral theory on the ethics of parenting, to see whether any principles can be extended to society's collective child-rearing efforts. The door should be open to anyone to bring in an approach or perspective that might improve our understanding.[67]

That a child-centered approach to education policy will yield policies that are non-neutral relative to the array of conceptions of the good that today's adults hold is irrelevant. As others have pointed out, any education policy, no matter how derived, will be non-neutral. Even a policy of empowering parents and schools to do whatever they want is non-neutral; it privileges a particular conception of the place of children in our society, of what children and parents are respectively entitled to, and of what the aims of education are (i.e., to serve the ends of parents). What matters in the child-rearing context is not neutrality but justice. If one particular, necessarily-non-neutral education policy appears most conducive to children's welfare, then an impartial balancing of the interests at stake suggests that the policy is just, regardless of whether it is disturbing to parents or other adults. That some parents will be upset, feel affront, fear for their children's salvation, and/or become dismayed at the prospect of their children rejecting their beliefs and way of life in and of itself has no direct bearing.[68] Children's interests trump. That some religious conservatives object to a liberal education out of fear that it might undermine their efforts to ensure their children think as they do is, in and of itself, unimportant. It is not their basic welfare that is at stake; it is the children's. What advocates for nonliberal religious groups need to argue is that *the state* should conclude that *the children* are harmed by a liberal education. They have yet to do so.

II. A CHILD-CENTERED ASSESSMENT OF SCHOOL VOUCHERS

A child-centered approach to state education policy will yield conclusions concerning both curricular issues—the content of a good secular education—and distributional issues—how education benefits are distributed. Because of the necessarily limited scope of this paper, I focus here on distributional issues, and I assume that an adequately developed basic political theory would generate certain conclusions about the basic rights of children and adults in connection with education.[69] This section principally examines the implications of those conclusions for the school voucher question.

Education benefits include both material resources and regulation. State-imposed requirements for instruction and treatment of students and standards of achievement, as much as state-provided funding, are a benefit to children, insofar as they induce schools to provide a better education. I assume for the sake of analysis here that the state can identify some components of a good secular education, that these are quite substantial—including fostering many cognitive skills such as critical and creative thinking, generating understanding of methods of inquiry in a variety of disciplines, and imparting a robust body of knowledge, and that this education would, from the state's perspective (since we are talking about state decision making), be good for all children in our society, including many whose parents would object to it on religious grounds.[70] Given this set of assumptions, how would a child-centered assessment of distributional issues differ from the prevailing adult-centered approaches?

First, a child-centered approach would eliminate adult rights from the analysis of how educational benefits should be distributed. Which schools receive state funding and which are subject to quality-promoting regulation are not, at least in the first instance, matters of parents' rights, taxpayer rights, or citizen voter rights.[71] They are matters of children's rights. Second, a child-centered approach would determine the content of children's rights without (direct) reference to parental choices, preferences, or beliefs.[72] This second difference has several implications. It means that we must look out for all children, not just those whose parents make claims on their behalf. It means that parental wishes cannot simply be assumed to serve as an adequate proxy for children's interests; whether they should be treated as such in particular circumstances requires analysis. And it means that the state must ultimately decide what the interests of children individually or collectively are; the state cannot decide that a child's interests are whatever his or her parent's religion says they are.[73]

These features of a child-centered approach have numerous implications. I will present just a few relating to the voucher question. One implication is that we must look more closely at the situation of children in private schools, particularly religious schools. It is often assumed that all private schools provide a

good education and that the only relevant question is whether
the state should support parents' desires to enroll their children
in private schools, or should instead devote public resources only
to making public schools better. To the extent that anyone is concerned about the internal practices of private schools, it is typically just to ensure that the state does not spend public money in-
appropriately—for example, by paying for religious instruction
or by supporting racial discrimination in admissions. Whether
the children attending those schools are receiving all they are entitled to by way of education is of little or no interest to philosophers, legal scholars, politicians, or the general public. This is in
large part, I believe, because people mistakenly equate children's
welfare and rights with their parents' choices; if their parents
choose to place them in a private school, they are *ipso facto* receiving that to which they are entitled.

In fact, though, many private schools in existence today fail to
provide a good secular education.[74] There are two reasons for
this. First, many private schools strive to provide a good secular
education but are resource-poor. I will refer to these as Type 1
schools. Some parents place their children in resource-poor private (usually religious) schools, even when a good public school
is available, for ideological reasons. It is a fixed point in our legal
and moral culture that parents may place their children in a private rather than a public school if they wish to do so.[75] Second,
many religious schools simply do not strive to provide a good secular education. In fact, they strive to accomplish the opposite—
that is, to prevent children from developing cognitive skills like
critical and creative thinking, from understanding methods of inquiry in core disciplines, and from acquiring the knowledge that
they would need to pursue careers in mainstream society. They
do this in an effort to ensure that, above all else, their children
remain believers. I will refer to these as Type 2 schools.

I argued in *Religious Schools v. Children's Rights* that Type 2
schools should not be allowed to exist. One could argue that
Type 1 schools should also not be allowed to exist, that parents
should be permitted to choose only private schools that strive to
provide a good secular education *and* that have adequate resources to do so. However, I want to provide an analysis here in
the mode of real-world theory, rather than ideal theory, in order

to try to say something relevant to policy discussion today.[76] And the reality is that there is virtually no political will to shut down either type of school. It is just not going to happen. In the real world, then, legislators are confronted with a situation in which there are, from the state's secular perspective, good public schools and bad public schools, good private schools and bad private schools. What decisions should they make about vouchers in this situation if they take a child-centered approach?

Legislators should first recognize that they have as much responsibility for the welfare of children in private schools as they do for the welfare of children in public schools. If any children have a right to a good education, then all presumptively have that right. Any liberal theory of justice will generate a right to equal protection of the laws, a right of non-discrimination, as between similarly situated groups of persons, in conferral of public benefits as well as imposition of public burdens. It will generate such a right for children as well as for adults. The Supreme Court's *Brown v. Board of Education* decision rested on just such a right. Children in private schools, like children in public schools, thus have a presumptive right to a good education. Importantly, the choices their parents make cannot extinguish that right; the children do not control those choices and so should not suffer as a result of them. Any liberal theory of justice will also endorse the proposition that while people may rightly bear the consequences of their own voluntary actions and choices, individuals should not suffer loss of important public benefits to which they are otherwise entitled because of choices other individuals make. Relative to children, parents are other individuals. In addition, the state bears responsibility for the fate of these children because state action is a but-for cause of their situation. They are in private rather than public schools only because the state (in the form of courts and legislators) has elected to give parents the power to put them there.

In light of the state's responsibility to children in private schools, and in light of the political reality that resource-poor private schools cannot be shut down and that many parents will place their children in those schools regardless of how much public schools are improved, the only way the state can fulfill its obligation to children in Type 1 schools is to enhance the resources of those schools. The conclusion therefore appears inescapable that state financial aid to religious and other private schools, whether in the form of vouchers or tuition reimbursement or tax credits, is not merely permissible but in fact is mandatory. Children in such schools have a right to a share of state education funding. This argument, grounded upon the rights of children in private schools, I believe to be the strongest theoretical (as opposed to politically effective) argument for vouchers. In contrast, the most that can be said on the basis of the rights of children currently in bad public schools is that vouchers might be *one way* of ensuring them a good education, while it would also be satisfactory for states instead to transform their public schools.[77] This theoretical point has no practical implications, though, since it might not be practically possible, and certainly would not be politically expedient, to design a voucher program only for those children whose parents would enroll them in a private school even in the absence of state aid and even if a good public school were available.

The prospect of vouchers raises several legitimate concerns. None of those concerns, however, is sufficient to justify a conclusion that the rights and interests of these children should be sacrificed. At most, they suggest that aid to private schools must be done in a particular way. For example, the church-state separation concern is not sufficient to rule out aid to religious schools that will improve the secular education those schools provide. Rather, it would simply require that state support for private schools be limited, to the extent possible, to the secular component of those schools. From the state's secular perspective, children in these schools cannot be said to have a right to state payment for inherently religious activities such as religious instruction and worship, and taxpayers have a legitimate objection to paying for those things. There is, admittedly, no perfect way of ensuring that no state money supports religion in any way in such schools, given the general religious ethos of the schools and given the imperfections of accounting procedures.[78] But it should be possible to ensure that the subsidy closely approximates the schools' cost of providing secular instruction, and that will have to be good enough. The fact that there will be some unavoidable conflict at the margins with Establishment Clause values is not sufficient reason to block the aid, because in a contest between the right of children to a good secular education and the interests of secularist taxpayers in not paying for religious practice, taxpayers lose.[79] Our interests in the matter as taxpayers are trivial compared to the interests of the children.

Another important concern is that vouchers would drain resources from public schools. This assumes, of course, a zero-sum game, and therefore invites the question, for philosophers at least, how much of the real-world situation to let into real-world theorizing. In ideal theory, I believe, we would conclude that states must appropriate sufficient public money for education that they could afford to provide vouchers *and* to give public schools all the resources they need to provide a great education. In this era of great economic prosperity, at least, there is no reason to think this would be impossible as a practical matter. Political will is a problem in this context, as it is with respect to closing bad private schools, but as noted above the potential for successful litigation is greater in this context. In any event, even assuming a zero-sum game, it is not obvious that the proper outcome is to deny children in resource-poor private schools any share whatsoever of public spending on education.

A conclusion that children in private schools have a right to share in the benefit of state financial support for education is not the end of the matter. There is also the regulation issue. While defenders of parental and community rights tend to oppose the attachment of regulatory strings to vouchers, and liberal statists urge minimal regulations principally to ensure equal access and non-coercion, a child-centered approach would lead to imposition of quite substantial regulations on voucher schools. Those regulations would go to the very content and methods of instruction, and would likely transform the character of many private schools.

The conclusion above that state funding must be limited, to the extent possible, to secular instruction itself requires some state oversight of private schools. States must determine on an ongoing basis how schools' budgets are allocated, or ensure that schools use all the state money given them only for secular instruction. In addition, the existence of Type 2 schools, which provide what from the state's perspective is an "anti-education," means that states must discriminate in their voucher programs. States simply may not fund such schools. To do so would actually harm the children in them, by encouraging and facilitating the denial of a good education. A state must therefore have regulations in place to ensure that such schools are weeded out of its voucher program. That some people will view this as discrimination among parents on the basis of their religious beliefs is, in a child-centered analysis, irrelevant. Parents have no rights in the matter. School funding is a benefit for children, not for parents.

In addition, the equal protection right of children in private schools again comes into play. To the extent that regulations and standards the state imposes on public schools constitute a benefit for the children in public schools (as recent discussion of tougher standards suggests), children in private schools are entitled to receive that benefit as well, to have their schools subject to rigorous academic standards. The adult-centered nature of popular thinking about child-rearing issues is apparent from the fact that while politicians today regularly spout off about holding public schools accountable, none speak of holding private schools accountable. The notion of private school accountability runs up against entrenched beliefs about parents' rights, beliefs that have undermined efforts by state education officials in the past to hold private schools accountable. The beauty of vouchers is that they might provide the first politically feasible means of imposing robust regulations on private schools.

A child-centered approach to the voucher question therefore yields the conclusion that states must enact voucher programs but also must attach thick regulatory strings to them. This conclusion is quite different from those reached by adult-centered modes of reasoning. Not only do liberal statists and conservatives view state subsidies for private education as merely permissible, and recommend attaching much less regulation if states do elect to create subsidies, but some of the regulations they do insist on actually appear, from a child-centered perspective, rather inconsequential, and even ironic. For example, why is it so important for parents to be able to opt their children out of religious services and instruction in religious voucher schools?[80] The services and instruction must not be inherently harmful to children; if they were, we should want to ban them altogether. Do they become harmful to children because the parents disagree with the views or simply belong to a different faith? These theorists do not make such a claim, nor do they provide any evidence for such a claim. In fact, courts faced with an analogous situation in divorce situations—namely, where ex-spouses are of different faiths and one objects to involvement of the child in the other's religion, uniformly find that children more likely benefit than suffer from exposure to more than one ideological perspective. One might expect a liberal theorist who values autonomy and training for critical thinking in public schools to actually see it as a good thing that some children in religious schools are being exposed to a worldview other than that of their parents. The underlying concern, therefore, must be with parental power and preference, not with children's welfare.

The outline of a child-centered approach to vouchers offered above leaves unanswered many difficult questions having to do both with the details of a permissible program and with problems of implementation. First, there is the question of which private schools that do strive to provide a good secular education should receive financial support. I have considered only those that cannot succeed because they lack adequate resources. Are those the only private schools that should receive state money? It seems implausible to say that children of very wealthy parents have a right to state education money, since their schools are likely to have all the resources they need, and then some. With many social welfare programs, the state uses income caps, and it seems justifiable to do that with education. Children do not have a right to state spending per se but, rather, to a good education. On the other hand, there are some children whose private schools have adequate resources but whose parents are not well off and have sacrificed a great deal to pay for tuition. These children presumably lose out on out-of-school educational activities because of the cost of school tuition; there is no money left over for lessons, camps, trips to national parks, etc. These children would benefit educationally if the state relieved their parents of the tuition burden, and they arguably have a right to that. Thus, an income cap is appropriate, but it should be higher than the caps in existing programs, which are one and a half to two times the poverty line.

A more complex question is how the state can enforce the requisite academic standards. Measuring compliance should not be too difficult. The state might measure performance solely by using tests, and thus minimize intrusion. Importantly, though, existing standardized tests are entirely inadequate to this purpose; in fact, they have proved counterproductive, insofar as they encourage schools to promote rote learning and to teach test-taking strategies rather than emphasizing higher-order cognitive skills. Much better tests would need to be devised and administered, tests that measure critical and creative thinking skills, mastery of methods of inquiry, and knowledge.

More difficult would be compelling compliance. We can state as a general principle that the state ought to do whatever it can to ensure that all Type 1 schools comply with the standards. But what can the state do if a school is unsuccessful? Cutting off funding as a penalty would create the problem that some children would fail to receive state monetary support for their schooling, even though their school is striving to provide a good secular education, because of the failings of their teachers and school administrators. They would suffer through no fault of their own, and this seems unjust. On the other hand, the interests of children would seem to demand that the state try to induce better performance by schools. This is a paradox that plagues public schools as well; states can grade public schools, but it is not clear how they can penalize failing schools, short of closing them, without harming the children in them. Using financial carrots rather than sticks does not seem much better; the worst schools might need more resources, not fewer, than the best schools.

One solution to this dilemma might be to rely on competition and consumer choice. Type 1 schools strive to provide a good secular education, so presumably the parents that patronize them value a good secular education. Therefore, the state might publicize performance results for private as well as public schools and rely on parents to choose among private schools on this basis. An additional solution, which could be done in tandem with the first, is to use the stick of increased supervision to induce improved performance. Schools that fall below standards might be subject to closer oversight by state education officials, something they presumably would want to avoid.

Another complex question is what to do with schools that do provide some secular benefit but that also engage in practices the state deems harmful to children. Even Type 2 schools will, after all, teach children to read and write, if only so the children can read and write Bible verses. For those schools, I am still inclined to say that they should receive no funding, because funding would not create an appreciable secular benefit for the children; the schools would not use the increased resources to add new secular components to the curriculum. In addition, funding those schools could lead their operators and parents to believe the state approves of what they are doing.

However, there are also among Type 1 schools some with internal practices that are problematic from the state's perspective. They might teach basic skills like reading, writing, and arithmetic, and also teach all the usual content of state-mandated courses but discourage independent and critical thinking. Or they might have sexist practices or teach sexist views. Presumably most parents who choose the school are aware of those practices and support them, so competition will not cure the problem. Should the state deny funding to such a school, based on the principle that the state should steer clear of supporting activities that it views as discriminatory or otherwise harmful to children?[81] Some schools might be induced by such a policy to change their practices, but others might be resolute, and increased oversight is unlikely to solve this sort of problem. Yet the children in the latter schools would suffer educationally by the denial of funding, again through no fault of their own. An adult-centered perspective allows one to avoid this paradox, by considering only what is fair to parents and leaving parents to bear the costs of their choice of schools. A child-centered perspective does not allow that easy way out. One adequate, though imperfect, solution might be to impose a modest financial penalty on—that is, slightly reduce the dollar value of vouchers going to—schools that refuse to commit to eradicating such practices, simply to communicate that the state condemns the practices.

There are many other questions that could be raised about the position on vouchers reached here.[82] And there is, of course, also the content question—namely, what is the content of "a good secular education"? I hope to have shown that a child-centered approach is the correct approach to all these questions, and to have interested others in the project of working out the details using that approach.

NOTES

1. The regulations of greatest interest have been those prohibiting discrimination in admissions and those requiring that parents be able to opt their children out of religious instruction and worship. See, e.g., Stephen Macedo, "Constituting Civil Society: School Vouchers, Religious Nonprofit Organizations, and Liberal Public Values," *Chicago-Kent Law Review* 75 (2000): 417–51, 418, 436–37 (also mentioning prohibition of teaching hatred on the basis of religion), 439, 440–41, 447; and Michael W. McConnell, "The New Establishmentarianism," *Chicago-Kent Law Review* 75 (2000): 453–75, 470.

2. Eamonn Callan, *Creating Citizens: Political Education and Liberal Democracy* (Oxford, 1997), at 9.

3. The problem I perceive might be better understood by considering an analogy to decision making about custody in divorce proceedings. Where a divorcing couple has children, state statutes command that judges allocate "legal custody"—that is, authority to make major decisions such as where the child will attend school—as well as physical custody (i.e., time spent in each post-divorce household) on the basis of the best interests of the child. This command reflects a legislative judgment that child rearing is first and foremost about the welfare of children, and that children have the most important interests at stake in the custody decision. Nevertheless, in practice, some judges fail to maintain a focus on the child's welfare, and instead slip into a mode of reasoning that focuses on fairness to the parents, on giving each parent some share of victory, or on rewarding perceived moral deservingness and punishing perceived moral failings. These judges are acting contrary to the law and to its moral underpinnings. Political theorizing about education has resembled this illicit form of judicial reasoning about legal custody, in the sense of focusing on arbitrating the competing claims of adults rather than on promoting the welfare of children.

4. Gutmann, *Democratic Education* (Princeton, 1989), p. 14.

5. Ibid., 13–14, 25–27, 38.

6. It is common, however, to overstate these difficulties. In the first place, the aim of child-centered thinking is not really to determine the absolute best way of raising children; it is, rather, to identify better and

worse ways of treating and teaching children, based on our best current knowledge, understanding, and capabilities. Secondly, much of the disagreement about what is better or worse stems not from lack of knowledge but, rather, from different ideological outlooks and different values. There is no real disagreement, for example, over whether critical thinking abilities are necessary to a wide range of careers in contemporary mainstream society, nor over whether sexist teaching and treatment undermine girls' equal opportunity to pursue careers in mainstream society. The problem for education policy arises from the fact that some parents do not want their children, especially not their daughters, prepared to pursue careers in mainstream society. The question the state must face, then, is not whether it has sufficient confidence in *its* conclusion that critical thinking and belief in gender equality are good for children but, rather, whether, despite this conclusion, it should empower parents to deny these things to their children—that is, whether the state should make parents' ideological perspective controlling.

7. Ibid., 7, 11–12.

8. Ibid., 14. See also ibid., 26–27, 36–37, 38.

9. Ibid., 11.

10. Ibid., 12 ("We can do better to try instead to find the fairest ways for reconciling our disagreements.").

11. Ibid., 27.

12. Ibid.

13. See Gutmann, "Civic Minimalism, Cosmopolitanism, and Patriotism: Where Does Democratic Education Stand in Relation to Each?" in this volume (2001), and Gutmann's new epilogue in a new edition of *Democratic Education* (Princeton 1999).

14. See Gutmann (2001) and Gutmann (1999), at 292 ("Schooling that is publicly mandated and subsidized by democratic citizens may legitimately pursue civic purposes . . .") and 294 ("If civic minimalism says that teaching about gender discrimination exceeds the minimum, it denies democratic citizens the discretion to mandate more than a minimal civic education in schools."). Gutmann also criticizes the civic minimalist position as substantively empty and/or internally contradictory. Ibid., at 295.

15. Gutmann (2001). See also Gutmann (1999), at xii.

16. See Gutmann (2001), and Gutmann (1999), at xiii ("Deliberation is not a single skill or virtue. It calls upon skills of literacy, numeracy, and critical thinking, as well as contextual knowledge, understanding, and appreciation of other people's perspectives. The virtues that deliberation encompasses include veracity, nonviolence, practical judgment, civic integrity and magnanimity. By cultivating these and other deliberative skills and virtues, a democratic society helps secure both the basic

opportunity of individuals and its collective capacity to pursue justice.")
The difficulties involved in determining what is good for children,
which Gutmann emphasized in *Democratic Education*, are apparently not
so great as to preclude her now providing a substantial list of such
things.

17. Gutmann (1999), at 297.

18. Gutmann (2001), Gutmann (1999), at 294.

19. Ibid.

20. Ibid., at 300.

21. I am not saying here that there is no child-centered argument for
making some decisions and some allocations of government benefits
turn on parental choice. Often parental support is necessary for child
welfare initiatives to benefit children. With respect to transfer of children to private schools, I suspect that strong parental *opposition* would
make transfer of a given child not conducive to his or her well-being.
However, where a child's parents are simply indifferent, a transfer determined best for the child without regard to the parents' position would
probably still be best for the child. My point here is that this is not the
sort of reasoning taking place in Gutmann's musings about school
vouchers.

22. Gutmann (1999), at 302.

23. Gutmann (2001). Cf. Macedo, supra note 1, at 441 ("The recourse for religious and other private institutions that wish to resist public values is to not become conduits for public monies dedicated to public purposes.").

24. For example, local majorities might be driven more by concern
with reducing taxes, or with channeling tax revenues to projects other
than schools, such as municipal golf courses, than by concern for children's welfare. Or they might be more concerned to make parents
happy or to avoid parental complaints, and for that reason water down
or abandon the requirements they would otherwise impose on schools.

25. See, e.g., Callan, supra note 2, at 135 ("The case for schools that
adhere closely throughout to the familial primary culture is typically presented as a matter of parents' rights. That is just the kind of argument
we should expect if we are asking about possible moral limits on the coercive pursuit of politically desirable ends.").

26. See, e.g., Callan, supra note 2, at 146 ("parents have a right to
make a choice that is bad for their children").

27. William Galston, "Two Concepts of Liberalism," *Ethics* 105 (1995):
516–534, 518.

28. See ibid., 527 ("The Reformation Project, which takes deep diversity as its point of departure, offers the best hope for maximizing oppor-

tunities for individuals and groups to lead lives as they see fit."). See also ibid., 521, 523, 524. At times, Galston writes as if the ultimate value is peace; prohibiting non-liberal ways of life would lead to civil war. E.g., ibid., 526. But if peace were the ultimate value, Galston's case for protection of diversity would be greatly weakened. The state would be free to pursue means of eradicating non-liberal ways of life—for example, various kinds of financial incentive—that are not likely to trigger social strife. In fact, the state might be duty-bound to minimize diversity in the long run, by means that produce the least strife in the short run, in order to lessen the likelihood of ideological conflict.

29. William Galston, *Liberal Purposes* (Oxford, 1991), at 252.

30. Ibid., 252–53. See also "Two Concepts of Liberalism," at 528 n.29 ("the scope of permissible diversity is constrained by the imperatives of citizenship").

31. Ibid., at 254. Galston also raises the specter of totalitarianism, which supporters of parental rights often throw in for good measure. For the liberal state to go beyond the civic minimum would be to impose on everyone "a single debatable conception of how human beings should lead their lives." *Liberal Purposes,* 256. As many others have pointed out, teaching children to think for themselves hardly has this effect. In fact, it might well increase diversity overall—some ways of life might die out, but many others may come into being. It does not rule out any conceptions of the good. At most, it makes less likely that anyone will adhere to any conception of the good unreflectively. (I say "less likely," rather than "impossible," because compulsory schooling occupies only about 15 percent of children's waking hours from birth to age eighteen, so regardless of what kind of schooling children receive parents will retain complete control over the vast majority of children's waking hours and so will have a much greater influence.) Galston and other conservatives thus need to argue that by making it less likely that any members of future generations will hold a conception of the good unreflectively, liberalism "will betray its own deepest and most defensible principles." Ibid.

32. See, e.g., Galston, *Liberal Purposes,* p. 255, Galston, "Two Concepts of Liberalism," pp. 531–33.

33. See, e.g., Stephen V. Monsma, *When Sacred and Secular Mix: Religious Nonprofit Organizations and Public Money* (1996), at 18–21, 183–84; Carl Esbeck, "A Constitutional Case for Governmental Cooperation with Faith-Based Social Service Providers," *Emory Law Journal* 46 (1997), at 27; Joseph Viteritti, "Choosing Equality: Religious Freedom and Educational Opportunity Under Constitutional Federalism," *Yale Law & Policy Review* 15 (1996), at 138.

34. Joel Feinberg defines a fundamental or "welfare interest" as "the 'basic requisites of a man's well-being,'" a "generalized means to a great variety of possible goals[,] whose joint realization, in the absence of very special circumstances, is necessary for the achievement of more ultimate aims." See Feinberg, *The Moral Limits of the Criminal Law, Vol. One: Harm to Others* (1984): 37. Feinberg gives as examples of fundamental interests: physical health, the integrity and normal functioning of one's body, basic intellectual abilities, emotional stability, "the capacity to engage normally in social intercourse," some minimum of financial resources, and "a certain amount of freedom from interference and coercion." Ibid. An interest in shaping the lives of other persons does not fit well with this definition or catalog of essential goods.

35. The question whether to sterilize mentally disabled women is a case in point. The law today requires a court order to perform this procedure, and judges are to render such orders only after applying a best interest or substituted judgment test—asking what is best for the disabled woman or what she would likely decide for herself if able. In addition, the law precludes courts from considering the interests of parents or other guardians for the incompetent woman in deciding whether to authorize sterilization. See Elizabeth Scott, "Sterilization of Mentally Retarded Persons: Reproductive Rights and Family Privacy," *Duke University Law Journal* 1986 (1986): 806, 817–22.

36. Imagine, for example, someone proposing that all the mentally disabled adults in a town be paraded down Main Street waving flags, for the purpose of shaming non-disabled adults who are insufficiently civic-minded. We would regard such instrumental treatment of persons to serve collective interests as immoral. In fact, we would probably say that it is worse to use incompetent persons than it is to use competent persons to serve collective ends, precisely because the former are more vulnerable and less able to protect themselves from harm.

37. Interpreting Callan on this point is somewhat difficult because he begins the pertinent section of the book by discussing a child-centered argument for parents' rights, but at some point shifts to discussing a child-centered argument against parents' rights. Callan, supra note 2, at 138–45. While Callan focuses on parental interests, one could make analogous arguments on the basis of citizens' interests. Those arguments would presumably be weaker, since a citizen's interest in how children in general are educated is presumably less pronounced than a parent's interest in how her children are educated. My responses to Callan below can easily be translated into arguments against sacrificing children's welfare for the sake of citizen interests.

38. Ibid., at 144.

39. Ibid., 145–46.

40. Ibid., at 143.

41. Ibid., at 144.

42. Ibid.

43. Ibid. (quoting Robert Nozick, *The Examined Life* (1989), at 28).

44. Callan, supra note 2, at 145. Callan defines a "zone of personal sovereignty" as "a sphere of conduct in which individuals are rightfully free to make *their own way* in the world" (emphasis added), states that personal sovereignty "is the social space where the traditional freedoms of liberal politics apply, such as freedom of conscience," and then proceeds to discuss child-rearing decisions as an aspect of personal sovereignty. Ibid.

45. Loren Lomasky explicitly compares child rearing to other projects people pursue to give their lives value: "Few people can expect to produce a literary or artistic monument, redirect the life of a nation, garner honor and glory, that lives after them. But it is open to almost everyone to stake a claim to long-term significance through having and raising children." Lomasky, *Persons, Rights, and the Moral Community* (1987), at 167. The thinking seems to be that if we cannot have those other things—and most of us will not, because they are not things to which we are entitled—most of us can at least use our children as vehicles for expressing our vision, for satisfying our will to power, or for making ourselves important in others' eyes. And some theorists appear to infer simply from our having the opportunity to use our children in this way that we must have a moral right to do so.

46. See generally James G. Dwyer, "Parents' Religion and Children's Welfare: Debunking the Doctrine of Children's Rights," *California Law Review* 82 (1994): 1371–1447.

47. See ibid., at 1416–20.

48. Thus, a child-centered approach to child-rearing law and policy is not "a moral theory of the family that says only the interests of children really count," ibid., at 144–45, nor does it "make individual parents no more than instruments of their children's good." Ibid., at 145. Rather, it demands that when the state makes decisions about the aims of child-rearing practices per se, it give primacy to the interests of children. Whether children receive training in critical thinking in school has no bearing on the self-determination of adults who happen to be parents, so nothing in liberal theory supports imputation of a right to those adults in connection with the matter. The interest parents have in satisfying their desire for *other*-determining power itself provides no justification for sacrificing the welfare of children as the state sees it. In fact, that desire should command no more solicitude than does the desire of a

husband to control the conduct of a spouse or the desire of a right-to-life advocate to control the conduct of a pregnant woman, both of which might also be infused with love and "momentous expressive significance." Ibid., at 144.

49. Callan, supra note 2, at 138–40. In fact, Callan's argument could be made stronger, by taking into account children's interest in their parents' self-confidence and satisfaction as parents, and children's interest in a stable family life, both of which can be threatened by state intervention. These interests of children counsel in favor of granting parents somewhat greater discretion in child rearing than one might otherwise attribute to them.

Callan commits a conceptual mistake, however, by characterizing the parental authority that children's interests support as a matter of parental right. If a certain rule of decision making regarding children's lives is predicated on the interests of children, it should be viewed as a right of the children, not of the decision makers. It is nonsensical to say that one person's interests generate rights in another person. Analogously, the law treats mentally incompetent adults as having a right to decisions being made according to certain procedures, and in some instances presumptively by an individual fiduciary—often a parent, rather than the state. The law does not attribute a decision-making *right* or *entitlement* to the fiduciary but, rather, accords a revocable power, constrained by an obligation to make decisions in accordance with the ward's best interests and by a prohibition on self-dealing. See Dwyer, supra note 46 at 1416–20.

50. Some theorists actually acknowledge after the fact that they have done this, yet do not recognize how problematic this is. In Galston's *Liberal Purposes*, 254, for example, there is at the tail end of an analysis of parent-state conflicts over schooling, the telling statement: "There are, after all, three parties to the educational transaction."

51. See, e.g., Stephen Macedo, "Liberal Civic Education and Religious Fundamentalism: The Case of God v. John Rawls?" *Ethics* 105 (1995): 468–496, 485 (asking whether "families have a moral right to opt out of reasonable measures designed to educate children toward very basic liberal virtues . . .").

52. See *Wisconsin v. Yoder*, 406 U.S. 205, 232 (1971) ("There is nothing . . . in the ordinary course of human experience to suggest that non-Amish parents generally consult with children of ages 14–16 if they are placed in a church school of the parents' faith.").

53. Callan, supra note 2, at 149. Will Kymlicka makes an analogous argument against imposing liberal educational mandates on cultural minority communities, protesting that doing so would threaten individu-

als' personal identity. See Kymlicka, *Liberalism, Community, and Culture* (1989), at 164–67. Kymlicka's argument confuses and conflates current adult members of cultural minorities, who have already-formed identities but who are not the persons whose education is at issue, and children born today to such adult members, who are the persons whose education is at issue but whose personal identity has yet to be formed. For an extended critique of Kymlicka's position, see James G. Dwyer, *Religious Schools v. Children's Rights* (Ithaca, NY: Cornell University Press, 1998), at Ch. 4.

54. At one point, Callan implicitly treats adults' "personal sovereignty" as including rule over their children's lives, Callan, supra note 2, at 145–46, but that is a conceptual error or misuse of language. My personal sovereignty and my autonomy mean rule over my life, not rule over anyone else's life. Directing my children's lives is no more a matter of my autonomy or personal sovereignty than would be control over the life of my wife.

55. *Liberal Purposes*, 254. Similarly, when Galston addresses the Amish question, he writes: "The issue is not simply the theological impulse to tyrannize over others. It is also the simple desire to be left alone. . . ." Galston, "Two Concepts of Liberalism," at 520. The later Rawls speaks in a similar fashion about education: "Justice as fairness honors, as far as it can, the claims of those who wish to withdraw from the modern world in accordance with the injunctions of their religion. . . ." John Rawls, *Political Liberalism* (Cambridge: Harvard University Press, 1993), 200. And Macedo writes that "we allow people to exclude themselves from public schooling and go to private schools, parochial and fundamentalist schools, and even school at home." Macedo, *Diversity and Distrust: Civic Education in a Multicultural Democracy* (2000), at 202. The children whose education is at stake are not wishing to be left alone, are not wishing to withdraw from the modern world, and are not excluding themselves. In addition, the parents do not wish to be left *alone*—they want to be left with their children in their exclusive power, and the parents are not excluding themselves from public schooling—they are seeking to exclude other selves, their children, from public schooling.

56. Alternatively, one could say that any theory of justice should give proper consideration to individuals' interests and rights over the course of complete lives, from birth to death. The Rawls of *A Theory of Justice* (1971) at times suggested such an approach, but the Rawls of *Political Liberalism* largely abandoned it. See Dwyer, supra note 537, at Ch. 6.

57. For an explanation of the distinction between parental rights and a parental privilege, and an argument for recognizing only the latter, see Dwyer, supra note 53, at Ch. 3.

58. I offer some thoughts on these questions in Dwyer, supra note 53, at Ch. 6.

59. "Two Concepts of Liberalism," p. 530.

60. Peter de Marneffe, "Is It Fair to Adults to Make Children Moral? Response to Robert P. George," *Arizona State Law Review* 29 (1997): 581–84. De Marneffe would balance against this aim the interests of parents and the need to protect children from known harms. See id. at 583 ("This argument . . . *might* be trumped if we *knew* that children were likely to be *harmed*. . . .") (emphasis added).

61. See Dwyer, supra note 46, at 1405–23. Amy Gutmann has criticized, on similar grounds, treatment of schooling as a matter of parents' free speech rights. See Gutmann (1999), at 299.

62. I presented an extended argument for this view in *Religious Schools v. Children's Rights*, and continue to develop that argument in a forthcoming book on the topic of school vouchers. In this short paper I can only state what the view is.

63. Two caveats: First, I assume certain current social circumstances continue—in particular, that our society remains sufficiently wealthy that a triage of fundamental interests of competing groups is not necessary. If it were the case that children could receive a good education only at the cost of adults starving, for example, the analysis would have to be much different. Second, I do not claim that adults' interests should not be considered at all but, rather, that children's welfare should be considered first, and should presumptively trump the interests of adults. A convincing showing that some adults have more important *self*-determining interests at stake might justify some sacrifice of children's welfare, but it is difficult to imagine such a situation in the education policy context. In addition, as between two policies shown to be equally conducive to children's developmental interests, it might well be appropriate to decide based on a balancing of societal interests and parental interests.

64. For examples of testimonials by adults who have experienced such regret and resentment, see Edward T. Babinsky, *Leaving the Fold: Testimonies of Former Fundamentalists* (1995), and Joanne H. Meehl, *The Recovering Catholic: Personal Journeys of Women Who Left the Church* (1995).

65. The original position approach is vulnerable to the general and familiar charge that real persons who attempt to reason from the original position will inevitably import a comprehensive moral view, which will largely pre-determine many conclusions before any reasoning takes place and will beg important meta-theoretical questions. The retrospective assent approach has its own set of problems. Relying on what actual individuals regret is problematic because of the difficulty of comparing different lives; we can, after all, live only one. Any person's belief that

her life would have been better (in terms of what she now values as an adult) if, for example, she had received a different sort of education, therefore cannot always or entirely be presumed accurate. And psychological propensities can distort perceptions in positive and negative directions—the "grass is always greener" personality and the "it's all for the best" personality. Relying on what actual individuals resent is problematic because what people resent depends on their views of what is just, which creates circularity. We would want to ask whether their resentment is appropriate, which is to ask whether they are correct about what is just. However, a convergence between the original position approach and the approach of looking to what actual people resent might show that the original position approach, and the conclusions reached by using it, are consistent with commonly shared moral intuitions.

66. See Dwyer, supra note 53, at Ch. 6. For a more fully developed account of why all children should receive an "autonomy-facilitating" education, see Harry Brighouse, *School Choice and Social Justice* (Oxford University Press, 2000), Ch. 4.

67. Any perspective, to be useful, would of course have to be one that state decision makers can properly adopt, since what we are discussing is public policy and legal rules—that is, decision making by organs of the state. This rules out, in particular, theological perspectives. Lest there be any mistake, I am taking no position here on from what perspective private citizens may argue for particular education policies but, rather, solely on the matter of what perspective legislators, state agency heads, and judges may adopt to make decisions about children's education.

68. It might have indirect bearing, insofar as children's well-being is affected by parents' reaction to state-imposed restrictions on their child-rearing choices. This is a complex matter I address in *Religious Schools v. Children's Rights*, Ch. 5. In addition, if parents believe a state policy threatens their children's temporal welfare, the state should seriously consider whether the parents are correct.

69. I argue for these conclusions in *Religious Schools v. Children's Rights* and in my forthcoming book on vouchers.

70. I am bracketing certain issues here in order to make the analysis manageable—for example, whether a different analysis would apply where parents object on non-religious grounds and whether some children in our society (e.g., children of Aleuts in the far reaches of the Alaskan archipelago) are so far removed from mainstream society that they would not benefit, and might in fact be harmed, by an education that prepares them for life in mainstream society. Children raised in Amish communities, who are often the focus of attention for political theorists, do not today fall into this category.

71. Adult rights, or at least adult interests, are relevant to a subsequent analysis of how state money may be spent after children's educational rights are satisfied. For example, if the state proposes not only to pay for secular instruction in private schools, which it might be required to do as a matter of the rights of the children in those schools, but also to pay for religious worship in private schools, the interests of taxpayers who object to state spending on religion would come into play. In addition, what total amount is spent on children's education relative to other state services, such as universities, roads, welfare, etc., is not solely a matter of children's rights. The interests of other groups of persons must weigh in at the outset in the decision how to allocate total state resources among child-rearing and non-child-rearing activities. That larger distributional issue is, unfortunately, ignored in the debate over vouchers; it is typically simply assumed that spending on private schools must translate into a decrease in funding of public schools, that the state will not appropriate new money to fund vouchers. But a decrease in public school funding is not logically entailed in spending on private schools, and it is also not inevitable as a political matter. In fact, several voucher bills considered by state legislatures in recent years have called for new appropriations and would have forbidden a decrease in spending on public schools. Those bills failed to pass, but not because it was thought that the state could not afford to spend any more money on education. In the analysis here, I address only the question of how to distribute appropriations for education among schools, not the question of how much should be appropriated for education relative to other public services.

72. As noted above, parents' wishes are indirectly relevant, insofar as children's welfare is affected by parents' emotional and mental states—for example, their happiness, their self-confidence, the extent to which they feel empowered and respected, etc.

73. Many philosophers and legal scholars overlook the fact that what is ultimately at issue in child-rearing situations is state decision making. Even an outcome that gives parents plenary legal rights of control over their children's lives is a state decision; laws come from the state, not from the sky. From a child-centered perspective, the state's decision as to how to assign presumptive legal authority to decide specific issues should be based on what is best for children generally. And if the state concludes on that basis that its own agencies should have presumptive authority over some aspects of children's lives, such as the 15 percent of children's waking hours spent in school, then its agencies should exercise that authority on the basis of what is best for individual children, as the agencies see it.

74. For a summary of the empirical literature on Catholic and fundamentalist Christian schools, see Dwyer, supra note 53, at Ch. 1.

75. I argue in *Religious Schools v. Children's Rights* that it is wrong to attribute parents an *entitlement* to do this. I believe, however, that granting parents this power is justifiable on child welfare grounds. Parents should, though, view their role in exercising this power as a fiduciary one, rather than a proprietary one. In any event, there is no point, even for philosophers, in arguing that the state should require that every child attend a public school, because that is so far outside the realm of possibility under current social circumstances. I therefore assume here that private schooling will continue to exist.

76. This is, admittedly, tricky business. One must decide to which imperfections in the real world one will make concessions. One cannot accept them all as given, since then one could make no recommendations for change. Here I rely on a rough distinction between things that can realistically be changed and things that cannot. Placing things on one side or the other admittedly involves a great deal of speculation.

77. There is also not much political will to transform public schools, so one might think that the only realistic way of fulfilling the right of these children to a good education is to subsidize their transfer to a private school. However, there is a potential for judicial intervention in the public school contexts that probably does not exist in the private school context. There has in fact been successful public school finance reform litigation in several states. In contrast, it is unimaginable that a court would order closure of any religious schools because of poor academic performance.

78. Contrary to what many believe, however, most religious schools are not "pervasively sectarian" in the sense that religion thoroughly shapes everything that they do. Catholic schools, which make up the largest segment of the religious school market, have separate classes for catechism and teach more or less the same content in state-required subjects that public schools teach. The term "pervasively sectarian" more aptly applies to the second type of school described above.

The "substitution" objection—that any state subsidy frees up private money for religious uses—is a non-starter. It is no concern of the state what people do with private money. There is also nothing to the objection that money from the state will go into the same bank account with the school's privately raised money and therefore will be used for all of a school's activities. The fungibility of money, both as between two sums of money and as between money and the things it can buy, makes it senseless to talk about where a particular dollar goes. From an economic perspective, limiting a subsidy to the amount of money an entity spends on a particular activity is what it means to pay only for that activity. This is a basic assumption of all government funding targeted for specific activities undertaken by private entities that also engage in activities other than the targeted ones.

79. This conclusion could be interpreted in two ways, as saying either that the Establishment Clause should be interpreted to allow for modest infringement upon separationist values, where this is an unavoidable and incidental effect of protecting important individual interests and rights, or that the Establishment Clause is trumped by the individual rights of children. Existing Establishment Clause doctrine in American courts does not clearly support either of these interpretations, and in fact is clearly contrary to the second. The Establishment Clause is generally, though only implicitly, treated as an absolute trump over all other considerations. In my view, this points out a defect in existing doctrine.

80. Macedo characterizes an opt-out requirement as "vital." See Macedo, supra note 55, at 271.

81. The United State Supreme Court reached this conclusion with respect to private schools that have racially discriminatory admissions policies, on the basis of Fourteenth Amendment Equal Protection Clause strictures. The Court held that states may not even provide textbooks to such schools. *Norwood v. Harrison*, 413 U.S. 465 (1973). All existing voucher programs accordingly mandate racial non-discrimination in admissions. The rationale of *Norwood* would presumably apply to internal practices as well as to admissions policies, and to sexism as well as racism. See James G. Dwyer, "School Vouchers: Inviting the Public Into the Religious Square," *William & Mary Law Review* 42 (2001), at 994–96. Prohibiting the state from supporting practices that are harmful to children in other ways, not having to do with discrimination, would require appeal to a different constitutional principle, perhaps substantive due process.

82. I endeavor to provide a fuller analysis of the questions raised above, and to answer other questions as well, in my forthcoming book on vouchers.

PART III

PRISONS, PUNISHMENT, AND MORAL EDUCATION

11

MORAL EDUCATION AND JUVENILE CRIME

RANDALL CURREN

Juvenile violent crime increased sharply in the United States during the 1980s, giving rise to a predominantly punitive and retributive public response which has persisted to the present, even as the incidence of serious juvenile crime has declined. Countless legislative measures have been enacted since the mid-1980s to facilitate the prosecution of juveniles as adults, to impose harsher prison sentences on them, and to abandon the presumption in favor of rehabilitative interventions which guided the juvenile justice system from its inception a century ago.[1] This legislative embrace of "adult time for adult crime" includes, in many states, laws which call for the automatic transfer of children fourteen years old or younger to adult court.[2] What the word "automatic" signifies in this context is that transfer is categorically mandated, and thus not dependent in any way on an assessment of the offender's maturity, developmental status, or life circumstances. An assessment of such factors typically does come into play in the adult courts in which juvenile offenders are subsequently prosecuted, but the judges in those courts lack the educative and rehabilitative alternatives which have been available within the juvenile system. The net result is a system less sensitive to the differences between children and adults, less occupied with enabling children to live within the law, and more indiscriminately punitive.

A secondary public and legislative response to juvenile violence and related problems has been to experiment with reintroducing moral education of various kinds into American schools. These educational interventions have been undertaken on a massive scale, and have often been grounded in public deliberations conducted in order to define and obtain consent to lists of "consensus values" to be taught. However, even combined with other efforts to improve the moral climate of schools and attempts to provide teenagers with more adult supervision, these represent a poorly funded, controversial, and unevenly researched and implemented attempt at prevention.[3] It is not clear how far such educative efforts may succeed in reducing the incidence of juvenile crime, but I shall argue that justice demands that we make serious and systematic efforts to ensure that all children receive an adequate moral education. I shall also argue that it is only when educational efforts of these and other kinds have been exhausted that it becomes appropriate to respond to criminal offenses with criminal sanctions. Because children continue to mature in relevant ways even into and through their late teens, a reasonable guiding presumption would be that educational interventions might succeed even with offenders in their late teens. It follows that the punishment of children as adults is unjust, even if it proved to be an effective means of controlling juvenile crime.

These arguments will rest on a principle which requires that our efforts to create good order in society be as much as possible educative and formative rather than punitive and retributive, and that the aim of our educative efforts be to nurture reasonableness or a degree of moral autonomy sufficient for recognizing and responding to the reasonableness of reasonable laws and for recognizing and resisting injustice. This principle will enable us to identify the morally significant difference between children and adults that should be determinative in this debate. Opponents of a separate system for juvenile offenders seem to hold that there is no significant difference, while proponents of a separate system often argue that imprisonment with adults is counterproductive, or rest their case in psychological evidence that children are generally less mature and less able to stay out of trouble than adults. Immaturity in itself does not appear to be the morally salient factor, however, for although children are on the whole less mature than adults, there are adult criminals properly liable to punishment who are no more mature in the relevant ways than children are. My thesis is that the morally salient difference between children and adults is that in a society which provides adequate and equitable opportunities for the young to overcome their immaturity, adults will have enjoyed a fair chance to overcome their immaturity and children will not have.

My topic thus falls within the general domain of debates about the nature of moral education and the state's proper role in its sponsorship, but my orientation differs from the recently dominant approaches in the political and legal theoretical literature in taking as its starting point the value of a just *rule of law*. Other approaches have been grounded in a democratic polity's claim to establish the citizen virtues essential to its own future flourishing;[4] in a conception of civic reciprocity which requires citizens and public officials to appeal in political argument to "reasons that are shared or could come to be shared by" all "who are motivated to find fair terms of social cooperation";[5] in the value of moral autonomy in individual lives;[6] in First Amendment rights of free speech and exercise of religion;[7] and in parental rights.[8] As important as autonomy, toleration, and the civic virtues are to an attractive political order, however, there are grounds for insisting that the rule of law is equally if not more fundamental, and that its demands are generally more compelling.

"Fair enough," many will say, "but what has the rule of law got to do with moral education? A rule of law requires promulgation or fair warning of the law's expectations, to be sure, but there is no reason to think that it requires education." The answer, in brief, is that what establishes a rule of law is in large measure not the apparatus of law itself but the civilizing—which is to say, educative—efforts of families, schools, and the like. These efforts are necessary, not only as a matter of feasibility but as a matter of justice, because the only alternative to providing the care and instruction essential to nurturing a responsiveness to reasoning and the reasonable demands of law is to use force and threats, and we can scarcely regard law that is imposed through force and threats and not through rational and voluntary consent as just.

The fundamental point, which derives from Socratic political thought, is that the respect for persons as rational or potentially rational agents inherent in a just rule of law requires that our efforts to secure compliance with law rely as much as possible on truthful and reasoned persuasion and instruction, rather than force and violence.

With regard to the goals and content of moral education, the approach I will take here is of a piece with the Aristotelian drift of recent work on moral education within moral theory. Discussion of moral education has played a remarkably small role in philosophical ethics in recent decades, but the moral theorists who have concerned themselves with moral education have been chiefly occupied with elaborating neo-Kantian and neo-Aristotelian accounts of what the aims and content of moral education should be.[9] The neo-Kantian "formalists" of the 1960s and 1970s displayed a uniquely modern faith in the natural development of reasonableness in children, and a resistance to inculcating substantive moral convictions, in arguing that children should learn the *form* of morality and become practiced in moral reasoning, in order to become morally autonomous, which is to say able and disposed to identify and apply rationally acceptable moral principles.[10] The intellectualism of these models, and of Lawrence Kohlberg's cognitive-developmental or Piagetian version of Kantianism, has been faulted quite reasonably for ignoring the motivational aspects of moral development and for exaggerating the extent to which form alone can generate moral content.[11] The neo-Aristotelian views, which have proliferated in the 1980s and 1990s, have combated the narrowness of this intellectualism by insisting on the importance of habituation and the inseparability of the development of good judgment from the formation of favorable desires, emotions, and perceptions.[12]

What we will find in the debate over juvenile crime is, in moral-psychological terms, interestingly similar to the path from these recent forms of intellectualism to neo-Aristotelianism, or from Socrates to Aristotle, with the proponents of criminalizing juvenile offenses offering narrowly intellectualistic defenses, and the critics pressing more balanced, if also problematic, accounts of moral development and criminal "capacity" or "competence," by which they mean the broad mental attributes a person must possess in order to be responsible for criminal acts (i.e., such things as knowing right from wrong, as opposed to the knowledge of a specific context of action that may be important to determining responsibility for a specific offense).

Having said this, I shall begin now by reviewing enough of the basics of Socratic intellectualism and its Platonic and Aristotelian successors to identify the classical precedents of the principles of justice and conceptions of moral capacity and education which I shall bring to bear on the debate. I shall then turn to the recent defenses and critiques of the criminalization of juvenile offenses, and conclude that attempts to distinguish children and adults simply in terms of the maturity of their capacity to live in compliance with the demands of law, and not in terms of the adequacy of the moral education they have received, are misguided.

I.

I have argued in detail elsewhere that Socratic moral and political thought rests in a *principle of fidelity to reason*, which demands respect for reason and for human beings as rational agents.[13] It follows from this principle that reason and evidence must be used as much as possible in moving others to action and belief, and thus that a legitimate rule of law—a system of governance through laws which are not mere commands but rules which create obligations of voluntary obedience whose violation is legitimately open to punishment—is one whose laws not only are reasonable in their substance but also are administered in a manner that puts truthful instruction and reasoned persuasion before force. On this account of the respect for persons inherent in a just or legitimate rule of law, governments cannot establish a general right to punish lawbreakers without providing for the education of all citizens, which is to say an education which encourages them to be rational and provides them with the reasons for the laws being as they are. By providing for the adequate education of some citizens but not others, a government might establish a right to punish the former when they commit offenses but not the latter, and in that event might be obliged as a requirement of justice to discriminate between the two in the course of criminal proceedings.

In Plato's account of the trial of Socrates, the latter argues famously that if he has corrupted the youth of Athens unwillingly, then the appropriate response to what he has done is not punishment but instruction. He held, equally famously, that human beings are so constituted that no one does wrong willingly, but only because of ignorance. On this exquisitely simple account of human conduct, the sole barrier to good conduct—conduct which conforms to the demands of law to the extent that conformity is warranted—is ignorance, which is presumably remediable through instruction and encouragement to reason things through and heed the stronger argument. Socrates may well have approved of moral education which is more complicated than this, but he provided no account which would justify such approval. His account of moral capacity and moral education is thus "intellectualistic," in according singular importance to a person's rational understanding of the requirements of law and morality and the nature of his or her conduct.

It remained to Socrates' student Plato, and Plato's student Aristotle, to elaborate accounts of moral development and education which assign plausible roles to desire, emotion, and perception. Socrates attempted to secure his intellectualism against the challenge posed by apparent instances of people "knowing the better, and doing the worse," by holding that what is really going on in such cases is that people aim to do what is best but are misled in their judgments of what is best by lapses of perception. Courage is thereby reduced to possessing knowledge of what to do in the face of danger and not being misled by a false perception that one's security outweighs a more important good. Plato saw, however, that courage, or the capacity and disposition to do the right thing in the face of danger, is not simply the product of a rational understanding of what is called for in dangerous situations but of *training* which provides practice in facing danger and overcoming fear. His view was that the accuracy and stability of one's perceptions of situations is a product of such training and experience, and he argued at length that this applies as much to acting with good judgment in the face of pleasure as in the face of danger.

On this account, which was developed and refined by Aristotle, one's desires, perceptions of what is good and bad, and capacity to do what there is good reason to do, all develop over time and are shaped—for better or for worse—by the kinds of actions that one practices. It is an account which regards the capacity for rational action, including action in accordance with reasonable laws, as a product of moral training, and as something inseparable from acquiring a good state of character. "Those who are able to rule themselves [in accordance with the demands of reason and common law] are good," writes Plato, "and those who cannot are bad."[14] In Aristotle's terms, the good man who has received adequate moral training and instruction can see the truth about what it is reasonable to do and has the capacity to do it, whereas one without such training will live "as passion directs" and "will not hear argument that dissuades him, nor understand it if he does."[15]

The upshot of this account of moral training as a prerequisite for rational conduct is to set *incapacity* beside *ignorance* as an obstacle to voluntary compliance with law which must be overcome through moral education, if we are to honor the dictum that a just rule of law demands putting instruction and persuasion before force as much as possible. To say that incapacity is such an obstacle is not to conceive of it simply or predominantly in terms of the *difficulty* an agent may encounter in doing the right thing. Rather, the Aristotelian thesis is that moral training not only makes it easier and more pleasant to do the right thing but shapes the desires and perceptions of what is good and bad that determine what an agent will do. Plato and Aristotle do not at all deny the Socratic notion that people feel justified in what they do when they do it; what they argue is that people do not come to have accurate and stable perceptions of what is justified simply through being talked to, and thus that it is quite predictable that people who grow up without appropriate moral habituation are likely to act badly, knowing perhaps that others disapprove, but believing they are justified. This is a very plausible view, and it is a view substantially at odds with the Augustinian image of all human beings standing at the crossroads of good and evil, equally capable of choosing both, and making a radical choice between the two.

The question, then, is who is to bear this burden of moral education essential to underwriting the state's claim to punish those who violate the law? Advocates of strong parental rights over the content of children's moral education may insist that parents are entitled to full discretion in the moral education they provide and bear full responsibility for providing it, but the upshot of the argument I have outlined is that the state bears a fundamental burden to ensure the adequacy of the moral education which all children receive. This is a burden of responsibility which cannot be shifted to parents, no matter how dominant the role of parents in *providing* moral education remains, because the state's position is that citizens who break the law are directly answerable to it, and the penalties it imposes cannot be shifted to third parties, however much at fault those third parties may be. More precisely, what is required is that each level of government which makes and enforces laws to which a person is subject must accept responsibility for the adequacy of that person's moral education in order to establish a right to punish that person in response to any violations of the law which may occur when those educative measures have run their course.[16] Further, until those measures *have* run their course (i.e., until there is good reason to conclude that further educative measures would be fruitless), any forceful measures taken in response to offenses must be justified not on retributive grounds but by their protective, educational, and possibly compensatory potential, and must be enacted in a manner reasonably calculated to be educative.

The thesis about responsibility which underlies this is not that all ignorance of the merits of the laws and all deficits of capacity to comply with the law are barriers in themselves to prosecution and punishment but that governments must be free of complicity in the existence of any such ignorance and incapacity to be in a position to justly censure and punish. How governments may best ensure the adequacy of moral education and the care that is inseparable from it remains an open question, but it is reasonable to assume that suitable measures would include in the United States both reforms in family policy to enable families to do better for their part and protect children from abuse that is damaging to their cognitive and moral development, and reforms in education policy.[17] While recognizing that families are the primary and most important units of moral socialization, we must also recognize that schools can provide a secondary setting, vital to the well-being of some children, in which the social bonds and expectations essential to a child's acceptance of a constructive social ethic can be nurtured.[18] In dealing with juvenile offenders, justice requires a system that is sensitive not simply to individual differences in criminal capacity but also to the extent to which educational interventions have been appropriate and have been exhausted, and it requires the aggressive and equitable use of the educational interventions which may yet be effective.[19]

An objection which could be reasonably anticipated at this point is that it is surely only an ideal state that should have the authority to oversee and ensure the adequacy of moral education. What could be more illiberal and dangerous than to place such power in the hands of a regime that might abuse it? This deserves a lengthier response than I can give it here, but a number of responses are in order. First, I am arguing that the least restrictive alternative is to grant governments this authority to the extent, but only to the extent, necessary to fulfill the responsibilities of educational oversight and provision which are foundational to a right to use coercive force in response to criminal wrongdoing. To say that those responsibilities rest squarely with the governments themselves is to lay down a very significant and consequential restriction on their right to use coercive force. This in itself is anything but illiberal, of course. Considered from an impartial point of view, and in light of what we know about the predictors of crime rather than on the dubious assumption of a natural human power of unconditional free choice,[20] the least restrictive policy would surely be to ensure adequate education, inasmuch as that could be expected to preempt a good deal of the vastly more restrictive penal confinement that would be needed in its absence. Those who take it for granted that they will never be convicted of a crime may, of course, still feel imposed upon. Why shouldn't they enjoy the even less restrictive alternative of having no compulsory moral education imposed on them while avoiding criminal penalties through their own good choices? One answer to this is that it does not rest in an impartial point of view, and would tolerate gross inequities in the risk of suffering criminal convictions that is imposed on people. A second answer is that those who take it for granted that they will never commit a crime are either self-deceived or *did* have a moral education imposed

on them. Is their worry that some children will have to endure
again at school what they will in any case endure in sufficient
measure at home? Or that what they get at school will be different from what they get at home, and in some way at odds with it
or dangerously heavy-handed?

These questions bring us to a second important point, which
concerns the extent and nature of the moral educative power these
arguments authorize governments to use. First, as regards the
scope of the morality to be inculcated, it can be no wider than the
minimal social ethic embedded in the law itself, where this means
not every and any system of laws but a system of just and constitutionally enacted laws that are administered in a manner conducive
to their voluntary and rational acceptance. Second, as regards the
aims of the moral instruction this authorizes, the principle of respect I have relied upon requires that the dominant aims be to cultivate respect for others, to promote rationality, good judgment,
and the capacity to act from good judgment, and to enable children to arrive at an accurate understanding of what is good about
having laws and the particular laws we have. The teaching of critical thinking is as central to this agenda as the inculcation of virtues
of social cooperation, and there is no place in it for the inculcation
of blind obedience or obedience to law as such. Third, as regards
the methods of this moral education, the real levers of power as it
were, it is very important to be clear about the conditions that must
be established in order to draw children into moral communities,
for drawing them in is exactly what must be done in order to succeed. What is required is to create social circles within schools
which welcome children into them as valued members, manifest a
willingness to promote those children's interests, and thereby induce a sympathetic attachment to the norms of social conduct on
which membership in those circles is predicated. The foundation
of moral education and its most important tool is thus to give children a social circle which they can belong to and feel valued in, and
which is itself a part of mainstream society. It is in this way above all
that the moral climate of schools can make a significant difference
to a child's degree of alienation from the pathways and norms of respectable society. To provide this is not to engage in a suspect exercise of governmental power, even if we also require children to attend school.

II.

The politically potent slogan "adult time for adult crime" seems to express the thesis that what matters to equity and justice is the outward form of a criminal act, the specific mental elements belonging to the definition of a crime, such as intent to kill, and nothing else. An intentional killing by an eleven-year-old becomes on this thesis an "adult crime," properly punishable in the same manner, and under the same retributive rationale, that an intentional killing by any adult would be. The question thereby begged is whether there are differences between adults and children which should make a difference to how we respond to their offenses.

Or does this miss the point? Perhaps there is an inference at work here to the effect that children who commit offenses which are more commonly committed by adults, such as homicides, are by that very fact no longer children in some important sense. Or, more likely, there is an inference that the commission of serious offenses is symptomatic of the fact that "kids are different now" and are "growing up faster."[21]

The suggestion that kids are growing up faster now is an almost universal article of faith among American parents, and it implies that the differences between adults and children are smaller and less legally significant than they used to be. The primary basis for this belief, however, is that American children are less shielded from ugliness and evil, less sheltered, less supervised, and less cared for than they used to be. Being more on their own, they also tend to be less accepting of attempts to exercise authority over them. The least fortunate of them grow up in conditions uncomfortably close to a Hobbesian state of nature, and learn quite young that neither their parents nor the police can protect them. Not surprisingly, their loyalties and strategies of mutual protection tend to shift and spin them out of the sphere of respectable society when they learn this.[22] Thus, it may well be true that it is more common in the United States now than in the recent past for children to be exposed to evil and have to fend for themselves at an early age. But although growing up faster in this sense is a risk factor for criminality, it does not enable children to become reasonable in their judgments and actions at a younger age. The evidence that children are committing vicious acts at earlier ages is not evidence that they are becoming capable of living well and within the law at earlier ages. It's not evidence that their education has run its course earlier, and that nothing feasible remains but to lock them away.

What the American public fears and alleges, perhaps, is that children who learn to survive on the streets through criminal means are irreparably ruined by it, and are thus indistinguishable from adult criminals in being beyond the reach of rehabilitative interventions. If this is true, then it does undermine a historically influential argument for a separate system of juvenile justice more oriented to rehabilitation than the adult criminal justice system is, but we cannot justly assume that it is true. Indeed, we must infer from the inadequacies of a child's moral upbringing that educative measures have not been given a reasonable chance to succeed, and that the child has been denied a share in the common foundation for uncoerced compliance with the laws which a just rule of law requires. There can be little doubt that the economic, social, and educational policies of the United States put some children at far greater risk of moral alienation and criminality than others, and it would be a morally unconscionable view of responsibility and justice that sanctioned giving up on those who have been put at greater risk, on the mere presumption that the advantages others have enjoyed could make no difference to the kind of people they become.

Another influential argument through the years when juvenile crime rates were climbing was that the juvenile justice system "wasn't working." A specific criticism which may have merit is that the responses to early offenses have been so insignificant in many cases that they have done nothing to discourage further offenses of escalating severity. If this is true, then the system has not functioned effectively on its own terms, and its rehabilitative and educative efforts have fallen far short of what they should have been. In itself this is no argument for a more punitive approach. More generally, the argument counsels harsher treatment as what will "work," presumably on the assumptions that children will be deterred from crime by the threat of punishment, and that if they are rational enough to be deterred then they surely possess the mental traits essential to criminal competence and can be justly treated as adults. The most obvious way to redeem the first of these assumptions would be to hold that human beings, juveniles included, are rational actors who are motivated by calculations of the expected cost of committing crimes, computed as a function of the likelihood of receiving a prison sentence and its probable length. The trouble with this assumption is that it is just as implausible in its own way as the Socratic view of human motivation. It identifies rationality, and the foresight, caution, and temperance that are essential to it, as universal gifts of human nature, and not the hard-won accomplishments that they are. Justice and a more plausible view of human nature would counsel moral educative efforts that are geared to nurturing both the cognitive and affective aspects of reasonableness, and that are conducted in a setting and manner which draw children into groups which care about and protect them, and thereby induce a sympathetic attachment to social morality and the reasonable demands of law.

A further and quite different argument for prosecuting children as adults grew out of the introduction of procedural rights into juvenile court proceedings in the 1960s. Until that time juvenile proceedings were considered non-adversarial, but in 1966 the U.S. Supreme Court held that the similarities with adult criminal proceedings gave juveniles the same rights of procedural justice as adults.[23] This assignment of equal rights to children is credited with diminishing the distinctiveness of the juvenile system and undermining the perceived need for it. The moral logic of this is obscure. Witness, for instance, the argument that "if children are enough like adults to warrant the same rights, are they not also like adults in knowing the difference between right and wrong?"[24] Since the only respect in which children need be like adults in order to warrant the same rights of procedural justice is in sharing a common vulnerability or having interests which may be compromised by violations of procedural justice, there is little need to dwell on the deficiencies of this argument. Its presumption that "knowing the difference between right and wrong" is a sufficient basis on which to regard children as subject to the full force of criminal sanctions is revealing, however.

The origins of this presumption go back at least to the common law doctrine of "infancy," which assumed its present form in the fourteenth century. Under this doctrine, the age of discretion or threshold of criminal capacity or competence is set at fourteen, children younger than seven are regarded as incompetent, and children between seven and fourteen are "presumed to lack the capacity to commit crime, but the presumption [can] be rebutted by proof of malice, which in turn [can] be shown by concealment of the crime."[25] Although there has not been complete agreement on what may suffice to rebut the presumption of incompetence for children seven to fourteen, the formulations which courts have used are all narrowly cognitive, the most modern test being "that the surrounding circumstances must demonstrate . . . that the individual knew what he was doing and that it was wrong."[26] Knowing the difference between right and wrong is thus all there is to criminal competence under these common law rules. Although these rules have been overridden by statutes in many states, and the juvenile justice system's presumption has been that children even older than fourteen are immature and can and should be rehabilitated, something like the common law's intellectualistic conception of criminal discretion or competence has evidently remained influential and has contributed to the widespread perception that there is no injustice in dismantling the juvenile justice system. If one believes that all that is essential to criminal capacity is knowing right from wrong, then one could readily believe that any sane ten-year-old is morally indistinguishable from an adult and no less answerable for his crimes. One could think that a moral education limited to informing children about which kinds of acts are wrong and which are right would render a child criminally capable and no less subject to criminal sanctions than an adult.

It would be neither true, nor necessary for my purposes, to maintain that the foregoing constitutes an exhaustive survey and refutation of the arguments which have moved the legislative and popular attacks on the juvenile justice system forward. My concern in this section has been to illustrate the deficiencies of these arguments, and in doing so to expose the weight that is ultimately borne by narrowly cognitive conceptions of criminal capacity. Advocates of the criminalization of juvenile offenses must hold that there is no morally relevant fact that distinguishes children from adults in this arena, no fact that makes the latter fully accountable and the former not, and the traditional and still most plausible way to do this is to hold that only certain cognitive traits widely possessed by children are necessary for criminal accountability. Let's turn now to the opposing arguments which draw on developmental psychology.

III.

"I am confident that a child is unlikely to succeed in the long, difficult process of rehabilitation when his teachers during his confinement are adult criminals," wrote Justice Skelly Wright in a dissenting opinion in *United States v. Bland*.[27] This is a much-repeated argument for preserving a juvenile justice system that promotes the well-being and rehabilitation of juvenile offenders, and it is buttressed by evidence that placing juvenile offenders in adult correctional facilities tends, for several reasons, to confirm them in patterns of criminal and violent behavior.[28] This evidence suggests that many juvenile offenders who are now tried and punished as adults are much the worse and more dangerous for it, and that their behavioral patterns and states of character are still being formed and may yet be improved by rehabilitative and educational means.[29]

Other evidence for the plasticity of adolescent character, and thus for the potential utility of educational interventions in rehabilitating juvenile offenders, has been marshalled by developmental psychologists in a series of articles on juvenile justice reform. The main thrust of these contributions, however, is to try to establish that criminal competence must be conceived of more broadly than it has been by those who defend a more punitive response to juvenile offenses, and to show that some aspects of criminal competence continue to develop through middle and late adolescence. In its intent, this is consistent with the broadening of the agenda for moral education implied by Aristotelian accounts, but the principle underlying its objection to punishing children as adults is different.

More specifically, the contributions of psychologists to the juvenile justice debate directly challenge the assumption that all the elements of criminal capacity can be safely assumed present by early adolescence. The value of developmental research, in their view, is its utility in identifying the age by which children will have developed good judgment and the capacity to act from it, not only in ideal circumstances but in the face of corrupting social pressure and conflicts which may engender violence if they are not handled in a calm and skillful manner.[30] They thereby assume that such attributes as independence of judgment, a mature perspective on risk and consequences, and self-restraint are essential to criminal capacity, and they argue that adolescents as a class are distinguished from adults by the absence of these attributes. The basic findings presented in this literature are summed up by Stephen Morse:

> As a class . . . adolescents: (1) have a stronger preference for risk and novelty; (2) subjectively assess the potentially negative consequences of risky conduct less unfavorably; (3) tend to be impulsive and more concerned with short-term than long-term consequences; (4) subjectively experience and assess the passage of time and time periods as longer; and (5) are more susceptible to peer pressure. All five differences diminish with maturation throughout adolescence. . . .[31]

The significance of these developmental findings for assigning criminal responsibility have been challenged, however. Morse argues that these forms of immaturity are compatible with meeting the minimal standard of rationality used in determining criminal competence (i.e., in judging insanity or incapacitating mental defect), and that they are also present in comparable degrees in many adults whom we do not excuse. "These factors decrease the probability that the agent will act wisely," he writes,

> But this is true of many characteristics that do not diminish responsibility. . . . A regrettable number of adults are immature and have dreadful judgment. Yet we do not excuse that minority of adults. Why, therefore, should adolescents be treated differently?[32]

They shouldn't be treated differently, he concludes, because even though it is true that immaturity is "normal" for adolescents and not for adults, the "moral relevance [of this fact] is obscure."[33]

Morse's line of argument is conducted on the narrow ground of orthodox excusing conditions as defeaters on judgments of responsibility. Though reasonable on its own terms, so too is the developmentalists' intuition that the immaturity of the young matters to how we may justly treat them. This creates something of a dilemma, as long as we hold that responsibility is sufficient to justify punishment and that the orthodox excusing conditions are the right ones to admit. The classical view, if I am right, is that the moral significance of the immaturity of the young lies in the responsibility of the adult community, in its legislative capacity, to provide adequate and equitable opportunities for the young to overcome that immaturity. In a well-ordered society which is conscientious about such things, an adult will have had such an opportunity, and will in that respect have a decidedly different moral status from a child or adolescent. It follows that the moral difference which eludes Morse is a difference which arises from a principle of putting instruction before force as much as possible, and need not be understood as a difference in responsibility *per se*. Indeed, it is hard to see how any test of criminal competence, or the capacities of judgment and choice which must be present for an individual to be legitimately judged responsible, could adequately capture the moral difference between children and adults. My inclination is thus to deny the premise that an individual's responsibility for an offense is sufficient to justify criminal punishment of that individual, and hold that the legitimacy of punishment also rests on a prior history of conscientious educative efforts.

If this is, as I believe, the obvious way through this dilemma, it points up a neglected aspect of the importance of moral education for the debate over juvenile justice reform, namely the role of adequate education in justifying the use of punishment. We can justly censure and punish those who have enjoyed the benefits of such education, but our response to those who have not enjoyed those benefits must continue to be guided by educative aims, even if it involves elements of force or constraint. This being so, justice also demands that we begin by establishing social and scholastic conditions in which all children are assured an adequate moral upbringing and education, and it demands that we pursue a vigorous program of research which will enable us to better judge when it is reasonable to infer that all appropriate efforts to instruct and guide children have been exhausted and justice permits recourse to criminal sanctions. A rule of law, established in a manner respectful of the reason in all citizens, rather than imposed by force, demands as much and certainly more.[34]

NOTES

I would like to thank John Bennett, Steve Macedo, and my audience at the Rochester Institute of Technology, where I presented a version of this paper on October 23, 2000, for their helpful responses.

1. For a comprehensive history of juvenile justice in the U.S., see Sanford J. Fox, "Juvenile Justice Reform: A Historical Perspective," *Stanford Law Review* 22 (1970): 1187–1239.

2. See Kelly Keimig Elsea, "The Juvenile Crime Debate: Rehabilitation, Punishment, or Prevention," *The Kansas Journal of Law & Public Policy* 5 (1995): 135–144; Marygold Melli, "Juvenile Justice Reform in Context," *Wisconsin Law Review* 1996 (1996): 375–398; Eric Fritsch and Craig Hemmens, "An Assessment of Legislative Approaches to the Problem of Serious Juvenile Crime: A Case Study of Texas 1973–1995," *American Journal of Criminal Law* 23 (1996): 563–609; Brenda Gordon. "Note: A Criminal's Justice or a Child's Injustice? Trends in the Waiver of Juvenile Court Jurisdiction and the Flaws in the Arizona Response," *Arizona Law Review* 41 (1999): 193–226.

3. On the controversies which have surrounded legislative mandates of moral instruction in some states, see e.g., "Morality Play: Today, It's Reading, Writing and 'Diligence' in Elementary Schools," *The Wall Street Journal* Monday, October 25, 1999: 1A, 8A. For an overview of various initiatives, approaches, and the research they rely on, see Maurice Elias, et al., *Promoting Social and Emotional Learning: Guidelines for Educators* (Alexandria, Va.: Association for Supervision and Curriculum Development, 1997).

4. See esp., Amy Gutmann, *Democratic Education* (Princeton: Princeton University Press, 1987).

5. Amy Gutmann and Dennis Thompson, *Democracy and Disagreement* (Cambridge: Harvard University Press, 1996), pp. 14 and 65. See also Stephen Macedo, *Diversity and Distrust: Civic Education in a Multicultural Democracy* (Cambridge: Harvard University Press, 2000).

6. See esp., Bruce Ackerman, *Social Justice in the Liberal State* (New Haven: Yale University Press, 1980), Eamonn Callan, *Creating Citizens*

(Oxford: Clarendon Press, 1997), and Harry Brighouse, *School Choice and Social Justice* (Oxford: Oxford University Press, 2000).

7. See e.g., Stephen Arons, *Compelling Belief* (Amherst, Mass.: University of Massachusetts Press, 1986).

8. See e.g., Stephen Gilles, "On Educating Children: A Parentalist Manifesto," *The University of Chicago Law Review* 63: 937–1034.

9. I set aside here a number of less fundamental topics of recent interest, such as the extent to which virtue can be taught or cultivated through university-level instruction. See e.g., Thomas Piper, et al., *Can Ethics Be Taught?* (Boston: Harvard Business School, 1993). I also set aside neo-Humean ethics of care, which have only begun to receive serious philosophical attention. See e.g., Michael Slote, "Caring versus the Philosophers," in R. Curren, ed., *Philosophy of Education 1999* (Urbana, Ill.: Philosophy of Education Society, 1999). For a more detailed overview of the debates, major positions, and literature of moral education, see my entry, "Moral Education," in Lawrence and Charlotte Becker, eds., *Encyclopedia of Ethics*, 2nd ed. (New York: Routledge, 2001).

10. See e.g., R. M. Hare, *The Language of Morals* (Oxford: Clarendon Press, 1952), and Kurt Baier, "Moral Autonomy as an Aim of Moral Education," in G. Langford and D. J. O'Connor, eds., *New Essays in the Philosophy of Education* (London: Routledge & Kegan Paul, 1973).

11. See F. Clark Power, Ann Higgins, and Lawrence Kohlberg, *Lawrence Kohlberg's Approach to Moral Education* (New York: Columbia University Press, 1989); and Robert Fullinwider, "Moral Conventions and Moral Lessons," *Social Theory and Practice* 15 (1989): 321–38.

12. See e.g., Edmund Pincoffs, *Quandaries and Virtues* (Lawrence: University Press of Kansas, 1986); Nancy Sherman, *The Fabric of Character* (Oxford: Clarendon Press, 1989); and David Carr and Jan Steutel, eds., *Virtue Theory and Moral Education* (London: Routledge, 1999).

13. My presentation in this section, and in places where I speak of the foundations of corrective justice, will be an unscholarly summary. For the full scholarly and analytical treatment, see *Aristotle on the Necessity of Public Education* (Lanham, Md.: Rowman & Littlefield, 2000).

14. *Laws* 644b. The translation here is Trevor Saunders', in John Cooper, ed., *Plato, Complete Works* (Indianapolis: Hackett Publishing Co., 1997).

15. *Nicomachean Ethics* X.9 1179b26-27. The translation here is Benjamin Jowett's, revised by Jonathan Barnes, in Jonathan Barnes, ed., *The Complete Works of Aristotle* (Princeton: Princeton University Press, 1984).

16. I have in mind here a native-born citizen or a permanent resident who arrives in a legal jurisdiction early in life. It is reasonable to think that the educational burden on the state is diminished in proportion to

the age at the date of entry of those who arrive later in life, or is diminished in the case of those who have reached some threshold, such as a threshold of contractual competence that could underwrite shifting the burden of responsibility to the individual as a condition of entry. Which of the possible positions on this matter is the most morally sound is not immediately obvious, however, and this is a complication which I will not attempt to resolve here.

17. On the cognitive and moral developmental impact of parental abuse and neglect, see D. Cicchetti and S. L. Toth, "A Developmental Psychopathology Perspective on Child Abuse and Neglect," *Journal of the American Academy of Child & Adolescent Psychiatry* 34, no. 5 (1995): 541–65; D. Cicchetti and S. L. Toth, eds. *Developmental Perspectives on Trauma* (Rochester: University of Rochester Press, 1997); A. Shields and D. Cicchetti, "Reactive Aggression among Maltreated Children: The Contributions of Attention and Emotion Dysregulation," *Journal of Clinical Child Psychology* 27, no. 4 (1998): 381–95.

18. On the role of such bonds, see R. Ryan and J. Stiller, "The Social Contexts of Internalization," in M. L. Maehr and P. R. Pintrich, eds., *Advances in Motivation and Achievement*, Vol. 7 (Greenwich, Conn.: JAI Press, 1991), pp. 115–49.

19. On some educational interventions which have shown success in teaching violent children self-control and alternatives to aggressive behavioral patterns, see Albert Reiss, Jr., et al., *Understanding and Preventing Violence* (Washington, D.C.: National Academy Press, 1993), 385 ff., and Brenda Gordon, "A Criminal's Justice or a Child's Injustice?" 195, n. 14 (citing findings reported by the U.S. Department of Justice, Office of Juvenile Justice and Delinquency Prevention).

20. The research establishes that "violent offenders tend to have experienced poor parental child rearing methods, poor supervision, and separations from their parents when they were children. . . . In addition, they tend disproportionately to come from low-income, large-sized families in poor housing in deprived, inner-city, high-crime areas." (A. Reiss, et al., *Understanding and Preventing Violence* (Washington, D.C.: National Academic Press, 1993), p. 367.)

21. See, e.g., Elsea, "The Juvenile Crime Debate: Rehabilitation, Punishment, or Prevention," 138, n. 48 and related text.

22. Ron Suskind recounts in his book, *A Hope in the Unseen* (New York: Broadway Books, 1998), a boy's experience of fearing for his life because he had witnessed a murder and might be suspected of cooperating with the police: "After that, something was extinguished in Phillip. He began a slow but steady shift" toward a "double life" in which his security away

from home was predicated on solidarity with those who ruled the streets outside the law (67).

23. In re: Gault, 385 U.S. 965 (1966).

24. Elsea, "The Juvenile Crime Debate," 137, quoting Mark Downie, "When Kids Commit Adult Crimes, Some Say They Should Do Adult Time," *California Lawyer* October 1993, at 57.

25. Wayne R. LaFave and Austin W. Scott, Jr., *Handbook on Criminal Law* (St. Paul, Minn.: West Publishing Co., 1972), 351. "Malice" amounts to intent to commit the criminal act, or an intent to commit the act while knowing it is wrong—knowing, at any rate, that others will think it wrong and make trouble if one is found out.

26. *Ibid.*, 352.

27. 472 F.2d 1329, 1349–50 (D.C. Cir. 1972) (Wright, J., dissenting).

28. See Martin L. Forst & Martha-Elin Blomquist, "Cracking Down on Juveniles: The Changing Ideology of Youth Corrections," *Notre Dame Journal of Legal Ethics and Public Policy* 5 (1991): 323–75; Zvi Eiskovitz & Michael Baizerman, "'Doin' Time': Violent Youth in a Juvenile Facility and in an Adult Prison," *Journal of Offender Counseling, Services & Rehabilitation* 6 (1983): 5–20; and Martin Forst, Jeffrey Fagan, and T. Scott Vivona, "Youth in Prisons and Training Schools: Perceptions and Consequences of the Treatment-Custody Dichotomy," *Juvenile and Family Court Journal* 40: (1989): 1–14.

29. It is also worth noting in this regard that "as a class, juvenile delinquents have lower IQs and educational attainment than their non-delinquent peers. They also have a higher incidence of learning disabilities and mental illness, may have lower levels of moral development, often lack social problem-solving skills. . . ." Richard E. Redding, "Juveniles Transferred to Criminal Court: Legal Reform Proposals Based on Social Science Research," *Utah Law Review* 1997 (1997): 709–63, at 725–726.

30. See, e.g., Jennifer Woolard, et al., "Theoretical and Methodological Issues in Studying Children's Capacities in Legal Contexts," *Law and Human Behavior* 20 (1996): 219–28; Laurence Steinberg and Elizabeth Cauffman, "Maturity of Judgment in Adolescence: Psychological Factors in Adolescent Decision Making," *Law and Human Behavior* 20 (1996): 249–72; Laurence Steinberg and Elizabeth Cauffman, "The Elephant in the Courtroom: A Developmental Perspective on the Adjudication of Youthful Offenders," *Virginia Journal of Social Policy and Law* 6 (1999): 389–417; Elizabeth Cauffman, et al., "Justice for Juveniles: New Perspectives on Adolescents' Competence and Culpability," *Quinnipiac Law Review* 18 (1999): 403–19.

31. Stephen Morse, "Symposium on the Future of the Juvenile Court: Immaturity and Irresponsibility," *Journal of Criminal Law & Criminology* 88 (1997): 15–67, at 52–53.

32. *Ibid.*, 56, 58.

33. *Ibid.*, 59, 61, and 58.

34. It follows from what I have said here that in a society that is not well ordered and conscientious about moral education, the basis for distinguishing between adult and juvenile offenders is diminished, and the legitimacy of trying juveniles "as adults" must be evaluated on a case-by-case basis. I explored this consequence of my view in "Punishment and Inclusion: The Presuppositions of Corrective Justice in Aristotle and What They Imply," *Canadian Journal of Law and Jurisprudence* 8 (1995): 259–74, reprinted in S. M. Griffin and R. C. L. Moffat, eds., *Radical Critiques of the Law* (Lawrence: University Press of Kansas, 1997), 273–92, and within the larger setting of the Socratic tradition of moral and political theory in chapter six of *Aristotle on the Necessity of Public Education.*

PART IV

EDUCATION AND THE IDEAL OF RACIAL INTEGRATION: RENEWAL OR RETREAT?

12

THE PROMISE OF RACIAL INTEGRATION IN A MULTICULTURAL AGE

LAWRENCE BLUM

A social commitment to school integration beat a hasty retreat in the 1990s. In a series of legal decisions at the federal and federal district levels, states and school districts have been permitted to dismantle programs (such as busing and magnet schools) aimed at increasing racial diversity in their schools. The districts have been declared, in the key legal terminology, "unitary"—that is, whatever segregation currently exists is declared not to be a result or vestige of state-sponsored or state-created segregation. Not all school districts legally permitted to avoid or jettison desegregation actually go this route. Many sponsor initiatives to bring white students and racial minority students into the same schools.[1] All told, however, racial segregation in schools itself continues to increase, with Latinos increasingly segregated.[2]

Deliberate efforts to racially diversify school populations are losing public support as well, most strikingly among blacks, the group most strongly behind the decades-long push for integration. Justice Clarence Thomas, in his Supreme Court opinion in the *Missouri v. Jenkins* case of 1995, articulated an increasingly heard plaint. It is insulting and even racist, Thomas said, to assume that a black child has to sit next to a white child in class in

383

order to learn. Thomas elaborates, "To presume that blacks must have a sufficient quota of whites in the classroom to learn is to presume that there is something inherently wrong with blacks."[3] Blacks are increasingly, or at least publicly, viewing efforts at integration as an *alternative* to energy put into enhancing the quality of schooling for black children.[4]

Defenses of desegregation—particularly of blacks or Latinos with whites—in the face of this opposition tends to focus on occupational benefits. Gary Orfield, a prominent researcher and advocate for school integration, replies directly to Thomas's argument by saying that integration works by providing "economically disadvantaged minority" students with greater life opportunities through "access to middle-class schools, and to the world beyond them."[5]

Many blacks still find the ideal of integration attractive but feel that given the current demographics of schools, the conditions for realizing important integrationist values are unlikely to materialize. Gloria Ladson-Billings articulates this sentiment well: "In a better world I would want to see schools integrated across racial, cultural, linguistic, and all other lines. But I am too much of a pragmatist to ignore the sentiment and motivation underlying the African American immersion school movement. African Americans already have separate schools. The African American immersion school movement is about *taking control* of those separate schools."[6]

The *mere* physical co-presence of children from distinct ethnoracial groups in the same school is not by itself a good.[7] Those who favor racial plurality in schools, and its intentional promotion, believe there to be vital goods to be secured in such schools not attainable, or much more difficult to attain, in schools composed entirely, or almost entirely, of one racial group. I argue in this paper that popular and to a large extent scholarly discussion of ethnoracial plurality in schools has lost sight of these goods, which are social, moral, and personal (to the individual student), as well as civic, the type of good to which I will devote most attention.

The neglect of these goods by both opponents and proponents of desegregation is connected with a public discourse that has tended to operate with an excessively narrow—consumerist, instrumentalist, and nondemocratic—conception of the appropriate goals and values of education itself. Recovering a richer conception of education will provide the foundation for a renewed concept of "racial integration" and its values.

I draw my conception of the value of racially mixed schools from the more general ideals of racial integration articulated by Martin Luther King, Jr. He said, "Integration is creative, and is therefore more profound and far-reaching than desegregation. Integration is the positive acceptance of desegregation and the welcomed participation of Negroes into the total range of human activities . . . [A] desegregated society that is not integrated . . . leads to 'physical proximity without spiritual affinity.' It gives us a society where men are physically desegregated and spiritually segregated, where elbows are together and hearts are apart."[8]

Randall Kennedy adds a more explicitly civic and democratic dimension to King's moral and spiritual vision. "Integrationists seek . . . to create a society in which the intimate and equal association for people of different races in all spheres of life . . . is *welcomed* as a normal part of a multiracial democracy."[9] We ignore King's and Kennedy's idealism at our peril in education policy decisions. Unless we are aware of these ideals, and their associated range of social benefits, we cannot know what we are losing when we retreat from them, and whether the abandonment is worth the price.

The "ideal" nature of my argument—the recognition that it is only under certain conditions that various components of the integrationist ideal are realized—means that I am by no means advocating racial desegregation as an overriding policy objective. Under less than ideal conditions—including those currently obtaining in many classes, schools and districts—it may be reasonable to favor policies that do not press toward racially mixed schools, or even that facilitate certain kinds of single-race (or single-race-dominated) schools. At the same time, I will also argue that, despite the retreat from both the social ideal of integration, and the more minimal goal of racially plural schools, we actually know a good deal more than we did when King wrote those words about how to *realize* integrationist ideals in racially diverse schools.

INTEGRATION AND ASSIMILATION

When King spoke of "desegregation," he meant a process by which schools that were monoracial (and generally created as such by the state) become deliberately racially mixed. ("Desegregation" can also be used to refer to the end-state created by that process.) In King's time, virtually the only schools that were racially mixed were ones that had been desegregated in this sense. Currently, however, racially mixed schools are frequently *not* a product of desegregation. While often called "desegregated," these schools draw a racially diverse group of students because of their location (schools in mixed neighborhoods, or located on the border of more than one monoracial neighborhood) or non-race-related features of the school (magnet schools), rather than by dint of race-based assignment or admissions policies.[10]

As King said, desegregation, or, more generally, the existence of a plurality of ethnoracial groups in a school, is a necessary step toward his conception of "integration," an embracing of that plurality and an attempt to establish humane, moral, and civic relationships among students of the different groups. Although schools have been in the process of becoming *less* racially mixed in the 1990's, reversing a trend prior to that point, a majority of students do attend schools that are racially plural in a meaningful sense. According to Orfield and Yun's findings, in 1996–97, the average urban black student attended a school with 35 percent blacks, 36.5 percent Latinos, and 15 percent whites. (To put this in some perspective, 35 percent of blacks as a whole attended schools that were 90–100 percent non-white.) In the suburbs the numbers for the average black student were 20 percent black, 30 percent Latino, and 40 percent white. In small cities, whites attended schools that were 14 percent black and 8.5 percent Latino; in the suburbs of large cities the percentages for the average white student were 6.8 percent black and 7.4 percent Latino.[11] If a racially plural school is defined as more than 10 percent of two groups (or more), the majority of Latino, black, Asian, and Native American children attend racially plural schools.[12] A not insubstantial minority of whites does so as well. (On average, whites attend schools with 81 percent white classmates.)[13]

The racial demography of a given school is quite relevant to its potential for attaining the personal, social, and civic goals I will address below. A minimal, critical mass of students of two or more groups is necessary for some of these goals, but the goals will be greatly facilitated if more than that number is present. Similarly a high percentage of one majority group poses greater challenges than a school with a lower percentage. And the ideal situation (present in very few schools) is one with no ethnoracial group in the majority. Beyond this, the ease of achieving some of the various aims is affected by the percentages of *whites* specifically. I am not able to comment further on the bearing of distinct ethnoracial demographic patterns on the forms of and possibilities for implementation of the goals I discuss below but want only to flag these demographics as important desiderata in achieving the goals of racial integration.

I will follow Dr. King and retain the language of "integration," at least some of the time. But I do want to enter a cautionary note regarding some of its associations. First, because of its history, "integration" has carried an implication that the groups involved are limited to blacks and whites. Latinos have fought their own battles for integrated schools and equal education,[14] but public recognition has been slow to incorporate that history. Given how irredeemably culturally plural the nation has become—with Latinos soon becoming as numerous as blacks, Asian-Americans the fastest-growing panethnic group, and other groups not readily classified under the familiar categories—the association of the term "integration" with only white and black is unfortunate, and should be jettisoned.

A related, but more subtle, implication is that integration concerns only the mixing of students of color with whites. While many central issues concerning integration do indeed concern whites, the potential benefits of racial diversity of schools are not confined to interactions between whites and other groups. Seldom a matter for legal action, integration of distinct non-white groups is nevertheless starting to be a significant social and policy issue; the city of Pasadena for example has crafted a school integration policy that mixes Latinos and blacks.[15]

Finally, for many, the term "integration" carries assimilationist overtones—as if its meaning were that the minority group were being "integrated into" a structure and culture fully defined by the majority group. The minority group's own culture's integrity is not respected, nor its impact on the larger culture that includes it recognized and welcomed.[16] As the National Research Council stated in its magisterial 1989 study, *A Common Destiny: Blacks and American Society*, "[T]he preservation of black culture and group identity" is a condition "that many blacks' definition of 'integration' requires."[17] And power must be shared with racial minorities also.[18]

These assimilationist overtones are not surprising. When the great battles for school integration were waged in the 1950's and '60's, *cultural* differences among different groups were not sufficiently recognized, either in the legal argumentation or in the minds of the white educators attempting to implement integration.[19] Blacks were seen by whites as something like "whites with black skin." Moreover, assimilation had been the reigning social philosophy since the 1924 immigration restrictions, and before. Cultural pluralism had become a fringe philosophy after a minor flurry of support early in the century.[20]

Post-1965 immigration and the rise of the multicultural movement has placed issues of culture and group identity at the forefront both of education and of intergroup relations. Assimilation in its traditional meaning as conformity to a European-based American culture can no longer serve as a worthy social aim, and the ideal of integration must definitively break with it.

Integrated education must respect the cultural and racial identities of students, and recognize when cultural differences bear on the task of education. For example, students whose home languages are other than standard English—for example, Spanish, Vietnamese, or African-American Vernacular English (sometimes called "Ebonics") and for whom such languages are important to their cultural identity—should not be discouraged from using those languages in social interaction in school settings other than classrooms. Nor should the school devalue these languages or dialects and the cultural identities of which they are an integral part. This culture-respecting practice should, however, in no way diminish the emphasis on teaching standard English and its use as the language of instruction. The world of education's understanding of how to take account of cultural and identity differences among students has increased exponentially since the 1950's, and we are much better positioned to put in place a non-assimilationist ideal of integration than we were at that time.[21]

For all these reasons, the ideal I wish to elaborate and defend here might most accurately be described as "educational ethnoracial pluralism," incorporating what the current imprecise (and in some ways misleading) term "diversity" is generally taken to signify—the importance and value of recognizing ethnoracial group identity, culture, and distinctness. Yet that cumbersome phrase fails to carry "integration's" historic moral associations.

Brown and the Genesis of the Ideal of Racial Integration in Schools

Any discussion of racial integration in schools must take account of the *Brown v. Board of Education of Topeka* decision, and I wish to place my own argument for integration in the context of those offered by the Court in that decision. The *Brown* ruling was a decisive moment in American legal and social history, striking a severe blow to the racial caste system in the South, and lending the highest official imprimatur to ideals of racial equality and integration. At the same time, the decision has been subject to much criticism for the insufficiency or misguidedness of its legal reasoning.[22]

The Court provided (at least) five rationales for ending segregation. These rationales occupy different levels of generality, and, in the decision, were not clearly laid out and separated from one another. They are:

(1) White-dominated school districts could not be trusted to give black schools material and educational resources equal to white ones.

(2) State-created segregated schools are premised on the inferiority of blacks to whites. Thus segregation implicitly conveys this constitutionally impermissible message, independent of the material resources of the two school systems.

(3) This message of inferiority is inevitably damaging to black students' sense of worth, and has a negative im-

pact on their motivation to learn. (Argument (2) did not depend on the actual psychological impact of the message of inferiority but only on the constitutional wrongness of its declaration by the state.)

(4) Segregation is *inherently* unequal, hence wrong.

(5) Equality of opportunity cannot be provided in separate schools.

The first argument still carries some force with desegregation advocates. By and large black-dominated school systems do receive fewer resources than white, and, perhaps more importantly, fewer than needed to secure equal educational opportunities for both groups. The large number of legal suits based on inequities in district funding within states (in some of which the courts have found in favor of the plaintiffs) testify to continuing inequity. (Many of these involve a racial dimension.) A pure resource equity argument is, however, less compelling now than it has been in the past. The gap in expenditures has certainly been greatly reduced since the 1950's. Apart from inequities in physical facilities and teacher salary, however, on the average, teachers in majority black and Latino schools are less well trained and have performed less well on tests designed to assess teacher knowledge and competence. Many blacks not otherwise attracted to the idea of sending their children to white-dominated schools feel that doing so is the only way to ensure that their children will receive adequate educational attention from the state.

The second argument is not applicable to current forms of segregation, since ("de facto") segregation in schools is no longer a matter of official state policy ("de jure"). The argument used in some cases subsequent to *Brown* that resulted in busing to achieve integration—that a certain district's segregated or insufficiently desegregated schools are a *legacy* from prior state-created segregation—objects to extant inequities and their genesis in earlier state-sanctioned segregation rather than to the official declaration of inferiority.[23]

The third argument, based on empirical connections between the declaration of inferiority, the children's sense of self-worth, and their resultant motivation to learn, is mooted by the same absence of state-declared inferiority just noted.[24] In any case, the empirical connections between segregation, self-worth, and academic motivation have never been well established and later desegregation cases seldom relied on them.[25]

The fourth argument, "inherent inequality," may come to no more than (2)—declaration of inferiority—in which case it is not a separate argument. However, Roy Brooks also points out that the *Brown* decision can be read as glossing "inherently unequal" as (3)—causing reduced self-esteem, motivation, and academic achievement (though he correctly notes the misleading character of that usage, since the language of "inherent" is generally understood to *contrast* with causal effects).[26] But the Court's statement "Separate educational facilities are inherently unequal" has often been understood more broadly, to condemn as unequal and wrong separate single-race or predominantly single-race schools in their own right, independent of how they are created or of specific effects those schools have on the children who attend them. The Court's language here lends itself to such a reading, though much of the rest of the decision does not dovetail with this "inherent inequality" idea. Much writing on racial integration draws at least partially on the idea that once a school has been shown to be segregated (by some measure), this renders it unequal and thus morally problematic, independent of other deficiencies in the school. This view has the virtue of retaining a strong morally critical edge to the idea of racial separation, but the conflation of separation and inequality makes it more difficult to pinpoint the basis of the moral ills involved. (I argue below that non-integrated schools *are* morally and civically problematic, but not necessarily because, or only because, they are *unequal.*)

The fifth and final notion is equality of opportunity. Argument (1), regarding equal educational resources, is one concretized form of that more general idea. The Court declared that "the opportunity of an education . . . where the state has undertaken to provide it, is a right which must be available to all on equal terms" and goes on to say that segregated schools "deprive the children of the minority group of equal educational opportunities."[27]

Yet the absence of a clear constitutional standing for the principle of equality of opportunity has made for some confusion. "Equal protection," the salient constitutional principle used in the *Brown* case to mandate equality, does not irrefutably supply a rationale for the more substantive principle of equality of opportunity, and the Court itself notes that the Fourteenth Amendment cannot be read as having intended to forbid segregated schools.[28] Yet the Court goes on to rely on the confused "inherent inequality" idea to bring school desegregation under the jurisdiction of "equal protection of the laws" in that Amendment.[29]

Nevertheless, whatever the weaknesses of its constitutional foundation, equality of opportunity has come to be the major argument, or family of arguments, used to support desegregation, and also constitutes a powerful idea in American political culture as a grounding for arguments in the domain of education. Let us look, then, at the relation between equality of opportunity and racial integration.

EQUALITY OF OPPORTUNITY

By linking desegregation and equality so closely, the *Brown* Court initiated a confusion between the two ideas that continues in current thinking. In Jonathan Kozol's passionate and influential attack on racial inequalities in education, segregation and inequality routinely serve as proxies for one another.[30] Gary Orfield's series of extremely valuable empirical studies of desegregation are marred, from a normative point of view, by a tendency to assume both that racial separation can virtually never be anything other than inequality-producing, and also that inequality (of opportunity) is the *only* thing wrong with racially separated schools.[31] Both racial segregation and inequality of opportunity are indeed bad things, and empirical connections do exist between them. But they are bad for somewhat distinct reasons, and cannot serve as automatic proxies for one another.

Broadly speaking, there are two types of equality of opportunity relevant to schools—equality of educational opportunity, and equality of life chances or occupational opportunity. Equality of educational opportunity is quite a complex notion once one pushes on it a bit,[32] but our purposes will be served by the intuitive idea of equivalent educations, taking individual differences into account. (For example, a dyslexic child may require special tutoring to gain an education equivalent to that of a non-dyslexic child who does not receive tutoring.)

Educational opportunity was a major focus in many of the early desegregation legal and policy battles. Historically the African-American community has placed great value on education, both in its own right and as a means to occupational mobility. Robert Carter, a lawyer in the early desegregation cases, eloquently states the view prevailing at the time, of the link between desegregation and equality of educational opportunity:

> I believe I accurately speak for the lawyers [involved in the *Brown* cases] in saying that we believed that the surest way for minority children to obtain their constitutional right to equal educational opportunity was to require the removal of all racial barriers in the public school system, with black and white children attending the same schools, intermingled in the same classrooms, and together exposed to the same educational offerings. Integration was viewed as the means to our ultimate objective, not the objective itself.[33]

Carter mentions these beliefs in part to say that subsequent developments prevented the hoped-for desegregation, and its conversion into equality of opportunity, from taking place. Districts resisted integration by various means; extensive desegregation did not really begin in the South until after 1964. After (and before) that many whites left school districts in which their children would have gone to school with a substantial number of blacks (so-called "white flight"). Continuing housing segregation in the context of neighborhood districting helped prevent schools from becoming racially mixed. Blacks and other integration advocates underestimated white parents' resistance to their children attending schools with blacks. While originally desegregation was seen as a southern issue, when it moved north, blacks were disappointed to witness white reluctance and outright racism as well. Undoubtedly *part* of the recent black retreat from the "dream" of integration is black bitterness over white rejection, and a defensive retreat into the security and warmth of a community where they will not have to worry about acceptance.[34]

In addition, Robert Carter's assumptions about how desegregation would lead to equality of opportunity were faulty, or at least limited. Equal education requires not only the co-presence of different groups of students in schools and classes, and equal exposure to educational content. It also requires teachers and schools to treat children of different racial groups equally, an assumption both Carter and the Court may have made but did not articulate.

Unfortunately the overwhelmingly white teaching force frequently failed, and still fails, to treat children of color and particularly black and Latino children, equally.[35] In their rich and comprehensive study of an ambitious desegregation program in St. Louis that buses urban black students to white-dominated suburban schools, Amy Stuart Wells and Robert Crain note that many of the white teachers do not believe in the black students' academic abilities, and hold various stereotypes and prejudices regarding them (for example, as unmotivated and disruptive).[36] Even independent of their distinct prejudices, the teachers often fail to understand the life situations and cultural backgrounds of their students, thus constraining their ability to deliver an equal education—to treat their students truly equally. (Earlier, I argued that schools had to recognize culturally distinct identities in service of a non-assimilationist, culture-respecting, integrationist ideal. Here, I am arguing that a related recognition is required for equality of educational opportunity.)

Wells and Crain contrast these teachers with a smaller number of what they call "visionary educators" whom the desegregation program has spurred to reevaluate their own pedagogies. "The visionary educators argue that showing students, especially African-American students, that white educators believe in them and support them is half the battle in trying to improve their academic achievement."[37] Thus there are racial, cultural, and class dimensions of what it would take for the largely white teaching force truly to provide equal education to students of color.[38] Doing so would be a significant achievement.

Apart from the behavior of teachers, a school can fail to provide equality of educational opportunity through a policy of tracking, defined here as assessing some measure of attainment (often thought of as "ability") in a cohort of students in the same grade, and then forming distinct classes according to results of that assessment. In desegregated schools, when (as is typical) the black and Latino children dominate the bottom track, with few in the top track, those children are almost inevitably deprived of equal educations.[39]

These complex forms of unequal treatment undermine equal educations. At the same time, a recognition of their character should be regarded as an important advance in our understanding of the range of factors involved in bringing about the ideal of equality of educational opportunity.

The unequal treatment of black students in urban or suburban, white-majority schools has persuaded some black parents to shun such schools. It is true that unless the equal treatment condition is met the equality of opportunity argument does not come fully into play as support for integrated schools. However, depending on the school's distance from this ideal, a black or Latino child might, all told, still be better off in a suburban school in which she was not treated fully equally than in an urban-majority black or Latino school with inferior educational resources. Many black parents send their children to such schools for precisely this reason.[40]

More recently, the focus on education as the domain of opportunity has been supplemented, and in some cases supplanted, by occupational or life chances opportunity, as the earlier quote from Gary Orfield suggests (above, p. 384). In the early years of desegregation, it might have been easier to believe that *educational* opportunity, and success, translated directly into *occupational* equality, and success. However, later research has indicated that occupational success functions partly independent of school success. Some researchers have shifted their focus to the longer-term issue of equal occupational opportunity as a distinct goal by which to assess desegregation, and have found that black students who attend racially integrated secondary schools do better in the world of work than their counterparts from monoracial schools.[41] If valid, this research provides not insubstantial support for racially mixed schools, especially a mixing of blacks and whites, though the argument is confined to middle-class whites.

I emphasize the distinguishing of equality of opportunity and racial integration primarily to *contrast* equality of opportunity arguments with other types of benefit of integrated education. While equality of opportunity (of either the educational or life chances variety) is indeed a vital goal by which to assess educational policy, racial integration included, it is nevertheless only one possible good and purpose of education, and of integrated education in particular.

In fact the notion of "equality of education" or "equality of educational opportunity" contains an ambiguity that has muddied the waters in this area. Equality of education is a good independent of the *quality* of education in question, as a matter of justice. And *race-based* inequalities in education (as elsewhere) are particularly odious, even where the superior education received by whites is still relatively poor in quality.

Yet we must obviously be concerned about the quality of education received by all groups, and not only about its equal or unequal distribution among the groups. Perhaps ironically, the focus on equality of educational opportunity among both proponents and detractors of racial integration has had two confounding effects on the debate. First, it has tended to deflect a clear focus on the character and quality of the education received by the different groups. It has kept us from inquiring into the range of appropriate educational goals for a democratic and liberal society, goals that could then serve as standards by which to assess various forms of racial integration and separation. When the Thernstroms say (echoing Clarence Thomas's remark cited above, p. 383–84), "[I]t is fortunate that there is no compelling evidence to support the belief that black students cannot learn, or cannot learn as well, when they attend schools with few white classmates," they seem to assume that we all agree what it is that these children are, or should be, learning.[42] The focus on the racial inequality issue encourages our failing to examine this assumption.

While the meaning of "education" in "equality of educational opportunity" can be neutral among conceptions of education, I believe that its general understanding in popular discourse, especially currently, tilts toward some conceptions of education and away from others. It tends to involve a consumerist, purely instrumental, and individualistic conception of education. The benefits of schooling are seen as accruing *only* to the individual student, rather than, for example, to the society or polity; it is individual students whose opportunities are at stake in "equality of opportunity."[43] What one student receives in the way of schooling is not seen as part of a larger picture in which other students are affected. Parents' search for good schools for their children has often become uncoupled from a sense that their child shares an educational fate with her cohort, that the education of one must be seen in the context of the education of others.

The educational benefits in the equality of opportunity framework also tend (again, not always, or necessarily) to be viewed in terms of cultural capital needed for the student to "get ahead" in the world, rather than in terms of their intrinsic educational, personal value. Schooling's social dimension—social development that accompanies participating with fellow students in a learning community—also drops out of this picture. So the reigning understanding of equality of opportunity tacitly omits the moral, social, and civic dimensions of schooling, both as benefits to the society, and as non-individualistic or non-instrumental benefits to the student.

I will argue that these essential moral, social, civic, and personal dimensions of education can either be provided *only* in ethnoracially plural settings or that such settings are *much more likely* than monoracial ones to provide them. In virtually no case can the good be attained through mere ethnoracial co-presence alone; in that sense I agree with the criticisms of busing and other measures designed to increase ethnoracial plurality for its own sake that such measures lose sight of their relationship to the genuine goods of that plurality and to the several distinct factors needed to attain them. Those factors are manyfold, but I will focus on three—curriculum, pedagogy, and (a general catchall category) other school-based factors. (Thus I omit the vital factors related to the structural relations between ethnoracial groups in the larger society, which have a strong impact on relations among ethnoracial groups in schools.)

MORAL GOODS IN INTEGRATED EDUCATION

While the civic, social, moral, and personal goods of integrated education are not entirely separable from one another, I will begin with moral goods, in part because Martin Luther King's paean to integration is cast in moral (and spiritual) terms, and also because this area has drawn extensive research. Moral growth among students regarding race involves at least the following goals: (1) reduction or elimination of racial prejudice, a goal that applies to all ethnoracial groups (because (ethno)racial prejudice has no racial boundaries),[44] and whose moral force derives in part from the more general moral principle of equal respect for all human beings;[45] (2) treating members of groups other than one's own as individuals (for example, by not stereotyping); (3) accepting members of groups other than one's own as co-equals in shared enterprises, and recognizing common interests with them in attaining superordinate goals; and (4) experiencing a sense of shared humanity with members of other groups, an exemplification of what Martin Luther King calls "a recognition of the solidarity of the human family."[46]

These goals have hardly been met in many ethnoracially plural schools. But at this point there is no excuse for accepting this unfortunate circumstance as an inevitable, or purely random, result of racial plurality. Largely spurred by court-mandated and voluntary efforts to desegregate schools, social scientists since the 1960's have engaged in extensive research on attaining these goals in ethnoracially plural settings. The language in which this research is couched is not always explicitly moral. For example, "improving intergroup relations" is a common formulation of a subject of research inquiry within social psychology, one that foregrounds a social, in contrast to a moral, aim. However, the moral aims are in fact presupposed. As a result of this research, we now know much about how racially mixed schools can reduce prejudice, increase mutual comfort and acceptance, weaken stereotyping, promote an appreciation of members of "racial outgroups" as individuals, promote a sense of shared attachment across ethnoracial boundaries to common goals and a consequent recognition of common interests, and, by implication at least, a recognition of common humanity. While many programs have not been fully tested, it is now clear that if teachers were appropriately trained and if school administrators would commit themselves to these goals, moral relationships between students of different races could be greatly improved, and the moral characters of students positively affected.[47] The education and education policy communities could make great strides toward King's vision of racial integration had they the will to do so.

All these moral/educational aims are extremely difficult to achieve in monoracial schools, of any race. Portions of some of them—aspects of multicultural curricula, or certain ways of teaching about stereotypes—could be accomplished in monoracial schools. But by and large the pedagogical programs and initiatives researched depend on the co-presence of students from different ethnoracial groups. They all concern ways to turn that presence into educationally and morally beneficial results.

CIVIC GOODS IN INTEGRATED EDUCATION

Racially integrated schooling plays, or can play, a vital *civic* role in a racially and ethnically plural democracy, a function not entirely distinct from the moral role just discussed. Civic education is increasingly recognized as an important component of schooling, as it was more explicitly in earlier historical eras, and a plethora of civic education programs have made their way into various schools, or have at least been crafted for this purpose. The *National Standards for Civics and Government* (created by the Center for Civic Education), and the esteemed California *History-Social Science Curriculum Framework* (which promotes a strong civic dimension in the study of history) are two prominent examples.[48]

Relations among ethnoracial groups are central to the requirements of civic education in the United States. Race has always been a central fault line in American life. Citizenship was formally limited to whites ("free white persons") in the 1790 Naturalization law, and racial restrictions on naturalization were not fully abandoned until 1952. Immigration policy was driven by racial considerations (not always acknowledged as such) until 1965, and initiatives to limit immigration in the mid-1990's (such as California's Proposition 187) are generally regarded as having a partly racist motivation as well.[49] While blacks were formally granted equal citizenship in the 13th, 14th, and 15th Amendments after the Civil War, their ongoing struggle for full status as equals in the American polity has suffered setbacks and reversals since that time, and has certainly not yet been completed.[50] The Supreme Court recognizes the deleterious yet historically central divisiveness of race by according laws containing racial distinctions the highest level of scrutiny among categories of social differentiation. While a staggering outpouring of major and/or popular general works on race in the United States in the 1990's disagreed on the extent and significance of improvement in the quality of lives of (primarily) blacks, there was much greater agreement on the large gulf of communication, perception, and social comity between the races.[51] This gulf is recognized by most to take its toll on the quality of civic cooperation and public interaction.

Yet, surprisingly, extant civic education programs give race very little attention. It is certainly not seen as a central civic concern. In general, the race-related civic goals such programs and guidelines propose consist in teaching that it is un-American to discriminate against people on the basis of race (as well as religion, creed, national origin, and the like).[52] These programs often also invoke a more general and vaguer idea of "equality" but without further elaboration of its implications for civic education regarding race.

Any attempt to spell out civic virtues is bound to be controversial. The burgeoning literature in this area within philosophy, political theory, and educational theory yields a wide range of qualities claimed as essential for citizens to sustain and reproduce the polity.[53] Differences stem from several sources—whether a minimalist or a more robust conception of civic education is sought; whether the liberal, democratic, market, republican, or other feature(s) of the society are particularly emphasized; how "moralized" the conception of citizenship; and others. Recognizing these controversies, I will offer a conception of citizenship specifically related to the domain of race that emphasizes the liberal, democratic, egalitarian, and participatory dimensions of our national traditions, and presupposes the recognition (1) of our history and continuing legacy of racial inequality and racialized understandings of (full) citizenship, (2) that ethnoracial differences constitute a particularly difficult and charged form of difference among our citizens, and (3) that, partly in consequence, ethnoracial differences mark significant lines of mutual ignorance and misunderstanding. Thus the model of civic education with which I operate goes beyond the minimal goal of cultivating those dispositions necessary to reproduce the current political order to encompass dispositions implied by ideals supposedly but not always actually embodied in current institutions and practices.

In this light I see at least four civic commitments, concerns, and abilities related specifically to the area of race that should be part of a civic education program. These incorporate but go beyond a commitment to non-discrimination just mentioned, and give substance to the idea of equality. One is a commitment to racial equity in the larger society, correcting the historical legacy of injustice. This involves, at least, a concern that the life chances of blacks and Latinos as groups be brought more in line with the life chances of whites, and, on the curricular level, presupposes students learning about the historical and current deficiencies of the American social order in the area of race.

This civic goal involves nurturing a general sense of social justice, directed specifically at racial inequities. That sense of racial justice is best promoted in a racially plural educational context, partly because students of color are more likely than white students to have had an experience of injustice and, especially in the case of blacks, Latinos, and Native Americans, to have been introduced by their families and communities to the idea of social justice as it bears on racial groups. Most (especially middle-class) white students, in the absence of direct educational exposure in this area, have little awareness or understanding of the experience of being racially discriminated against, being thought inferior, being an object of demeaning stereotyping, and the like. They have little understanding of how the world looks and feels to blacks, Mexicans, Puerto Ricans, or immigrants of color. They do not recognize the historical factors that have shaped the differing lives of distinct ethnoracial groups.[54]

White students' education in racial justice will thus be enhanced by exposure to the personal and familial experiences of students of color. Discussion of race and ethnicity-based experiences of injustice or insult personalizes the civic issues at hand, making them more compelling and accessible to white students than they would be through bare curricular study. (Explicit curricular study, however, must be a central part of this civic education, whether in racially plural or monoracial schools.) Even independent of the character of education and interaction in integrated schools, Orlando Patterson claims, "The sociological evidence is

now overwhelming that Euro-Americans who went to school with
Afro-Americans tend to be more tolerant and more in favor of greater
educational and economic opportunities for Afro-Americans."[55]

A second, related but more general, aim is a broader sense of
equal civic attachment and regard for members of all groups. As
mentioned above, Smith has convincingly traced the historical
sources of the deeply rooted failure of American society to regard its non-white members as full citizens. In addition, Thomas
and Mary Edsall and others have convincingly argued that whites'
failure to experience a sense of full civic attachment to blacks
permeates many issues of public policy. Part of the opposition to
government programs that has become a stable reference point
in contemporary American politics stems, often on an entirely
unacknowledged level, from a sense that people of color, and especially blacks, are the primary beneficiaries of such programs,
whether this is true in any particular case or not.[56] For much of
the white electorate, blacks and poorer Latinos are not experienced as fully part of the "we" whom they reflexively embrace in
their view of the appropriate subjects of social policy. Equal civic
attachment involves a sense of being bound up with those of
other ethnoracial groups in a national, as well as local, community of shared fate, accompanied by a conception of social good
that embraces these other groups as well as one's own. That sense
of shared fate frequently eludes members of many ethnoracial
groups (not only whites) with regard to other groups, although
its consequences are much more deleterious for the groups most
in need of public attention and concern than they are for whites.

This sense of civic attachment can be promoted by ethnoracially plural education in a manner similar to the way the sense of
racial justice can be promoted. Respectful classroom interchange
that draws on differing experiences and perspectives of students
of different groups tends to promote that sense of connection
that can be expanded into a sense of civic attachment, while it
still recognizes and validates the distinct ethnoracial identities
that students bring to the classroom interchange.

Beyond this, schools can more directly promote civic attachment by explicitly constructing the school itself, its subunits, and
to some extent its classes, as civic spaces. Being sensitive to promoting a sense of ownership of the school on the part of mem-

bers of all groups by promoting participation in policy making and rule setting, in extra-curricular activities, in community-affirming rituals, and the like, serves to encourage a sense of shared attachment among students, and shared responsibility for the school as a civic community.[57]

A third civic aim is to decrease social segregation and the social discomfort, strain, and absence of relation that so often currently exists among persons of different racial groups. This absence of social connection is, as a civic concern and a social phenomenon, distinct from social injustice and inequity (though they are sometimes conflated), and also distinct from equal civic attachment. This aim is civic in a broader sense. It concerns the quality of public life, not only engagement with processes related to the making of official policy.

The related educational task is for students to learn ways of being with members of other racial groups without perpetuating this sense of ethnoracial strain and disconnection. For this they need to learn to be interpersonally comfortable, including sharing public spaces in the school, with ethnoracial others. Students must learn to engage one another across these divides, and not be paralyzed by fear that what they say will offend someone of another group, yet be open to learning about what does offend, and able to discuss these matters further. None of this can be learned in monoracial schools. Stephan's work, mentioned earlier in connection with moral aims, is pertinent here.[58] Classes themselves must be mixed, and forms of cooperative education (including group projects with ethnoracially mixed groups) utilized that promote mutual respect.[59] Other venues for providing superordinate goals are drama, sports, and other extra-curricular activities, service and civic projects, and the like.

A fourth civic aim is the ability to communicate and engage with those of other distinct ethnoracial groups in the process of public deliberation, compromise, and shared institutional commitment necessary to the functioning of democratic institutions in a racially plural society. This cross-racial civic deliberation requires the more general civic skill of communicating honestly and fruitfully across the socially salient gulf of race difference about issues related to race. While common interests across ethnoracial lines can sometimes be identified without engaging

ethnoracial differences, by and large the process of public deliberation across ethnoracial lines regarding most issues of general concern will require some such engagement.[60] Yet many, perhaps most,
Americans lack this ability, and have precious few occasions to learn
and practice it. A potentially extremely valuable dimension of integrated education is acquiring this ability with regard to fellow students. Schools present a particularly favorable venue for overcoming barriers to interracial communication. Students are thrown together for a good portion of their lives during formative years.
Because schools are explicitly dedicated to learning and growing,
and especially to civic purposes, a rationale exists for schools' promotion of the skills and personal sensibilities necessary to communicating about race. (Workplaces also generate imperatives requiring cross-racial cooperation and communication, but not generally
about racial matters nor with broader civic purposes.)

How is this communication to be fostered in schools? Undoubtedly, its current presence in classrooms is scant. Yet in my
experience students generally welcome acknowledgment and validation of their race-based experience (as they see it) and their
ethnoracial identity.[61] They often feel that other groups fail to appreciate these experiences and viewpoints. (This may include
wanting others to realize that they do *not* regard their racial identity as being as important to themselves as others may think.) In
addition, all groups resent being stereotyped in what they recognize to be an especially charged area and are grateful for settings
in which this resentment can be acknowledged and the stereotypes begun to be dissipated. When confident of this acknowledgment by their peers and teachers, students are willing and eager
to learn from others and to engage in conversation about these
charged matters.[62] Knowledgeable educators are coming to recognize the importance of fostering these cross-racial conversations as part of building a sense of civic community in the classrooms and in schools.[63]

PARTICULARISTIC GROUP RECOGNITION AND SHARED CIVIC ENGAGEMENT

I argued earlier that a culturally sensitive form of racial integration should validate students' desire for racial and cultural recog-

nition. Here I am suggesting that such recognition can play an important role in facilitating cross-racial conversations about charged racial matters in classes. The capacity to engage in such conversations becomes an important skill that is a component of the more directly civic ability to deliberate with those of different groups concerning matters of public concern. Yet some critics of multicultural education fear that validating distinct cultural and racial identities in school contributes to a debilitating separatism rather than a healthy shared civic engagement. They would wish to focus only on commonalities among the students, ignoring these ethnoracial differences, and would press universalistic norms of equality and respect for individuality as values that can bind students together.

I very much agree that the direct teaching of such universalistic values is vital, and they have been part of my moral and civic panoply of values. At the same time, leaving unrecognized the distinct ethnoracial identities that are socially and personally significant to students in general (not in every single case perhaps) prevents the students from truly understanding one another, appreciating one another as individuals, and developing the empathy necessary for a genuine personal appropriation of the universalistic values of respect and equality.[64] The form of civic education I advocate is likely to prevent such particularistic ethnoracial recognition from either encouraging or legitimating an ethnoracial group separatism that involves distrust or hostility toward outgroup members. While acknowledging that in-group socializing and ethnicity-based organizations can be healthy and supportive to students in ways unappreciated in the assimilationist model of integration,[65] the encouragement of discussion and engagement across ethnoracial lines is likely to have the effect of blurring those lines themselves to some degree. The more students of differing groups feel comfortable socializing with and partaking of cultural and other group-based activities of groups other than their own, the more difficult it will be for any group to erect strong barriers that shield in-group from out-group members.

Indeed, it will be difficult even to maintain a sharp in-group self-definition within the school itself, if some members of group A start being accepted as school friends by members of group B.

There will be white kids who become part of a black social group, blacks who do the same with an Asian-American group. This does not mean the white kids stop being white, or the black kids black, though in some cases, especially if there is some racial ambiguity in the student's family background or upbringing, something like this can happen as well. But it does mean that within that school, the boundaries of who counts as "in the black group" will become flexible and blurred. In addition, the increasing number of interracial children (all groups are experiencing an increase in out-marrying), who can be expected to be present in the kinds of mixed schools discussed here, have the effect of pressing those ethnoracial boundaries to become even more permeable, subject to change, and incapable of sharp definition.

The result of this permeability is not assimilation as traditionally understood—a shedding of cultural distinctness in favor of a dominant cultural norm defined by dominant groups. Nor is it even a cultural uniformity with a more truly multicultural character, itself an advance over the older model of "Anglo-conformity." In any school, as in the society as a whole, ethnoracial groups with a critical mass of members will retain their distinctness. The distinctness remains historically, socially, and educationally important to recognize and respect, as it expresses itself in students' individual identities. At the same time, in the context of schools infused with the civic education I have been describing, students of all groups will be encouraged, directly and indirectly, to cross those boundaries in numerous ways. The resultant muting of boundaries is to be welcomed both for its expanding of the individual horizons of the students, as well as for its facilitating the sense of social and civic connection essential to a multiracial democracy.[66]

TRANSFER OF CIVIC ATTITUDES FROM SCHOOL TO THE PUBLIC ARENA

Is the form of civic education I have been sketching likely to be significant in forming citizens committed to equality and democracy in a multiracial context? Would students take their experience of the face-to-face "society" of their class, racially pluralistic as it may be, and generalize it to the much more impersonal world of civic relationships in a city or nation-state? It is a standard objection to one type of communitarian or fraternalistic view of the polity that it misleadingly, and even dangerously, wishes to model civic relations on the intimate ties of friendship or close communities.[67]

On one level, this is an objection, or at least an expression of caution, regarding *any* civic or moral education taught and practiced in schools. A child might well not practice the civic or moral virtues learnt in school in the world outside it. Civic education even at its best would do well to face up to the disjunct between the sort of trusting and nurturing school and classroom setting conducive to internalizing civic values, and the outside world, where a range of other norms and expectations may pull for different qualities, and discourage the civic or moral ones in question.[68]

Nevertheless, although the civic-minded school is a face-to-face community, it is not necessarily or generally a community of intimates, with strong personal ties. Students who learn to work and learn together in cooperative activity, and who engage one another in honest conversation about race, need not be friends with one another. Their connection often does not extend beyond the bounds of the school. A school, especially at the junior high level or above, where students share classrooms with several distinct groupings of fellow students each day, is much more like an intermediate association between intimacy and the impersonality of a large polity. In this regard it is like a church or synagogue, a neighborhood organization, or a bowling league. It is as reasonable to think that a class or school has the potential to be at least as important a context for forging a civic-minded character as are these other associations. Moreover, if connections to the outer world are explicitly emphasized in the civic and moral education itself (as they should be), and especially if that education sometimes takes the form of civic projects engaged with the world outside the school (for example, in service learning with a strong civic component), the carryover from school to polity is that much more likely.

In addition, there is some reason to think that racial attitudes formed in the kind of school setting I have been describing are *more* likely to have an impact on students' racial attitudes in general (outside school) than are other civic attitudes likely so to generalize. This may seem paradoxical, for we are all familiar with individuals who divide racial "others" into a smaller number of "acceptable" persons (often friends of theirs), leaving the majority the target of the same objectionable stereotypes the moral and civic education is attempting to undermine.

However, set in the context of curricular material that teaches the complex history and circumstances of group Y, honest conversations about race that will inevitably lead to a questioning of stereotypes of the group, and a pedagogy that avails itself of proven or near-proven insights about reducing prejudice and stereotypes,[69] a member of racial group Z is more likely to appreciate the internal diversity of racial group Y. She will thus become more likely to treat members of group Y (in general, not only in her circle of school acquaintances) both as individuals and as fellow human beings.

Moreover, racism and its legacies (residential racial segregation, general social segregation), and a pervasive ignorance about one another's lives, situations, and cultures set up distinctive barriers between racial groups. The very idea of "race" does so as well, implying a kind of unbridgeable gulf and dissimilarity.[70] Even though the school setting involves direct connections only between *particular* members of distinct racial groups, forging these connections in the way I have described involves an assault on the *general* barriers between the racial groups in question.

For these reasons, other things being equal, successful civic education concerning race is more likely than civic education in some other areas to transfer from the school context to civically valuable attitudes and commitments in public arenas.

Personal Benefits of Integrated Education

I have dwelt on the moral and especially the civic benefits of ethnoracially plural schooling because these are particularly striking lacunae in much dispute about integration and desegregation. But the individual student benefits in other ways, also not captured on the equality of opportunity model. The moral and civic virtues enable one to "live well," as Aristotle said. They provide richer and more meaningful forms of engagement with one's fellow citizens and human beings, and with the larger society.

Beyond this, learning about the experiences, outlook, and histories of ethnoracial groups other than her own is a vital part of a student's learning about the character of her own society and world. Any education with a plausible claim to being called "quality" must involve a deep understanding of the social reality of one's society. I mentioned earlier that, in an instrumental sense, children of color suffer more in the loss of social capital from an ignorance of their society. Whites can much *better* afford to be ignorant of the lives of non-whites than the reverse. Still, my point here is not this socially related cost but the intrinsic educational loss to the student of a lack of knowledge of other groups.

Of course some of this knowledge can be provided through a rich multiculturally sensitive curriculum, even in monoracial or near-monoracial schools. But, first, while some teachers in such schools may provide such a curriculum, the pressure and perceived need for it is likely to be much greater in ethnoracially plural schools.[71] Second, and more important, my argument has been that a school that draws on the experiences of students and their families in multiracial classroom settings will be the most felicitous setting for students of all groups to see the point, retain knowledge, and achieve a deeper understanding of the social realities of groups other than their own.

The second personal educational benefit is that knowledge of one's society involves a form of *self*-knowledge. In understanding the race-based experience of groups other than one's own, one comes to understand not only "the other" but also oneself. This is so on several levels. One is as an American. The plurality of ethnoracial groups is a deep part of the fiber of American life, so in understanding them one gains a deeper appreciation of one's Americanness as a social and cultural identity. In particular, all major ethnoracial groups have had an impact on the shape of popular and political culture that form the fabric of social existence for all Americans. Many whites recognize that certain styles of dress, modes of personal interaction, language, music, films, dance, and the like, originated with distinct non-white groups. Blacks are unquestionably the most prominent group in this regard; their cultural influence far outstrips their proportion of the population. But, especially in certain parts of the country, and increasingly everywhere, Latinos have had an impact on food, language, music, and the like. Fewer whites may recognize that cultural forms they think of as "white" or—more vaguely but still with an implication of whiteness—as "mainstream" have been decisively influenced by Latinos, blacks, Native Americans, and others.[72] Political culture and institutions too have been decisively shaped by the European encounters early in our history with Native Americans and Africans, and, later, especially with Mexicans. More recently, the Civil Rights movement has had a profound effect on public and legal understandings of equality and justice, American-style.

Expanding the Horizons of White Students

Echoing the equality of opportunity argument, Orlando Patterson says, "Integration is about the acquisition of social and cultural capital [by Afro-Americans]."[73] Yet all the benefits discussed in the previous sections accrue to whites as well as to students of color, or to the society as a whole. Segregated schooling and a segregated life are very constricting to white students.[74] These sheltered white students do not learn how to "read" the behavior of individuals in other ethnoracial groups. They do not get to know members of these groups as individuals. They cut off a large source of friendships and friendly acquaintanceships.

Sheltered white students fail to develop what some have called "multicultural and multiracial competence"—a recognition of and knowledge about cultural and racial differences that allows individuals to negotiate a culturally pluralistic world.[75] Lack of such competence will affect white students who will have to function in an increasingly culturally plural work environment. Janet Schofield cites a report commissioned by the U.S. Department of Labor, which concluded that "the ability to work effectively in a context of cultural diversity is one of the basic competencies which is required to perform effectively in the U.S. labor force."[76] An absence of integrated education could thus have a materially deleterious effect on whites. (As mentioned above, racial minorities are *more* harmed by lack of multicultural competence, a point integral to the occupational form of the equality of opportunity argument.)

In closing this discussion of the potential benefits of ethnoracial diversity in schools, let us note how it provides the answer to Clarence Thomas's oft-echoed show-stopper, "It is insulting to say that blacks need to sit next to whites in order to learn." The response given by proponents of the equality of opportunity argument, such as Orfield, and Wells and Crain, is "But for access to higher status knowledge and personal/occupational networks, blacks do need to sit next to whites." That answer is compelling as far as it goes, but its still-lingering sense of insult stems from a failure to recognize that white students have much to learn from black students also. Such mutual interchange among students of different ethnoracial background is of great value to blacks too, and to Latinos, Asian-Americans, whites, and so on. That benefit is to the individual student but also to the larger society.

Conclusion

The retreat from a commitment to integrated education betokens a loss of faith in the democratic promise of schooling in a culturally pluralistic society. I have not explored whether that pessimism about schools is empirically justified. My argument has been more minimal. A range of vital personal and civic goods—communication, cooperation, understanding, civic attachment, commitment to racial justice, multiracial competence and personal comfort, social and self-understanding—is virtually unattainable without, or is greatly facilitated by, racial and cultural plurality in the student bodies of our schools. These goods have dropped out of sight in public discourse concerning both desegregation and school reform more generally.

Regarding desegregation, equality of opportunity—either of education or of life chances—has taken center stage as the prime argument in its favor. I hope that the empirical case for a link between desegregation and equality of opportunity stands up to scrutiny, and further hope that this link will have an impact on public policy in this area. Nevertheless, my own task has been to indicate the limits of equality of opportunity as an argument for integrated education. Equality of opportunity does not by itself supply the civic skills and commitments needed to reproduce and strive to perfect a multicultural democracy, and tends to operate with an instrumentalist, individualistic, and non-civic conception of education.

The moral, civic, and personal sensitivities, concerns, and abilities must be deliberately taught; students do not acquire them through mere contact, in school, with members of other ethnoracial groups. Disappointingly, these goals are not given a central place even in most programs of civic and moral education, much less in teacher education more generally. Their full realization requires teachers and schools sensitive to cultural and life situation differences among students; who themselves believe that all students have contributions to make to the education of other students; who are committed to facilitating interracial understanding, conversation, and cooperation as an integral part of their educational goals; who have learned, or are in the process of learning, the pedagogical skills necessary to facilitate this goal. It also requires that teachers so described have the support of their institutions and its key administrators. The institution must not set the cultural identity of students against the school's own cultural norms but must manifest a culture of inclusion, respect, and faith in all children's ability to learn.

Is it asking too much that teachers learn to provide safe and trusting settings in which they can facilitate cross-racial connections, the frank expression and discussion of racial issues and experiences—in which they can teach racially oriented civic virtues? One hesitates to add new demands to teachers already grappling with new mandates of standardized tests and enhanced accountability. Nevertheless, racial and ethnic pluralism and the legacy of historical injustice will be with us for the foreseeable future, and will continue to play a large role in the real world of schools and classrooms. Teachers often conceive of their roles in narrow ways that prevent them from acknowledging the impact of these responsibilities—that it is not their place to deal with social development of students, that merely mixing students is sufficient to teach respect and acceptance, that they must totally ignore race and color in interaction with students.[77] But educators cannot really afford not to pay attention to racial matters, any more than they can afford not to deal with moral and civic issues generally.

While Martin Luther King, Jr.'s vision of deep moral and civic relationships across racial lines has lost its luster among all ethnoracial groups, a re-visioned conception—shorn of its assimilationist associations, and aware of the complexities or racial prejudice and division—remains as valid today as it was in King's time. The *Brown* Court was right to brand both educational inequality and racial separation as moral wrongs, even if its reasoning was not entirely adequate, and some of its specific arguments no longer applicable. Moreover, in the world of education, we now know better how to create the integrationist vision than we ever have known before. The future of the highest ideals of our democracy requires that we not abandon it.

NOTES

Earlier versions of this chapter were presented to the American Society for Political and Legal Philosophy (in December 1998) and to the Committee on Philosophy, Politics, and Public Policy. I am grateful to both audiences, and especially to my commentators at the ASPLP, Anita Allen and William Galston.

1. Examples in large metropolitan areas are Wilmington (Delaware), Louisville (Kentucky), and St. Louis. See Gary Orfield and John T. Yun, "Resegregation in American Schools," report of the Harvard University Civil Rights Project, 1999, 18. J. S. Fuerst and Roy Petty in their 1992 study of school integration add, "[M]anaged integration—achieved largely through intelligent use of busing—is working in hundreds of small and medium-sized communities all across the country." "Quiet Success: Where Managed School Integration Works," *The American Prospect*, Summer 1992, 65.

2. Orfield and Yun. Gary Orfield and Susan Eaton, *Dismantling Desegregation: The Quiet Reversal of Brown v. Board of Education* (New York: New Press, 1996), ch. 3, "The Growth of Segregation."

3. *Missouri v. Jenkins*, 115 S. Ct. 2038 (1995).

4. See, for example, Glenn Loury, "Integration has had its day," *New York Times*, April 23, 1997. The lead article in the August 5, 1998, edition of *Education Week* begins, "African-American parents, by an overwhelming margin, want the public schools to focus on achievement rather than on racial diversity and integration, a survey released last week says." It goes on to say that white parents express anxiety about integration.

5. Orfield and Eaton, xv. David Shipler captures a related attitude among blacks, stated by Laura Washington, an editor and publisher: "My mother's not a real big fan of white people. But she said to me: 'You've got to live with them. If you're going to be professional and go out into the world you're going to have to work with them every day . . . You need to learn how to understand how they think and how they live and the cultural differences, and you better learn it as early as you can. So go to an integrated high school.'" David Shipler, *A Country of Strangers: Blacks and Whites in America* (New York: Vintage, 1997), 102.

6. Gloria Ladson-Billings, *Dreamkeepers: Successful Teachers of African American Children* (San Francisco: Jossey-Bass, 1994), 3.

7. I adopt David Hollinger's useful phrase "ethnoracial" group to emphasize the partly racial, partly panethnic/pancultural character of the five major such groups—African-Americans, Native Americans, Latinos, Asian-Americans, and Euro-Americans. Pluralism as an ideal must also be cognizant of distinct cultural groups within each of these ethnoracial groups (e.g. Haitian-Americans, Chicanos, Korean-Americans). David Hollinger, *PostEthnic America* (New York: Basic Books, 1995).

8. Martin Luther King, Jr., "The Ethical Demands for Integration," in James M. Washington (ed.), *A Testament of Hope: The Essential Writings and Speeches of Martin Luther King, Jr.* (San Francisco: HarperCollins, 1986), 118.

9. Randall Kennedy, "In Praise of Racial 'Integration,'" In *IntellectualCapital.com,* July 24, 1997.

10. An argument could also be made that the term "desegregation" or "desegregated schools" should be completely abandoned except where it involves the process of altering racial demographics in a school previously intentionally created as racially segregated. Stephan and Abigail Thernstrom point out that the notion of "desegregation" (understood as a process rather than an end state) regnant in the 1970's— breaking up clusters of black students and placing them in majority white schools—is obsolete, if we confine ourselves to extant school district boundaries, for the cities to which desegregation orders of that era were applied no longer have white majority schools. Stephan and Abigail Thernstrom, *America in Black and White: One Nation Indivisible* (New York: Touchstone, 1997), 337–338.

11. Orfield and Yun, 25, 14. Since the authors' figures do not supply the percentage of actual schools with different racial demographics, one is unable to determine the percentage of students sharing schools with students of particular percentages of ethnoracial groups other than their own.

12. As Fuerst and Petty note, "With little fanfare, integration has become a fact of life for the majority of African-American school children in the United States." ("Quiet Success," 65.)

13. Orfield and Yun, 15.

14. Antonia Darder, Rodolfo D. Torres, and Henry Gutierrez (eds.), *Latinos and Education: A Critical Reader* (New York: Routledge, 1997).

15. Peter Schmidt, "California district strives to mix blacks and Hispanics," *Education Week*, April 12, 1995, 3. See also Lynn Beck and Rebecca Newman, "Caring in One Urban High School: Thoughts on the Interplay among Race, Class, and Gender," in Deborah Eaker-Rich and Jane Van Galen (eds.), *Caring in an Unjust World: Negotiating Borders and Barriers in Schools* (Albany: SUNY Press, 1996), concerning both tensions and positive relations among blacks and Latinos (mostly Central American immigrants) in a high school.

16. A black parent cited in an article about black disenchantment with integration makes this point about the reality, and whites' understanding, of integration: "Some blacks are rethinking integration for the simple reasoning that it never happened . . . We have extended the olive branch only to find that whites don't want integration, they want assimilation. People aren't willing to give up that much of their own identity for integration." Wil Haygood, "Race in American life: Ideals giving way to reality," *Boston Globe*, Sept. 14, 1997, A1.

17. Cited in John Brenkman, "Race Publics," *Transition*, issue 66 (undated), 27.

18. David Shipler, *A Country of Strangers*, 34 and elsewhere, cites blacks making this point.

19. Many blacks were of course aware of the distinctness of black culture, which had been articulated in this period by Ralph Ellison, Langston Hughes, and others. Perhaps the black legal activists at the NAACP were equally aware that cultural differences might play a role in the success of integration. But such issues had no legal standing, and there was no reason to bring them into the desegregation arguments.

20. Horace Kallen, Randolph Bourne, Alain Locke, and W. E. B. DuBois were influential proponents of cultural pluralism in the first decades of the 20th century.

21. There exists a burgeoning literature on the importance of respect for and sensitivity to cultural and racial factors in providing effective, quality education to racial-minority children, and on methods for incorporating that respect into pedagogy. Some of the most important works are Sonia Nieto, *Affirming Diversity: The Sociopolitical Context of Multicultural Education*, 2nd edition (White Plains, NY: Longman, 1996); Gloria Ladson-Billings, *The Dreamkeepers*; Theresa Perry and Lisa Delpit,

The Real Ebonics Debate (Boston: Beacon Press, 1997); Ann Locke David-
son, *Making and Molding Identity in Schools: Student Narratives on Race,
Gender, and Academic Engagement* (Albany; SUNY Press, 1996); Lisa Delpit,
Other People's Children: Cultural Conflict in the Classroom (New York: New
Press, 1995); Rosina Lippi-Green, *English with an Accent: Language, Ideol-
ogy, and Discrimination in the United States* (New York: Routledge, 1997);
Sonia Nieto, *The Light in Their Eyes: Creating Multicultural Learning Com-
munities* (New York: Teachers College Press, 1999).

22. For criticisms of the *Brown* Court's reasoning, see Andrew Kull,
The Color-Blind Constitution (Cambridge: Harvard University Press, 1992);
Thernstrom and Thernstrom; David Armor, *Forced Justice: School Desegre-
gation and the Law* (New York: Oxford, 1995).

23. The important cases making explicit the legal standing of the
legacy argument are *Green v. New Kent County* 430 U.S. 391 (1968) and
Swann v. Charlotte-Mecklenburg Board of Education 402 U.S. 1 (1971).

24. A variation on this argument claims that in American society
racial separation itself damages the self-worth of blacks. I argue elsewhere that *de facto* school segregation that results primarily from residential segregation partakes of something like the inferiority-declaring
force of what was objectionable about *de jure* segregation. "'Racial Integration' Revisited," in Joram Graf Haber and Mark Halfon (eds.), *Norms
and Values: Essays on the Work of Virginia Held* (Lanham, MD: Rowman and
Littlefield, 1998), p. 211.

25. For an extended critique of the alleged empirical connections
between segregation, self-worth, and academic motivation stated or
implied in the *Brown* decision, see Roy Brooks, *Integration or Separation:
A Strategy for Racial Equality* (Cambridge: Harvard University Press,
1996), 13–21. As Brooks points out (citing Walter Stephan) there are
reasons for thinking that white-dominated schools in which blacks are
a minority may well involve factors tending toward the *lowering* of
black self-esteem—whites' racism against blacks, blacks' comparison of
themselves to better-prepared white students, loss of power and status
(compared to majority black schools) merely from being a minority.
Brooks, 23.

26. Brooks, 12.

27. From text of Court's opinion, cited in Richard Kluger, *Simple Justice*, (New York: Vintage, 1975), 781.

28. *Brown* in Kluger, 780.

29. *Brown* in Kluger, 782.

30. For example, the statement "In no school that I saw anywhere in
the United States were nonwhite children in large numbers truly inter-
mingled with white children" is proffered early in the book in the con-

text of a discussion of unequal education, as if it were barely conceivable that a group of black children could become educated in any significant sense in the absence of whites. Jonathan Kozol, *Savage Inequalities: Children in America's Schools* (New York: Harper Collins, 1991), 3.

31. Two of Orfield's studies are cited above, footnotes 1 and 2, and there have been many others over the past decades, with the Harvard University Civil Rights Project sponsoring them approximately every two years since the early 1990's.

32. See, for example, the issue of *Social Philosophy and Policy* devoted to "Equal Opportunity", vol. 5, issue 1, Autumn 1987; Kenneth Howe, *Understanding Equal Educational Opportunity* (New York: Teachers College Press, 1997); and Amy Gutmann, *Democratic Education* (with new preface and epilogue) (Princeton: Princeton University Press, 1999), 128–139.

33. Robert Carter, "The Unending Struggle for Equal Educational Opportunity," *Teachers College Record*, vol. 96, #4, Summer 1995: 621.

34. Shipler, *A Country of Strangers*, 34 and elsewhere.

35. Nor are black teachers entirely immune from prejudice against especially poor black and Latino children.

36. Robert Crain and Amy Stuart Wells, *Stepping Across the Color Line: African-American Students in White Suburban Schools* (New Haven: Yale University Press, 1997). Personalizing this general insight about unequal treatment, a black male student, interviewed by Sara Lightfoot in her study of "good high schools," speaks of white teachers in one school who seem repelled or afraid of darker-skinned black students, contrasting them with the school's principal, "who does not draw back from him." Sara Lawrence Lightfoot, *The Good High School: Portraits of Character and Culture* (New York: Basic Books, 1984).

37. Wells and Crain, 290.

38. Delpit, *Other People's Children*.

39. Wells and Crain describe a modification of a common three-tiered tracking system, namely a two-tiered one, used in some of the St. Louis schools they studied. The two tracks are "honors" and "everyone else." While the honors classes were often all-white, Wells and Crain plausibly claim that the presence of a strong racial mixture in the other track, and the absence of an almost-all-black bottom track, makes this form of tracking substantially superior for the black children to the three-track model. There are other lesser forms of tracking—for example, having permanent ability groups *within* a single desegregated classroom, but not creating the classes themselves by ability group sorting.

There is a good deal of literature on tracking debating its pros and cons, but a substantial body of research suggests that non-tracked schools are better for the "lower ability" students while not being detrimental to the "higher ability" ones. See Jeannie Oakes, *Keeping Track: How Schools Structure Inequality* (New Haven: Yale University Press, 1985).

40. The METCO program in Boston, in which racial minority children can choose to attend suburban (generally overwhelmingly white) schools, at great inconvenience (long bus rides, culturally alien environments, difficulty of parental contact with school, and the like), has been a going concern for several decades.

41. Amy Stuart Wells and Robert Crain, "Perpetuation Theory and the Long-Term Effects of School Desegregation," *Review of Educational Research*, Winter 1994, vol. 64, #4: 531–555. The relevant literature cites three factors that convert black attendance at white majority schools into enhanced occupational success, independent of student school achievement. The first comprises skills of interaction in a white world, which enhance the student's self-presentation in applying for jobs, and his or her subsequent ability to negotiate the cultural terrain of white-dominated workplaces, thus enhancing job performance. The second is access to information about colleges and jobs that would not be attained at schools serving a less-middle-class clientele, a climate of support for pursuing higher education, school counselors pushing and helping students to make application to colleges, and the like. The third is the school's reputation; in general, an employer, or college, is more likely to select a black graduate from the integrated than the segregated school. (Note that the first two aspects concern class factors as well as, or intertwined with, racial ones.) It is worth noting here that one of the important pre-*Brown* integration cases, *Sweatt v. Painter* 339 U.S. 629 (1950)—ruling against a segregated law school in Texas with facilities and expenditures comparable to the then-white-only University of Texas Law School—makes use of very similar arguments.

42. Thernstrom and Thernstrom, 342.

43. "Equality of opportunity" can also take a more group-based focus, where the groups in question are defined by race, class, or gender. While this conception is less individualistic, it still does not engage with the larger social good of education; moreover, some conceptions of this group-based good see the group as simply standing in for the interests of individuals within the group, rather than involving a good to the group in its own right. Such a conception is made explicit in Brooks, *Integration or Separation*.

44. The *consequences* of racial prejudice and their moral seriousness are not symmetrical across racial groups, however. For a discussion of this issue, see L. Blum, "Moral Asymmetries in Racism," in S. Babbitt and S. Campbell (eds.), *Racism and Philosophy* (Ithaca: Cornell University Press, 1999).

45. Not all forms of departure from the principle of equal respect are equally objectionable. Among such forms, race-based discrimination is particularly invidious, because of the historic evils that have attended it.

46. King, "Ethical Demand for Integration," 121. Randall Kennedy speaks of seeing oneself and racial others as "neighbors united by ties that run deeper than those of racial kinship" and "not as members of separate racial tribes." ("In Praise of Racial 'Integration.'") This absolute prioritizing of common humanity over ethnoracial solidarity is not, I think, required by a true integrationist vision, including King's, and is not consistent with the pluralist version of integration that I advocate here. While in *some* sense our common humanity is deeper than our ethnoracial particularity, in other ways the solidarity of discriminated-against racial groups is no less meaningful or valid than the common humanity.

47. Walter Stephan, *Reducing Prejudice and Stereotyping in Schools* (New York: Teachers College Press, 1999). A substantial body of literature in social psychology (summarized by Stephan, a major figure in the development of this literature) explores the conditions (in schools and classes) under which individual racial prejudice is reduced and interracial acceptance and liking promoted. Much of the literature operates within a paradigm deriving from Gordon Allport's 1954 work, *The Nature of Prejudice* (Reading, MA: Addison-Wesley, 1979 [1954]), known as the "contact hypothesis." That hypothesis asserts that contact between groups is more likely to lead to reduction in prejudice and greater acceptance when the contact is characterized by equal status; when it involves cooperative activity in the service of shared, superordinate goals; when it is supported by the authority of the surrounding institution(s); and when it involves the perception of common interests and common humanity between members of the two groups.

48. Center for Civic Education, *National Standards for Civics and Government*, 1994. *History-Social Science Framework* (for California Public Schools Kindergarten Through Grade Twelve), (adopted by California State Board of Education, 1987).

49. See Juan Perea, *Immigrants Out: The New Nativism and the Anti-Immigrant Impulse in the United States* (New York: New York University Press, 1997) and Rogers Smith, below, footnote 50.

50. In a recent exhaustively researched work on the history of American citizenship, Rogers M. Smith argues convincingly that the conception of American citizenship as inclusive of all who swear allegiance to (what are taken as) American values and institutions, independent of race, religion, and ethnicity, is seriously deficient, and that American laws and public understandings of citizenship have historically been

bound up with racial (and other ascriptive) hierarchies. Only if we face up to the contamination of our understandings of citizenship by these racialist views can we fully achieve the liberal, democratic conception of citizenship that many wrongly regard as already triumphant. Rogers Smith, *Civic Ideals: Conflicting Visions of Citizenship in U.S. History* (New Haven: Yale University Press, 1997). Matthew Frye Jacobson's *Whiteness of a Different Color: European Immigrants and the Alchemy of Race* (Cambridge: Harvard University Press, 1998) argues that notions of "whiteness" have been and are deeply intertwined with ideas about "Americanness."

51. A small sample of major popular or scholarly works on race in this period: Cornel West, *Race Matters* (Boston: Beacon Press, 1997); Jennifer Hochschild, *Facing Up to the American Dream: Race, Class, and the Soul of the Nation* (Princeton: Princeton University Press, 1995); Andrew Hacker, *Two Nations: Black and White, Separate, Hostile, and Unequal*; Patricia Williams, *The Alchemy of Race and Rights* (Cambridge: Harvard University Press, 1991). Other works mentioned herein: Thernstrom and Thernstrom, Sniderman and Piazza, Shipler, Tatum, Patterson.

52. It is the burden of books like Smith and Jacobson to argue that racial discrimination is only partly, and ambiguously, "un-American."

53. A good summary of some of the most influential trends in recent citizenship theory is Will Kymlicka and Wayne Norman, "Return of the Citizen: A Survey of Recent Work on Citizenship Theory," *Ethics*, 104 (January 1994): 352–381.

54. Conversely, school may well be the one setting in which blacks, Latinos and other people of color can learn how the world looks to white people. It is sometimes said (in contrast to the converse) that racial minorities do understand whites, since they must learn something about the white world in order to make their way in it. The truth in this insight can be greatly overstated. Racially isolated blacks and Latinos often carry around extremely oversimplified and overgeneralized views of whites; and the knowledge necessary to navigate a white-dominated society may remain at a surface level. In addition, the different groups of color themselves may well be isolated from one another socially, and school may provide the best, or the only, venue in which they can learn about one another as well.

55. Orlando Patterson, *The Ordeal of Integration: Progress and Resentment in America's "Racial" Crisis* (Washington, DC: Civitas, 1997), 191.

56. Thomas and Mary Edsall, *Chain Reaction: The Impact of Race, Rights, and Taxes on American Politics* (New York: Norton, 1992). See also Donald Kinder and Lynn Sanders, *Divided by Color: Racial Politics and Democratic Ideals* (Chicago: University of Chicago Press, 1996). Paul M. Sni-

derman and Thomas Piazza, *The Scar of Race* (Cambridge: Harvard University Press, Belknap Press, 1993). While Sniderman and Piazza are concerned to demonstrate that far from all opposition to government programs benefitting blacks stems from racial prejudice, their findings nevertheless support the idea that *some* of the opposition lies in this source and that there is still a good deal of racial prejudice among whites, even if (as I agree) many social analysts misleadingly overstate both the degree of white racism and its impact on stances on policy issues.

57. Lawrence Kohlberg, better known for his paradigm-creating work in moral development theory, also did pioneering work in creating democratic communities in schools. See F. Clark Power, Ann Higgins, and Lawrence Kohlberg's misleadingly titled *Lawrence Kohlberg's Approach to Moral Education* (New York: Columbia University Press, 1989).

58. See note 47.

59. "Cooperative learning," which brings groups of racially heterogeneous students together in working groups, with a common task, and scope for all to make distinctive and recognizable contributions to the group effort, is generally regarded as facilitating more positive intergroup relations. See the summary by two of the leading researchers in this area, David W. Johnson and Roger T. Johnson, "Social Interdependence: Cooperative Learning in Education," in Barbara Benedict Bunker and Jeffrey Z. Rubin (eds.), *Conflict, Cooperation, and Justice: Essays Inspired by the Work of Morton Deutsch* (San Francisco: Jossey-Bass, 1995).

60. Roger Sanjek's *The Future of Us All: Race and Neighborhood Politics in New York City* (Ithaca: Cornell University Press, 1998) provides a rich and hopeful description of how an extremely ethnoracially mixed neighborhood succeeded in bridging its ethnoracial differences to find common ground, in part through acknowledgment of those differences themselves and working through and with them to produce mutual understanding, compromise, and constructive public deliberation.

61. On the importance of recognition of one's cultural identity in public venues, see Charles Taylor, "The Politics of Recognition," in Amy Gutmann (ed.), *Multiculturalism* (Princeton: Princeton University Press, 1994). Some typical experiences that students from different ethnoracial groups have had and that relevant literature suggests they wish acknowledged are the following. Many black students want non-blacks to acknowledge a barrage of slights and put-downs they feel they suffer outside the awareness of many whites. Many white students want to talk about ways they have tried to avoid prejudicial attitudes or behavior, or that they have grievances too that may be unrelated to race but are important to them. Many Asian-Americans want to say how they feel the

"model minority" image of their group is constricting to their aspirations and often conveys a tone of derision and lack of full acceptance, whether conscious or not. Some Latino students want to talk about being caught in the middle between white and black, or being pushed to adopt a race-like identity when they see their ethnocultural identity, one which embraces both light and dark-skinned Latinos, as more salient in their self-understanding. Both Latinos and Asians often resent the insistent focus on black and white that dominates discussion of racial and ethnic matters in the public domain and in schools and colleges.

62. For further discussion of interracial dialogue in classrooms (higher education in this case, but largely applicable, with modifications, to secondary education) see Lawrence Blum, "Can We Talk? Interracial Dialogue in the College Classroom," in *Change: The Magazine of Higher Education,* November/December 1998: 26–37.

63. Sonia Nieto's *The Light in Their Eyes: Creating Multicultural Learning Communities* is particularly insightful in this regard. See also Mary Dilg, *Race and Culture in the Classroom: Teaching and Learning Through Multicultural Education* (New York: Teachers College Press, 1999), and Beverly Daniel Tatum, *"Why Are All the Black Kids Sitting Together in the Cafeteria?" and Other Conversations about Race: A Psychologist Explains the Development of Racial Identity* (New York: Basic Books, 1997) (discussed below, note 65).

64. Sanjek's study (note 60) makes a good case that in local communities, productive alliances toward shared civic goals actually require engagement with ethnoracial differences.

65. Beverly Daniel Tatum's *"Why Are All the Black Kids . . . "* provides the best account of which I am aware of the developmental pressures and personal value of in-group socializing among racial minorities in schools and colleges, set within a general normative framework that assumes that a complementary connectedness to groups *other* than one's own ultimately represents a more personally and morally mature form of racial identity.

66. In *Integration or Separation,* Roy Brooks makes a case for a stronger validation of separatism than I do, though this form is itself a good deal weaker than a full-scale ethnic nationalist who wishes to have as little to do with society beyond the borders of the group as is economically and socially possible. Brooks argues that blacks (the group on whom he focuses his argument) may need (what he calls "limited") separation in order to develop the self-confidence and self-affirmation necessary to function in a white society that will almost inevitably be insensitive to their needs. "Limited separation provides an option to scores of African Americans who do not have the superhuman strength or extraordinary

good fortune to make it in racially hostile, predominantly white mainstream institutions" (190).

Blacks, and other racial minorities, can, certainly, experience this hostility, and black groups can be a vital source of support. But Brooks's argument appears to lock that white hostility in place as a permanent feature of our society and of the institutions in question; at least it involves no frontal attack on that hostility. By contrast, in the schools I am describing, institutional pride and the teachers' professional identity would be bound up in making the school a welcoming rather than hostile environment. Teachers would be committed to taking a stand against racial prejudice, and the form of education too is likely to mean that, at least, there is not a united front of hostility toward black students on the part of the majority white student group. White teachers, and some students, would be part of the "affirming" group for black, and other minority, students.

67. Cf. William Galston, "A Public Philosophy for the 21st Century," in *The Responsive Community*, vol. 8, issue 3, Summer 1998, 36.

68. Nancy Rosenblum rightly cautions that the effects of an association cannot be automatically inferred from its purposes. Not everything structured to be a "school of virtue" will end up being one. "The Moral Effects of Associational Life," *Report from the Institute for Philosophy and Public Policy*, vol. 18, #3, Summer 1998, 12.

69. See above, note 47: Walter Stephan, *Reducing Prejudice and Stereotyping in Schools*.

70. Audrey Smedley very convincingly makes this point about the concept of "race" in *Race in North America: Origin and Evolution of a Worldview*, 2nd edition (Boulder, CO: Westview Press, 1999).

71. This is a purely pragmatic argument. On my view, the need for a rich multicultural curriculum is not dependent on the ethnoracial demographic of a school (though the details of it may be—for example, a district with a large Laotian immigrant population has reason to give more attention to Laotian culture, history, and experience than a district that does not).

72. Almost all forms of what most whites think of as distinctively "American" music for example (even including country and western music) have been shaped, often decisively, by the black presence in America.

73. Patterson, *Ordeal of Integration*, 191. Patterson does not entirely believe that this is the *only* value of integration since, as noted earlier, he cites the increase in tolerance and concern for justice for Afro-Americans on the part of whites as an important effect of integration. (See above, p. 401–402.)

74. To note one pointed example, a middle-class white girl who attended a mixed school reported how acquaintances of hers who attended all-white schools rolled up the windows of their cars when a car of black kids pulled up alongside them. H. Andrew Sagar and Janet Ward Schofield, "Integrating the Desegregated School," in *Advances in Motivation and Achievement,* volume I (JAI Press), 230.

75. This argument does not distinguish between racial groups and ethnocultural groups. These are by no means the same. First generation Haitian-Americans have cultural norms distinct from African-Americans, though both are "black" and may be subject to similar racism. There are important cultural differences among different "white" groups. Every so-called "racial" group in the United States—that is, groups thought of racially even when a geographical term like "Asian" or "Latino" is used to designate them—contains myriad cultural groups within it. Nevertheless, the way that cultural and racial group identity are so intertwined in the United States makes the above argument applicable to both.

76. Janet Ward Schofield, "Review of Research on School Desegregation's Impact on Elementary and Secondary School Students," in Kofi Lomotey and Charles Teddlie (eds.), *Readings in Equal Education,* vol. 13 (New York: AMS Press, 1996), p. 92.

77. Janet Ward Schofield, *Black and White in School: Trust, Tension, or Tolerance* (New York: Teachers College Press, 1989), a superb study of the effects of desegregation in a middle school, masterfully articulates attitudes held by teachers (both white and black, though somewhat less by the latter group) that stand in the way of their being proactive in civic education in the area of race. See especially chapter 2: "The Teachers' Ideology."

13

INDIVIDUAL EXPERIENCE AND SOCIAL POLICY: THINKING PRACTICALLY ABOUT OVERCOMING RACIAL AND ETHNIC PREJUDICE

WILLIAM A. GALSTON

My comments on Professor Blum's paper are of limited philosophical interest. Few will challenge the ideal of an integrated society; few will reject the propositions that racial and ethnic prejudice lacks a rational basis, is the source of grave injustice for its victims, and demeans those who espouse it. I endorse his core thesis, that the mission of our public schools is civic as well as economic, moral as well as academic. The inquiry that animates his paper—how public schools can contribute to meaningful racial integration in our society—is appropriate and important. To the extent that Blum and I disagree, it is over means and tactical priorities rather than ends. For the most part, the issues between us are matters of empirical assessment and political judgment.

I do not believe that these practical concerns are outside the four corners of Blum's argument. Blum may disagree. Early on, he distinguishes between "philosophers" and "social analysts." Because he is writing as a philosopher, he suggests, he need only spell out the "potential benefits" of racially mixed classrooms and schools. How likely it is that the conditions needed to achieve these benefits will in fact be realized is a matter of social analysis for which he as a philosopher is not responsible.

This gesture toward ideal theory is not entirely satisfying, for two reasons. First, even ideal theorists are required to sketch the conditions under which they regard their theories are operative. (So, for example, we find Rawls describing the circumstances of justice and acknowledging that in situations of severe scarcity the strict priority of this theory of justice will not apply.) Second, Blum is not doing pure ideal theory. As he defines and justifies it, school integration is in part a remedy for current ills in our society—for example, the "social distance" between races and ethnic groups that diminishes the sense of shared equal citizenship and weakens the civic solidarity needed to sustain justice-based social policies. So his argument presupposes certain empirical assumptions—that school integration is effective in reducing social distance, that the benefits outweigh the costs, and so forth.

These assumptions do real work in the real world. Blum reports the view, common among black educators, that it is more important to be concerned about safety, order, and academic quality than about racial balance in schools. He replies, "Of course parents prefer a safe, monoracial school to an unsafe integrated one, and a monoracial one that does a good job of teaching its students to an integrated one that does a poor job. But why should these be presented as alternatives?" The answer is grounded in experience, not theory; many black educators have concluded that during the past generation, the focus on racial balance has come at the expense of other academic objectives, and that—given realities on the ground—it could not have been otherwise. From their standpoint, the strenuous efforts needed to overcome segregation inevitably diverted energy, attention, and resources away from teaching and learning.

This does not mean that these black educators have given up on integration, either as an ideal or as an achievable result of actual social processes. But many of them have developed an alternative, less-school-based view of how integration is most likely to come about: improved academic attainment will lead to upward economic mobility, which will lead to new geographical and housing opportunities, which will lead to increased school (and social) integration. This view rests on the hypothesis that much of what is usually understood as racial and ethnic prejudice in fact reflects class differences, which educational attainment can mute, at least when careers are open on the basis of talent and merit.[1] When class differences are superimposed on racial differences, gaps among students may be too wide for even the most dedicated and skilled educators to bridge.[2]

This raises the question whether school integration is better understood as a necessary condition for racial progress or rather as a consequence of that progress. Statistically, there has been little movement toward racially mixed schools over the past quarter century, and even less toward implementing Blum's pedagogical proposal for those schools. If meaningful school integration were a precondition for racial progress, then there could have been no progress. But there has been. Even after we allow for the possibility that whites are less likely to reveal racial prejudice than they once were, the improvement in racial attitudes over the past generation is hard to deny. We may argue about the extent of these changes, but the basic direction is hard to deny.

How is this possible? A part of the answer is that while integration has lagged in public schools, it has advanced in many other areas: workplaces, the military, government institutions, the media and popular culture, sports, and even the family, where rates of intermarriage across ethnic and racial lines have surged. Nancy Rosenblum suggests that history may have led us to overemphasize the impact of schools on civic attitudes while underrating the importance of adult experiences.[3]

Still, Blum is surely right to point to the continuing social distance between blacks and whites. These groups tend to live apart and worship separately. There are relatively few friendships across black/white lines, and the level of mutual misunderstanding is high.

These facts raise a number of questions. It may well be inevitable that we will tend to identify more closely with those with whom we share a racial, ethnic, religious, or even geographic heritage. This is not always a bad thing: social relations tend to be richer and more satisfying when we can presuppose and draw upon a rich fund of shared experiences. The problem, explored by Thomas Schelling among others, is that even a modest degree of group self-preference can translate into a significant level of self-segregation through the voluntary acts of individuals.[4] The tendency is exacerbated when groups define "integration" differently. For example, if whites regard a school or neighborhood as integrated when the percentage of blacks reaches the national average (about twelve percent) while blacks interpret integration as requiring rough numerical parity, the interaction between these divergent conceptions may perpetuate or even reinforce segregation. Whites who might be perfectly comfortable with schools and neighborhoods conforming to their definition of integration will tend to exit as the percentage of blacks rises toward parity, and blacks acting on the basis of their own definition may well interpret white behavior as motivated by unreconstructed prejudice.[5]

Blum's proposal for frank discussions among students across racial lines presupposes racially mixed schools, which are (as he notes) in distressingly short supply. Is a renewed push for school integration a promising course of action? The experience of recent decades does not offer much hope. As a nation, we have been far more successful in integrating voting booths than schools. The reason is instructive. The integration of the political system required the dismantling of state-sponsored obstacles to black participation, while the integration of the schools required as well state-imposed restrictions on the choices of individuals. Whites did not have to be restrained by law from leaving the political system while blacks entered; they had no place else to go. By contrast, when the state protected and promoted the ability of blacks to enter previously all-white schools, whites typically had exit strategies, and many used them.

To be sure, it was possible to use legal instruments to increase the difficulty of exit. But too often, this resulted in racially polarized communities whose antipathies penetrated the internal life of their schools. Blum's description of the potential civic advantages of racially mixed schools is persuasive. But he barely acknowledges the real-life costs of achieving racial balances—costs that are bound to affect the possibility of productive dialogue across racial lines.

Blum is not entirely silent on the gap between the ideal and the real, however. He cites with evident approval Gordon Allport's well-known hypothesis that contact between groups is more likely to lead to the reduction of prejudice and greater mutual acceptance when the members of different groups are of equal status, when the contact involves cooperative activities in the service of shared overarching goals, and when it is supported by the authority of surrounding institutions. The difficulty is that this hypothesis is not fully consistent with Blum's assertion that schools represent a "particularly favorable venue" for overcoming prejudice. In many cases, the interaction of race with class and culture produces the appearance of unequal status. Relations among students do not always (or even regularly) involve cooperative activities and shared goals. And when parents, communities, and governing institutions are bitterly divided, school integration can hardly be said to be supported by the relevant authorities.

Compare schools and the U.S. military. The equal status of new recruits is reinforced by the shared rigors of basic training; the military is a classic example of cooperation in the service of overarching goals; and racial harmony is strongly supported by public authorities, in part because the military cannot carry out its mission effectively in circumstances of racial division. It is no accident that while hardly trouble-free, the armed forces have moved farther in the direction of effective integration, solidarity, and equal opportunity than have our schools.

For the sake of argument, let me set all these doubts aside and address directly Blum's proposal for school-based civic education on racial and ethnic issues through direct, frank discussions of differences among students, moderated and guided by teachers. Is this course advisable, all things considered? There are three reasons for doubting that it is.

First, such discussions would not enjoy democratic authorization in typical U.S. communities. A recent in-depth survey of public opinion among parents of public school students revealed the following results: 89 percent of all parents (and 88 percent of African-American parents) believe that too much attention is paid these days to what separates racial and ethnic groups, and not enough to what they have in common. Seventy percent of parents (69 percent of African-American parents) believe that schools pay too much attention to what divides us. Eighty percent of parents (81 percent of African-Americans) believe that the best place for children to learn to take pride in their racial and ethnic heritage is at home, while school is for learning what it means to be an American. Eighty-four percent of parents (81 percent of African-Americans) would be upset or concerned if our schools were to teach that America was and still is a fundamentally racist country. Fifty-nine percent of parents (68 percent of African-Americans) would be upset or concerned if schools were to emphasize that the United States has mistreated minority groups throughout its history.[6] These finds create some difficulties for Blum's proposal, and especially for his suggestion that school-based civic education should convey to students "a recognition of the current deficiencies of the American social order in the area of race" and nurture "a sense of social justice, directed at racial inquiries."[7] To be sure, majorities can be wrong, and Blum could be right in spite of majority disapproval. But when whites and African-Americans are united in rejecting a course of action as inappropriate and unwise, one suspects that at least one of Allport's key conditions will not be met.

The second reason for doubt is that in the name of making things better, Blum's proposal could end up making things worse. After all, it requires teachers to serve as skilled moderators in discussion of highly sensitive topics. I have no doubt that Professor Blum is up to the task and that his students have benefitted from the discussions he has catalyzed. But what fraction of teachers share his distinctive combination of experience, professional preparation, and personal commitment? The sensitivity of parents to school-based controversies is legendary. Even relatively minor miscues by well-intentioned but inept teachers could well trigger an outpouring of parental and community protests. Perhaps the ensuing conflicts would be the civic equivalent of "teachable moments." It is at least as likely that the ill feeling would prove the reverse of constructive.

These uncertainties point to a larger difficulty: the gap between individual moral experience and social or political analysis. During the constitutional convention of 1787, everyone understood that George Washington, a man of exemplary virtue, would be the first president. But the delegates also understood that most of his successors were likely to be less virtuous and that it would therefore be a mistake to design the institution of the presidency as though Washington were the norm rather than the exception. Similar considerations are at work in the design of social policy. We cannot safely generalize from the success of skilled and charismatic individuals in confined settings. Sound policies provide both freedom of action for talented individuals and protections against the consequences of mistakes by the less talented. In my judgment, Blum gives insufficient weight to these considerations and moves too briskly from his personal experiences to broader systemic recommendations.

My final doubt about Blum's proposal concerns its empirical basis. It appears to rest on two premises about the reduction of prejudice, neither of which is evidently true.

Premise One: the reduction of prejudice requires an increased understanding of the experiences of groups other than one's own. Perhaps so, but let me suggest an alternative account: prejudice is reduced when clear institutional and civic messages undermine its legitimacy and when members of different groups have the experience of working together toward shared overarching goals. The attack on prejudice in the military followed a model closer to mine than to Blum's.

Premise Two: the reduction of prejudice is preceded—and facilitated—by the explicit discussion of deep feelings of anger, hurt, injustice, and victimization. I do not wish to deny that such discussion can sometimes be productive, but I am skeptical that this is so as a general rule. Some discussions of this sort just intensify a sense of disagreement and social distance. Even in the most intimate settings (marriage, for example) there are good reasons to doubt that frank discussions of negative feelings are uniformly productive. Judicious silence and a deliberate effort to forget are sometimes wiser. The same may be said, mutatis mutandis, of societies. There may be a tension between the past and the future. To secure a modus vivendi and move forward on pressing social problems, it may be necessary to downplay grievances, however justified, rooted in past events. "Truth" sometimes points in one direction, "reconciliation" in another.

None of this is intended in any way to gainsay Blum's underlying point, that schools must recommit themselves to a civic mission that includes building the beliefs and traits of character necessary for the successful operation of a multiracial, multiethnic society. I am inclined to believe, however, that a strategy quite different from Blum's would prove more generally effective, a strategy that builds on the convictions of parents and on the experiences of national (or community) service and the U.S. military. This form of civic education would begin by emphasizing what we have in common, across racial and ethnic lines. And it would provide students the opportunity to work in groups toward shared goals. No doubt group-based differences would emerge in the course of this sort of civic education. But they would be negotiated within a framework constituted by unity of principle and practice. In my view, the approach holds out more hope for generalized progress in these matters than does a strategy that tries to surface and then domesticate raw feelings.

NOTES

1. In a recent study, Jencks et al. report that academic attainment is far more closely correlated with occupational opportunity for African-Americans today than it was thirty years ago.

2. When Blum presented his paper at a University of Maryland colloquium, a colleague of mine reported his youthful experiences at a Rochester, New York, elementary school whose student body was divided between the white children of university faculty and black children from impoverished, poorly educated families. These background differences yielded patterns of behavior and belief that created mutual incomprehension and fear. One wonders whether even the most skillful teachers and administrators could have turned these differences into "teachable moments."

3. See her comments in this volume on Amy Gutmann's essay.

4. See Thomas C. Schelling, *Micromotives and Macrobehavior* (New York: Norton, 1978), chapters 1 and 4.

5. See Schelling, pp. 147–165.

6. These results are reported in "A Lot to Be Thankful For: What Parents Want Children to Learn About America" (New York: Public Agenda, 1998).

7. The subtext of Blum's proposal is that whites need to have their consciousness raised about racial justice and that without something like his strategy, the "nurturing of that sense of justice in whites" will be far more difficult to achieve. For obvious reasons, this line of argument is

likely to prove divisive . . . to say nothing of the fact that the public debate has shifted significantly since Bull Connor's day. People not deficient in a sense of justice about racial matters are now deeply divided about issues ranging from welfare reform to affirmative action, testing for public school students and teachers, community policing, and urban policy. The fact that neither whites nor blacks are pushing as hard for school integration as they were twenty-five years ago is not convincing evidence that the United States has retreated from a commitment to racial justice.

14

CIVIC VIRTUE, CULTURAL BOUNTY: THE CASE FOR ETHNORACIAL DIVERSITY

ANITA L. ALLEN

American schools are segregated.[1] That is, most children in the United States attend schools whose populations are dominated by a single race or ethnic group. Many attend public schools that are virtually all white, black or Hispanic. Is ethnoracial school segregation a problem? Professor Lawrence Blum believes it is a serious problem, and I agree. His essay "The Promise of Racial Integration in a Multicultural Age" offers an insightful account of why the United States needs "educational ethnoracial pluralism."[2]

The United States teems with racial and ethnic diversity. In 2000, some 75.1 percent of the population was white; 12.3 percent was black; .9 percent was Native American; 3.6 percent was Asian/Pacific Islander; 12.5 percent was a racially diverse group of Hispanics (Hispanics can be white, Asian, native, or black); 5.5 percent was "other"; and 2.2 percent was of mixed race.[3] Of course, American ethnic and cultural diversity is far greater than these Bureau of the Census data suggest. Numerous cultural, religious and linguistic sub-groups constitute each of the five racial and ethnic categories employed by government statisticians and administrators. The "white" population, for example, includes people who identify themselves as Italian, Irish, Arab,

German, Armenian, Amish, Mormon, Episcopalian and Jewish. The "black" population includes people who call themselves Ghanian, Nigerian, Haitian, Muslim, Catholic and Methodist. The "Asian/Pacific" group is exceedingly diverse, including people of many religions and of Vietnamese, Chinese, Korean, Hawaiian, Japanese, and Indian ancestry, to name a few.

How can a population of diverse peoples acquire the skills and understandings required for cooperative self-government? Ethnoracially integrated education is key. Americans should revive the ideal of integration. Although there is a civic case for school integration, many Americans who embraced integration at one time abandoned it before integration policies had exhausted their potential to secure promised "educational, civic, social, moral, and personal benefits."[4] Because integrationism, in Professor Blum's words, "beat a hasty retreat," pupil and nation are paying a heavy price.[5]

The rationale for public education has long included a civic justification. Effective citizens who vote, labor, parent and defend need basic learning. As explained by the United States Supreme Court in its most famous education decision:

> Today, education is perhaps the most important function of state and local governments . . . It is required in the performance of our most basic responsibilities, even service in the armed forces. It is the very foundation of good citizenship. Today it is the principal instrument in awakening the child to cultural values, in preparing him for later professional training, and in helping him adjust normally to his environment.[6]

Professor Blum argues that, just as there is a civic case for public education generally, there is a special civic case for ethnoracially integrated public education. Blum is on solid ground when he emphasizes the civic aims primary and secondary school integration can further.

I would like to evaluate Blum's defense of integration both on its own terms and as part of wider, international defenses of diversity. Blum's concerns about the ethnoracial segregation of American primary and secondary schools echo concerns in the United States and in Europe about segregation by race, ethnicity and sex within higher education, employment and business. In a number of contexts, the ideal of integration or diversity appears to conflict with the ideal of equal opportunity. Defending integration and diversity thus require setting aside particular conceptions of equality.

INTEGRATION VERSUS EQUAL OPPORTUNITY

The Civil Rights Act of 1964 brought about widespread integration of employment and places of public accommodation. Some occupations, industries and employment tiers are still segregated on the basis of race, ethnicity and/or sex, but employment integration has been, on the whole, successful and increasingly successful. The same cannot be said of school segregation. Neither *Brown v. Board of Education* nor the massive civil rights legislation enacted by Congress in the 1960s managed to eradicate *de facto* school segregation.[7]

In the 1960s when integration efforts were in their infancy, white critics charged desegregation would degrade or impair whites' supposed higher standards of educational achievement. Black critics charged that integrationist public policies would destroy black communities and culture, as blacks would naturally assimilate into white society. Although the Supreme Court first declared state-mandated segregation of the public schools unlawful in the 1954 decision *Brown v. Board of Education*, many school districts delayed desegregation efforts for more than a decade.[8] When public schools were finally desegregated in the 1960s and 1970s, desegregation was often pursuant to a court order, and often implemented without any special programs or curricula in place to foster mutual respect and understanding among the black, white, brown, yellow and red children brought together under the same roofs.[9] When twenty years of sometimes halfhearted integration efforts failed to undo the evils perpetuated by more than two hundred fifty years of segregation, people of all races, some of whom had originally supported integration efforts, began to conclude that integration policies had failed. The critics condemned integration and the things they associated with it: bussing, quotas, minority underachievement, and the destruction of neighborhood schools.

When it comes to primary and secondary education, policies promoting the ideal of integration are out of favor.[10] Policies promoting equality of opportunity are the vogue. Policies promoting integration commend assigning students to schools, classrooms and programs with an eye toward mixing students of dissimilar racial and ethnic backgrounds. Proponents say that integration entails diversity and that diversity enhances learning and citizenship. Policies promoting equal opportunity commend allocating educational resources—facilities, equipment, programs, and teachers—to provide students similar access to a quality education, whether in integrated or segregated schools. Proponents of equal opportunity point out that current public school segregation is the result of voluntary segregated residential housing patterns and the market for private schooling. They argue that school segregation is benign, even educationally beneficial, when it is not compelled by government.

Professor Blum argues that policymakers who accept ethnoracial homogeneity simply because it is not the direct result of government coercion are overlooking important values. Blum contends that well-designed racially integrated education is necessary for the realization of *inter alia*, certain civic aims. According to Blum, integration (1) signals a commitment to racial equity; (2) fosters seeing those of other races as equal fellow citizens; (3) addresses concerns about social segregation and social discomfort; and (4) improves the ability to communicate and engage with others of distinct ethnoracial groups.[11] American youth will enter the adult world unprepared for its pluralism to the extent that they are permitted to attend segregated primary and secondary schools. Blum's case for ethnoracially integrated schooling thus links integration to the aim of molding citizens prepared to participate effectively in a pluralistic democratic political economy.

Professor Blum clearly understands that merely physical integration, that is, getting an ethnoracially diverse group of young people into the same school building, must be accompanied by a genuine pedagogy and curriculum of integration. Students (and therefore teachers and parents) will need opportunities for cross-racial engagement, racially explicit studies, and moral education about the requirements of justice. Although Blum's essay does not focus on methods of achieving the integration he favors, one can assume that he defends integration fully cognizant of the controversy surrounding court-ordered bussing, redistricting, quotas, affirmative action, multicultural curricula and diversity training. Blum may assume that the moral case for integration, premised on the requirements of equal respect, common interests and shared humanity, when combined with the civic case for integration, premised on the formation of virtues required of pluralistic democracy, justifies policies that impose costs.

To survive legal and political controversy, as well as the ascendant philosophy of equal opportunity, any concrete proposal for integration today will probably have to rely heavily on the use of moral suasion and voluntary incentives. A few parents could be counted on to cooperate with novel integration policies precisely to reap the moral and civic benefits Blum emphasized. Other parents would cooperate conditionally. They would go along if, for example, a proposed integrated school boasted special educational benefits beyond ethnoracial diversity—benefits like intensive extra foreign language instruction, advanced science and math, art programs, or higher test scores on standardized tests. The so-called "magnet school" is one type of voluntary incentive that has worked in some districts to draw pupils of diverse ethnoracial and economic backgrounds to a common school in search of special educational benefits. About 1.2 million students in 230 school districts attend magnet schools.[12] However, the magnet school movement and similar programs and experiments have not fully eradicated problems of overall school segregation. Critics say that in a world of scarce resources, magnet schools (which, essentially, bribe whites to associate with minorities) create distributional inequities. Districts set up well-endowed schools that in practice serve highly motivated, high-income families, and sustain mediocre neighborhood schools to serve other families.[13]

Brown v. Board of Education abolished the sham regime of "separate, but equal" schools that dominated the southern states.[14] Professor Blum took pains to distinguish his civic benefits–focused argument for integration from the equal protection legacy of *Brown*. According to Blum, *Brown* argues first, that white-dominated school districts could not be trusted to allocate resources to black schools comparable to those allocated to white schools;

second, that state-created white-only schools are premised on the inferiority of blacks; third, that the message of inferiority harms blacks' self-esteem and motivation; fourth, that segregation is inherently unequal; and fifth, that equal opportunity cannot be provided in separate schools. Indeed, the Court did not justify its *Brown* decision by reference to the affirmative civic and personal benefits of integration as such. It stressed instead the general civic and personal value of education, and the equal right of blacks to share the same education given white children.[15] *Brown* upheld the principle of substantive equality of opportunity but was no affirmative celebration of racial diversity or civic pluralism as such. Blum was critical of some of the core factual premises of *Brown*. Still applicable and compelling, Blum suggested, are the claims of *Brown* that whites may unfairly allocate resources among black and white schools under their purview and that segregation may impair equal opportunity for status, jobs and careers. Assessing the equal protection arguments of *Brown*, Blum concludes that current school segregation, unlike the segregation of previous generations, is not a product of official state policy, and therefore is not premised on black inferiority. This means blacks can no longer claim that segregation is a badge of inferiority. Or can they? In truth, although official state policies no longer call for segregation, some current school segregation is premised on minority inferiority in two respects. First, the current segregated housing pattern is in part a reflection of public policies of the past designed to sustain race and class segregation. Restrictive covenants barred sales of white homes to blacks; public housing initiatives of the past eschewed mixed-income housing in favor of low-income "projects" and "high-rises." Black children know that whites prefer housing segregation, and that whites' reasons for preferring housing segregation have historically included racist reasons. Black children older than seven or eight cannot help but believe that their single-race neighborhoods and schools exist because of white antipathy for blacks. Blacks may have antipathy towards whites but know that their own attitudes towards whites have little to do with why blacks typically live in segregated neighborhoods. Segregation is a community builder, and many blacks value their communities. Still, low-income blacks who feel stuck in run-down, crime-infested neighborhoods may feel stuck in segregated neighborhood schools. They may feel, contrary to Blum's assessment, that their school options are premised on the false belief of black inferiority. There is no way to explain all-minority neighborhood schools that does not casually link school segregation to active prejudice or unequal economic opportunity.

Professor Blum doubts the empirical connections between segregation and impairment of the sense of self-worth, arguing that they have never been well established. The basis for doubt is apparent. Jim Crow did not prevent the emergence of proud African American artists, scientists, teachers, statesmen and activists of considerable courage and self-possession. I am less skeptical than Blum of social science research suggesting that segregation can cause blacks to doubt their self worth. To be sure, segregation may enhance the self-worth of minority group members who develop a sense of their own value through living and working wholly within their sub-group. Yet blacks in segregated communities with access to the wide world of experience and opportunity reported on television, in newspapers, in magazines or on the Internet, may feel trapped and confined in certain narrow roles. Such persons could easily come to suffer from forms of low self-esteem that could undercut motivation needed for academic excellence. Blacks in racially segregated neighborhood schools in poorer neighborhoods may question their equal worth; and even middle-class blacks may develop performance-reducing low self-esteem as they negotiate a world in which they feel their talents, virtue and appeal are doubted.

Blum's civic case for integration, like *Brown*'s equality arguments, depend upon controversial empirical claims. I believe Blum is surely right, though, that integration can help to nurture a sense of justice and convey recognition of deficiencies in the social order. In his discussion of integration as a way of teaching civic attachment, Blum makes the interesting assumption that civic attachment runs with race; that education is needed to create civic attachment to persons outside one's ethnoracial group, comparable in character to the attachment persons have for members of their own group. We cannot assume that civic attachment to people of one's own race is always greater than civic attachment to people of other races. It is likely that class differences among whites and African Americans, and class and ethnic differences among Hispanics, complicate the picture. Upper-income African Americans and Cubans may feel a degree of civic attachment to the whites in their income group, among whom they live, work, shop, worship and vote, that is equivalent or in excess of the attachment they feel to their own peoples. Of course, this may simply go to show that the integration needed in our schools includes class integration.

Can the United States get by with less integration than Blum believes is ideal? Blum's civic defense of integration could be thought too refined, too idealistic a vision of the practical virtue requirements of democratic pluralism. The American military is integrated, as are most workplaces and public facilities. The failure of school integration has not, and perhaps will not, ruin us. Indeed, Western democracies have proven that nations do not need all that much ethnoracial integration in order to be viable world powers. Blum arguably needs to amend his argument with closer evidence that the polity is at serious risk. However, I believe the readily available evidence of the increasing ethnoracial diversity of the United States is evidence enough of its vulnerability. Moreover, Blum's collateral moral case for integration stands, even if the civic case fails. The moral case is not diminished by pointing out that our nation is the most powerful and effective democracy in the world, even without school integration.

INTEGRATION VERSUS EQUAL OPPORTUNITY: BEYOND THE SCHOOLS

The policy dilemma of "equal opportunity" or "integration" has analogues outside the context of childhood education. In other contexts, proponents of integration urge laws, policies and practices designed to insure ethnoracially mixed colleges, workplaces and business communities; while proponents of equal opportunity urge that we outlaw discrimination and adopt color-blind, sex-blind policies for positions and offices open to all under conditions of equal opportunity.

One such context is the content of affirmative action. Americans are actively debating the future of affirmative action in higher education, employment, and government contracting.[16]

Proponents say affirmative action lawfully aims at integration (diversity), representation and inclusion.[17] The University of Michigan decided to fight lawsuits challenging affirmative action programs in its college and law school admissions on the grounds that an ethnoracially integrated, that is diverse, student body enhances education in ways that benefit the individual student, the university community and, ultimately, the state and nation. The case for diversity is, according to the University of Michigan, "compelling."[18] Officials in the formerly *de jure* segregated city of Atlanta, Georgia, decided to defiantly maintain its minority business contracts set-aside plan under which 35 percent of city contracts go to minority-owned firms, on the ground that minority firms would otherwise be virtually excluded from government contracts.[19]

The policy dilemma of "equal opportunity" or "integration" also has analogues in affirmative ("positive") action debates outside the United States.[20] Europeans are actively debating whether public and private employers should be asked to create diverse, integrated workforces reflecting their pluralistic population groups, or whether mere equal opportunity is enough.[21] Some Europeans say "positive action" should be undertaken to include women and minority group members under-represented in various occupations and professions. Others say "equal opportunity" in the form of non-discrimination policies are all justice will allow.

A product of colonialism and labor migration, diversity in European countries includes differences of race, ethnicity, culture, language, national origin, citizenship, ancestry, religion, sex and sexual orientation. Great Britain has large East Indian, Caribbean and African populations. Persons of Chinese heritage live in England and Ireland. France has a significant minority of persons of North African and black African ancestry. There are many persons of Turkish ancestry living in Germany. Traveling peoples, "Gypsies," and North Africans live in Spain. The Netherlands is home to many people of Indonesian ancestry. The black population of Italy has grown in recent decades. Sweden has tan-skinned immigrant minorities and an economically-less-privileged indigenous white minority group. No European country has a minority population rivaling the United States, but the number of minority-group members is significant in several nations. Nations with the largest populations of so-called "visible" minorities are Britain, with a 4.7 percent minority population; France, with 8 percent; the Netherlands, with 4.9 percent; and Germany with 2.6 percent. Sex and sexual orientation are additional sources of meaningful diversity in Europe. According to Professor Erna Appelt:

> Since World War II, international organizations have repeatedly declared themselves for the principle of anti-racism. International human rights instruments generally prohibit racism and racial discrimination. Systematic discrimination is often listed as a gross violation of human rights.[22]

Appelt identified a dozen legal instruments opposing racism or discrimination.[23] Most of the European Community countries have ratified United Nations Conventions against racial discrimination in employment adopted in the 1950s and 1960s. However, these decades-old conventions subsist as hortatory measures and have not been implemented into national law.

The Treaty of Amsterdam contains an important article—Article 13, EC Treaty—authorizing the Council of the European Community to "take appropriate action to combat discrimination based on sex, racial or ethnic origin, religion or belief, disability, age or sexual orientation."[24] The European Union has recently taken steps to require member states to create laws against sex discrimination. The Maastricht Treaty was silent on the question of sex discrimination, but the European Court of Justice has held that sex equality is one of the fundamental human rights presupposed by European Union law. Principles of equal pay for equal work are embodied in the Union's Equal Pay Directive and Equal Treatment Directives.[25] But what about "positive" or affirmative action to achieve gender diversity or ethnoracial diversity?[26]

The European Court of Justice first heard a case squarely raising the question of whether preferential treatment of women to achieve gender diversity in public employment was consistent with the Union's ideal of "equal opportunity" for all in 1995.[27] Many praised the court's decision in *Kalanke v. Freie Hansestadt Bremen* for its seeming vindication of the principle of "equal opportunity" over the principle of gender diversity. Prof. Gabriel

Moens, for example, said the decision to deny Bremen the right to require that women be granted a preference in public service appointments until they constituted half the workforce in the relevant pay bracket, was a vindication of equal opportunity.[28] Using race or sex as employment criteria, Moens argued, is wrong. The goal of proportionate representation of women, gender diversity in that sense, is wrong. But the European Court of Justice swiftly changed its mind.[29] In 1998, in the case *Hellmut Marschall v. Nordrhein-Westfalen*, the court upheld an affirmative action plan similar to the one it struck down in the *Kalanke* decision.[30] The court held that where there are fewer women than men in a job category within a sector of public service, women can be given preference over equally qualified men, so long as no particular factors favoring specific male competitors militate against the preference. The court distinguished *Kalanke* on the grounds that the law at issue there had no "savings clause" entitling male candidates to an objective individual assessment of factors that might tilt the selection process in their favor. In short, affirmative action creating presumptive preferences for women is lawful, consistent with the European Union's conceptions of equal opportunity. As a direct result of the *Hellmut Marschall* case, local authorities in Germany were permitted the option of favoring a woman for employment as a teacher, over a similarly qualified man.

Now that affirmative action has been established for European women, the question arises whether affirmative action policies should be adopted and upheld to benefit members of racial and ethnic minority groups. The visible minorities in member nations tend to be poorer, less well employed if employed and discriminated against in employment and promotions. Government aid programs in heterogeneous nations may favor persons belonging to racial majorities. Employers may deliberately or inadvertently subject unpopular minority groups to systematic discrimination, by limiting their employment to low-paying jobs with few opportunities for promotion to higher-paying jobs.

The value of Professor Blum's contribution is that he has effectively articulated a set of key moral and civic virtues for a pluralistic democracy that require diversity as the context of education. As noted above, others are making the case for diversity in higher education and employment. It remains to be seen whether diversity will become a policy goal throughout the nations of Europe.

DEFENDING DIVERSITY

Population diversity is a fact. But should it also be an objective of institutional design within good and just societies? There is reason to think it should. First, diversity ought to be established so that the talent, knowledge, understanding and experiences of all groups are incorporated and preserved as contributions to public life. This is a benefit of integration that Blum does not emphasize. Second, as Blum does emphasize, diversity should obtain so that citizens can learn to live effectively with others of different races and beliefs and appreciate their equal worth as fellow citizens. Third, diversity is needed so that no person need be undercut by reasonable suspicions that he or she is being excluded solely by virtue of arbitrary traits such as his or her sex, race or ethnicity. Because in the past the homogeneity of race, sex and ethnicity was associated with discrimination of a sort we must be vigilant to guard against today, diversity is an important feature of our institutions. I believe the moral basis of the diversity program found in U.S. education and employment inheres in these basic considerations.

U.S. industry is finding that there is also a prudential basis for diversity: gaining competitive advantage in the labor market.[31] Corporate proponents of affirmative action sometimes argue that ethnoracial integration of corporate employment must become a reality in order to cope with changes in the available labor pool.[32] Ethnoracial minorities in the United States now make up about 30 percent of the population. Firms inhospitable to minority laborers, professionals, and executives will suffer with a reduced labor pool and will be less competitive.

In the U.S. we hear about diversity mainly in the bitter contexts of the school desegregation and affirmative action debates. In the United States, "affirmative action" policies have arisen alongside comprehensive civil rights statutes to fight the problem of educational and economic disadvantage traced to discrimination. Professor Blum has noted the shift in the context of debates over school desegregation from integration (diversity) ideals to equal opportunity ideals. In the context of affirmative action, ideals of substantive equality of opportunity gave way to a new focus on diversity, which is now under fire.

Among those taking the shots is philosopher George Sher.[33] Professor Sher argues that it is immoral to base the treatment of persons on diversity objectives, even to achieve social benefits. According to Sher, racial, sexual and ethnic diversity are neither morally important nor morally worthy goals. Justice should aim at equal opportunity and color blindness, not diversity. Sher condemns the use of diversity criteria in higher education admissions at schools like the University of Michigan and Harvard University. The U.S. Supreme Court condemned admissions quotas in the *Bakke* decision, but praised Harvard University's use of diversity criteria in undergraduate admissions.[34] To Sher's way of thinking, though, diversity policies are simply quota policies in disguise; diversity criteria and quotas are equally unjust and immoral. Presumably Sher would support the decision of the federal courts in Texas to outlaw affirmative action at the University of Texas.[35]

Sher is thus a vigorous critic of policy makers who now stress the goal of diversity rather than the goals of equalizing opportunities and correcting injustice as the primary goal of affirmative action. In the 1980s, political and legal problems with the discourse of "quotas" and "rigid numerical goals" caused some liberal proponents of affirmative action in higher education and employment to turn to a diversity discourse. It was a strategy. Yet, valuing human diversity is not merely a "strategy" liberals cooked up in a dark cabal one night to prevail in a lawsuit. The diversity argument cannot be reduced by its opponents to the status of a "last ditch effort" to salvage affirmative action, bussing and set-asides. Nor can it be reduced to a matter of irrational aesthetics, like preferring color TV to black and white or rainbow sherbet to peach. Diversity is much more than a minor aesthetic consideration about how we think human affairs ought to be ordered.

Professor Sher's and similar perspectives fail to account for the great depth of the widespread attachment to human diversity. I take the following to be facts and good evidence of the importance and felt importance of human diversity. First, many people think that mass murder is a horrid crime against humanity, and that genocide is even worse. How can we account for this intuition about justice? By understanding human diversity as a value. Second, the great international human rights declarations and conventions of this century contain provisions for the perpetuation not only of individual people and countries but of religious, ethnic and cultural groups. Why does international justice require this group focus? Because it presupposes that human diversity is a value. Third, those same documents grant children a right to a national identity—a nationality. Why isn't a stable individual identity enough? Because we value the existence and perpetuation of distinct and diverse sources of national affiliation. Fourth, we take an interest in the distinctive practices of the many groups and sub-groups that inhabit our nation and the world. We build museums of natural history (devoted to bio-diversity of human and animal and plant life). We build ethnic museums (of Italian art, African American history, of Asian Art, of Jewish history etc.) that display the ways of life and contributions of the many peoples of the world. Why do we care? Why are we willing to devote time and resources to support such institutions? The answer, I think, is that we treasure diversity and the diverse contributions of world peoples. Fifth, we are entertained by the diversity of foods, entertainment styles, and clothing and hairstyles associated with large cities, such as New York, Hong Kong, London, Paris, and Rio de Janeiro. This is one reason we travel. To broaden our minds. We believe there is a connection between experiencing other cultures and the diversity of our culture and the breadth of our minds. Sixth, protecting our own group's distinctive ways of life, appearances etc. is a goal of marriages. "Mixed" marriage is legal and common, but not nearly so common as marriages that promise to retain and perpetuate group identities. Why do people feel duty-bound to preserve their groups-based distinctiveness, if not because they value their own group's diversity? Finally, even when American colleges and universities were highly segregated on the basis of race and class, some schools' admissions practices recognized the value of certain forms of diversity—e.g., diversity of talent (sports, science, music); diversity of demographics (north, south, east, west, rich, middle class, poor); diversity of religion (Catholic, Protestant,

Jewish, Hindu, Muslim, Buddhist); and diversity of aspiration (dancer, librarian, accountant, banker, housewife). In light of these considerations it is not surprising human diversity would arise in the post-WWII, post–civil rights era as a value for higher education and employment, and to be widely embraced as legitimate.[36] In light of how we otherwise view diversity in the U.S. and around the world, it should come as no surprise that many people take racial/ethnic homogeneity in public institutions to be per se a sign of injustice requiring affirmative action and perhaps preferential treatment.

Sher complains that diversity criteria in education do not reward and include the best minds. In theory, human diversity does not map perfectly onto intellectual diversity and intellectual excellence; but in practice, intellectual diversity has resulted from affirmative action; it is also arguable that, for all the talk of lowering standards, the intellectual quality of formerly white schools has been improved as a consequence of affirmative action (to the detriment, I might add, of historically single-race and single-sex schools, some of which have experienced brain drain).

As to intellectual diversity resulting from increased human diversity in the university, affirmative action with respect to women and minorities has led to the creation of new fields, subfields and styles of inquiry in the humanities and social sciences. The creation of women's studies and minority studies programs and departments may have been a matter of politics early on, but no one can reasonably deny that women and minority scholars and white men, too, are now asking worthwhile, previously unasked questions and pioneering new approaches to scholarship. Philosophy is a good example of a field that has been greatly broadened and improved by women and minority scholars, particularly in the areas of feminism, ethics, bioethics, political philosophy, and legal philosophy.

As to intellectual quality resulting from increased human diversity, affirmative action with respect to women and minorities has turned white male academics into better scholars, by compelling them to confront issues and perspectives they could once ignore or marginalize, such as the role of women in the western migration or in national defense. Affirmative action is responsible for the rise of African American intellectuals as among the most important public intellectuals of our day.

On a typical American college campus, diversity is a welcome mat. In the past, homogeneity was not an accident. Students from backgrounds known to have been deliberately excluded in the past may feel better on campus and perform better and be able to pursue desired courses of studies if faculty, staff and student bodies are more diverse. Diversity creates same-kind role models. It makes good intellectual sense to not allow the lack of diversity to lead to the loss of tomorrow's Annette Baier, Judith Thomson, Martha Nussbaum, Iris Young or Amy Gutmann.

Professor Blum's case for integration presupposes that social change is a legitimate goal of primary and secondary schools. Sher complains that social change, and hence social change through diversity, is not a legitimate goal of universities. And yet social change is a traditional goal of elite universities, such as the University of Michigan, many of which have professional schools devoted in part to public service. Social change is an inevitable product of scientific, humanistic and technical excellence, precisely because the world is not already perfect. Major universities measure their own success by the impact of their faculties. Social change works in tandem with other, inwardly focused goals of universities and colleges.

Human diversity in social and economic institutions is a legitimate goal for higher education and employment.[37] And while it is not always clear what kind of diversity should matter most, it hardly seems unjust or unintellectual to consider race or gender diversity that matters from historical and economic viewpoints, along with talent, regional origins and other forms of diversity.[38] Today, serious proponents of diversity embrace all forms of diversity relevant to identity and perspective, including being of Arab ancestry, having superior organizing skills, or being from a poor farm town in Iowa. Serious proponents of diversity understand that there are obvious problems with dividing the nation into four racial groups (white, black, native, Asian/Pacific islander) and two ethnicities (Hispanic or not). Sophisticated proponents of affirmative action operating in a policy and legal context defend the use of the government statisticians' categories as a means to doing practical, if imperfect good: focusing assistance on some of the nation's largest or poorest or most identifiable or most excluded minority groups. Questions about whether particular individuals belong in these minority groups (mixed-race people, rich kids, etc.) are complex; but such questions in no way invalidate efforts to achieve diversity.

HUMAN DIVERSITY AND CULTURAL BOUNTY

We might need less affirmative action to achieve integration and diversity in adult contexts if we had more integration to achieve integration and diversity in childhood educational contexts. If children of all backgrounds were learning together with comparable resources, we might expect minority achievement to improve, reducing "white flight" and thereby eliminating the need for overt diversity preferences. The diversity would just be there. Workplaces are integrated, the military is integrated, and government is integrated. But families, schools, neighborhoods and places of worship are not. The lack of integration in those key contexts explains school segregation and independently burdens the development of civic virtues tied to ethnoracial understanding and justice.

Blum makes an important case for integrated schooling, one I fear will not be taken seriously enough by a nation of habitual segregationists. We can compare the civic case for integration Blum has made stressing the needs of democratic pluralism with two others, the cases for integration premised on distributive justice and on corrective or compensatory justice. The arguments for integration in Europe are primarily arguments about fair (usually, more equal) distribution of economic and social goods. The claim is that members of minority population groups and women deserve a larger share of economic and social goods beyond their reach. While claims of a civic nature are not unheard of in Europe, the economic justice claims predominate. The case for integration in the United States and Europe has been made by appeal to ideals of distributive justice, but also to ideals of corrective or reparative justice. Whereas distributive arguments demand goods in the name of current inequalities, corrective or reparative arguments demand school admissions, jobs and set-asides to make up for overt public and private discrimination.

All of the above arguments for integration have an imperative, cautionary, "integrate or else" tone. Yet, as previously noted, there seems to be a positive passion for human diversity implicit in so many dimensions of Western life, a passion that makes Sher's claims of the irrelevance of diversity and the immorality of diversity programs border on the bizarre. Diversity is something worth celebrating as well as mandating and prescribing. Encouraging people of different races and ethnicities to mingle seems to have a positive value distinct from mere aesthetics, and beyond concerns of justice, morality and civic virtue. It is true, as Blum says, that we are a pluralistic nation with a poor history of dealing with racial differences; and that without integration, we may fail as a pluralistic democracy. However, we should want integration even if blacks and other minorities were educationally and economically thriving to the exact same extent as whites, and even if the races lacked historic animosities. The reason: different peoples represent different, generally benign and interesting, cultural contributions. Ethnoracial integration amounts to human diversity and human diversity represents cultural bounty. If *Brown* did not go far enough in making the affirmative civic case for integration, perhaps Blum does not go far enough in making the affirmative cultural case for integration. There is an irony, though, in my suggestion that we focus on cultural bounty as well as civic virtue. If we are very successful in making institutions diverse, a degree of cultural homogenization and cross-assimilation is inevitable, effectively reducing diversity's cultural bounty.

NOTES

1. See "The Expert Report of Thomas J. Sugrue," in *The Compelling Need for Diversity in Higher Education*, the University of Michigan's compilation of expert testimony used in its defense of *Gratz, et al. v. Bollinger, et al.*, No. 97-75231 (E.D. Mich) and *Grutter, et al. v. Bollinger, et al.*, No. 97-75928 (E.D. Mich.). Sugrue cites data establishing racial homogeneity as the norm in American primary and secondary schools, p. 35–39.

2. Lawrence Blum, "The Promise of Racial Integration in a Multicultural Age," in this volume at 383.

3. *Profiles of General Demographic Characteristics 2000, Issued May 2001: 2000 Census of Population and Housing,* U.S. Department of Commerce, Economics and Statistics Administration and U.S. Census Bureau, Table DP1.

4. Blum, *op. cit.*

5. Blum, *op. cit.*

6. *Brown v. Board of Education,* 347 U.S. 483 (1954).

7. *Ibid.; Brown v. Board of Education,* 349 U.S. 294 (1955).

8. Court intervention was common. See, for example, *Swann v. Charlotte-Mecklenburg Board of Education.*

9. Anita LaFrance Allen, "The Half-Life of Integration," in ed. Stephen Macedo, *Reassessing the Sixties* (New York: W. W. Norton & Company, 1997), 207–227, at p. 215.

10. I lament the decline of the integration ideal in a memoir of my involvement in southern school desegregation efforts; *Ibid.*

11. Blum, *op. cit.*

12. Carmel McCoubrey, "Magnet Schools and Class," *The New York Times,* June 23, 1999, Sec. B, p. 11, col 2.

13. In their study of magnet schools in St. Louis and Cincinnati, researchers Claire Smrekar and Ellen Goldring found increased racial integration but class segregation. Magnet schools "creamed" higher-income pupils of all races off the top of non-magnet schools. They speculate that social class creaming can be explained by the fact that higher-income parents can more easily provide private transportation (in family cars) to magnet schools, and are more likely to be in the community information loop, enabling them to find out about when and how to apply to magnet schools. See Claire Smrekar and Ellen Goldring, *School Choice in Urban America: Magnet Schools and the Pursuit of Equity* (New York: Teachers College Press, 1999).

14. *Plessy v. Ferguson,* 163 U.S. 537 (1896), upheld state laws requiring "separate, but equal" public facilities for blacks and whites.

15. *Brown v. Board of Education,* 347 U.S. 483 (1954).

16. For a brief overview of the history of affirmative action through the 1990s see, Anita L. Allen, "Affirmative Action," in eds. A. Saltzman, D. Smith and C. West, *Encyclopedia of African-American Culture and History* (New York: Macmillan, 1996).

17. All sides of the debate are represented by the following sampling of publications. See D. Bok and William G. Bowen, *The Shape of the River: The Long-term Consequences of Considering Race in College and University Admissions* (Princeton: Princeton University Press, 1998); Bernard Boxhill, *Blacks and Social Justice* (Totowa, New Jersey: Rowman and Littlefield, 1984); Steven M. Cahn, *The Affirmative Action Debate* (New York: Routledge, 1995); Nicholas Capaldi, *Out of Order: Affirmative Action and the Cri-*

sis of Doctrinaire Liberalism (Buffalo, New York: Prometheus Books, 1985); Linda Chavez, *The Color Bind: California's Battle to End Affirmative Action* (Berkeley: University of California Press, 1998); W. Avon Drake and Robert D. Holsworth, *Affirmative Action and the Stalled Quest for Black Progress* (Urbana: University of Illinois Press, 1996); Gertrude Ezorsky, *Racism and Justice: The Case for Affirmative Action* (Ithaca: Cornell University Press, 1991); Robert K. Fullinwider, *The Reverse Discrimination Controversy: A Moral and Legal Analysis* (Totowa, New Jersey: Rowman and Littlefield, 1980); Nathan Glazer, "In Defense of Preference," *The New Republic*, April 6, 1998, pp. 18–25; David Theo Goldberg, *Multiculturalism: A Critical Reader* (Boston: Blackwell Publishing, 1997); Alan Goldman, *Justice and Reverse Discrimination* (Princeton: Princeton University, 1979); Kent Greenawalt, *Discrimination and Reverse Discrimination* (New York: Knopf, 1983); Kathanne W. Greene, *Affirmative Action and Principles of Justice* (New York: Greenwood Press, 1989); Barry R. Gross, *Discrimination in Reverse: Is Turn-about Fair Play?* (New York: New York University Press, 1978); Alex M. Johnson, "Defending the Use of Quotas in Affirmative Action: Attacking Racism in the Nineties," *University of Illinois Law Review* 1992 (1992): 1043–1073; Augustus J. Jones, *Affirmative Talk, Affirmative Action: A Comparative Study of the Politics of Affirmative Action* (New York: Praeger, 1991); Richard Kahlenberg, *The Remedy: Class, Race and Affirmative Action* (New York: Basic Books, 1996); Andrew Kull, *The Color-Blind Constitution* (Cambridge: Harvard University Press, 1992); John C. Livingston, *Fair Game? Inequality and Affirmative Action* (San Francisco: W. H. Freeman, 1979); Glenn Loury, "Why Should We Care About Group Inequality?" *Social Philosophy and Policy* 5 (1988): 249–71; Howard McGary, Jr., "Justice and Reparations," *Philosophical Forum* 9 (1977–78): 250–263; Mari Matsuda and Charles Lawrence, *We Won't Go Back: Making the Case for Affirmative Action* (Boston: Houghton Mifflin, 1997).

18. See endnote 1, above.

19. "Atlanta's Mayor Defies Threat to End Affirmative Action," *New York Times*, July 16, 1999 Section A, page 10, col 3.

20. Julio Faundez, *Affirmative Action: International Perspectives* (Geneva: International Labour Office, 1994).

21. These debates were the subject of a conference sponsored by the European Union, "Combating Racial Discrimination: 'Affirmative Action' as a Model for Europe?" held September 17–18, 1998, at Innsbruck University, Innsbruck, Austria. See also the associated Report of Professor Erna Appelt, *Combating Racial Discrimination: "Affirmative Action" as a Model for Europe?* Department of Political Science, University of Innsbruck, Austria.

22. Appelt, Report, p. 11.

23. She identifies the UN Convention of Human Rights (1948); European Convention on Human Rights (1950); United Nations Conventions Relating to the Status of Refugees (1951); Convention of the International Labour Organization Concerning Discrimination in Respect of Employment and Occupation (1958); European Social Charter (1961); UNESCO Convention Against Discrimination in Education (1960); International Covenant on Economic, Social and Cultural Rights (1966); International Covenant on Civil and Political rights (1965); International Convention on the Elimination of All Forms of Racial Discrimination (1965); European Charter for Regional or Minority Languages (1992); and the Framework Convention for the Protection of Minorities (1995). Appelt, Report, p. 11.

24. Appelt, Report, p. 14.

25. See *Gillespie v. Northern Health & Social Services Board*, Case C-342/93, (1996) ECR I-475. This case held that, as a requirement of the EU's Equal Pay Directive or Article 119, women absent from work during a maternity leave should receive a pay hike other workers received after collective bargaining, but that they were not necessarily entitled to full pay during their leaves. See also *P. v. S.*, Case C-13/94, (1996) ECR I-2143, holding that the Equal Treatment Directive, Council Directive 76/207/EEC, which requires equal, nondiscriminatory treatment of men and women, precludes dismissal of a transsexual worker for reasons linked to reassignment of gender.

26. *Hellmut Marschall v. Nordrhein-Westfalen*, Case C-409/95, [1997], ECR I-6363.

27. *Kalanke v. Freie Hansestadt Bremen*, Case C-450/93, [1995], ECR I-3051.

28. Gabriel A. Moens, "Equal Opportunities Not Equal Results: 'Equal Opportunity' in European Law After Kalanke," 23 *Journal of Legislation* 43 (1997).

29. See Austin Clayton, "*Hellmut Marschall v. Land Nordrhein-Westfalen*: Has Equal Opportunity Between the Sexes Finally Found a Champion in European Community Law?" 16 *Boston University International Law Journal* 423 (1998).

30. *Hellmut Marschall v. Nordrhein-Westfalen*, Case C-409/95 (1997), ECR I-6363.

31. Texaco discovered the hard way that hiring minorities only to disparage and discriminate against them was self-defeating. See Bari-Ellen Roberts, with Jack E. White, *Roberts v. Texaco: A True Story of Race and Corporate America* (New York: Avon Books, 1998). See also, Adam Bryant, "How Much Has Texaco Changed," *New York Times*, page 1, col. 1, November 2, 1997.

32. Keynote Address of Roberta Gutman, Corporate Vice President and Director of Global Diversity, Motorola, September 30, 1999, "Global Diversity and Institutional Change," at the University of Michigan Symposium "Contexts for Diversity: Europe and North America."

33. See George Sher, *Approximate Justice: Studies in Non-Ideal Theory* (Lanham, Md.: Rowman and Littlefield (1999), pp. 8, 80–81 88–93). I am mainly responding here to Sher's unpublished paper, "Diversity," delivered at the American Philosophical Association Meetings, December 27, 1998; the paper develops points made in the book on the pages cited above. Professor Sher is on the faculty of Rice University.

34. *Regents of the University of California v. Bakke*, 438 U.S. 265, 287 (1978).

35. *Hopwood v. Texas*, 78 F.3d 932 (5th Cir. 1996), struck down affirmative action in higher education admissions in Texas. In 1996, voters approved California Proposition 209 to end affirmative action in admissions and hiring in public universities in California. One result of this referendum was that the University of California at Berkeley felt compelled to turn away 800 black applicants with 4.0 grade point averages and SAT scores of at least 1200. See Steven A. Holmes, "Rethinking Affirmative Action," *New York Times*, April 5, 1998, p. 5., quoting Glen Loury.

Some diversity opponents in Sher's camp do not object to the so-called Ten Percent Solution adopted in Texas. This affirmative action surrogate achieves diversity through offering automatic admissions to the University of Texas of all students in the top ten percent of their high school classes. The brightest students segregated in black or Latino schools are thus guaranteed admission to the state university because they excelled at their high schools, not because of their race. See David Orentlicher, "Affirmative Action and Texas' Ten Percent Solution: Improving Diversity and Quality," 74 *Notre Dame Law Review* 181–210 (1998).

36. Compare Dan A. Oren, *Joining the Club: A History of Jews and Yale* (New Haven and London: Yale University Press, 1985).

37. Bok and Bowen argue that the consequences of affirmative action have been overwhelmingly positive.

38. Steven M. Cahn, like Sher, argues that the distinctions of race, gender and ethnicity offer no evidence that these types of diversity deserve more consideration than others. Blum effectively answers this argument by linking these types of diversity to civic virtues appropriate for our national composition and history. See Steven M. Cahn, "Two Concepts of Affirmative Action," 83 *Academe* (January–February 1997, no. 1): 4–19.

15

THE BROKEN PROMISE OF
RACIAL INTEGRATION

ANDREW VALLS

Optimism about progress toward racial justice has fallen on hard times. That optimism, which was perhaps strongest in the 1960s and '70s, has been replaced over the last two decades by pessimism that a non-racist American society will ever be achieved. What Derrick Bell calls "racial realism" holds that racism is a permanent feature of our society, and that those fighting for racial justice should resign themselves to this, even while they fight on.[1] This point of view is largely shared by legal scholars and philosophers who identify with "critical race theory." Critical race theorists generally believe that racism is far more deeply rooted in American society than is often recognized, and that any progress toward racial justice must begin by acknowledging this fact. One conclusion that follows from this line of reasoning is that the usual approaches to racial injustice must be rethought, and conventional wisdom questioned. In particular, the traditional civil rights strategy of integration, with its assimilationist tendencies, must be scrutinized and perhaps discarded in favor of alternative strategies that favor black-dominated institutions, institutions that both reproduce black culture and offer a refuge from racism.[2]

It is in this context that we should interpret Professor Blum's observation that "a social commitment to school integration beat a hasty retreat in the 1990s" (p. 383). Of course, the administrators and judges who have effected policy changes in this area are not critical race theorists, but Clarence Thomas and his ilk are not the only ones who are part of this "retreat." Black parents and educators too have come to question the value of integrated education, especially as it has been practiced until now, and even in principle. While integrated education certainly has its benefits, it carries inevitable costs as well, and more people are questioning whether the trade-offs are worth it. Blum sees this as an unfortunate development because it indicates a turning away from the benefits both achieved and achievable with integration. He eloquently articulates the benefits that could result from racially and ethnically integrated education, focusing on the moral and civic virtues that can be developed in students. While I agree that there can be many benefits to integrated schools, both to the students who attend them and to society at large, I wish to take issue with Blum's position that the trend away from integrationism is on the whole an unfortunate one. Blum tells only part of the story, emphasizing only the benefits of integration, and neglecting both its costs and the benefits of non-integrated education. Before a judgement can be reached on the issue, these other costs and benefits must be considered. Hence in what follows I focus on the costs of integration and the benefits of separatism. I hope that by my doing so, we will have a more balanced picture than that drawn by Blum alone, and therefore we will be in a better position to make a judgement about the promise of integration and its alternatives.

One limitation to my argument should be noted before proceeding. My focus will be on African Americans, the costs to them of integration, and the benefits they might enjoy from separation. This means that I will neglect the interests of both whites and, to a lesser degree, other minorities. This focus seems justified in light of the fact that African Americans have been the focus of most desegregation and integration litigation in the United States since *Brown v. Board of Education* (1954). African Americans have historically faced a high level of segregation and exclusion, and integration is usually intended as the remedy for this injustice. I am therefore most concerned with the way African Americans are actually helped or hurt by integration.

How successful has integration been as a remedy for the legacy of segregation that African Americans have experienced? How successful might it be, and are alternatives more promising?

I begin by addressing the "ideal" character of Blum's argument, and by advancing the position that even under ideal conditions, a good case can be made for the existence of non-integrated, black-dominated schools. I then review the record of integration and suggest that this record gives us little hope that Blum's goals will be achieved through the means he recommends. Finally, I argue that present conditions are far from conducive to pursuing the integrationist ideal, and that the ideal itself is limited and flawed.

INTEGRATION IN AN IDEAL WORLD

Professor Blum emphasizes the "ideal" nature of his argument, granting that "[u]nder less than ideal conditions . . . it may be reasonable to favor policies that do not press toward racially mixed schools" (p. 385). Unfortunately, Blum does not indicate *how* idealized a world he envisions in advancing his argument, and it seems that he must strike a delicate balance here. If his ideal conditions are too far from actual ones, his argument risks irrelevance. For example, many of the problems that his recommendations seek to address would not exist in the first place. Members of racial and ethnic minorities would not need to talk about their experiences of being discriminated against or stereotyped, because these would not occur. By the same token, members of the majority would not need to learn of such experiences. On the other hand, if conditions are too non-ideal, then presumably Blum's proposals have little chance of succeeding. He seems to concede as much when he notes that white teachers are often insensitive to the needs of their black students (p. 394), and that integrated schools often fail to create conditions that foster constructive communication across racial lines (pp. 398, 404). That is, he grants that some aspects of the actual, non-ideal world create serious barriers to the success of integration. These features of the world, it seems, must be "idealized away," but Blum is unclear about how many and which features must be set aside for his prescriptions to work. A cynic might suggest that Blum wants to have it both ways: he wishes to advance his argument at the ideal level where aspects of the actual world would support a case for racial separation, but he draws on problems in the actual world when doing so supports his argument for integrated schools. Hence he counts the existence of racism as a reason for integration when it supports the need for dialogue among students but minimizes the significance of racism as a barrier to constructive dialogue.

Furthermore, if we are comparing the benefits and costs of both integrated and separate schools, the comparison must be fair. Both kinds of schools must be considered under the same conditions, either ideal or non-ideal. Integrated schools under ideal conditions are surely better than separate schools under (sufficiently) non-ideal conditions, but the reverse is also true: ideal separate schools are better than non-ideal integrated schools. If Blum wishes to argue at the ideal level, we must compare integrated schools and separate African American schools under similarly ideal conditions, and we must specify how ideal those conditions are. Blum does not give us much guidance about this; however, his rejection of assimilation implies that the ideal conditions he has in mind include a society where cultural differences between racial groups remain but are not accompanied by racism. Beyond this, I assume that it is a society in which educational resources are adequate and fairly distributed, and teachers are well trained and culturally sensitive. Further, I assume that in Blum's ideal world, residential segregation has been eliminated, or at least has diminished to the point that school integration does not involve the high cost to students of being bussed great distances. Under these highly idealized conditions, what are the costs and benefits to African Americans of integrated and separate schools?

At one level, Blum's ideal of "educational ethnoracial pluralism" is unobjectionable and even inspiring. Who could object to his conception of multicultural education, where students learn to communicate across their differences and develop the civic virtues he endorses? Surely African Americans have nothing to lose and much to gain from the existence of such schools. Surely African American students have a great interest in attending such schools, and in having whites and other minorities attend them.

Yet there is something to lose. Blum states that "the ideal situation . . . is one with no ethnoracial group in the majority" (p. 387). Blum's ideal would leave African Americans (and other groups) with no choice but to be a perpetual minority in their school throughout their educational experience. This involves a serious cost to black students who would prefer to attend a majority-black school. Given that in our idealized American society cultural differences would remain, some black students would probably feel that Blum's integrated schools are not *their* schools to the same extent as black-dominated schools, no matter how non-racist and welcoming the integrated schools may be. The integrated schools would not be culturally black, focused on black history and experience, or run by a predominantly black administration and faculty. Blum's ideal of integrated schools would rule out the existence of such black-dominated institutions. This is a serious cost to the students who would wish to attend them.

Achieving Blum's ideal would, then, require the destruction of existing historically and predominantly black schools. These would have to be either closed entirely or integrated so that African Americans no longer would constitute a majority within them. It is true that some of the *raison d'être* for historically and predominantly black educational institutions is the racism and discrimination that African Americans have faced and continue to face in American society. One might argue, then, that under ideal conditions where racism has been eliminated, predominantly black educational institutions would not be needed. But this is mistaken. Predominantly black schools, in addition to providing a refuge in a racist world, are also important sites for the protection and reproduction of African American culture, history, and experience. Even in an ideal world, they would still perform this function better than integrated schools where African Americans are a minority. As David Carroll Cochran has recently written, "Predominantly black primary and secondary schools are institutions that help provide critical cultural, social, and economic resources to group members. They are places where black children interact with each other and with adult role-models, form relationships, pick up cultural meanings and values, and learn social skills."[3]

As Will Kymlicka has argued, minority groups are at a disadvantage vis-à-vis majorities, and are therefore vulnerable to them in a way that sometimes justifies a measure of autonomy and separatism. Institutions in society inevitably reflect the outlook of the majority group, and minorities therefore face the choice of assimilating or being outsiders within these institutions, both of which involve important costs that members of the majority do not have to bear. Liberal equality, then, requires compensation for these costs to minorities, and one important strategy of equalization is the support of minority-controlled institutions. Of course, Kymlicka makes this argument on behalf of national minorities, groups with a geographic concentration in an historic homeland, with their own distinct language, culture, traditions, and the full range of institutions that make up what Kymlicka calls a "societal culture."[4] African Americans as a group do not satisfy all of these criteria, so it would require a modification of Kymlicka's account before it would be adequate to support the argument for separate black schools (something that I cannot do here). Still, Kymlicka has shown that minority rights and group-conscious policies are compatible with, and even required by, liberal political principles, and this general position would seem to support the case for predominantly black schools. Even if Blum's schools could be truly multicultural, and white culture would not dominate them, it would remain the case that the society at large and other institutions within it would be white-dominated. Since Blum sees cultural differences as persisting into an ideal, nonracist future, and since he rejects assimilation, he should endorse institutions that help African Americans resist the assimilationist pressures created by a white-dominated society. Predominantly black schools are one such resource of resistance.

Even in a non-racist world, then, cultural differences would mean that there would continue to be good reasons for the existence of black-dominated schools. These schools play, and would continue to play, an important role in protecting and reproducing black culture and keeping alive black history and experience. Some African American students might want to attend such schools, while others might prefer a more integrated education. Hence, in my ideal world, in contrast to Blum's, there would exist both the integrated schools he describes and black-dominated schools as well. Both would be seen as legitimate and as serving important functions, and both would offer high-quality education to their students. Ideally African American students would have a choice between these two kinds of schools, and would not be forced into integrated settings, as Blum would have it.

Could separate, predominantly black educational institutions provide the benefits that Blum seeks? Could they foster civic virtue? Doing so may be more difficult than in a multiracial setting, but certainly to some extent they could provide these benefits, especially with the proper curriculum. In addition, some of the racial and cultural integration that Blum advocates could take place in sites other than schools. Blum provides no evidence that the ends he seeks cannot be achieved through other means such as these. He cites research that shows that a properly structured multicultural educational environment can achieve many benefits, and then concludes, without evidence, that they cannot be achieved in other contexts or with alternative strategies (397, 399, 403, 411). In doing so, he seems to commit (or to come close to committing) the logical fallacy of denying the antecedent: A brings about B, therefore not-A means not-B.[5] No doubt multiracial and multicultural schools can provide many benefits, but given the fact that they can also involve important costs to African Americans, it is worth considering whether and how these benefits can be achieved through other means or in other contexts. Blum's argument leaves these other possibilities entirely unexplored.

The Record of Integration

Many of the considerations advanced above in favor of some black-dominated schools are only strengthened if we drop the "ideal" assumptions that American society is not racist, all teachers are well qualified and culturally sensitive, and little or no residential segregation exists. Under present conditions, it is all the more important that black students and parents have a choice between attending a predominantly white school and a predominantly black one, between confronting the hostile or indifferent conditions often experienced at the former or postponing one's entry into white-dominated institutions. Furthermore, if no such choice is practicable, then the focus ought to be on quality education itself, rather than the racial and ethnic mix of the school. The resources expended on bringing about integration—busing, litigation, etc.—would be better spent on educational resources for African American students.

Even in the pre-*Brown* era, under state-mandated racial segregation, there were certain benefits for African American students from being in all-black schools. Some of these schools, despite the odds and despite scarce funds and other resources, provided quality education to their students. They provided a caring environment that addressed the students' needs.[6] Often the school was a focal point of the black community, and this enhanced parent and community participation in the education of African American children.[7] I do not mean to paint too rosy a picture of conditions in black segregated schools under Jim Crow, and I am not, of course, advocating a return to state-sponsored racial segregation. Rather, the point is that even under these very adverse conditions, there were some positive features of some all-black institutions. These benefits are still attainable in predominantly black schools, especially if the separation is chosen (or at least not state-enforced) and if resources are distributed fairly.

Many of the benefits of all-black educational institutions were lost in the drive to integrate. Far more black schools than white were closed, and black teachers and principals often either lost their positions or were demoted, while most whites kept their jobs.[8] Integration, then, involved a heavy cost for black educators. But it was African American children who paid the most for integration, and not just from losing the services of black educators. Many black students were bussed to predominantly white schools (far more than were white students bussed to predominantly black schools). When they got there, they found themselves in more anonymous, if not hostile, environments, and their distance from home meant that parent and community involvement in their education declined substantially. Many black communities themselves suffered the loss of an institution that played a major role in the community. Integration, then, involved great costs to black educators, black students, and the African American community at large.

One could respond that none of this was necessary, that integration need not have been implemented this way. Integration could have taken place in a more even handed manner, with the burdens more fairly shared. Students could have been bussed equally in both directions, and teachers and principals could have been retained or fired more equitably. Hence the problem is not with the integrationist ideal but with the way that it was implemented, and therefore none of this touches Blum's argument. However, I would argue that at least some of the costs to African American students and the African American community were a necessary consequence of integration, and not merely contingent. There are simply some goods that a predominately black institution can provide to its African American students that an integrated one cannot or would not. Furthermore, before we take up the challenge of pursuing Blum's integrationist ideal, we should have some assurance that the pattern just described—where African Americans are forced to pay most of the costs of integration, often without receiving the benefits promised—would not persist. There seems to be little basis for such an assurance.

It might be objected that this portrayal of the situation is too bleak. After all, haven't there been some benefits of integration that make it all worthwhile? No doubt for some students there have been benefits, and some African Americans have benefitted a great deal. However, overall the picture is quite mixed, whether one considers black academic achievement or the self-esteem of black students. A review of 35 years of empirical research on the effects of integration concluded that "no consistent evidence of the positive effects of school racial composition or desegregation on black learning has been forthcoming."[9] There is also evidence that the self-esteem of black students is higher among those at predominantly black schools than among those at more integrated schools.[10] In higher education, one major study found that black students at predominantly white institutions viewed that environment as hostile, and that "black students in black schools show more academic progress than their counterparts in white colleges."[11] So there is little evidence that the academic and psychological benefits of integration for African American students that *Brown* and its progeny envisioned have materialized. On the contrary, the evidence suggests that black students often do better in majority-black schools.

This, among other things, has led some civil rights lawyers to express regret about the litigation strategy that was pursued in *Brown* and its aftermath. Derrick Bell argues that the lawyers involved were "serving two masters," black parents and children on the one hand, and civil rights organizations on the other. The former, he argues, wanted first and foremost quality education with equal resources, whereas the latter were ideologically committed to integration. While the lawyers were ostensibly representing the parents and children, the civil rights organizations were paying for the litigation, with the predictable result that integration became the goal of the litigation, rather than directly pursuing the interest of the clients in quality education.[12]

It turns out that some of the doctrines that have emerged out of desegregation litigation have done positive harm to legal arguments for equal educational resources for African Americans. As Alan Freeman has pointed out, one thing that can be said for the pre-*Brown* "separate but equal" doctrine is that at least unequal facilities was "a litigable claim."[13] Now, once a district has been declared free of the legacies of de jure segregation, no constitutional redress exists for unequal facilities. Black schools with inferior resources are "merely" the result of local funding of education, not of racial discrimination, even if many poorer urban districts are predominantly black and other minority districts and wealthier suburban districts are predominantly white. In addition, the drive for integration encouraged "white flight," which exacerbated residential segregation and made school integration all the more difficult to achieve. The Supreme Court has contributed to this by ruling, in *Milliken v. Bradley* (1974), that federal courts may not integrate urban and suburban school districts unless the districts actually conspired to achieve segregation. In short, by and large, whites who did not want their children to go to school with black students, and did not want to provide equal educational facilities either, have essentially won. Under current circumstances and legal doctrines, it is difficult to imagine a realistic strategy for achieving integration in many parts of the country, and it is even more difficult to imagine those circumstances and doctrines changing any time soon.

So the record of integration is a poor one from the point of view of the interests of black students and the African American community. This record gives us reason to doubt that the continued pursuit of Blum's ideal in the existing, decidedly non-ideal world will achieve the benefits he envisions. It seems more likely that the continued drive toward integration would impose heavy costs on African American students, without such costs being imposed on white students, and without counterbalancing benefits for black students. The historical record indicates that in the real world, integration is far less promising than Blum suggests.

THE LIMITS OF INTEGRATION

Despite the poor record of integration, Professor Blum thinks it an ideal still worth pursuing in the name of developing the civic virtues necessary in a multicultural democracy. But the main educational interest of black parents and children, I have suggested, is not integration but quality education and a fair distribution of educational resources. Much of the motivation of black parents for sending their children to predominantly white schools is the belief that they are more likely to receive a quality education there. The evidence shows that if quality education could be obtained close to home, black parents would prefer not to bus their children to predominantly white schools further away.[14] Generally, African American parents want quality education for their children, first and foremost. They want integration only secondarily, if at all. I believe that educational policy should respect these preferences. Blum, on the other hand, sees these preferences as mistaken, and as obstacles to be overcome rather than as positions to be respected.

Perhaps Blum's attitude is explained by a belief that one cannot have quality education in racially separate institutions, since part of educational quality is fostering civic virtues that cannot be fostered in non-integrated settings. Blum comes close to taking this position when he states that "Any education with a plausible claim to being called 'quality' must involve a deep understanding of the social reality of one's society," and goes on to say that, while this understanding might be gained in a monoracial school, it is "likely to be much greater in ethnoracially plural schools" and that these are "the most felicitous setting" for developing this deep understanding (409). Blum wants to tie the notion of quality education to the existence of multicultural schools but must stop short of saying that one cannot have the former outside the latter. Indeed there are no grounds to conceive of quality education as necessarily involving integration, or to suppose that it cannot take place in predominantly black schools.

The emphasis on quality education for African Americans rather than integration seems all the more appropriate when one considers that many of the benefits of integration that Blum envisions would be disproportionately enjoyed by whites. Consider the moral goods to be fostered by integrated education. The moral growth Blum foresees includes the reduction or elimination of racial prejudice, treating others as individuals, seeing them as equals, and experiencing a sense of shared humanity (398). While it is true, as Blum says, that no group is free from prejudices and stereotypes toward other groups, it is also true that on the whole, in our society whites stand in greater need than blacks of these kinds of moral improvement. Generally speaking, it is not blacks who see whites as inferior but whites who see blacks that way. Blum seems to acknowledge this by his emphasis on "expanding the horizons of white students" (pp. 410).

Of course, there is no doubt that it is in the interest of African Americans to reduce white prejudice, so if integrated education were to have the effects supposed by Blum, African Americans would have a double interest in it: their own moral improvement and the benefits they might enjoy from the improvement of whites. Similarly regarding the civic virtues that Blum sees as coming out of integrated education: African Americans no doubt have an interest both in developing these virtues themselves and in having them fostered in others.

Granting this, two questions must be asked. First, under current, non-ideal conditions, how likely is it that integration will achieve these goals? While Blum presents some grounds for optimism regarding this question, he also must often admit that the kind of dialogue he envisions takes place very rarely. The current state of educational resources, racial prejudice, and other factors are formidable obstacles to pursuing Blum's vision. Even if these obstacles could be overcome, the second question is, does the interest that African Americans have in the achievement of Blum's objectives override their interest in having the option of attending a predominantly black school? It is presumptuous, to say the least, to give an unequivocal "yes" as an answer to this question. Given that both integration and separation carry costs and benefits, risks as well as rewards, either position is reasonable and neither type of school should be imposed to the exclusion of the other.

Blum's emphasis on integration faces yet another difficulty when one considers the fact of residential segregation, which makes integrated education much more difficult to achieve in many places. The fact is that most big city school districts have very small proportions of white enrollment: most of the largest districts "have 85% or more non-white enrollments and serve virtually no middle class white families."[15] Under these circumstances, one must ask which strategy for improving educational opportunities for African Americans is most likely to be successful, a continued pursuit of integration or the pursuit of an equitable share of resources for predominantly black schools? With so much working against the success of integrated schools, one cannot be sanguine about the prospects for success of Blum's recommendations.

It is in light of all of these considerations that people of many perspectives—not just Clarence Thomas—have begun to question the pursuit of integration. For example, the case for separate schools has been made by Alex Johnson in his critique of the Supreme Court's decision in *United States v. Fordice* (1992). In this case, the Court refused to order equal funding for Mississippi's public historically black colleges and universities (HBCUs) as a remedy for the history of state-sponsored segregation in higher education. Johnson emphasizes the role of HBCUs as "transmitters and preservers of African-American culture" and as a "cultural buffer" against the majority white culture.[16] He also elaborates the costs of integration, arguing that "students are forced into a hostile environment whether they are ready for it or not"[17] and concludes that African Americans should have a choice about when they take up the challenges of being in a predominantly white institution. Many have come to agree with Johnson and to see that black-dominated schools are important both to the preservation of black culture and experience, and to the protection of black students from potentially hostile predominantly white schools.

As others have suggested, a similar position has been taken by advocates of all-women's colleges.[18] The general argument is that women's colleges (as well as primary and secondary schools) provide a haven in which young women can develop, free from the anxieties that may be associated with attending school with men. Male students often dominate classroom discussion, and women who attend single-sex schools often do better academically than those who attend gender-integrated schools. It is widely acknowledged as a good thing for young women to have the option of attending such schools. Why, then, is the analogous position applied to African Americans so controversial?

I think that the answer to this question lies, at least in part, in the overwhelmingly dominant integrationist ideology that took hold during the civil rights movement. As a response to the injustice of state-mandated segregation, all forms of racial separatism became equated with racism and therefore seen as inherently suspect. Not everyone took this view—black nationalists did not—but most "respectable" opinion, black and white, was thoroughly integrationist. As a result, defenders of black institutions have been on the defensive ever since. They find that they must defend these institutions against the well-meaning but (on their view) misguided emphasis on integration as the solution to America's continuing racial disparities.[19]

In this light, Blum's argument places him in a long and proud tradition, but one that has failed to fulfill its promise and that was incomplete and inadequate from its inception. The contrast between the integrationist perspective and one that sees a legitimate role for some separatism is demonstrated in Blum's response to Roy Brooks's argument for "limited separation." Brooks's book *Integration or Separation?* is a major recent critique of integration and a defense of voluntary separation by African Americans as a strategy for black advancement. Brooks argues that integration has largely failed, and that separation in some institutional contexts, including education, is a more promising strategy for dealing with racism and for achieving racial equality.

Blum's response to this position is that "Brooks's argument appears to lock that white hostility in place as a permanent feature of our society and of the institutions in question; at least it involves no frontal attack on that hostility" (note 66, p. 423). The problem with Blum's approach, from the point of view I have been defending, is that it places African American students on the front lines in his "frontal attack," whether they want to be there or not. As a result they may be not the beneficiaries of integration but some of its first casualties. If a "frontal attack" is needed, surely those on the front lines should be volunteers, not conscripts.

Perhaps what lies at the bottom of this disagreement is the level of optimism or pessimism about the prospects of eliminating racism in the United States. Blum is rather optimistic that integrated education, with a multicultural curriculum, sensitive teachers, and the like, will create a welcoming atmosphere for minority students and, in the long run, substantially reduce the racism of society at large. Others, with whom I am inclined to agree, have argued that racism is a deeply rooted feature of our society, and that we must base our attack on racism and racial injustice on the premise that racism will be difficult if not impossible to eliminate, at least for the foreseeable future. If this is the case, it is most likely that pursuit of Blum's strategy will bring more of what integration has already brought: benefit for some black students, no doubt, but also long bus rides to hostile territory for many others. This perspective does not, as Blum suggests, "lock in" white racism. It sees that racism as already locked in and asks, given this, what is in the best interest of African American students? It seeks ways of combating racism and racial injustice that do not sacrifice the interests of black students themselves. Blum asks us to have faith that, properly structured, integrated education will work out well for everyone. I worry that in pursuing his noble values, especially under current conditions, we risk doing much more harm than good.

CONCLUSION

I have argued that even under ideal conditions, African Americans would have an interest in the existence of black-dominated schools, and that they should have a choice between attending one of these and attending an integrated school. Under the non-ideal conditions that currently obtain, it is all the more important that this option be available. If such a choice is impractical, then the primary focus of educational policy should be quality education and a fair share of educational resources. As Cochran suggests, voucher programs and charter schools are worth considering as ways of making choice available,[20] though they may be problematic for other reasons. Perhaps quality neighborhood schools or magnet schools are preferable. It is not my purpose to enter into this important debate here but merely to establish that integration has serious costs, and separation some benefits, that Blum does not acknowledge.

From a perspective that does not place integration above all else, it is not to be lamented if some black-dominated schools continue to exist. If the students are receiving quality education, and particularly if they have chosen their predominantly black schools, there may be nothing to lament. I disagree, then, with Blum's assertion that "racial separation" is necessarily a "moral wrong" (p. 413). Under some circumstances, it should be seen, rather, as a normal aspect of a multiracial and multicultural society, especially if it is a society that is racist. Many white students are certainly in need of the moral and civic improvement Blum envisions, and they may be more likely to experience it if some African Americans and members of other minorities are present in their schools. But African Americans and other minorities have no obligation to attend mostly white schools for the sake of the moral improvement of whites.

If predominantly black schools have a legitimate place in our educational system, the same cannot be said of schools that are all, or nearly all, white. The situations are entirely asymmetrical. As suggested above, the work of Kymlicka demonstrates that minority cultures are vulnerable in ways that majority cultures are not, and this justifies differential treatment on liberal grounds. Minorities are entitled to certain forms of separation and autonomy as a protection against their vulnerability to the majority. But minorities are also entitled to inclusion in majority-dominated institutions, and members of the majority may not exclude minority members from the institutions they dominate. In the present context, I would argue that this means that African Americans are entitled to black-dominated educational institutions but whites are not entitled to all-white institutions.[21] Hence majority-white schools should do everything they can to attract and retain black students, and the existence of privileged, lily-white schools is certainly to be lamented.

Let me conclude by reiterating that I do not take issue with the idea that, under favorable conditions, integrated educational institutions can do a great deal of good. Nor do I deny that they can foster the virtues Blum defends, virtues that I join him in endorsing. Rather, I have argued that even under ideal conditions, something would be lost if we had only integrated institutions, with no option for members of minority groups to attend schools where they are the majority. Further, I have argued that, under the non-ideal conditions that currently obtain, it would certainly be a mistake to pursue integration above all else. In particular, it should not be pursued at the expense of the well-being and quality education of minority students themselves. These latter values must take precedence over integration, and we must be aware that, under some conditions, we risk sacrificing them in the name of integration.

NOTES

I wish to thank Madge Willis, who brought Mwalimu Shujaa's *Beyond Desegregation* to my attention, and Lincoln Turner, for sharing with me his B.A. thesis, "Metropolitan School Desegregation in the 1970's: The *Swann* and *Milliken* Cases" (Morehouse College, 1999).

1. Derrick Bell, "Racial Realism," in *Critical Race Theory: The Key Writings That Formed the Movement*, ed. Kimberlé Crenshaw, Neil Gotanda, Gary Peller, and Kendall Thomas (New York: The New Press, 1995), 302–12.

2. See generally *Critical Race Theory*, ed. Crenshaw et al.; and *Critical Race Theory: The Cutting Edge*, ed. Richard Delgado (Philadelphia: Temple University Press, 1995).

3. David Carroll Cochran, *The Color of Freedom: Race and Contemporary American Liberalism* (Albany: State University of New York Press, 1999), 159.

4. See generally Will Kymlicka, *Liberalism, Community, and Culture* (Oxford: Clarendon Press, 1989); and Kymlicka, *Multicultural Citizenship: A Liberal Theory of Minority Rights* (Oxford: Clarendon Press, 1995).

5. I say "seems" because Blum equivocates about whether ethnoracially plural schools are necessary and/or sufficient to bring about his ends.

6. Emilie V. Siddle Walker, "Can Institutions Care? Evidence from the Segregated Schooling of African American Children," in *Beyond Desegregation: The Politics of Quality in African American Schooling*, ed. Mwalimu J. Shujaa (Thousand Oaks, CA: Corwin Press, 1996), 209–26.

7. Patricia A. Edwards, "Before and After School Desegregation: African American Parents' Involvement in Schools," In *Beyond Desegregation*, ed. Shujaa, 138–61.

8. Derrick Bell, *And We Are Not Saved* (New York: Basic Books, 1987), 109; Van Dempsey and George Noblit, "Cultural Ignorance and School Desegregation: A Community Narrative," in *Beyond Desegregation*, ed. Shujaa, 115–37; Christine J. Faltz and Donald O. Leake, "The All-Black School: Inherently Unequal or a Culture-Based Alternative?" in *Beyond Desegregation*, ed. Shujaa, 227–52.

9. H. J. Walberg, "Involuntary School Desegregation versus Effective Education," in *Cultural Diversity and the Schools: Prejudice or Progress?* ed. J. Lynch, C. Modgil and S. Modgil (Bristol, PA: Falmer, 1992), 363, cited in Faltz and Leake, "The All-Black School," 230.

10. Roy L. Brooks, *Integration or Separation? A Strategy for Racial Equality* (Cambridge: Harvard University Press, 1996), 22–23.

11. Jacqueline Fleming, *Blacks in College* (San Francisco: Jossey-Bass, 1984), cited in Andrew Hacker, *Two Nations: Black and White, Separate, Hostile, Unequal* (New York: Scribner's Sons, 1992), 148, 154.

12. Derrick Bell, "Serving Two Masters: Integration Ideals and Client Interests in School Desegregation Litigation," in *Critical Race Theory*, ed. Crenshaw et al., 5–19; Bell, *And We Are Not Saved*, chapter 4.

13. Alan David Freeman, "Legitimizing Racial Discrimination Through Antidiscrimination Law: A Critical Review of Supreme Court Doctrine," in *Critical Race Theory*, ed. Crenshaw et al., 29–46: 32.

14. D. L. Cuddy, "A Proposal to Achieve Desegregation Through Free Choice," *American Education* 19 (1983), 25–31, cited in Faltz and Leake, "The All-Black School," 233.

15. Gary Orfield and John T. Yun, "Resegregation in American Schools" (Cambridge: The Civil Rights Project, Harvard University, 1999), 7. Available at: http://www.law.harvard.edu/groups/civilrights/publications/resegregation99.html. Accessed September 27, 1999.

16. Alex M. Johnson, Jr., "Bid Whist, Tonk, and *United States v. Fordice*:

Why Integrationism Fails African-Americans Again," *California Law Review* 81 (1993), 1401–70: 1432.

17. *Ibid.*, 1444.

18. See, for example, Hacker, *Two Nations*, 158.

19. See generally Gary Peller, "Race-Consciousness," in *Critical Race Theory*, ed. Crenshaw et al., 127–58.

20. Cochran, *The Color of Freedom*, 163–64.

21. Hence I disagree with Brooks as to whether all-white institutions could be defended on the same grounds as all-black institutions. He says "the option should be left open," but I fail to see how the exclusion of African Americans and other minorities from predominantly white schools could ever be justified. See Brooks, *Integration or Separation?* 230–31.

INDEX

Abington Township v. Schempp, 105–6, 202
Accreditation, 33, 88, 101, 105, 154, 180,
   221, 238, 240
Ackerman, Bruce, 136n, 242n, 376n
"Adult time for adult crime," 15, 359, 369.
   See also Children, punishment as adults
Affirmative action, 441–42, 444–46,
   448–50. *See also* Quotas, racial
Aiken, Lisa, 260–61
Allen, Anita, 18, **434–55**
Allport, Gordon, 419n, 428–30
American Federation of Teachers (AFT),
   247–48
Amish, 13, 55n, 86n, 160, 227, 237–38,
   243n, 269, 275–76, 278, 281, 300
Appelt, Erna, 443
Appiah, Anthony, 56n, 57n
Aristotle, 15, 203, 362–65, 373, 408; neo-
   Aristotelianism, 362
Arneson, Richard, 243n
Arons, Stephen, 377n
Asians and Asian-Americans, 386–87, 406,
   411, 421–22n, 434
Assimilation, racial, 387–89, 406, 459, 461.
   See also Integration, racial
Atheism, 105, 112, 117, 172–73, 226, 230–31
Augustine, 365
Autonomy: individual, 11–13, 196–98,
   207–8, 210–12, 215, 242n, 247, 254–72,
   290–95, 297–99, 301–3, 323–25,
   327–28, 330, 332, 341, 360–62; mini-
   mal, 290–95, 298–99, 301–3; minority
   right to, 461, 471; parental, 60, 65,
   69–70, 79, 83, 186–87; teacher, 81–82.

See also Children; Education; Liberalism; Teachers, role of in moral education

"Backstop" role of the state, 135n, 286,
   288, 297, 310n
Baier, Annette, 449
Baier, Kurt, 377n
Bailyn, Bernard, 136n
Baizerman, Michael, 379n
"Balkanization," social, 10, 129, 148, 156,
   161
Bates, Stephen, 218n, 273–74n
Bell, Derek, 456, 465
Berkowitz, Peter, 203, 218n
Berlin, Isaiah, 260
Bible, the, 11, 54n, 64, 107, 108, 110–12,
   118, 128, 140n, 184, 202, 204, 209, 210,
   266, 343
Blacks, 3, 16, 99, 126–27, 130, 150,
   176–77, 383–90, 393–95, 399–402, 406,
   409–11, 421–22n, 426–28, 434, 438–41,
   451, 457–72
Blaine, James G., 112
"Blaine Amendment," 112–13
Blomquist, Martha-Elin, 379n
Blum, Lawrence, 16–18, **383–424**, 425–35,
   437–41, 444–45, 451, 456–62, 464,
   466–72, 473n
*Board of Education, Island Trees School Dis-
   trict v. Pico*, 68–69, 81
Bob Jones University, 128
Boettner, Loraine, 140n
Boggs, Circuit Judge, 219n